Well Seasoned

A Southern Classic

Les Passees, Inc.
Memphis, Tennessee

Les Passees, Inc.
Memphis, Tennessee
1982

A community service organization founded in Memphis in 1910, Les Passees, Inc., has supported a range of medical and civic activities financially and through volunteer service. Since 1950, when the Club became dedicated to the establishment of an outpatient treatment center for children with cerebral palsy, the Les Passees Children's Services Center has grown into a nationally recognized, innovative facility for children with developmental disabilities.

Les Passees is a volunteer organization which provides for, and enhances, community awareness of the services provided by Les Passees Children's Services Center. All proceeds from Well Seasoned *directly support the Center's expanding role in the field of treating infants and children with special needs.*

Library of Congress 82-081148
ISBN 0-939114-42-9

1st Printing	1982	20,000
2nd Printing	1985	10,000
3rd Printing	1987	15,000
4th Printing	1990	15,000
5th Printing	1995	10,000

To order other copies of *Well Seasoned* use order blanks provided in the back of the book or write to:

Les Passees Publications
40 South Idlewild
Memphis, Tennessee 38104

Manufactured by
Favorite Recipes® Press
P.O. Box 305142
Nashville, Tennessee
1-800-358-0560

Table of Contents

Trade names of products used only when specified by donor of recipe.

Cookbook Production Committee

Chairman: Mrs. Charles D. Schaffler

Mrs. R. Franklin Adams
Mrs. Jack Bellows
Mrs. Thomas J. Becktold, Jr.
Mrs. Henry Hancock
Mrs. William C. Harris
Mrs. Russell G. Henley, III
Mrs. Michael Hewgley
Mrs. Carl H. Langschmidt, Jr.
Mrs. Phillip H. McNeill

Mrs. Charles Richard Patterson
Mrs. Peter R. Pettit
Mrs. Daniel Randolph Ramey
Mrs. Burdette Russ
Mrs. Richard Simmons
Mrs. Philip Strubing
Mrs. Hershel P. Wall

Marketing and Promotions Committee

Chairman: Mrs. James A. Breazeale

Co-Chairman: Mrs. William E. Denman, III

Mrs. Scott A. Arnold, III
Mrs. Gus Denton
Mrs. Jere Fones
Mrs. Allen Holt Hughes

Mrs. Forrest N. Jenkins
Mrs. E. G. Mankey
Mrs. Thomas Shipman, III

We wish to thank the members of Les Passees, Inc., their friends and relatives who graciously contributed and tested over 2000 recipes from which Well Seasoned *is compiled.*

Acknowledgments

A direct descendant of one of the founders of Memphis, *IMOGENE HUDSON FARNSWORTH* is a self-trained artist who began painting seriously in 1973. She quickly became recognized as one of the foremost wildlife artists in America. Her first watercolor (1974), reproduced as limited edition prints, won a prestigious Printing Industries of America Award, an honor she receives consistently. The Les Passees Children's Rehabilitation Center deeply appreciates her support and friendship in donating her painting for the cover of *Well Seasoned.*

CYNDY GRIVICH, a Teaching Assistant in Graphic Design at Memphis State University and a free-lance illustrator, is the recipient of several Awards of Excellence and Merit from the Art Directors' Club of Memphis. Les Passees, Inc., receives the contribution of her ink illustrations for the divider pages of *Well Seasoned* with great appreciation.

LES PASSEES CHILDREN'S SERVICES CENTER

Founded in 1950 by Les Passees, Inc., the Les Passees Rehabilitation Center at 49 North Dunlap, Memphis, Tennessee, specializes in the treatment of children from birth to four years of age with developmental disabilities. Approximately a thousand children benefit annually from services provided by the Center.

Renamed Les Passees Children's Services Center, Inc. in 1995, the Center operates under the conviction that success lies in early detection and treatment. Each child, upon physician referral, receives a comprehensive medical and psycho-social evaluation. A Medical Director, a full-time Director of Clinical Services, and a dedicated professional staff provide innovative, individualized services. Treatment and equipment designed by the staff have served as models through the years for other centers throughout the country. In 1980, under a Department of Transportation grant, a van designed especially to transport handicapped infants was designed as a national prototype.

The Center, a United Way agency, has long been supported by the entire Memphis medical, business and civic communities. With this support a brighter future for these children can become a reality—not just a dream.

Foreword

Breaking bread together is a ritual for all seasons. Sharing a meal—whether midweek meatloaf or an eight-course dinner for twelve, blind eye to the budget—is a universal, intimate tradition that cuts across age and culture. Today, however, we often lose sight of the significance of this daily ritual that binds family and friends together. We are busy, we are pressured, we are running late and tired. We become seduced by the siren song of fast food outlets, the neon promise of empty calories. Simply because we are so busy, however, because so much of life has become harried and fragmented, the communal experience of sharing a meal is increasing more essential to the quality of our lives.

Well Seasoned is a cookbook for all seasons. The selections range from regional to international, classic to nouvelle, exotic to convenient, simple to complex. All recipes have been tested and retested for taste, accuracy and reliability; many offer serving suggestions. The appendix includes herb and sauce charts and metric measurements and equivalents. The index is thoroughly cross-referenced for convenience. It is a cookbook for the eclectic.

The *Well Seasoned* cook, confronted relentlessly by the cliché that eating (and therefore preparation) is a necessity, gives double meaning to the belief that Necessity is the mother of invention. Necessity's culinary mothers have spent years evolving recipes that raise this necessity to the level of an art. Balancing time, pressures, and budgets daily with the desire to honor the ritual of mealtime transforms one into an artist. May *Well Seasoned* inspire you to be not just a cook but an artist for all seasons.

We wish to thank Justine Smith, owner of Justine's Restaurant, recipient of numerous Holiday Magazine awards, for serving as honorary editor of Well Seasoned.

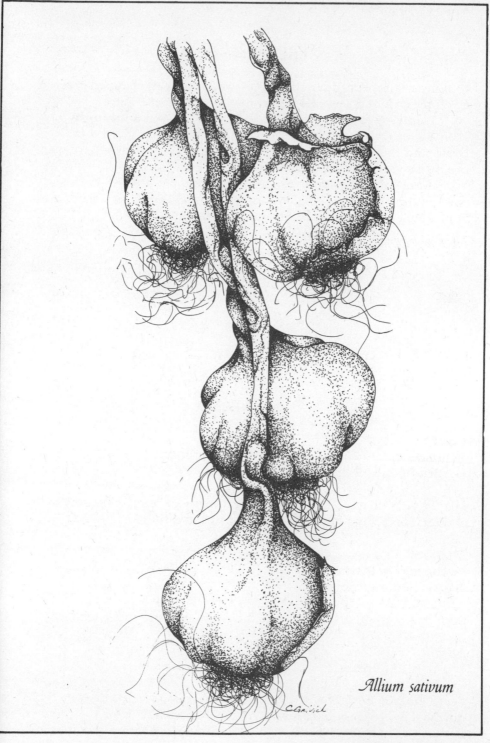

Allium sativum

C.Grivich

Appetizers

Chili Cheese Bars

6 ounces sharp Cheddar cheese
6 ounces white cheese, Swiss or
   Monterey Jack

1 4-ounce can chopped green
   chilies, and juice
5 eggs, beaten until frothy

Grate and mix cheeses together. Line bottom of 9-inch square oven-proof dish with ½ of the cheese mixture. Spread green chilies and juice over cheese mixture. Layer remaining cheese. Pour eggs over cheese-chili mixture. Bake for 20-25 minutes at 350° F. Cut in bars or squares. For a spicier appetizer, add cayenne pepper. Serves 6-8.

This may be frozen. Try this for a main dish brunch.

Mrs. Calvin Ozier (Brenda Witt)

Baby Quiches

Crust
3 ounces cream cheese
1 stick butter

1 cup flour

Mix all ingredients. Chill dough. When ready to bake, make tiny balls of dough and press into greased miniature muffin pans.

Mixture
¼ cup grated Swiss cheese
6 green onions, chopped

7 slices bacon, cooked and
   crumbled

Combine ingredients. Put small amount of mixture into each crust.

Filling
1 cup heavy cream

2 eggs, beaten

Scald cream and mix with eggs. Pour 1 teaspoon of filling over each quiche. Can freeze or bake now. If frozen, bake at 425° F. for 10 minutes. If thawed, bake at 325° F. for 12-15 minutes. Makes 24 individual quiches.

Mrs. Thomas Hollomon (Jayne Pressgrove)

Fred's Spinach Quiche

4 eggs, beaten
4 tablespoons flour
8 ounces cottage cheese, small
   curd
8 ounces Cheddar cheese,
   grated

1 10-ounce package frozen
   chopped spinach, thawed
   and well drained
½-⅔ stick butter, melted

Mix all ingredients together and pour in an oblong Pyrex dish. Bake at 350° F. for 1 hour. Cool for 30 minutes before cutting into bite size pieces. Makes 20 squares or serves 8-10 as a side dish.

Good party hors d'oeuvre.

Mrs. Ernest B. Portis (Diana Gene Wallin)

Party Puffs

1 loaf firm unsliced white
   bread
3 ounces cream cheese
1 stick butter

2 4¾-ounce cans Underwood
   Chunky Chicken Spread, or
   4 ounces sharp cheese,
   grated
2 egg whites, stiffly beaten

Trim crust from bread. Cut bread into 1-inch cubes. Melt cream cheese and butter in double boiler. Remove from heat. Fold in either chicken spread or sharp cheese. Fold in egg whites. Dip bread into mixture until well coated. Place on cookie sheets and bake at 400° F. for 12-15 minutes. Can be frozen before baking. Makes 60-80 puffs.

Mrs. William M. Fay (Sally Harding)

Mrs. Sam A. Gassaway, Jr. (Barbara Billings)

Olde English Cheese Ball

16 ounces cream cheese
1 5-ounce jar Old English
   Sharp Cheese Spread
2 tablespoons mayonnaise
1 tablespoon Parmesan cheese

1 tablespoon grated onion
1 tablespoon chopped pimiento
1 tablespoon lemon juice
1 cup chopped pecans
½ cup finely chopped parsley

Mix first 7 ingredients. Shape into ball and roll in mixture of pecans and parsley. Freezes beautifully.

Mrs. Henry T. V. Miller (Alice Anne Bolling)

Parmesan Delights

⅓ cup Hellmann's mayonnaise
⅓ cup Parmesan cheese
1 teaspoon Worcestershire
   sauce

2 tablespoons minced onion
1 loaf party rye bread
Paprika (optional)

Blend first 4 ingredients. Spread on toasted party rye bread. Sprinkle generously with more Parmesan cheese and paprika if desired. Broil until bubbly. Serves approximately 25.

Mrs. Thomas J. White, III (Carol Pickens)

The Now-Famous Cheese Ring

16 ounces sharp Cheddar cheese,
   grated
1 cup pecans, chopped
¾ cup mayonnaise

1 medium onion, grated
1 clove garlic, pressed
½ teaspoon Tabasco
1 cup strawberry preserves

Combine all ingredients except preserves and mix well. Mold into ring and chill. Fill with preserves. Serve with crackers.

Chutney may be substituted for strawberry preserves. Really different and looks pretty!

Mrs. Richard E. Charlton (Sandra Cummings)

Homemade Boursin Cheese

24 ounces cream cheese,
   softened
3 garlic cloves, crushed
2 tablespoons dry white
   vermouth
2 teaspoons minced parsley
¾ teaspoon salt

½ teaspoon dried basil
¼ teaspoon tarragon
¼ teaspoon minced chives
¼ teaspoon thyme
¼ teaspoon sage
¼ teaspoon white pepper

Process all ingredients together in food processor or blender. Pack into crocks or form into logs and serve with crackers.

Mrs. Hershel P. Wall (Jean Harrington)

Mushroom Turnovers

Pastry
8 ounces cream cheese,
   softened
2 sticks margarine, softened
⅛ teaspoon salt

2 cups sifted flour
1 egg yolk
2 teaspoons milk

Combine cheese and margarine. Add salt and work in flour until smooth. Chill. Roll pastry ⅛-inch thin on floured board. Cut with 2¾-inch biscuit cutter. Use 1 teaspoon of filling on each round. Fold pastry over and press edges firmly. Mix egg yolk with milk. Brush tops of turnovers with this glaze. Freeze. Bake frozen at 375° F. for 15-20 minutes.

Filling
½-¾ pound fresh mushrooms,
   chopped
1 onion, minced
3 tablespoons butter
½ teaspoon salt

Pepper to taste
2 teaspoons flour
½ cup sour cream
1 teaspoon dried dill

Sauté chopped mushrooms and onion in butter. Add salt and pepper. Add flour and cook 1-2 minutes. Remove from heat. Add sour cream and dill. Cool. Makes 50-75.

Everyone will want this recipe!

Mrs. Preston D. Miller (Mary Jane Greene)

Mushroom Squares Rosemary

1 4-ounce can mushroom stems
   and pieces, drained and
   chopped
2 slices bacon, fried and
   crumbled
2 tablespoons shredded Swiss
   cheese

2 tablespoons mayonnaise
1 tablespoon dried parsley
⅛ teaspoon crumbled rosemary
⅛ teaspoon salt
6 slices thin white bread with
   crusts removed
½ stick butter, softened

Mix first 7 ingredients. Spread butter lightly on one side of bread and cut into 4 squares. Place squares, buttered side down, on cookie sheet. Spread with mushroom mixture. Bake for 5 minutes, or until lightly browned, at 400° F. Makes 24 canapés.

Mrs. Martin McNamara
Nashville, Tennessee

Mushroom Marbu

12-16 large mushrooms
1   stick butter
1   bunch green onions,
    chopped
¾   cup Italian style bread
    crumbs
1   4¼-ounce can shrimp,
    drained

1 6½-ounce can crabmeat,
   drained
½ cup dry white wine
   Lemon-pepper marinade
   Garlic salt
   Juice of one lemon

Clean mushrooms, chop stems and reserve caps. Sauté chopped stems and green onions in butter. Stir in crumbs, add wine, and remove from heat. Gently stir in shrimp and crabmeat. Season with lemon-pepper marinade and garlic salt to taste. Place mushrooms on ungreased cookie sheet and fill with crumb mixture. Bake at 325° F. until topping is crisp, 10-30 minutes, depending on mushroom size. Top with fresh lemon juice prior to serving.

Mrs. Jerry Nations
Brookhaven, Mississippi

Mushroom Marinade

¾ cup salad oil
3 tablespoons soy sauce
⅛ cup Worcestershire sauce
1 teaspoon salt

3 tablespoons lemon juice
¼ teaspoon garlic powder
⅓ cup red wine
1½ pounds mushrooms

Mix all ingredients in large skillet. Place mushrooms, stem up, in skillet and cook on medium heat for 15 minutes. Turn mushrooms over and cook 10 minutes more. Let cool covered in refrigerator overnight. Reheat before serving. Serves 4.

Mrs. James J. Madison, III (Gloria Bethay)
Paris, Tennessee

Zippy Mushrooms

⅔ cup tarragon vinegar
½ cup salad oil
1 clove garlic, minced
1 tablespoon sugar
1½ teaspoons salt
⅛ teaspoon pepper

2 tablespoons water
Dash hot pepper sauce
1 medium onion, sliced in rings
2 6-ounce cans broiled whole
   mushrooms, drained

Combine first 8 ingredients. Pour over onions and mushrooms in a bowl. Cover and refrigerate for at least 8 hours. Serve with toothpicks and Melba toast rounds.

Mrs. James J. Madison, III (Gloria Bethay)
Paris, Tennessee

Mushrooms Vaughan

Fresh small mushroom caps
½ cup fresh bread crumbs
¼ cup grated Parmesan cheese

Salt and pepper to taste
½ cup flour
2 eggs, beaten

Boil mushrooms for 1 minute and drain. Combine crumbs with cheese and seasonings. Dip mushooms in flour, then egg, then cheese-crumb mixture. Freeze for at least one hour. Fry in deep fat at 400° F. until brown. Serve with cocktail sauce. (see Index)

Mrs. William Meade Vaughan, Jr. (Carmine Baker)

Mushrooms Boursin

2 pounds mushroom caps
½ stick butter
1 pound sausage

5 ounces Boursin cheese
¼ cup milk
   Salt and pepper to taste

Sauté mushroom caps in butter 1-2 minutes. Cook sausage in separate skillet and drain well. Mix sausage, cheese and milk until blended. Stuff mushroom caps and broil until hot and bubbly.

Mrs. Clyde L. Patton, Jr. (Leslie Wilsford)

Mushroom Canapé

2 cups sliced fresh mushrooms
2 tablespoons butter
   Salt, pepper and cayenne
      pepper to taste
1 tablespoon soy sauce

1 tablespoon Hellmann's
      mayonnaise
8 ounces cream cheese
   Toast rounds

Sauté mushrooms in butter for 2 minutes. Add seasonings and soy sauce. Stir in mayonnaise and cream cheese until melted. Spread on toast and cook at 400° F. for 10 minutes. Serves 6-8.

Mrs. Charles Schaffler (Mickey Pooley)

Marinated Artichoke Hearts

2 tablespoons lemon juice
2 tablespoons salad oil
⅛ teaspoon garlic salt
1 tablespoon sugar
¼ teaspoon dried oregano

¼ teaspoon dried tarragon
2 tablespoons water
1 15-ounce can artichoke
      hearts, drained
   Paprika

Combine all ingredients, except paprika. Cover and chill several hours or overnight. Drain and sprinkle with paprika. Serve with toothpicks and Melba rounds.

Everyone loves these!

Mrs. George Davis
Murphy, North Carolina

16

Antipasto Spread

1 8-ounce can mushrooms, stems and pieces
1 14-ounce can artichoke hearts
1 2-ounce jar pimiento
1 5-ounce jar green olives, chopped
¼ cup chopped green pepper
½ cup chopped celery

Drain first 4 ingredients and finely chop. Mix with celery and green pepper.

Marinade
⅔ cup white vinegar
⅔ cup Mazola oil
¼ cup minced dry onion
2 teaspoons Italian seasoning
1 teaspoon salt
1 teaspoon seasoned salt
1 teaspoon onion salt
1 teaspoon sugar
1 teaspoon Aćcent
½ teaspoon seasoned pepper

Mix marinade and bring to boil. Cool. Pour over artichoke mixture and refrigerate at least 24 hours. Serve with Melba rounds. Makes about 2 pints.

Must make ahead. Great holiday gift.

Mrs. John Franklin Holmes (Jeanie Hobby)

Stuffed Artichoke

1 artichoke
½ cup Italian seasoned bread crumbs
½ cup grated Romano or Parmesan cheese
2-4 cloves garlic, finely chopped
¼ cup finely chopped parsley
Salt and pepper to taste
¼ cup olive oil
1 tablespoon lemon juice

Cut top and bottom from artichoke and clip each leaf tip with scissors. Mix together all other ingredients, except oil and lemon juice. Fill each leaf with mixture, starting at bottom and going up. Pour oil over artichoke and sprinkle with lemon juice. Steam in covered pot in small amount of water for about 45 minutes. It is done when leaf pulls off easily. Serves 1 for dinner, or more as appetizer.

This stuffing is also good in mushroom caps.

Mrs. Michael Lynch (Susan Corcoran)

Marinated Artichoke

1 fresh artichoke
Juice of ½ lemon
Salted water

¼ cup olive oil
1 8-ounce bottle French or
Italian dressing

Wash, cut stem and tips of leaves of artichoke. Brush cut edges with lemon juice. Place in saucepan with enough salted water to cover bottom of pan ½-inch deep. Add olive oil and bring to a boil. Lower heat and simmer, covered, until leaf pulls out easily, about 30 minutes. Drain upside down and place in a wide-mouth jar. Fill with salad dressing. Marinate overnight. Drain well before serving.

Must be done ahead.

Mrs. John Howser (Josie Matlock)

Artichokes, Cream Cheese and Caviar Ball

1 14-ounce can artichoke
hearts, drained and
chopped
8 ounces cream cheese,
softened
1 tablespoon Hellmann's
mayonnaise

1 tablespoon sour cream
1 teaspoon grated onion
Salt and pepper to taste
1 2-ounce jar red caviar
Parsley

Blend cheese, sour cream and mayonnaise. Mix with artichokes and onion. Season with salt and pepper. Mold mixture into a flattened ball. Spread caviar over top. Surround with parsley and serve with assorted crackers.

Mrs. Wayne H. Woods
Monroe, Louisiana

Guacamato

First Layer

1 envelope unflavored gelatin
¼ cup cold water
¼ cup boiling water
1½ cups mashed avocado
3 tablespoons lemon juice
½ cup heavy cream, slightly
   whipped

1 teaspoon salt
¼ teaspoon Tabasco
¼ cup sliced ripe olives
5 teaspoons grated onion
  Dash of cayenne
½ scant teaspoon chili powder

Soften gelatin in cold water; then dissolve gelatin in boiling water. Combine remaining ingredients and fold in gelatin. Pour into oiled loaf pan and chill until thickened.

Second Layer

3 cups tomato juice
1½ bay leaves, crumbled
½ teaspoon salt
1 thick slice onion
6 whole cloves
12 whole peppercorns

2 envelopes unflavored gelatin
1½ tablespoons lemon juice
1½ tablespoons tarragon vinegar
  Tabasco to taste

In saucepan, place 2 cups of tomato juice, bay leaves, salt, onion, cloves and peppercorns. Bring to boil and simmer 10 minutes; strain. Soften gelatin in remaining 1 cup tomato juice, then dissolve in hot mixture. Add lemon juice, vinegar and Tabasco. Allow to cool slightly; pour over first layer. Chill until firm. Unmold. Slice and serve garnished with cooked, crumbled bacon and, if desired, more olives.

Good as an hors d'oeuvre served with crackers; also great with chicken salad. This recipe may be seasoned more, or less, according to taste.

Mrs. Thomas Hollomon (Jayne Pressgrove)

Miniature Avocado Appetizers

1 large mashed avocado
1 tablespoon lemon juice
¼ teaspoon salt
⅛ teaspoon cayenne pepper
⅛ teaspoon garlic powder

2 tablespoons mayonnaise
8 slices whole grain bread,
toasted with crusts
removed

Mix all ingredients, except toast. Spread toast with mixture and cut each slice into quarters. Arrange on serving platter.

Toppers
⅓ cup finely chopped green
onions with tops
½ cup sliced cherry tomatoes
8 slices bacon, crisply fried and
crumbled

1 4½-ounce can tiny shrimp,
rinsed and drained
½ cup shredded Cheddar cheese
⅓ cup chopped parsley

Garnish with toppers or place toppers in separate bowls, allowing each person to garnish his own appetizer. Makes 32 appetizers.

Mrs. Mickey Moran (Pat Taylor)

Asparagus Delights

8 teaspoons prepared mustard
2 6-ounce packages smoked,
cooked ham slices
2 6-ounce packages pasteurized
process Swiss cheese slices

16 uncooked fresh asparagus
spears
2 eggs, beaten
1 cup dried bread crumbs
Salad oil for frying

Spread ½ teaspoon mustard on each ham slice. Top with slice of cheese. Place an asparagus spear at one end, trimmed to fit. Roll up jelly-roll style and secure with 3 toothpicks. Repeat until all ham, cheese and asparagus are used. Dip each roll in beaten egg, then bread crumbs. In medium saucepan, heat 1-inch of oil to 350° F. on deep fat thermometer. Fry rolls, 2 or 3 at a time, for 1 minute. Drain on paper towels. Keep warm in 200° F. oven up to 1 hour. Cut each roll in 3 pieces. Makes about 48 tidbits.

Mrs. Dennis Higdon (Joanna Coss)

Zucchini Appetizer

3 cups unpared, grated zucchini
1 cup Bisquick
½ cup chopped onion
½-¾ cup Parmesan cheese
2 tablespoons chopped parsley
½ teaspoon salt
½ teaspoon seasoned salt
½ teaspoon marjoram or oregano
Dash of pepper
1 garlic clove, minced
½ cup oil
4 eggs, beaten

Grease a 13x9-inch pan. Mix all ingredients in a mixing bowl by hand. Pour into pan. Sprinkle Parmesan cheese on top. Bake at 350° F. for 25 minutes. Cut into squares.

Mrs. Jerry B. Martin (Carolyn Cowser)

Caviar Mold

3½ envelopes unflavored gelatin
2 cups chicken broth
1 2-ounce jar black caviar
2 hard cooked eggs, pressed through sieve
1 2-ounce jar red caviar
6 ounces cream cheese
1½ teaspoons milk or cream
½ teaspoon grated onion
1 teaspoon lemon juice
Seasoned salt to taste
Parsley

Soften gelatin in chicken broth. Stir over medium heat until dissolved. Chill until slightly thickened. Divide into 3 portions. Fold black caviar into first portion; eggs into second; red caviar into third. Pour red mixture into 3-cup mold. Chill until set but not firm. Add egg mixture. Chill. Add black mixture and chill until firm. Beat cheese, milk or cream, onion, lemon juice and seasoned salt to make a frosting. Turn mold onto platter. Frost and garnish with parsley.

Mrs. Leo J. Fairchild
Monroe, Michigan

Party Caviar Pie

6   eggs, hard-boiled and
      chopped
3   tablespoons mayonnaise
1½ cups minced onion
8   ounces cream cheese,
      softened

⅔ cup sour cream
1 4-ounce jar Iceland lumpfish
    caviar
Lemon wedges
Parsley sprigs

Combine eggs with mayonnaise. Spread over bottom of well-greased 8-inch springform pan. Sprinkle with onion. Blend cream cheese and sour cream until smooth. Spread over onion with wet spatula. Cover. Chill 3 hours or overnight. Before serving, top with caviar spread to pan edges. Run knife around sides to loosen. Remove from pan. Garnish with lemon wedges and parsley sprigs. Serves 10-12.

Mrs. Harland Smith (Betty Bouton)

Salmon Delight

1   15½-ounce can red salmon,
      drained and boned
2   tablespoons horseradish
1   teaspoon lemon juice
1   cup mayonnaise

½ teaspoon lemon-pepper
    seasoning
8 ounces cream cheese
    (optional)

Mix first 5 ingredients. Pour over cream cheese and serve with Triscuits, or omit cream cheese and serve with large Fritos. Chill before serving.

Mrs. William Hackett (Sandra Childress)

Clam and Chutney Mold

1 8-ounce can clams, drained
16 ounces cream cheese,
   softened
1 green onion, minced
   Worcestershire sauce to taste
Tabasco sauce to taste
Lemon juice to taste
Chutney
½ cup finely chopped green
   onions

Blend clams, cream cheese, green onion, Worcestershire sauce, Tabasco and lemon juice in food processor. Pack into 3-cup mold and chill until time to serve. Unmold and spread top with chutney and then green onions. Serve with Sesame Toast Rounds. Yields 3 cups.

Do try this unusual and pretty combination!

Mrs. John Turley, III (Barbara Barham)

Marinated Shrimp and Vegetables

3 pounds large shrimp, cooked,
   peeled and deveined
2 14-ounce cans quartered
   artichoke hearts, drained
1 pint small cherry tomatoes
1 pound fresh mushrooms

Combine shrimp and vegetables in an airtight plastic container. Add marinade. Stir gently. Cover tightly and chill 8-24 hours. Drain well. Place in bowl to serve. Serves 24-30.

Marinade
1½ cups tarragon vinegar
1 onion, quartered
2 tablespoons crushed garlic
2 tablespoons lemon juice
1 teaspoon brown sugar,
   packed
½ teaspoon prepared mustard
   Salt and pepper to taste
4 cups salad oil
1 cup olive oil

Combine all ingredients, except oils, in blender. Blend at medium speed for 5 seconds. Add oils and blend well. Makes 6½ cups marinade.

Mrs. Rowe Belcher (Susan Ramsay)

Marinated Shrimp

5 pounds shrimp
2 cups oil
1 tablespoon salt
¼ teaspoon paprika
¼ teaspoon Tabasco

2 cloves garlic, chopped
Juice of 3 lemons
1 large onion, sliced paper thin
1 3-ounce jar capers

Clean, shell and cook shrimp. Combine next 6 ingredients for marinade. In large casserole, layer shrimp, onions and capers, alternating until all shrimp are used. Cover with marinade and let sit 48 hours in refrigerator. Stir 3 or 4 times. Serve cold on cocktail picks.

Mrs. John K. Lawo (Paula Domke)

Pickled Shrimp

1½ cups vinegar
1½ cups oil
1½ cups chili sauce
1½ teaspoons garlic salt
2 tablespoons dry mustard
5 drops Tabasco

1 tablespoon celery seed
5 pounds large shrimp, cooked
    and peeled
2 medium onions, thinly sliced
    and separated into rings
8 bay leaves

Blend first 7 ingredients together. Layer shrimp, onions and bay leaves. Pour sauce over all and marinate at least 24 hours. Serve in bowl with toothpicks. Serves about 50 at a cocktail party.

Mrs. Neal G. Clement
Florence, Alabama

Shrimp Cake

11 ounces cream cheese,
    softened
1 tablespoon mayonnaise
2 tablespoons milk

1 4-ounce jar horseradish
Dash of Worcestershire sauce
2 4½-ounce cans shrimp,
    chopped

Blend cheese, mayonnaise and milk until smooth. Add remaining ingredients. Blend well and pour into mold. Freeze. Thaw before serving. Unmold. Serves 10-12.

Mrs. L. Draper Hill
Grosse Pointe, Michigan

Shrimp Chaussons

2 sticks butter	2 teaspoons Dijon mustard
8 ounces cream cheese	½ teaspoon tarragon
½ teaspoon salt	2 teaspoons lemon juice
2 cups flour	6 tablespoons mayonnaise
1¼ cups shrimp, cooked and chopped	⅛ teaspoon salt
	1 egg yolk
4 green onions, chopped	2 teaspoons cream

For pastry, cream butter, cheese and salt. Work flour into mixture with fingers and flatten dough into 8x6-inch rectangle. Chill overnight in foil. For filling, mix together next 7 ingredients. Set aside. Divide dough into 6 equal parts, keeping all parts in refrigerator until ready to work. Roll each part into rectangle ⅛-inch thick. Fold in thirds and roll into ⅛-inch thick rectangle again. Cut 2 inch rounds. Place 1 teaspoon of filling on each round, then fold into half-moon shape. Crimp with fork to seal and place on ungreased cookie sheet. Chill for 1 hour. Whisk egg yolk and cream together and brush tops with this glaze. Bake at 375° F. for 18-20 minutes. Makes 4-5 dozen.

These freeze beautifully before baking. Can be baked frozen as needed.

Mrs. Charles A. Williams, III (Elise McDonald)

Shrimp Squares

6 slices sandwich bread	¾-1 teaspoon curry powder
24 large shrimp	24 thin slices Kraft Cracker Barrel sharp cheese
¾ cup mayonnaise	

Remove crusts from bread and toast. Cut into quarters. Clean and boil shrimp in seasoned water. Drain and cool. Season mayonnaise with curry powder. Spread generous teaspoon of seasoned mayonnaise on toast. Place a shrimp on mayonnaise and a cheese slice on shrimp. Bake at 325° F. for 15 minutes. Brown on cookie sheet under broiler if desired. Can be done ahead and refrigerated. Serves 6-8.

Can also be made as 6 whole open-face sandwiches for lunch.

Mrs. Leo J. Fairchild
Monroe, Michigan

Crabbies

1 stick butter, softened
1 5-ounce jar Kraft Old
   English Cheese Spread
1½ teaspoons mayonnaise
¼ teaspoon garlic salt

¼ teaspoon Lawry's seasoned
   salt
1 7-ounce can crabmeat,
   drained
6 English muffins

Cream first 5 ingredients together, adding crabmeat last. Spread on English muffins. Freeze. To serve, broil until golden brown, and quarter. Can save leftovers and rebroil. Makes 48 appetizers.

Mrs. Jackson W. Moore (Betty Wilson)

Crabmeat Cocktail Pie

8 ounces cream cheese,
   softened
1 7-ounce can crabmeat,
   drained

½ lemon
4 ounces cocktail sauce (see
   Index)

Place cream cheese in middle of serving tray and spread out from center until you form circular shape. Spread crabmeat on top of cream cheese. Leave cream cheese border by not spreading crabmeat to the edge. Squeeze lemon over top of crabmeat. Pour cocktail sauce on top of this, again leaving a border. Place Melba rounds or other crackers around edge of dish.

Fresh crabmeat is even better!

Mrs. William Lee (Pam Reviere)
Dallas, Texas

Crab Balls with Rémoulade Sauce

½ stick butter
1 small white onion, chopped
2 green onions with tops,
   chopped
1 cup mashed potatoes
   Salt and pepper
1 tablespoon Worcestershire
   sauce

1 teaspoon poultry seasoning
Dash Tabasco
Dash nutmeg
1 pound crabmeat
2 eggs, beaten
½ cup milk
½ cup cracker crumbs
Oil

Sauté onions in butter. Add next 7 ingredients and mix well. Roll into small balls. Mix together egg and milk. Dip balls into egg-milk mixture, then roll in crumbs. Fry in deep oil at 350° F. until brown. Makes 50 balls. May be frozen after rolling in crumbs; thaw and fry.

Rémoulade Sauce
8 tablespoons mayonnaise
3 tablespoons horseradish
   mustard
1 tablespoon vinegar
2 tablespoons olive oil

½ clove garlic and equal
   amount minced onion
Few drops Tabasco
Black pepper

Mix all ingredients. Serve with hot crab balls.

Mrs. Rex Amonette (Johnnie Dacus)

Crab Canapés

3 ounces cream cheese,
   softened
1 tablespoon mayonnaise
2 ribs celery, finely chopped,
   or ¼ teaspoon celery salt
¼ teaspoon Worcestershire
   sauce

1 tablespoon grated onion
1 6-ounce package frozen
   crabmeat, thawed and
   drained
Small rounds of bread,
   toasted on one side
Paprika

Mix all ingredients except bread and paprika, and spread on untoasted side of bread rounds. Sprinkle with paprika and broil until bubbly. Makes about 20 1½-inch rounds.

Mrs. David Alexander
Claremont, California

Bacon Roll-Ups

5 green onions, thinly sliced
6 ounces cream cheese
3 tablespoons sour cream
1 tablespoon chopped chives
½ teaspoon garlic salt

⅛ teaspoon pepper
1 sandwich loaf Roman Meal bread
1¼ pounds bacon

Mix green onions, cream cheese, sour cream, chives and seasonings. Cut crust from bread. Roll with a rolling pin. Spread cheese mixture on each slice and cut into thirds. Cut bacon into thirds. Roll up each piece, wrap with bacon and secure with toothpicks. Refrigerate 24 hours. Bake on cookie sheet at 400° F. for 20-30 minutes. Makes 75.

Mrs. Preston D. Miller (Mary Jane Greene)

Ham Roll-Ups

3 ounces cream cheese
1 envelope onion soup mix
1 2½-ounce package smoked ham slices

Midget sweet pickles

Let cream cheese soften, then mix in onion soup to taste. Spread cream cheese mixture on a dry slice of ham. Place pickles lengthwise on bottom edge of ham, then roll up. Place seam side down in a pan and cover with a moist towel. Chill for several hours, then slice and serve. Serves 8-10.

Unusual and good. Can substitute stuffed olives for the pickles.

Mrs. Max B. Ostner, Jr. (Mary Margaret Buffa)

Deviled Ham Puffs

8 ounces cream cheese
1 egg yolk
1 teaspoon onion juice
1 teaspoon baking powder
⅛ teaspoon salt

¼ teaspoon horseradish
Dash of Tabasco
1 2¼-ounce can deviled ham
Bread

Blend all ingredients except ham and bread. Cut and toast 24 small rounds of bread on both sides. Spread deviled ham on toast pieces and cover with cheese mixture. Bake at 375° F. for 10 minutes. Makes 24 appetizers.

Mrs. William Herington (Corrie Bozeman)

Easy Chicken Drumsticks

1 stick butter
Juice of 2 lemons
2 cups saltine cracker crumbs

20 chicken drumsticks
Salt and pepper, to taste

Melt butter and pour into shallow bowl. Add lemon juice. Dip each drumstick into mixture, then roll in cracker crumbs. Arrange in shallow baking dish. Pour any remaining butter sauce over top. Salt and pepper to taste. Bake at 350° F. for 1 hour. Baste once or twice. Serve hot or lukewarm. Serves 8-10.

How easy can it get!

Mrs. James Bettendorf (Berkeley Blake)

Chinese Chicken Wings

3 pounds chicken wings
1 cup soy sauce
1 cup brown sugar

1 stick butter
1 teaspoon dry mustard
¾ cup water

Disjoint wings and discard tips, using only large two pieces of wing. Arrange in baking pan or casserole. Heat remaining ingredients until butter and sugar dissolve. Pour over wing pieces. Marinate 2 hours or longer, turning occasionally. Place in oven and bake at 325° F. for 1 hour, turning or basting occasionally. Serves 10-12.

Can be used as a main dish for 4.

Mrs. Gavin Gentry (Mary Jane Coleman)

Sesame Chicken Bits

3   ounces sesame seeds
2   eggs, beaten
1   cup water
1½ teaspoons salt

1   cup flour
8   chicken breast halves
    Oil

Mix all ingredients except chicken. Bone chicken and cut into bite-size pieces. Dip chicken in batter and fry in hot oil.

Great for picnics, too.

Mrs. Mike Marshall

Beef Tidbits

8   ounces cream cheese,
       softened
1   tablespoon Worcestershire
       sauce
4   teaspoons horseradish

1   small onion, finely chopped
1   tablespoon chives
2   2½-ounce packages Leo's
       smoked beef slices

Mix cheese and seasonings. Spread each beef slice with mixture and roll tightly. Refrigerate for 24-48 hours. Slice and serve on toothpicks. Makes 12 rolls or 72 slices.

A favorite with men.

Mrs. John C. Aldinger (Ann Hadaway)

Sweet-Sour Meatballs

4½ pounds ground beef
       Salt and pepper to taste
2   tablespoons parsley flakes
2   teaspoons Accent

2   teaspoons onion flakes
¼   cup oil
3   10-ounce bottles chili sauce
3   8-ounce jars grape jelly

Combine meat and seasonings. Form into walnut-sized balls and sauté in oil until browned. Drain and add chili sauce and jelly. Simmer slowly, covered for one hour. Serve in chafing dish with toothpicks.

A cocktail favorite! Freezes well.

Mrs. Jerry B. Martin (Carolyn Cowser)

Pizza on Rye

1   pound ground beef
1   pound mild sausage
1   pound Velveeta cheese,
      chopped
1   teaspoon basil

1   teaspoon oregano
¼   teaspoon garlic powder
2   tablespoons parsley flakes
1½ loaves party rye bread

Brown meats together and drain well. Return to heat and add cheese. Let melt, then add rest of ingredients. Spoon onto slices of bread. Place on a cookie sheet and freeze. Do not thaw. When ready to serve, broil 5 to 7 minutes and serve hot.

Great with soups or salads.

Mrs. Edward W. Miller

Sweet and Sour Sausage Balls

3   pounds pork sausage
¾   cup brown sugar
¾   cup red wine vinegar

¾   cup ketchup
½   teaspoon ginger
1½ teaspoons soy sauce

Make balls out of sausage and bake at 350° F. for 45 minutes. Drain well. Mix all other ingredients together and pour over hot meatballs. Marinate for 24 hours. Reheat and serve in a chafing dish. Makes about 100 balls.

Mrs. Wallace T. Grogan

Mrs. Robert W. Knapp (Barbara Robertson)

Shrimp Pâté

1   pound shrimp, boiled and
      peeled
¼   teaspoon salt
⅛   teaspoon pepper
½   teaspoon thyme

2   tablespoons minced onion
1   egg, beaten
⅔   cup white wine
6   tablespoons butter, softened

Grind shrimp in blender, turning off and on to finely mince. Add remaining ingredients, mixing well. Place in lightly greased 2-cup mold and bake in 350° F. oven for 50 minutes. Chill. Unmold and serve with crackers.

Mrs. John McQuiston (Robbie Walker)

Smoked Trout Pâté

1 1-2 pound trout
¼ cup homemade mayonnaise
1 tablespoon Shedd's
      Old-Fashioned Sauce

1 tablespoon lemon juice

Smoke trout (see Index). When cool, bone, skin and flake. Place in blender or food processor, add remaining ingredients and mix well. This should be moist. Mold and chill. Unmold and serve with toast points.

Mrs. William C. Harris (Ann Clark Quinlen)

Pâté

4 sticks butter, divided
2 pounds chicken livers,
      drained and patted dry
2 tablespoons cognac
1 apple, chopped

1 onion, chopped
   Salt and pepper
2 tablespoons sour cream
1 truffle, chopped (optional)

Sauté livers in ½ stick butter in large pan. Pour off fat. Add cognac and ignite. Pour livers into a bowl. In same pan, heat ½ stick butter. Cook apple and onion over medium heat until onion is translucent. Add to chicken livers. Mix seasonings and sour cream with bowl ingredients. Purée in food processor and then press through sieve. Let mixture cool to room temperature. Soften remaining 3 sticks butter. Combine with liver mixture and mix well. Pour into earthenware crock and chill. Garnish with truffle, if desired.

Mrs. Gardner Brooksbank (Kaye Dodds)

Chicken Liver Terrine

1 medium onion, chopped	1 tablespoon salt
1 clove garlic, chopped	1 teaspoon white pepper
2 eggs	½ stick butter
1 pound chicken livers	1 cup heavy cream
¼ cup flour	Party-size pumpernickel
½ teaspoon ginger	bread
½ teaspoon allspice	Tiny dill gherkins

Combine onion, garlic and eggs in blender at high speed for 1 minute. Add livers and blend 2 minutes longer. Add next 7 ingredients. Blend at high speed 2 more minutes. Pour into well greased 1-quart baking dish and cover with foil. Set in pan of hot water and bake 3 hours at 325° F. Remove foil and cool. Re-cover and chill at least 4 hours or overnight. Serve with pumpernickel bread and dill gherkins.

Dr. John L. Hooker

Braunschweiger Pâté

½ 10¾-ounce can tomato soup	1 teaspoon Worcestershire
1½ cups Braunschweiger	sauce
1 tablespoon unflavored	1 clove garlic, pressed
gelatin	Salt to taste
¼ cup water	1 tablespoon chopped parsley
1 10½-ounce can consommé	

Mix tomato soup and Braunschweiger. Dissolve gelatin in water. Bring consommé to a boil and add gelatin. Pour ⅓ of gelatin mixture into mold and chill. Add remainder of gelatin mixture to liver mixture. Add remaining ingredients. Mix and pour into mold. Chill. Serves 8-10.

This also makes wonderful sandwiches.

Mrs. Bob Sargent
Nashville, Tennessee

Larane's Bacon Spread

2 slices raw bacon
1 teaspoon Worcestershire
   sauce
2 teaspoons mayonnaise
¼ cup sharp Cheddar cheese

1 small onion
½ green pepper
½ teaspoon dry mustard
   Sliced French bread

Put all ingredients, except bread, through fine chopper or food processor. Spread on bread and toast under broiler. Serve hot. Freezes well. Makes 10 canapés.

Delicious on rye bread also.

Mrs. Harry McKee (Larane Wilson)

Two-Day Swiss Spread

1 12-ounce package Swiss
   cheese
2 large green peppers,
   chopped
1 teaspoon dry mustard

½-1 cup mayonnaise
1 teaspoon seasoned salt
4 dashes Tabasco
   Triscuits, rye crackers or
   party rye rounds

Chop peppers and cheese. Mix with rest of ingredients and refrigerate for 24-48 hours before serving. Aging improves taste. Yields 2½-3 cups.

Excellent on bran or rye bread for sandwiches

Mrs. Patricia Taylor

Mushroom Spread

4 slices bacon
2 tablespoons bacon drippings
½ pound fresh mushrooms, chopped
1 medium onion, finely chopped
1 clove garlic, whole
2 tablespoons flour
¼ teaspoon seasoned salt
¼ teaspoon lemon-pepper seasoning
8 ounces cream cheese, cubed
2 teaspoons Worcestershire sauce
1 teaspoon soy sauce
½ cup sour cream
1 teaspoon chopped parsley

Cook bacon until crisp; drain and set aside. In 2 tablespoons of drippings, sauté mushrooms, onion and garlic until tender and most of the liquid has evaporated. Blend in flour, seasoned salt and lemon-pepper. Add cheese, Worcestershire and soy sauce; stir until cheese melts. Remove garlic. Stir in sour cream, crumbled bacon and parsley. Heat but do not boil. Serve warm on rye rounds or crackers.

Mrs. Max Lucas (Ruth Plyler)

Cold Eggplant Spread

1 large eggplant
1 large onion, chopped
1 green pepper, chopped
2 cloves garlic, minced
¼-½ cup olive oil
2 fresh tomatoes, peeled and chopped
Salt and pepper to taste
Cayenne pepper to taste
2 tablespoons white wine

Bake whole eggplant in 400° F. oven until soft. Cool, peel and chop. Sauté onion, green pepper and garlic in oil until tender. Add tomato, eggplant and seasonings to onion mixture. Add wine and cook until thick, about 10 minutes. Chill and serve with Melba rounds.

Be liberal with the cayenne pepper in this recipe! Chopped green olives also add a special touch.

Edwina Theresa Thomas

Shrimp Mayonnaise

3 cups mayonnaise
½ cup ketchup
3 eggs, hard-boiled and grated
½ large dill pickle, finely chopped

¼ cup stuffed green olives, finely chopped
¼ cup celery, finely chopped
2 cups chopped, cooked shrimp

Mix all ingredients the day before to bring out shrimp flavor. Makes 6 cups dip.

Try filling fresh tomatoes with this for a salad!

Mrs. Robert G. Allen (Sally Ball)

Shrimp Butter

8 ounces cream cheese, softened
1½ sticks butter, softened
4 tablespoons mayonnaise
1 tablespoon minced onion

Juice of 1 lemon
Salt and cayenne pepper to taste
1 12-ounce package frozen shrimp, cooked and cooled

Mix all ingredients except shrimp. Gently fold in shrimp. Refrigerate at least 12 hours. Serve with crackers. Serves 10-12.

Mrs. J. Walker Hays, III (Helen Scanlin)

Smoked Oyster Spread

4 ounces cream cheese, softened
1 3½-ounce can smoked oysters, chopped
1 tablespoon mayonnaise

1 tablespoon milk
1 teaspoon onion juice
½ teaspoon paprika
Finely minced chives

Mix first 6 ingredients. Chill. Sprinkle with chives and serve with crackers. Makes 1 cup.

Pretty covered with parsley.

Mrs. G. Thomas Vaughan

Creamy Braunschweiger Spread

1   8-ounce package
    Braunschweiger
8   ounces cream cheese
¼   cup mayonnaise
¼   cup sweet pickle relish

¼   teaspoon garlic salt
1   tablespoon Worcestershire
    sauce
¼   teaspoon onion salt

Blend all ingredients in blender or food processor until smooth. Delicious served with dill, white or party rye bread. Makes approximately 2 cups.

Mrs. Charles E. Frankum (Linda Lacey)

Pataveritt

½   pound Braunschweiger
2   tablespoons finely chopped
    onion
½   rib celery, finely chopped
2   tablespoons sweet pickle
    relish

2   tablespoons mayonnaise
2   drops Tabasco, or more
1   teaspoon Worcestershire
    sauce
    Capers or parsley for garnish

Blend all ingredients in blender or food processor until smooth. Serve cold, garnished with capers or parsley. Serves 8-12.

Mrs. Douglas Averitt, Jr. (Frances Keenan)

Hot Mushroom Dip

½   stick butter
2   cloves garlic, minced
1   pound fresh mushrooms,
    sliced
3   tablespoons minced parsley

½   teaspoon salt
½   teaspoon pepper
    Cayenne pepper to taste
8   ounces sour cream

Sauté garlic in butter for 3 minutes. Add remaining ingredients, except sour cream. Sauté for 1 more minute. Fold in sour cream and serve on Melba toast or Triscuits.

Mrs. William S. Mitchell

Vegetable Dip

1   onion
2   large ripe tomatoes
1   4-ounce can chopped green
    chilies
6   black olives, sliced
1   tablespoon vinegar
2-3 tablespoons olive oil

Coarsley chop onion and tomatoes. Add chilies and olives. Toss vegetables in oil and vinegar. Refrigerate and serve with chips.

Excellent dip, but use only summer's best tomatoes!

Mrs. Charles W. McCrary (Janie Stone)

Dip for Vegetables

1   cup mayonnaise
¼   cup minced parsley
¼   cup minced green onion
2   thin slices onion
⅓   cup chopped fresh spinach
¼   cup sour cream
2   tablespoons lemon juice
    Salt and pepper to taste

Combine all ingredients in blender or food processor. Chill. Serve with fresh vegetables. Makes 1½ cups.

Mrs. Bill Summey
Sanford, North Carolina

Artichoke Dip

2   8½-ounce cans artichoke
    hearts
1   cup mayonnaise
1   cup Parmesan cheese
1   tablespoon lemon juice
8   drops Tabasco
2   green onions, chopped
½   teaspoon garlic salt

Drain and mash artichokes. Mix all ingredients and heat in a saucepan. Serve hot in a chafing dish with chips.

Pretty with paprika on top.

Mrs. Joseph W. Teagarden, III (Diana Wilborn)

Mexicali Dip

2 chopped avocados
1 8-ounce jar El Paso Taco
  Sauce
8 ounces sour cream

6 ounces grated Monterey Jack
  cheese
4-5 chopped green onions

Layer ingredients in bowl in order listed. Serve as dip with Doritos.

Also good topped with layer of sliced ripe olives and layer of crumbled bacon.

Mrs. Dennis Higdon (Joanna Coss)

Guacamole Dip

2-3 medium avocados
2 tablespoons chopped onion
1 14-ounce can Italian
  tomatoes, drained

4 tablespoons lemon juice
2 teaspoons Tabasco
1 teaspoon garlic salt
1 cup Hellmann's mayonnaise

Place all ingredients except mayonnaise in blender; mix well. Pour into bowl; add mayonnaise. Refrigerate. Placing avocado seed in dip will help prevent guacamole from turning brown if made in advance. Makes about 3 cups.

Mrs. Phil Hickey, II

Spinach Dip

1 10-ounce package frozen
  chopped spinach
¾ cup mayonnaise
¾ cup sour cream

1 tablespoon parsley flakes
½ 4-ounce package Original
  Hidden Valley Dressing
Dash of Tabasco

Defrost spinach and squeeze dry. Mix all ingredients together and serve with chips or crackers. Keep chilled.

Quick and easy. Great stuffing for squash.

Mrs. Charles Alfred Williams, III (Elise McDonald)

Vera's Dip

⅓	cup olive oil	1	6-ounce can tomato paste
3	cups peeled, cubed eggplant	2	tablespoons wine vinegar
⅓	cup chopped green pepper	¾	cup chopped green olives
1	onion, chopped	1½	teaspoons sugar
1	4-ounce can sliced mushrooms	½	teaspoon oregano
		1	teaspoon salt
2	or more cloves garlic, crushed	¼-½	teaspoon pepper
			Tabasco to taste

Heat oil. Add eggplant, green pepper, onion, mushrooms and garlic. Cover and cook 10 minutes. Stir. Add remaining ingredients; simmer 30-40 minutes. Serve hot with Fritos or crackers. May be done ahead, frozen and reheated.

Also makes a super vegetable dish.

Mrs. Peter Rosato, III (Vera Wood)

Cajun Dip

1	16-ounce can kidney beans, undrained		Salt to taste
			Tabasco to taste
1	pound lean ground beef	8	ounces sharp Cheddar cheese, grated
1	cup finely chopped onion, divided		
½	cup ketchup	1	5-ounce jar salad olives, chopped

In blender, mash beans with liquid to a paste. Brown ground beef and half of onions. Add beans, ketchup, salt and Tabasco. Simmer for 30 minutes. To serve, place meat mixture in chafing dish. Cover completely with grated cheese. Make a circle of onions about half way in from the edge. Fill center with olives. Replenish cheese, onions and olives as needed. Serve with plain Doritos. Serves 15-25.

Mrs. William C. Lewis

Clarkie's Caviar Dip

8 ounces cream cheese,
   softened
5 tablespoons mayonnaise
1 clove garlic, pressed
2 teaspoons finely minced
   onion

2 teaspoons Worcestershire
   sauce
4 drops Tabasco
1 teaspoon lemon juice
1 4-ounce jar Icelandic caviar

Mix well all ingredients except caviar. Place in serving bowl. Chill. Top with caviar. Serve with bland crackers.

Mrs. William L. Quinlen, Jr. (Ann Clark Miller)

Hot Clam Dip

1 medium onion, minced
1 green pepper, minced
6 tablespoons butter
2 7½-ounce cans minced clams,
   well drained
1 8-ounce package Velveeta
   cheese, cubed

½ cup ketchup
2 tablespoons Worcestershire
   sauce
¼ teaspoon cayenne pepper

Sauté onion and pepper in butter for 5 minutes. Put onions, peppers and remaining ingredients in double boiler and stir until cheese has melted. Serve hot with Fritos.

Mrs. William A. Coolidge

Easy Shrimp Dip

1 4½-ounce can small shrimp,
   drained
3 ounces cream cheese,
   softened
2 tablespoons mayonnaise
8 ounces sour cream

1½-2 tablespoons lemon juice
¼   teaspoon seasoned salt
½   teaspoon lemon-pepper
    seasoning
1   tablespoon chopped chives

Mix all ingredients well and chill. Serve with Wheat Thins. Makes approximately 2 cups.

Mrs. Scott Allison Arnold, III (Anne Dillard)

Chipped Beef Dip

2 2½-ounce jars dried beef, chopped finely
8 ounces cream cheese, softened
½ green pepper, chopped
1 medium onion, chopped
8 ounces sour cream
1-2 tablespoons finely chopped celery
1-2 tablespoons finely chopped parsley
3 tablespoons horseradish
½ cup chopped pecans

Combine all ingredients, except pecans. Place in baking dish; sprinkle pecans over top. Bake, covered, for 20 minutes at 350° F. Serve with crackers.

Mrs. Ruffner Murray (Jean Magee)

Taco Dip Supreme

1 pound ground beef
¼ cup chopped onion
   Salt and pepper to taste
2 tomatoes, chopped
2 avocados, chopped
6 ounces Cracker Barrel cheese, grated
½ cup Ortega Taco Sauce
8 ounces sour cream

Brown onion and ground beef. Drain. Season with salt and pepper. Place in bottom of glass bowl. Layer tomatoes and avocados on top of ground beef. Then layer cheese. Fold in taco sauce. Spread sour cream on top. Serve hot with taco-flavored Doritos. Serves 6-8.

Men especially love this.

Mrs. Richard A. Miller, Jr. (Shelley Brodnax)

Laurus nobilis

C. Grivich

Soups

Chilled Salmon Bisque

1 onion, chopped	1 teaspoon dill weed
½ cup chopped green pepper	1 tablespoon Worcestershire
1 clove garlic, minced	sauce
1 tablespoon butter	1 teaspoon salt
2 6-ounce cans pink salmon,	½ teaspoon pepper
drained and picked	2 tablespoons sherry
2½ cups light cream	2 tablespoons lemon juice

Sauté onion, pepper and garlic in butter. Combine all ingredients, except sherry and lemon juice, in blender or food processor. Blend at high speed until smooth. Refrigerate until chilled. Add lemon juice and sherry before serving. Makes 1½ quarts.

Excellent! Good on a hot summer night.

Mrs. John W. McQuiston (Robbie Walker)

Borscht

1 16-ounce jar pickled beets	Tabasco to taste
and juice	1 clove garlic, minced
2 cups V-8 juice	Sour cream or chopped hard-
3 whole dill pickles, chopped	boiled eggs
3 tablespoons finely grated	
onion	

Place all ingredients in blender or food processor and blend until smooth. This may be served hot or cold. Garnish with a dollop of sour cream or chopped hard-boiled eggs. Serves 4.

Mrs. Harry McKee (Larane Wilson)

Cold Cucumber Soup

½ medium onion, chopped
1 medium cucumber, peeled and coarsely cubed
¾ cup chicken broth
1 10¾-ounce can cream of chicken soup
8 ounces sour cream
¼ teaspoon Tabasco or less
½ teaspoon Worcestershire sauce
¼ teaspoon celery salt
⅛-¼ teaspoon curry powder
Chopped chives for garnish

Place first 5 ingredients in blender. Blend until smooth. Add seasonings to taste. Chill 2 hours or more. Garnish with chopped chives. Serves 4-6.

Mrs. Thomas Hollomon (Jayne Pressgrove)

Chilled Mushroom Soup

1½ pounds fresh mushrooms
1 onion, chopped
1 rib celery, chopped
1 carrot, thinly sliced
1½ teaspoons peppercorns
1½ teaspoons salt
1 bay leaf
3 cups dry vermouth
1 chicken bouillon cube
3 tablespoons olive oil
2 tablespoons flour
½ teaspoon thyme
2 cups heavy cream

Wash mushrooms and break off stems. Combine stems and next 8 ingredients in saucepan. Bring to a boil, reduce heat and simmer 10 minutes. Thinly slice mushroom caps and briefly sauté in olive oil. Stir in flour and thyme and cook, stirring constantly, for about 3 minutes. Strain vermouth mixture over mushrooms. Discard vegetables. Bring to a boil, reduce heat and simmer 10 minutes. Chill and skim off any grease. Just before serving, stir in cream. Serves 6-8.

Mrs. William E. Denman (Julie Moss)

Soup Verde

2 10-ounce packages frozen
   green peas
½ cup minced green onion
½ teaspoon salt

¾ cup water
1 chicken bouillon cube
1 10¾-ounce can chicken broth
½ cup heavy cream

Combine first 5 ingredients in pan and bring to boil. Cover and simmer 15 minutes. Purée in blender. Add chicken broth and chill. Stir in cream before serving. Serves 6.

Mrs. Bill Summey
Sanford, North Carolina

Chilled Tomato Soup

4 large tomatoes, cut into
   sections
1 large onion, coarsely chopped
2 cloves garlic, minced
2 cups water, divided
1 teaspoon salt
   Freshly ground pepper to
   taste

1 teaspoon dill weed
4 tablespoons flour
1 cup light cream
   Chopped chives, parsley or
   dill for garnish

Combine tomatoes, onion, garlic, 1 cup water, salt, pepper and dill in large saucepan. Bring to boil and simmer 30 minutes. Stir remaining water slowly into flour and add to hot soup. Cook 3 minutes, stirring. Pour soup into blender and blend in batches. Strain. Refrigerate when cooled. To serve, stir in cream and garnish as desired. Serves 8.

For extra richness, substitute heavy cream for light cream.

Mrs. J. T. Jabbour

Chilled Watercress Soup

1 bunch watercress
1 green onion, chopped
1 10¾-ounce can chicken broth
1 sprig fresh basil or mint

1 teaspoon salt
1 cup heavy cream
Watercress, mint or chives for garnish

Remove tough stem ends from watercress. Blend all ingredients, except cream and garnish, in blender until greens are chopped. Place in saucepan and simmer for 3-5 minutes. Chill. To serve, add cream and garnish as desired. Serves 4.

Mrs. William B. Trimble, Jr. (Becky Johnstone)

Jade Garden Soup

6 cups strained chicken stock, or 5 10¾-ounce cans chicken broth
1 large onion, chopped
1 carrot, sliced
2 ribs celery, sliced
⅓ cup rice
1⅓ cups spinach, packed down

1⅓ cups lettuce, packed down
1⅓ cups parsley, packed down
Salt
Pepper
Cayenne pepper
Accent
Sour cream, paprika and dill weed, for garnish

Cook stock, onion, carrot, celery and rice for 35 minutes, covered, or until rice is soft. Place spinach, lettuce and parsley in saucepan. Cover with water and bring to a quick boil. Drain immediately. Add to soup. Adjust seasonings. Mix in blender until smooth. May be thinned with more broth. Refrigerate overnight. Garnish as desired. Serves 6-8.

Can be served hot or cold.

Mrs. Miki Mall

Gazpacho Soup

1 cucumber, peeled and chopped	1 tablespoon minced parsley
6-8 green onions and tops, chopped	1 46-ounce can tomato juice
	1 24-ounce can V-8 juice
3-4 ribs celery, chopped	1 lemon, juiced
1 green pepper, chopped	Salt and pepper to taste
1 28-ounce can tomatoes, coarsely chopped	10-15 drops Tabasco
	1 teaspoon Worcestershire sauce

Put chopped vegetables in large container. Add juices and seasonings. Refrigerate for several hours before serving. Serves 10-12.

The flavor of soup enhances with age.

Carolyn Mitchell Kittle

Gazpacho Andaluz

2 cucumbers, peeled and chopped	4 cups cold water
5 tomatoes, peeled and chopped	¼ cup red wine vinegar
1 large onion, chopped	4 teaspoons salt
1 green pepper, chopped	4 tablespoons olive oil
2 teaspoons chopped garlic	1 tablespoon tomato paste
4 cups coarsely crumbled French bread, crust removed	

Combine first 6 ingredients in deep bowl. Stir in water, vinegar and salt. Make a smooth purée of this mixture in blender or food processor. Pour purée into a bowl and whisk in olive oil and tomato paste. Cover and refrigerate at least 2 hours before serving. Serves 6-8.

Garnishes

Bread cubes	Cucumbers, chopped
Onions, chopped	Green peppers, chopped
Tomatoes, chopped	

Garnishes should be put in separate bowls and used according to each individual taste. Never omit the garnish.

This is the true Andalusian way of making gazpacho.

Dorsey Mathis

White Gazpacho

2 10¾-ounce cans chicken
   broth
3 green peppers, chopped
3 cucumbers, peeled, seeded
   and chopped
4 green onions, chopped
3 tablespoons white wine
   vinegar
12 ounces sour cream
3 garlic cloves, minced
1 tablespoon powdered chicken
   bouillon

¼ cup olive oil
6 medium mushrooms,
   chopped
3 tomatoes, peeled and
   chopped
2 tablespoons Worcestershire
   sauce
   Salt and pepper to taste
½ teaspoon summer savory

Put ¾ can chicken broth in blender or food processor. Add peppers, 2 cucumbers, 1 onion, vinegar, sour cream, garlic and powdered chicken bouillon. Blend. Combine olive oil, remaining broth and remaining vegetables, Worcestershire sauce, salt, pepper and summer savory in a large bowl. Add ingredients from blender to bowl and mix well. Chill. Serves 12.

Mrs. William Craddock

Cream of Avocado Soup

1 onion, chopped
1 clove garlic, minced
4 tablespoons butter
1 tablespoon flour
4 cups chicken broth or stock

4 ripe avocados
1 8-ounce can crabmeat
2 cups light cream
   Salt and pepper, to taste

Sauté onion and garlic in butter until limp. Add flour. Blend. Stir in chicken stock and whip until smooth. Mash avocados and crabmeat and stir into liquid. Simmer 20 minutes. Stir in cream. Season to taste and heat, without boiling. Serve either hot or very cold. Serves 4-6.

Do not cook or store in aluminum container.

Mrs. Charles W. McCrary (Janie Stone)

Cream of Artichoke Soup

3 tablespoons butter
½ cup chopped green onions
1 rib celery, finely chopped
1 carrot, finely chopped
1 bay leaf
⅛ teaspoon thyme
1 quart chicken broth

1 10-ounce package frozen
  artichoke hearts, cooked
  and sliced
2 egg yolks, beaten
1 cup heavy cream
  Salt and white pepper to
  taste

Sauté onions, celery, carrot, bay leaf and thyme in butter until tender. Add broth. Simmer 10-15 minutes. Add artichoke hearts. Continue simmering another 10 minutes. Remove from heat. Add egg yolks, cream, salt and pepper to taste. Serves 6.

Mrs. Lucian Wadlington (Patsy Mullins)

Cuban Black Bean Soup

1 pound black beans
2 quarts water
2 tablespoons salt
5 cloves garlic, peeled
½ tablespoon cumin
½ tablespoon oregano
1 ounce white vinegar
5 ounces olive oil

½ pound onions, chopped
½ pound green peppers,
  chopped
1 cup raw rice
½ cup chopped onion
½ cup olive oil
¼ cup vinegar

Wash beans thoroughly and soak in water overnight. Boil beans and salt in enough of the water to cover beans. Cook until beans are soft. Crush garlic, cumin, oregano and mix with 1 ounce of vinegar. Heat 5 ounces of oil in skillet. Sauté onions and peppers until tender. Add crushed ingredients, sautéing slowly. Add this mixture to the bean mixture and cook slowly until ready to serve. Cook rice according to directions on package. Marinate rice and ½ cup of the chopped onion in ½ cup of oil and ¼ cup vinegar. Add one spoonful of rice to each serving of soup. Serves 4-6. This soup takes about 4 hours of cooking.

Mrs. Dudley Bridgforth (Donna Kay Byrd)

Annie's Cream of Broccoli Soup

1½ pounds fresh broccoli
2 tablespoons butter
½ cup chopped onion
1 cup diced potatoes
2 13¾-ounce cans chicken
   broth

½ teaspoon salt
1 cup light cream
⅛ teaspoon ground nutmeg

Chop broccoli and parboil in salted water for 5 minutes. Drain well. Sauté onion in saucepan in butter for 5 minutes. Add potatoes, broth and salt. Heat to boiling, lower heat, and simmer 15 minutes. Add broccoli. Simmer 5 minutes longer or until vegetables are tender. Pour mixture, half at a time, into blender. Blend. Return to saucepan and add cream and nutmeg. Bring to boil. Season to taste with salt. Serves 6-8.

A delicious garnish for this and other cream soups is a dollop of whipped cream with nutmeg.

Mrs. Thomas C. Scott (Bette Thomas)

Cream of Carrot Soup

2 tablespoons butter
½ cup coarsely chopped onion
1 pound carrots, peeled and
   sliced
1 pound potatoes, peeled and
   cubed
6 cups chicken broth
1½ teaspoons dried thyme

2 bay leaves
1 cup heavy cream
1 cup milk
⅛ teaspoon Tabasco
½ teaspoon sugar
⅛ teaspoon nutmeg
Salt
Freshly ground pepper

Heat butter in soup kettle and sauté onion. Add other vegetables and broth and bring to a boil. Add thyme and bay leaves. Simmer 40 minutes or until vegetables are tender. Put mixture in blender or food processor in batches. When all is processed, repeat blending, in batches, until very smooth. Transfer back to kettle. Bring to boil and add remaining ingredients. May be served hot or very cold. Serves 12.

Beautiful color. Delightful for a summer luncheon.

Carolyn Mitchell Kittle

Cream of Corn Soup

2 strips bacon, finely chopped
2 tablespoons finely chopped
   onions
2 cups fresh corn, or 2 10-ounce
   packages frozen corn
2 tablespoons butter

2 tablespoons flour
2 cups milk
1 teaspoon salt
½ teaspoon pepper
2 cups light cream

Fry bacon until crisp. Add onion and sauté until soft. Chop corn in blender or food processor and add to onion and bacon. Cook slowly until it begins to brown. Add butter, then flour. Cook slowly for 3 minutes. Add milk, salt and pepper. Cook until thickened. Add cream and heat until smooth. Serves 6.

Use kitchen scissors to snip raw bacon.

Mrs. Pat Roach (Nell Magee)

Cajun Corn Soup

6 tablespoons cooking oil
6 tablespoons flour
2 large onions, chopped
1 cup chopped celery
3 large potatoes, cubed
3 fresh tomatoes, peeled and
   chopped
5 pints boiling water
1 10-ounce package frozen tiny
   lima beans

2 tablespoons salt
1 teaspoon cayenne pepper
3 pounds peeled shrimp
2 17-ounce cans whole kernel
   corn
2 17-ounce cans creamed corn
8 sprigs parsley, chopped

Using a heavy iron skillet, cook oil and flour, stirring constantly, until dark brown. Be careful not to burn. Add onions and celery. Continue cooking on low heat, stirring, until vegetables are soft. Add tomatoes and potatoes. Stir well to dissolve roux. Add water and cook until boiling. Add next 6 ingredients. Cook for 30 minutes. Garnish with parsley. Serves 12.

Mrs. Joseph D'Geralamo (Dianne Dupepe)

Special Corn Chowder

4 slices bacon, diced
1 large onion, chopped
3 cups peeled, diced potatoes
3 cups water
3 tablespoons butter
¼ cup flour
2 cups milk

1-2 cups diced, cooked ham
2 12-ounce cans whole corn, undrained
2 teaspoons salt
¼ teaspoon pepper
2 tablespoons parsley
1 tablespoon dill weed

Cook bacon until almost crisp. Add onion and cook until soft. Add potatoes and water and cook over moderate heat until tender, about 10 minutes. In separate pan, melt butter and blend in flour. Gradually add milk, stirring constantly. Add this mixture to potato mixture. Add remaining ingredients. Heat without boiling. Makes 3 quarts or twelve 8-ounce cups.

Great for "football watching" parties.

Mrs. Charles Richard Patterson (Helen Reynolds)

Alfredo Soup

3 cloves garlic, pressed
1 onion, thinly sliced
2 ounces olive oil
4 tablespoons butter
3 cups sliced mushrooms
Pepper to taste
2 ounces tomato paste
2 ounces dry sherry

3-4 13¾-ounce cans chicken broth
3 egg yolks
2½ ounces Parmesan cheese, grated
2 tablespoons chopped parsley

Sauté garlic and onion in olive oil and butter. When tender, add mushrooms and sauté very slightly. Add pepper to taste. Do not salt. Add tomato paste, sherry and broth. Simmer about 30 minutes. Recipe may be done ahead to this point. For last minute completion of this recipe, whisk together egg yolks, Parmesan cheese and parsley. Add one cup of very warm broth mixture to egg mixture and stir. Then add egg mixture to rest of broth in saucepan. Serve hot. Serves 6.

Mrs. Charles Schaffler (Mickey Pooley)

Mushroom Soup

1 pound fresh mushrooms,
   sliced
½ onion, thinly sliced
7 tablespoons butter, divided
4 tablespoons flour
2 cups milk

¼ teaspoon salt
3 peppercorns
1 teaspoon minced parsley
2 10¾-ounce cans beef bouillon
   Whipped cream
   Ground nutmeg

Sauté mushrooms and onion in 3 tablespoons butter. Set aside. Melt 4 tablespoons butter in saucepan, then add flour, 1 tablespoon at a time. Gradually add milk, stirring until smooth. Add salt, peppercorns and parsley. Put sauce and mushrooms in blender or food processor and blend until smooth. Pour into saucepan; add bouillon and heat. Serve warm with dollops of cream and a sprinkling of nutmeg. Serves 6.

Dreamy luncheon soup.

Mrs. Charles Richard Patterson (Helen Reynolds)

French Onion Soup

6 small onions, thinly sliced
2 tablespoons butter
1 teaspoon flour
6 cups beef or chicken broth
½ cup dry white wine

   Freshly ground pepper
6 slices day-old French bread
6 tablespoons grated Swiss
   cheese

Lightly brown onions in butter. Sprinkle in flour and continue to cook. Add broth, wine and pepper. Simmer 10-15 minutes. Toast bread on both sides and place in soup tureen or individual casseroles. Pour soup over toast and sprinkle with cheese. Put in moderate oven to melt cheese. Serve very hot. Serves 8.

Mrs. Jimmy Haskins
Union City, Tennessee

Leek and Potato Soup

8 slices bacon, chopped
6 ribs celery, chopped
8 leeks, sliced
4 potatoes, peeled and sliced
3 quarts chicken broth or
  stock, divided

2 teaspoons salt
4 cups light cream
1-3 Polish sausages, cooked and
  sliced
Chives, for garnish

Sauté bacon in heavy, large pot until transparent. Add celery and leeks. Cover and steam for 10 minutes. Add potatoes, 2 quarts stock and salt. Cook until potatoes are tender. Cool. Purée in batches, then add rest of stock. May be frozen at this point. Add cream and sausage. Season to taste with salt and pepper. Heat slowly and serve garnished with chives. Serves 12.

Hearty and good! Good with Italian bread, cheese and apples.

Mrs. Roy Moore (Pat Patteson)

Pimiento Soup

½ cup chopped onion
4 tablespoons butter
1 4-ounce jar whole pimientos
4 tablespoons flour
2 cups milk
1 cup heavy cream
2 cups chicken stock
1½ cups grated Cheddar cheese

1 teaspoon salt
⅛ teaspoon white pepper
¼ teaspoon Accent
¼ teaspoon Worcestershire
  sauce
Chopped fresh parsley for
  garnish

Sauté onion in butter until soft but not brown. Add pimientos and heat for 2 minutes. Add flour gradually and cook, stirring constantly, for 2 minutes longer. Add milk, cream and chicken stock. Heat, stirring constantly, until the soup is slightly thickened. Do not boil. Add cheese and stir until melted. Add seasonings. Put soup in blender or food processor and blend until smooth. Garnish with parsley. Serves 4-6.

Mrs. Clyde L. Patton, Jr. (Leslie Wilsford)

Cream of Spinach Soup

3 10-ounce packages frozen
   chopped spinach
2 cups milk
2 tablespoons butter
3 tablespoons grated onion
2 cups light cream

1 2¾-ounce package Knorr's
   dry leek soup mix
2 cups chicken broth
   Dash of cayenne pepper
   Dash of Tabasco sauce
   Parmesan cheese

Cook spinach as directed on package. Drain well. Blend with enough milk to make a smooth mixture. Melt butter in saucepan and sauté onion until tender. Stir in cream. Gradually add soup mix. Add blended spinach, remaining milk, chicken broth and seasonings. Heat soup and sprinkle with grated Parmesan cheese. Serves 8.

Mrs. Gwin Scott (Wynn Skipper)

Cream of Herb Soup

3 tablespoons butter
1 cup chopped green onions
1 cup chopped spinach
½ cup chopped fresh basil, or 3
   tablespoons dried basil, or
   ½ cup chopped watercress
¼ cup chopped parsley

5 cups chicken broth
1 teaspoon sugar
1 cup light cream
   Salt and pepper to taste
2 tablespoons butter, softened
2 tablespoons flour
   Chopped parsley, for garnish

Melt butter in large saucepan. Sauté onions until tender, about 10 minutes. Add spinach, basil or watercress and parsley. Cover and simmer 10 minutes. Add broth and sugar. Simmer, covered, for 30 minutes. Slowly stir in cream. In separate pan, blend together butter and flour. Whisk in a little of the hot soup, beating until smooth. Pour slowly into soup, stirring constantly. Bring just to a boil and remove from heat. Serve in warm bowls with parsley garnish. Serves 8-10.

Mrs. Huey L. Holden (Barbara Hopper)

Squash Soup

6-8 green onions, green part
    discarded
4 tablespoons butter
2 pounds summer squash,
    diced
4 cups chicken stock or broth

1 cup heavy cream
    Salt
    White pepper
6 tablespoons sour cream
    Chopped chives

In large saucepan, sauté white parts of onions in butter until softened. Stir in squash. Add chicken broth; bring to a boil and simmer, covered, for ½ hour, or until vegetables are soft. Purée in blender or food processor and return to pan. Stir in cream, salt and pepper to taste and reheat. Garnish with one tablespoon sour cream and sprinkle of chives per serving. Serves 6. Crumbled bacon can also be used as garnish.

Mrs. Charlie Carr
Chapel Hill, North Carolina

Curried Zucchini Soup

3 tablespoons butter
2-3 medium onions, thinly sliced
1 large clove garlic, thinly
    sliced
1 teaspoon curry powder
6 large zucchini, sliced ¼-inch
    thick

2-3 teaspoons salt
    Freshly ground pepper
3 cups chicken stock
    Lemon juice
    Cayenne pepper
1½ cups heavy cream
1½ tablespoons dark rum

In large saucepan, sauté onions and garlic in butter until soft. Stir in curry powder and cook slowly, about 2 minutes. Add zucchini, cover, and cook over low heat for 6 minutes. Season with salt and pepper to taste. Add chicken stock, cover, and simmer about 8 minutes, or until zucchini is tender but still retains some crispness. Purée in blender or food processor. Do not let this purée become too smooth. Season to taste with salt, pepper, lemon juice and a few dashes of cayenne pepper. Stir in cream and rum immediately before serving. Serves 8.

Mrs. Mickey Moran (Pat Taylor)

Lady Curzon Soup

2 15-ounce cans turtle soup
⅓ cup minced mushrooms
2 tablespoons sherry
½ teaspoon curry powder

¼ cup heavy cream
2 egg yolks, lightly beaten
1½ tablespoons brandy
Parmesan cheese for garnish

In a saucepan, bring soup to boiling point over moderate heat. Transfer ¾ cup to small saucepan. Add mushrooms and simmer for 5 minutes. Stir in sherry and add this mixture to soup. In small bowl, dissolve curry in cream. Add egg yolks and brandy. Add 1 cup of soup to cream mixture and return to rest of soup. Cook over low heat until slightly thickened. Serve, sprinkled with Parmesan cheese. Serves 4-6.

Mrs. Charles Richard Patterson (Helen Reynolds)

Crab Bisque

1 cup crabmeat
½ cup sherry
1 10¾-ounce can tomato soup
1 10¾-ounce can green pea soup
1 soup can light cream

½ teaspoon curry
½ teaspoon paprika
Sour cream (optional)
Chives (optional)
2 eggs, hard-boiled (optional)

Put crabmeat in a bowl, pour sherry over and let stand 1 hour. Blend remaining ingredients. Heat slowly. Do not boil. Add crabmeat. Reheat to boiling point and serve immediately. Top with a dollop of sour cream and sprinkle with chives or grated hard-boiled egg. Serves 6.

Mrs. John Parsons (Frances Urquart)

Susan's She Crab Soup

3 cups milk
3 lemon slices
½ teaspoon mace
3 cups light cream
1 pound crabmeat

1 stick butter
½ cup crumbled saltine
  crackers
Salt and pepper to taste
2 tablespoons sherry

Heat milk, lemon and mace in double boiler for 2 minutes. Add cream, crabmeat and butter and cook 15 minutes. Thicken with crumbs and season to taste. Before serving, add sherry. Keep over low heat until serving time. Serves 4-6.

Mrs. Jon K. Thompson (Susan Taylor)

Seafood Bisque

4 cups chicken stock
2 cups heavy cream
2 cups milk
½ stick butter
1 teaspoon Worcestershire
  sauce
2 generous dashes of cayenne
  pepper

1 pint oysters, chopped, reserve
  liquid
1 pound crabmeat, flaked
1 pound shrimp,peeled and
  chopped coarsely
6 tablespoons dry sherry
2 dashes nutmeg

Combine first 6 ingredients and oyster liquid in a pot. Simmer, but do not boil. Add seafood to liquid and simmer for 15 minutes. Remove from heat. Add sherry and nutmg and serve immediately. Serves 10-12.

Mrs. Ann H. Roy
Florence, Alabama

Oyster-Artichoke Soup

3 tablespoons butter
4 green onions, chopped
1 clove garlic, minced
1 14-ounce can artichoke
   hearts, drained and rinsed
1 14½-ounce can chicken broth
⅛ teaspoon red pepper flakes

¼ teaspoon anise seed
¼ teaspoon salt
1 teaspoon Worcestershire
   sauce
¾ pint oysters, undrained
2 10¾-ounce cans cream of
   potato soup

Sauté onion and garlic in butter until soft. Quarter artichoke hearts and add to pot. Add chicken broth and seasonings. Simmer 15 minutes. Add oysters and their liquid and simmer 5 minutes. Add potato soup. Purée in batches in blender or food processor. Reheat, but do not boil. Serves 6-8.

Mrs. Hershel P. Wall (Jean Harrington)

Oyster-Spinach Soup

4 tablespoons butter
4 shallots, minced
½ cup dry white wine
1 pint raw oysters, drained
1 teaspoon salt
⅛ teaspoon white pepper
½ 10-ounce package frozen
   chopped spinach

2 cups chicken broth
4 cups light cream
2 tablespoons cornstarch
1 teaspoon Worcestershire
   sauce
Cayenne pepper to taste

Melt butter in saucepan. Add shallots and sauté for 2 minutes. Stir in wine and bring to a boil. Cook until reduced by half. Finely chop oysters and add to wine mixture. Add salt and pepper, and stir over medium heat for 5 minutes. Remove from heat. In separate saucepan, bring spinach and broth to a boil; reduce heat. Cook until spinach is tender. Add cream and cook until thoroughly heated. Combine mixtures and let stand until cool. Dissolve cornstarch in 2 tablespoons cold water. Process soup in blender on high speed. Return to heavy pan over low heat. Add cornstarch and seasonings. Serves 8-10.

Dress up with whipped cream or a hint of lemon.

Mrs. Charles E. Frankum (Linda Lacey)

Oyster Stew

1 stick butter
½ bunch parsley, finely chopped
½ cup green onions, finely chopped
½ cup finely chopped celery
1½ pints oysters and juice

4 cups light cream
2 cups milk
Beau Monde to taste
White pepper to taste
1 teaspoon Accent
Tabasco to taste

Melt butter. Sauté parsley, green onions and celery until soft. Add oysters and juice and cook until the oysters curl. Add cream, milk, spices and lightly simmer. Do not overcook. If desired, add arrowroot to thicken. Serves 4-6.

This is especially festive during the holidays served in "Santa" cups.

Mrs. Kay K. Butler (Kay Kendall)

Shrimp Chowder

2 large onions, sliced
2 tablespoons butter
½ cup boiling water
3 medium potatoes, pared and cubed
½ tablespoon salt
¼ teaspoon seasoned pepper

3 cups milk
1 cup grated sharp Cheddar cheese
2 pounds raw shrimp, shelled and deveined
1½ tablespoons chopped parsley

In Dutch oven, sauté onions in butter until tender. Add boiling water, potatoes, salt and pepper. Simmer, covered, for 20 minutes, or until potatoes are tender. Do not drain. Meanwhile, heat milk with cheese until cheese has melted and milk is hot. Do not boil. Add shrimp to potatoes and cook until they turn pink, about 5 minutes. *Slowly* add hot milk mixture. Heat, but do not boil. Sprinkle with parsley. Serves 6.

Mrs. John Sorrells

Clam Chowder

2½ cups chopped onion
5 slices bacon, coarsely
  chopped
3 tablespoons butter
3 cups diced potatoes
2 6½-ounce cans minced clams

4 tablespoons flour
4 cups milk
Seasoned salt
Freshly ground pepper
Chopped parsley

Combine onion, bacon and butter in Dutch oven and cook over medium-low heat until onion is very tender and bacon begins to cook. Stir frequently. Cook potatoes in salted water to cover. Drain and reserve liquid. Drain clams and reserve liquid. When onions are tender, stir in flour. Slowly add clam juice, one cup of potato water and one cup of milk. Stir until thick and boiling. Add clams and potatoes and enough milk to make desired soup consistency. Season with seasoned salt and pepper to taste. Garnish with chopped parsley before serving. Serves 8.

Good with hearty meat sandwich, white wine and a warm fire.

Mrs. Henry Hancock (Peggy Fairchild)

Clam Chowder au Vin

2 cups diced potatoes
½ cup chopped onion
½ cup chopped celery
¼ teaspoon salt
1 cup water
1 10½-ounce can condensed
  Manhattan-style clam
  chowder

1 cup milk
1 7½-ounce can minced clams,
  drained
3 tablespoons dry white wine
½ cup heavy cream, whipped
Salt
Pepper
2 tablespoons snipped parsley

In large saucepan, combine first 5 ingredients. Cover and cook until potatoes are tender, about 10 minutes. Mash slightly. Add chowder, milk, clams and wine. Heat, but do not boil. Stir cream into chowder and season with salt and pepper. Garnish with parsley. May be served over toast or pastry shells. Serves 4.

Mrs. Alan Carey (Nancy Brunson)

Creole Bouillabaisse

2 tablespoons butter
2 tablespoons olive oil
¼ cup flour
1 cup chopped onion
½ cup chopped celery
1 clove garlic, minced
5 cups water
1 28-ounce can tomatoes, cut up and undrained
½ cup dry white wine

2 tablespoons chopped parsley
1 tablespoon lemon juice
1 bay leaf
½ teaspoon salt
¼ teaspoon saffron
¼ teaspoon cayenne pepper
2 pounds fish filets
½ pound raw shrimp, peeled
1 pint oysters
1 pound crabmeat

Make roux by mixing butter, oil and flour in skillet. Stir over low heat until light brown. Add onion, celery and garlic. Cook until tender. Gradually stir in water. Add next 8 ingredients and ¼ of fish filets. Bring to boil and simmer for 20 minutes. Add remaining fish and cook 5-10 minutes. Add shrimp, oysters and crab. Cook additional 3-5 minutes. Serves 8-10.

Mrs. Ann H. Roy
Florence, Alabama

New Orleans Gumbo

4 tablespoons flour
4 tablespoons oil
4 10¾-ounce cans chicken with rice soup
4 soup cans water
1 cup chopped onion
1 cup chopped green pepper
1 cup chopped celery
4 cloves garlic, minced
2 bay leaves

1 tomato, chopped
1 tablespoon Worcestershire sauce
¼ teaspoon cayenne pepper
1 pound fresh okra, sliced
Bacon drippings
1 pound shrimp, shelled and cleaned
1 pound crabmeat, picked
Gumbo filé

Make dark brown roux with flour and oil. Set aside. In a large pot, combine next 10 ingredients. Cook on medium-high heat until very hot, but not boiling. Brown okra in heavy skillet with bacon drippings, stirring frequently. Add okra and roux to gumbo, mixing well. Cover and simmer for 1½ hours, stirring occasionally. Add seafood and simmer for 15 additional minutes. Correct seasonings. Sprinkle filé lightly over individual servings. Serves 8-10.

Gumbo is best served over rice in a large flat soup bowl.

Mrs. Michael Lynch (Susan Corcoran)

Spicy Seafood Gumbo

2-3 pounds shrimp
1 gallon water
4 bay leaves
1 teaspoon salt
4 strips bacon, fried and
   crumbled
8 whole green onions, sliced
1 tablespoon flour
1 28-ounce can tomatoes,
   cut up
2 10-ounce boxes frozen cut
   okra

1 pint lump crabmeat
1 teaspoon thyme
1 tablespoon crushed red
   pepper
1 pint oysters
1 cup rice, uncooked
1 tablespoon gumbo filé
Salt, pepper, Tabasco and
   thyme to taste

Boil shrimp in water with bay leaves and salt for 5 minutes. Remove shrimp and reserve liquid. Peel shrimp and return to liquid. Fry bacon and reserve grease. Crumble bacon and add to liquid. Sauté onions in bacon grease. Add 1 tablespoon flour to grease, stirring well to make a roux. Add onions and roux to liquid. To mixture, add tomatoes, including liquid, okra, crabmeat, thyme and red pepper. Cover and simmer 3 hours. Add oysters, oyster liquid and rice. Cover and simmer 1 hour. Add gumbo filé, salt, pepper, Tabasco and thyme to taste. Simmer 5 minutes. Do not boil after adding filé as it will destroy the flavor. Serves 6-8.

Any boned fresh fish may be substituted for crabmeat.

Mrs. L. P. Daniel (Betty Hurt)

Sausage-Mushroom Soup

½ pound bulk mild sausage
6-8 green onions, sliced
1 pound fresh mushrooms,
   sliced
1 stick butter

2 10¾-ounce cans cream of
   mushroom soup
2 cups light cream
Salt and pepper to taste

Sauté sausage and green onions; drain. Sauté mushrooms in butter and set aside. Combine soup and cream and cook until hot, stirring constantly. Combine sausage mixture and mushrooms with the soup mixture and season to taste. Serves 6.

A life-saver for the working person.

Mrs. Aimee Gianotti (Aimee Lee Guthrie)

Minestrone with Pesto Sauce

Soup

1 cup dried great northern beans	1 stalk celery
2 10¾-ounce cans condensed chicken broth	2 zucchini
	1 large tomato
2 teaspoons salt	1 clove garlic
1 small head cabbage	2 medium onions
2 medium potatoes	¼ cup olive oil
4 carrots	¼ cup chopped parsley
1 16-ounce can Italian-style tomatoes	1 cup broken-up spaghetti

Soak beans overnight. Drain. The next day, add enough water to broth to make 1 quart. Pour into a Dutch Oven with 2 more quarts water, salt and beans. Bring to a boil, reduce heat and simmer, covered, for 1 hour. Wash and quarter cabbage. Remove core and slice. Slice potatoes ½-inch thick and cube. Slice carrots. Add these vegetables and canned tomatoes to soup. Cook for ½ hour. Meanwhile, slice celery diagonally. Slice zucchini. Peel, slice and cube tomato. Peel, cut in half and slice onions thinly. Mince garlic. Sauté both in olive oil. Add celery, zucchini and tomato. Cover. Cook until limp, about 20 minutes. Add to soup mixture along with parsley and spaghetti. Cook 2 hours. Makes 4½-5 quarts.

Pesto Sauce

½ stick butter, softened	1 teaspoon dried basil
¼ cup Parmesan cheese	½ teaspoon dried marjoram
½ cup chopped parsley	¼ cup olive oil
1 clove garlic, crushed	¼ cup chopped walnuts

Blend first 6 ingredients. Gradually add oil, beating constantly. Add nuts and mix well. Top each bowl with a dollop of sauce. Serves 6.

Mrs. Harry McKee (Larane Wilson)

Kielbasa Soup

2 tablespoons butter
1 pound kielbasa sausage,
   sliced into ½-inch slices
1 cup chopped onion
2 cups chopped celery with
   leaves
4 cups shredded cabbage

2 cups sliced carrots
1 bay leaf
½ teaspoon dried thyme
2 teaspoons salt
1½ cups beef bouillon
5 cups water
3 cups cubed potatoes

Melt butter in large kettle and add sausage, onions and celery. Cook until onions are tender. Add remaining ingredients, except potatoes. Cover and simmer 1-1½ hours. Add potatoes and cook 20 minutes longer, or until potatoes are tender. Serves 8. This recipe does not freeze well.

A truly hearty cold weather soup.

Ben Gilliland

Hungarian Soup

6 slices bacon, chopped
½ cup chopped onion
1½ pounds ground chuck
1 28-ounce can tomatoes,
   undrained
1 10¾-ounce can condensed
   potato soup
1 10½-ounce can beef
   consommé

2 cups water
2 cups sliced carrots
1 cup celery leaves
1¼ teaspoons salt
¼ cup cornstarch
½ teaspoon black pepper
   Grated Parmesan cheese

In soup kettle, sauté bacon until transparent. Add onion and cook until golden. Add meat. Stir over medium heat until browned. Add next 7 ingredients. Cover and simmer 45-50 minutes. Blend cornstarch to a smooth paste in small amount of water. Add to soup. Stir and bring to a boil. Add pepper and sprinkle with cheese. Serves 6-8.

Mrs. Philip Vaiden (Lynda Woodward)

Easy Shrimp and Crabmeat Gumbo

3 tablespoons bacon grease
1 large onion, chopped
1 10-ounce package frozen
   chopped okra, thawed
4 cups water
2 tablespoons chopped parsley

1 15-ounce can tomato sauce
   with tomato bits
1 bay leaf
1½-2 tablespoons gumbo filé
1 pound shrimp, peeled
1 7-ounce can crabmeat

In a Dutch oven, sauté onion in bacon grease until golden. Toss okra in grease until completely coated. Add remaining ingredients, except seafood. Simmer 2½ hours, adding additional water if needed. Add seafood and cook 30 more minutes. Serve over rice. Serves 6.

Freezes well.

Mrs. Dan Conaway (Nora Ballenger)

Chicken Gumbo

3-4 pound hen
   Salt and black and red
   pepper to taste
1 cup oil
¼ cup flour
1 cup chopped onion
1 cup chopped celery
½ cup chopped green pepper

3-4 quarts hot water
1 cup chopped green onion
   tops
½ cup minced parsley
1 teaspoon powdered thyme
1 teaspoon filé per serving
¾ cup cooked rice per serving

Cut chicken in serving pieces. Season with salt and peppers. Heat oil and add seasoned chicken. Cook to golden brown. Remove chicken. Add flour to make a roux. Cook to medium brown, stirring constantly. Add onion, celery and green pepper. Cook slowly until soft, about 5 minutes. Add chicken. Pour in all water, a quart at a time. Simmer until chicken is tender. Add green onions, parsley and thyme for last 15 minutes. This will be a thin consistency. Sprinkle filé over hot cooked rice at serving time. Add about 2 cups of hot gumbo with a piece of chicken per bowl. Serves 8-10.

Mrs. S. R. Pooley, Sr.
Jackson, Mississippi

Duck Gumbo

3 ducks, cooked and boned
  Onion, celery leaves, salt,
    and pepper
6 tablespoons shortening
6 tablespoons flour
2 cups minced onion
3-4 cups diced celery
2 green peppers, chopped
1 bunch green onions,
    including stems, chopped
3 cloves garlic, minced
½ cup chopped parsley
7 cups boiling duck broth

3 cups boiling water
2 tablespoons salt
2 teaspoons pepper
1 teaspoon Aćcent
1 6-ounce can tomato paste
1 28-ounce can tomatoes,
    including juice
1 teaspoon oregano
½ teaspoon red pepper
1 16-ounce package frozen cut
    okra
2 teaspoons gumbo filé

To cook ducks, cover with water and season with onion, celery leaves, salt and pepper. Simmer on top of stove until meat falls off bone, about 1½-2 hours. Save the strained broth for gumbo. Melt shortening, add flour and cook over medium heat, stirring constantly, until dark brown. Add next 6 ingredients to roux and cook about 5 minutes. Add boiling liquid slowly and stir until roux is dissolved. Add next 7 ingredients. Can be frozen at this point. Cover and simmer 2-2½ hours. Add duck and okra and cook about 1 hour longer. Add filé immediately before serving. Do not boil after adding filé, as this may cause the gumbo to be stringy. Serve over rice. Serves 10-12.

Mrs. Allen H. Hughes (Marily Davis)

Hearty Winter Soup

3 onions, chopped
2 tablespoons butter
1 pound ground beef
1 clove garlic, minced
3 cups beef stock
2 28-ounce cans tomatoes,
    coarsely chopped
1 cup diced potatoes

1 cup diced celery
1 cup green beans
1 cup diced carrots
1 cup dry red wine
2 tablespoons chopped parsley
½ teaspoon basil
½ teaspoon thyme
  Salt and pepper to taste

Sauté onions in butter in soup kettle until tender. Stir in ground beef and garlic and cook until brown. Add remaining ingredients and bring to a boil. Reduce heat and simmer 1¼ hours. Serves 8-10.

Mrs. Millard Bailey (Chrystine Gilmore)

Vegetable Soup

4 pounds beef short ribs	1 tablespoon paprika
3 pounds canned tomatoes	½ teaspoon pepper
5 medium carrots, sliced	1 10-ounce package frozen peas
4 cups diced celery with leaves	1 10-ounce package frozen
3 large onions, diced	baby lima beans
4-5 medium potatoes, diced	1 17-ounce can Niblets corn
1 tablespoon salt	½ medium cabbage, shredded

In large pot, cover meat with water. Bring to boil and simmer over low heat 1½ hours. Add next 8 ingredients. Cook over low heat 1 more hour. Remove meat and bones and let cool. Cut meat in small pieces and return to soup which has been simmering. Cook 1 more hour. Add remaining ingredients and more water, if needed. Let simmer until ready to serve. Season to taste. Makes 1-1½ gallons.

Wintertime treat.

Mrs. Henry Hancock (Peggy Fairchild)

Turkey Soup

Leftover roasted turkey, bones
and skin

To each 7-8 cups broth add:

¼ cup chopped carrots	½ teaspoon salt
1 cup chopped celery with	¼ teaspoon paprika
leaves	1 cup chopped canned
½ cup chopped onion	tomatoes
¼ cup chopped parsley	½ bay leaf
3 tablespoons rice	½ cup chopped turnips

Remove turkey from bones and put aside. Put bones and skin in a pot. Break up very large bones. Cover with water and simmer at least 4 hours. With large carcass, simmer overnight. Strain through a colander and skim off excess grease. Measure broth and add vegetables and remaining ingredients. Simmer until vegetables are tender. Add enough chopped turkey meat to make a thick soup. Season to taste. If you have any leftover turkey gravy and dressing, add to soup. Serves 8-10.

Yummy.

Mrs. Henry Hancock (Peggy Fairchild)

Capsicum annum, frutescens

C. Grivich

Eggs & Cheese

Eggs Eisenhower

1 cup cracker crumbs
1 cup white sauce (see Index)
½ pound Cheddar cheese,
   grated

1 7-ounce jar pimientos,
   drained and chopped
4 hard-boiled eggs, sliced
½ cup buttered bread crumbs

Butter 1½-quart casserole. Sprinkle bottom and sides with half of the cracker crumbs. Add ½ cup white sauce to bottom of casserole. Layer half of the cheese, pimientos and eggs. Repeat layers, starting with crumbs and ending with egg slices. Top with buttered bread crumbs. Bake at 350° F. for 25 minutes. If casserole has been refrigerated, bake for 45 minutes. Serves 4-6.

Mrs. Marilyn S. Adams

Becky's Brunch

8 slices white bread
1 stick butter, softened
1 small jar Kraft Old English
   Cheese

3 eggs, beaten
2 cups milk

Trim crusts from bread. Spread butter and cheese on one side of each bread slice. Place 4 slices in 2-quart casserole dish. Mix together eggs and milk. Layer half of egg-milk mixture over bread. Then layer remaining bread slices and top with remaining egg-milk mixture. Cover and refrigerate 4-6 hours or overnight. Bake uncovered at 350° F. for 45 minutes. Serves 6-8.

Seafood Filling Variation

1 6½-ounce can shrimp or
   crabmeat
1-2 ribs celery, finely chopped
1 green onion, finely chopped
   Juice of 1 lemon

1½ tablespoons mayonnaise
1 teaspoon prepared mustard
½ teaspoon garlic powder
   Pepper to taste

If using variation, mix all ingredients well. Add all filling after first egg-milk mixture layer. Continue layering as stated above.

Makes a delicious brunch or luncheon main dish.

Mrs. Spence L. Wilson (Becky Webb)

Cheese Brunch

6 slices white bread
12 ounces extra sharp Cheddar
    cheese, grated
2 cups chopped ham
3 eggs

1¾ cups milk
1 teaspoon dry mustard
1 teaspoon salt
4 drops Tabasco

Butter a 3-quart casserole. Cut crust from bread. Cut each slice into 4 sections. Line casserole with bread sections. Mix rest of ingredients together and pour over bread. Cover and refrigerate overnight. Bake 45 minutes at 325° F. Serves 8.

Mrs. Roy Stauffer (Melanie Province)

Sunday Soufflet

6 tablespoons butter, melted
6 eggs
1 teaspoon salt

1 cup sifted flour
1 cup milk

Preheat oven to 450° F. Melt 6 tablespoons butter in 8-inch heavy skillet, coating the bottom and sides. Beat eggs at medium speed. Gradually add salt and flour, blending well. Add milk and blend thoroughly. Pour batter into skillet and bake until crust is brown, about 20 minutes.

Sauce
6 tablespoons butter
4 tablespoons lemon juice, not
    reconstituted

½ cup maple syrup
Powdered sugar

Heat butter, lemon juice and syrup. To serve, cut into wedges, sprinkle with powdered sugar and top with sauce. It will rise then fall when served. Serves 6.

This is a cross between an omelette and a soufflé. This can be doubled in a 12-inch skillet.

Mrs. Ann H. Roy
Florence, Alabama

Eggs Sardou

2 packages frozen, chopped
 spinach, cooked and
 drained
1 cup medium-thick white
 sauce (see Index)
 Salt and pepper to taste
½ teaspoon garlic powder
1 teaspoon Worcestershire
 sauce
1 tablespoon Parmesan cheese

1 clove garlic, pressed
½ stick butter
4 tomato halves
4 artichoke bottoms
1 tablespoon butter
4 poached eggs
 Hollandaise sauce (see Index)
 Freshly chopped parsley
 Paprika
 Salt and pepper to taste

Mix first 6 ingredients together. Keep warm. Lightly sauté garlic in butter. Add tomato halves and gently cook for 2 minutes. Keep warm. Sauté artichoke bottoms in butter over medium heat about 5 minutes. Transfer to a heated serving plate. Top each artichoke bottom with a poached egg, creamed spinach and hollandaise. Garnish serving dish with tomato halves, parsley and paprika. Salt and pepper to taste. Serves 4.

Allison Lynch

Eggs à la Nouvelle Orléans

1 cup white sauce (see Index)
½ teaspoon garlic powder
¼ teaspoon nutmeg
¼ cup chopped parsley
¼ cup grated Cheddar cheese
 Salt and Tabasco to taste

8 ounces lump crabmeat
2 English muffins
4 poached eggs
1 cup grated Cheddar cheese
 Paprika

Combine first 6 ingredients. Fold in crabmeat. Split and toast muffins. Place a poached egg, some of crabmeat mixture and some of grated cheese over each muffin half. Sprinkle lightly with paprika. Place under a very hot broiler until cheese has melted. Serves 4.

Adrien Lynch

Lynch Party Eggs

2 English muffins, split and
  toasted
4 thin tomato slices (optional)
4 slices turkey or chicken
4 poached eggs
1 14-ounce can quartered
  artichoke hearts, drained

2 tablespoons butter
8 slices bacon, cooked until
  crisp
Hollandaise sauce (see Index)
Grated mozzarella cheese

Butter each muffin half. Place a tomato slice, chicken slice and poached egg on each half. Heat artichoke hearts in butter. Place 2 artichoke quarters and 2 slices bacon, halved, on each egg. Top all with hollandaise and then grated cheese. Broil for about 1 minute until cheese has melted and slightly browned. Serves 4.

Adrien Lynch

One-Dish Brunch

1 14½-ounce can asparagus
  spears, drained
8 hard-boiled eggs, peeled and
  halved
7 tablespoons butter, divided
¼ teaspoon prepared mustard
1 tablespoon grated onion
½ cup minced ham or chicken

4 tablespoons flour
1 cup chicken bouillon
Salt, pepper and paprika to
  taste
¾ cup light cream
½ cup grated Cheddar cheese
Parsley or paprika, for
  garnish

In greased 2-quart flat casserole, layer asparagus. Remove yolks and mash with 4 tablespoons butter, mustard, onion and meat. Stuff egg whites with mixture and layer on top of asparagus. Melt 3 tablespoons butter with flour in saucepan. When well blended, slowly add bouillon while stirring constantly. Add seasonings and cream. Heat and stir until thick. Pour over egg layer. Sprinkle top with cheese and parsley or paprika. Bake at 350° F. for 20 minutes. Serves 6-8.

Mrs. John W. Dillard, Jr. (Ann Rogers)

Sunday Brunch Casserole

6   eggs, lightly beaten
2⅔ cups light cream
1   tablespoon brown sugar
¼   teaspoon paprika
1   tablespoon minced onion
½   teaspoon dry mustard
½   teaspoon salt
½   teaspoon Worcestershire
     sauce

⅛   teaspoon pepper
⅛   teaspoon red pepper
2   pounds sausage, 1 mild and
     1 hot, cooked and drained
8   slices bread, crusts removed
½   pound sharp cheese, grated

Mix all ingredients except sausage, bread and cheese. Butter 3-quart casserole and layer bread, sausage and 1½ cups cheese in dish. Cover with liquid mixture. Top with remaining cheese. Refrigerate overnight. Take out two hours prior to cooking. Cook 1 hour at 350° F. Let casserole sit 20 minutes before serving. Serves 8.

Serve this for a brunch or luncheon with hot fruit and homemade rolls.

Mrs. Charles Frankum (Linda Lacey)

Mrs. Kay K. Butler (Kay Kendall)

Sausage Surprise

8   slices white bread
1½ pounds link sausage
12 eggs, beaten
½   pound sharp Cheddar
     cheese, grated

1   teaspoon dry mustard
2   cups milk
1   6-ounce can evaporated milk
1   10¾-ounce can mushroom
     soup

Butter a 3-quart casserole. Trim crusts from bread and cut into 4 squares. Line casserole with bread. Brown sausage and drain. Cut each link into 3 pieces. Combine eggs, sausage, cheese, mustard and milk. Pour into casserole and refrigerate overnight. When ready to bake, mix evaporated milk and soup. Pour over casserole. Do not remix. Bake at 300° F. for 1½ hours. Serves 8.

Serve with fruit salad and muffins.

Mrs. Richard A. Williamson (Norma Jane Buffington)

Chiles Rellenos Casserole

6 slices bread
½ stick butter or margarine, softened
½ pound Cheddar cheese, shredded
½ pound Monterey Jack cheese, shredded
1 4-ounce can green chilies, chopped

6 eggs
2 cups milk
2 teaspoons salt
2 teaspoons paprika
1 teaspoon oregano
½ teaspoon pepper
¼ teaspoon garlic powder
¼ teaspoon dry mustard

Trim crusts from bread. Spread each slice with butter and put buttered side down in 11x7x2-inch baking dish. Top with cheeses. Sprinkle with chilies. Beat eggs until frothy. Add remaining ingredients, mixing well. Pour egg mixture over casserole. Cover and chill at least 4 hours. Uncover and bake at 325° F. for 50-55 minutes or until lightly browned. Let stand 10 minutes before serving. Serves 6-8.

Mrs. Ernest B. Portis (Diana Wallin)

Colorado Huevos Rancheros

2 pork chops or equal amount of pork shoulder, cut in pieces
2 tablespoons oil
4-5 cloves garlic, minced
4 tablespoons flour
1 16-ounce can tomatoes, undrained and chopped
2 teaspoons beef bouillon powder

¼ cup picante sauce
1 4-ounce can chopped green chiles
Salt to taste
4 tortillas
Oil
4 eggs, soft-fried
Grated Cheddar cheese

Brown pork in oil. Add next 7 ingredients. Simmer 1-2 hours, covered, stirring frequently. Fry tortillas in oil until warm. Top each tortilla with egg and ½ cup warm sauce. Sprinkle with cheese. Serve immediately. Serves 4.

Sauce may be made ahead and refrigerated. Reheat and assemble at serving time.

Mrs. Jon K. Thompson (Susan Taylor)

Mexi-Crêpes

Crêpes

12 flour tortillas, thawed
12 thin slices ham
1 pound Monterey Jack cheese,
   cut into ½-inch strips

1 canned chili pepper, cut into
   ⅛-inch wide strips

Place ham slice on each tortilla. In center of ham, place strip of cheese and strip of chili pepper. Roll up and secure with toothpick. Place side by side in buttered 9x13-inch baking pan.

Sauce

1 stick butter
½ cup flour
4 cups milk
¾ pound sharp cheese, grated

1 teaspoon dry mustard
1 teaspoon salt
⅛ teaspoon Accent
⅛ teaspoon pepper

Make roux of butter and flour. Add milk, then cheese and seasonings. Stir until smooth and thick over medium heat. Pour over crêpes. Bake at 350° F. for 45 minutes. Serves 12.

Mrs. Fred Hodges (Charlotte Jackson)

Artichoke Quiche

2 6-ounce jars marinated
   artichoke hearts
1 onion, chopped
1-2 cloves garlic, minced
½ pound sharp cheese, grated
4 eggs, beaten

¼ cup bread crumbs
⅛ teaspoon pepper
⅛ teaspoon Tabasco
⅛ teaspoon oregano (optional)
2 tablespoons minced parsley
1 9-inch pie crust, unbaked

Drain artichoke hearts, reserving juice from 1 jar. Sauté onion and garlic in reserved juice. Slice artichokes. Mix onions, garlic, artichokes and remaining ingredients. Pour into pie crust. Bake at 350° F. for 1 hour. Serves 6.

Especially good for a luncheon dish.

Mrs. John William Barnes (Cynthia Wooten)

Mrs. Claude Springfield, III (Ann Shannon)

Zucchini Quiche

3-4 medium zucchini
3 tablespoons butter
2 tablespoons flour
 Milk
1 small white onion, thinly
 sliced

1½ cups grated Swiss cheese
2 eggs, beaten
 Salt and pepper to taste
1 9-inch pie crust, unbaked

Slice and boil zucchini until tender. Drain. Melt butter. Add flour and enough milk to make a medium-thick cream sauce. To the sauce, add onion and ½ cup cheese. Cook until well blended. Cool. Add eggs to cooled sauce. Add zucchini. Pour into pie crust. Sprinkle remaining cheese on top. Bake at 350° F. for 25-30 minutes or until golden brown. Serves 8.

Serve with tomato aspic or marinated tomatoes. Easy!

Mrs. Michael Heffernan (Tracy Plyler)

Cheese Onion Pie

4 cups thinly sliced onions
1 tablespoon butter
2 cups shredded Cheddar
 cheese
3 eggs
⅔ cup light cream

1 teaspoon salt
¼ teaspoon pepper
6 tomato slices
1 9-inch deep-dish pie crust,
 unbaked

Sauté onions in butter until golden. Spread alternate layers of onion and cheese in crust, ending with cheese. Combine next 4 ingredients, beating lightly. Pour over cheese and onion filling. Bake at 400° F. for 25 minutes. Place tomato slices on top and bake for 5 more minutes. Serves 6.

Unusual and easy.

Mrs. James Martin Greene (Cissy Bell)

Crabmeat Quiche

3 tablespoons butter
3 green onions, minced
½ cup water
8 ounces crabmeat
2 tablespoons dry vermouth

3 eggs
1 cup light cream
1 tablespoon tomato paste
1 9-inch deep-dish pie crust
½ cup grated Swiss cheese

Melt butter in skillet. Add onions and water. When water boils away, add crabmeat and vermouth. Allow to come to a boil. Add eggs, cream, and tomato paste which have been beaten lightly with a wire whisk. Pour into pie crust which has been pricked and partially baked for 5 minutes at 375° F. Cover with grated cheese. Place on baking sheet and bake at 375° F. for 30 minutes. Serves 6.

Mrs. Dorsey Mathis, Jr. (Margaret Jones)

Salmon Quiche

1 9-inch pie crust
3 eggs, well-beaten
1 5⅓-ounce can evaporated milk
2 tablespoons margarine, melted
1 tablespoon flour

1 envelope onion soup mix, single serving size
1 7¾-ounce can salmon, drained and flaked
½ teaspoon salt
¼ teaspoon pepper
1-2 cups grated Cheddar cheese

Prick bottom and sides of pie crust with fork, and partially bake at 400° F. for 5-10 minutes. Thoroughly blend remaining ingredients, except cheese. Sprinkle half of cheese in pie shell. Pour salmon mixture over cheese. Bake at 375° F. for 35-40 minutes. Sprinkle remaining cheese on top and return to oven until melted. Cool slightly before cutting. Serves 5-6.

Mrs. William C. Lewis

Beef and Spinach Quiche

1 10-inch pie crust	¾ teaspoon salt
3 tablespoons butter	½ teaspoon pepper
1 cup diced onion	⅛ teaspoon nutmeg
1 pound round steak, ground	2 large eggs
1 10-ounce package frozen	1 cup heavy cream
chopped spinach, thawed	½-¾ cup grated sharp cheese

Heat oven to 400° F. Bake pie crust for 10-12 minutes. In a medium skillet, sauté onion in butter. Add beef and brown lightly, draining off fat. Drain spinach thoroughly. Mix spinach, beef, onions, salt, pepper and nutmeg. Beat eggs with cream and stir into other ingredients. Pour mixture into pie crust and cover with grated cheese. Bake at 375° F. for 30 minutes or until filling is set. Serves 6.

Mrs. William S. Mitchell

Hamburger Quiche

½ pound ground beef	1½ cups shredded sharp
½ cup mayonnaise	Cheddar or Swiss cheese
½ cup milk	⅓ cup chopped onion
2 eggs	Salt and pepper to taste
1 tablespoon cornstarch	1 9-inch pie crust, unbaked

Brown ground beef in skillet; drain and put in unbaked pie crust. Mix all other ingredients and pour over ground beef. Bake at 350° F. for 40 minutes. Serves 6-8.

This is a busy day special. Make it ahead and bake later.

Mrs. Richard Collins (Barbara Watson)

Pepperoni Quiche

¾ cup shredded Swiss cheese
¾ cup shredded mozzarella
cheese
½ cup chopped pepperoni
1 tablespoon chopped green
onion

1 9-inch pie crust, unbaked
3 eggs, beaten
1 cup light cream
½ teaspoon salt
¼ teaspoon oregano

Combine first 4 ingredients and sprinkle into bottom of pie crust. Mix together remaining ingredients and pour into pie crust. Bake at 325° F. for 1 hour or until firm. Allow to stand a few minutes before cutting. Serves 6.

Also makes a unique appetizer.

Mrs. David Sims (Carol Mauney)

Easy Cheesy Soufflé

1 tablespoon butter or
margarine
3 cups seasoned croutons
4-5 ounces sharp cheese, grated
4 eggs
2 cups milk
½ teaspoon salt

½ teaspoon dry mustard
½ teaspoon pepper
½ teaspoon garlic powder
½ teaspoon onion salt
4-5 slices bacon, cooked and
crumbled

Melt butter in 1½-quart casserole. Add croutons and cheese. Mix next 7 ingredients and pour over croutons and cheese. Top with bacon. Bake at 325° F. for 55-60 minutes. If cooking too fast, reduce heat to 300° F. Serves 6-8.

A good and easy Sunday night supper.

Mrs. Phillip H. McNeill (Mabel McCall)

Never-Fail Cheese Soufflé

1 tablespoon butter	3 egg yolks
2 tablespoons flour	1 cup grated sharp Cheddar
1¼ cups milk	cheese
Salt and pepper to taste	3 egg whites, stiffly beaten

Melt butter and blend in flour. Gradually add milk, stirring constantly, and cook until thickened. Add salt and pepper. Cool slightly. Add egg yolks and cheese. Fold in egg whites. Bake at 350° F. for about 45 minutes. Serve immediately. Serves 2-3.

Mrs. Richard De Saussure (Phyllis Falk)

Zesty Cheese Grits

3 cups water	½ teaspoon paprika
1 teaspoon salt	1½ teaspoons seasoning salt
¾ cup quick grits	⅛ teaspoon Tabasco
¾ stick margarine	2 eggs, beaten
½ pound medium Cheddar cheese, grated	⅛ teaspoon onion salt
	½ teaspoon Parmesan cheese
½ teaspoon Worcestershire sauce	¼ teaspoon celery salt

Bring salted water to a boil. Add grits and cook 3 minutes. Remove from heat. Add remaining ingredients and mix well. Pour into a greased 2-quart casserole. Bake 1 hour at 250° F. Microwave instructions: Bake 10-15 minutes until bubbly. Stir once. Serves 6.

Mrs. Raymond E. Henley (Kim Baxter)

Cheese Grits for a Mob

4 cups quick-cooking grits	6 sticks margarine
4 quarts water	4 pounds Velveeta cheese,
1½ tablespoons salt	cut up
1½ dozen eggs, beaten	1½ teaspoons Tabasco

Cook grits in boiling water for 3-5 minutes. Add remaining ingredients and pour into 3 greased 3-quart casseroles. Bake at 250° F. for 1¼ hours. Can be prepared ahead and left out for hours, or cooked and reheated. It is better not to refrigerate. Serves 40-50.

Mrs. Kenneth Jack (Betty Clark)

Pimiento Cheese Frankum

2 pounds hoop cheese
2 7-ounce jars pimiento
1 large onion
2 large Kosher dill pickles,
   chopped

4 stalks celery
  Pinch of salt
2 cups mayonnaise

Put all ingredients into food processor until blended. This can be refrigerated for about a week.

Mrs. Charles E. Frankum (Linda Lacey)

Cheese Nut Loaf

1 cup cooked brown rice
1 cup wheat germ
1½ cups chopped pecans or
   walnuts
1 onion, minced
½ cup thinly sliced mushrooms

1 pound sharp Cheddar cheese,
   shredded
1 clove garlic, minced
¼ teaspoon salt
⅛ teaspoon pepper
4 eggs, beaten

Combine first nine ingredients in a large bowl. Mix well. Add eggs and mix thoroughly. Pack mixture into a well-greased 9x5-inch loaf pan. Bake at 350° F. for 50 minutes, or until firm. Remove from oven and let stand 10 minutes. Loosen sides with a knife and turn onto a warm platter. Slice and serve plain or with Mushroom Sauce (see Index). Serves 6-8.

Mrs. Huey L. Holden (Barbara Hopper)

Citrus monachello

Fish & Seafood

Stuffed Fish Mornay

3 tablespoons butter
¼ cup flour
1 10½-ounce can chicken broth
¼ cup grated Swiss cheese, packed
1 tablespoon grated Parmesan cheese
1 tablespoon light cream
Drops of lemon to taste
2 tablespoons diced tomato
Generous dash crushed tarragon
½ cup flaked crabmeat
½ cup chopped shrimp

2 tablespoons chopped mushrooms
2 tablespoons chopped green onions
¼ teaspoon salt
¼ teaspoon tarragon, crushed
½ small garlic clove, minced
8 filets of flounder, red snapper, sole, ocean perch or pompano, about 2 pounds of fish
8 oysters, halved
2 tablespoons melted butter

For sauce, melt butter in saucepan over medium heat. Add flour and whisk until smooth. Cook, stirring, for 2 minutes. Remove from heat and stir in 8 ounces chicken broth. Return to heat and stir until mixture thickens and boils. Remove from heat and add cheeses. At this point, reserve ¼ cup of sauce for stuffing. To remaining sauce, stir in remaining broth and 1 tablespoon of light cream. If necessary, add more cream to make desired consistency. Season with drops of lemon juice to taste. Add tomato and tarragon and cook on medium heat 2-5 minutes. Keep warm to serve with fish. Combine ¼ cup reserved sauce with next 7 ingredients. Arrange 4 filets in shallow baking dish. Spread sauce-seafood mixture evenly over filets. Top with oysters, then remaining filets. Brush with melted butter and bake in 375° F. oven for 30 minutes. Serve remaining sauce with fish. Serves 4.

For an onion sauce, omit tomato and substitute 1 tablespoon finely chopped green onion.

Mrs. Dayton Smith (Justine Holloway)

Fried Flounder Almondine

2 pounds fresh flounder filets
Salt and pepper to taste
2 tablespoons lemon juice
¾ pound Ritz crackers
¾ cup sliced almonds

3 eggs, beaten
⅔ cup milk
2 cups flour
½ cup oil
1 stick butter

Cut flounder into 6 portions and season with salt, pepper and lemon juice. Coarsely crumble crackers and mix with almonds. Beat eggs and milk. Dredge flounder in flour and dip into egg mixture. Roll in cracker-almond mixture and pat down firmly so mixture will adhere. Heat oil and butter. Fry fish about 5 minutes on each side or until it is golden brown and flakes easily. Drain on paper towel and serve. Serves 6.

May use any firm white fish.

Mrs. Mickey Moran (Pat Taylor)

Flounder Wrightsville

1½-2 pounds flounder filet, fresh
1 stick butter, cut in pieces
¼ cup dry white wine

Salt and pepper to taste
Juice of ½ lemon
½ pound lump crabmeat

Place all ingredients, except crabmeat, in order in Pyrex dish. Bake at 350° F. for 20 minutes. Add crabmeat for last 5-10 minutes and baste several times with pan juices. Serves 4.

Use only the freshest fish and crabmeat!

Mrs. John Franklin Holmes (Jeanie Hobby)

Swiss Salmon Bake

1 7¾-ounce can red salmon,
   drained and flaked
¾ cup chopped celery
1 tablespoon chopped green
   onion

3 tablespoons sour cream
¼ teaspoon dry mustard
1 cup shredded Swiss cheese,
   divided

Combine first 6 ingredients. Stir in ¾ cup cheese. Spoon into 2 individual au gratin dishes. Sprinkle with remaining cheese. Place casseroles on a baking sheet and bake at 350° F. for 20 minutes. Serves 2.

Mrs. Richard DeSaussure (Phyllis Falk)

Aunt Sarah's Baked Red Snapper

Sauce

1 clove garlic, minced
1 small onion, chopped
1 15½-ounce can tomatoes
3 whole cloves
¾ teaspoon ground allspice
2 bay leaves

2 large ribs celery, finely
    chopped
1 teaspoon Worcestershire
    sauce
⅛ teaspoon cayenne pepper

Mix ingredients and cook 12-20 minutes. Press through sieve. Add Worcestershire sauce and cayenne.

Fish

¼ cup oil
    Flour, seasoned with salt and
    pepper

4 red snappers, whole or filets
1 lemon, sliced
    Butter

Heat oil in skillet. Dredge fish in flour and brown lightly on both sides. Place in a large baking dish. Put lemon slices on filets and top with sauce. Top with bits of butter and cook for 30-45 minutes in a 350° F. oven, or until fish flakes easily, depending on thickness of filets. Serves 4.

Mrs. Robert K. Armstrong (Betty Hunt)

Grilled Red Snapper

    Olive oil, bacon grease
3 pounds filet of red snapper
    Salt, white pepper and
    paprika to taste

1 stick butter, melted
2 cloves garlic, crushed
    Juice of ½ lemon

Heat large griddle to smoking point. Grease liberally with olive oil and bacon fat. Season and sear fish on both sides, turning carefully. Cook quickly for 3-5 minutes per side. Heat butter, garlic and lemon juice to bubbling and serve over fish. Serves 6.

Mrs. John Turley, III (Barbara Barham)

Filet de Sole à l'Orange

2 pounds sole filets, cut into
3x1-inch strips
2 oranges
2 egg yolks
1½ sticks butter, softened
4 cups white fish stock or
salted water

1 pound fresh spinach, cooked,
drained and chopped, or
two 10-ounce packages
frozen spinach, cooked,
drained and chopped
1 tablespoon butter
Fresh parsley

Salt and pepper filets. Remove rind from oranges with a vegetable peeler. Reserve oranges. Cut rind into short julienne strips and blanch in boiling water for 2-3 minutes. Drain. Pour cold water over rind and pat dry in paper towel. Section one orange. Set aside. Squeeze juice from remaining orange into a saucepan. Add egg yolks and heat over low heat, whisking until thickened. Whisk in butter, bit by bit. Keep sauce warm but do not allow to boil. In large saucepan, bring stock or water to boil and poach sole strips for 45 seconds. Remove, drain and keep warm. In enamel saucepan, toss spinach in 1 tablespoon butter. Put in serving dish. Top with sole strips. Finely chop reserved rind and add to sauce according to taste. Top spinach and sole with sauce. Garnish with reserved orange slices and parsley. Serves 4.

Dr. Richard J. Reynolds

Smoked Trout

Charcoal
Hickory chips
2 cups white wine

Juice of 2 lemons
2 tablespoons marjoram
Cleaned fish

In bottom pan of smoker, build fire with charcoal. When lit, cover with wet hickory chips. In water pan, pour wine, lemon juice, marjoram and fill with water. Split fish all the way down the underside. Place fish on rack with underside down and sides spread as flaps to make fish stand up. Cover and smoke 2 hours for larger fish, 1-2 pounds, or 1½ hours for smaller ones.

This can be done in a covered grill by building fire at one end and placing fish at other end. Put foil or pan under fish and baste with wine, lemon juice and butter.

Mr. Nick Patton

Tuna Mousse

1 7-ounce can white tuna
1 package unflavored gelatin
1 cup cold water
1 10¾-ounce can tomato soup
3 ounces cream cheese, cut up
½ cup mayonnaise
Salt to taste

¼ cup chopped green olives
¼ cup chopped green pepper
1 cup chopped celery
1 tablespoon grated onion
1 tablespoon lemon juice
Tabasco to taste

Rinse, drain and dry tuna. Dissolve gelatin in cold water. Bring undiluted soup to boil in large saucepan. Add cream cheese and stir until melted. Add gelatin and blend well. Set aside to cool. Add remaining ingredients and tuna. Pour into oiled mold or bowl and chill. Unmold and serve on lettuce for lunch or with crackers as an appetizer. Serves 4 as main dish.

Can substitute one can of shrimp for tuna.

Mrs. Steve Keltner (Jane Farrimond)

Crab-Asparagus Newburg

6 ounces crabmeat
2 tablespoons butter
2 tablespoons flour
1 cup heavy cream
3 tablespoons ketchup
2 teaspoons Worcestershire
   sauce

2 tablespoons white wine or
   sherry
Salt
Paprika
16 fresh or frozen asparagus
   spears, cooked until barely
   tender

Drain crabmeat and clean. Melt butter in saucepan. Add flour and blend well. Stir in cream until thick and smooth. Add crabmeat and next 5 ingredients. Heat gently and serve over hot asparagus. Serves 4.

This is also delicious served over toast, biscuits, rice or cooked broccoli.

Mrs. William C. Lewis

Crab-Broccoli Pie

2 tablespoons butter
3 tablespoons chopped onion
3 tablespoons chopped celery
1 10-ounce package chopped broccoli, slightly cooked and drained

1 7½-ounce can crabmeat
1 cup grated Cheddar cheese
1 cup Hellmann's mayonnaise
1 9-inch pie crust, unbaked

Sauté onions and celery in butter until tender. Mix with other ingredients and put in unbaked pie crust. Bake at 375° F. for 45 minutes. Serves 6.

Mrs. Clyde Craig
Webster Groves, Missouri

Crab Coquilles

3 tablespoons butter
2 tablespoons flour
1 cup milk, heated
1 teaspoon salt
1 teaspoon prepared mustard
1 teaspoon Worcestershire sauce
1 tablespoon instant minced onion

⅛ teaspoon cayenne pepper
2 egg yolks, lightly beaten
2 cups crabmeat
1 tablespoon chopped parsley
1 teaspoon lemon juice
2 tablespoons sherry
3 tablespoons butter, melted
⅔ cup soft bread crumbs

Melt butter, stir in flour and heated milk. Season with salt, mustard, Worcestershire sauce, onion and cayenne pepper. Cook, stirring constantly, until thick. Add egg yolks, crabmeat and parsley. Cook several minutes. Stir in lemon juice and sherry. Spoon into slightly buttered individual baking shells. Combine butter with bread crumbs and sprinkle over top. Bake at 350° F. for 20 minutes. Serves 6-8.

Mrs. Thomas W. Jones (Janis Cox)

Crabmeat Delicious

4 tablespoons butter
3 eggs, hard-boiled
4 tablespoons flour
4 tablespoons vinegar
2 teaspoons prepared mustard
2 teaspoons Worcestershire
  sauce
½ teaspoon salt

¼ teaspoon pepper
2 egg yolks, lightly beaten
1 small onion, chopped
1 cup heavy cream
1 pound crabmeat
2 egg whites, lightly beaten
½ cup buttered bread crumbs

Melt butter in double boiler. Separate hard-boiled eggs. Mash yolks in butter and stir in next 6 ingredients. Chop cooked egg whites and combine with beaten egg yolks and onion. Add to double boiler. Pour in cream and cook over hot water until very thick. Add crabmeat. Remove from heat and fold in beaten egg whites. Pour in 2-quart greased casserole. Sprinkle with crumbs and bake 20 minutes at 350° F. Serves 6-8.

Mrs. Rex Amonette (Johnnie Dacus)

Heavenly Crabmeat

1 stick butter
3 tablespoons minced onion
½ cup flour
4 cups heavy cream, heated to
  boiling point
½ cup Madeira wine
  Salt and pepper to taste
2 tablespoons lemon juice
4 cups fresh crabmeat

3 9-ounce packages frozen
  artichoke hearts, cooked
  according to directions
2½ cups dry shell macaroni,
  cooked and drained
2 cups grated Gruyère or
  Swiss cheese
⅛ teaspoon paprika

Melt butter in heavy sauce pan. When butter sizzles, add onion and sauté until golden: Stir in flour, cooking over low heat until flour is pale yellow. Remove from heat. Add cream, stirring vigorously. Return to moderate heat and stir until sauce comes to a boil. Reduce heat and add Madeira. Season with salt and pepper. Pour lemon juice over crabmeat and toss lightly. Combine crabmeat, artichoke hearts, macaroni and sauce together in two 3-quart buttered casseroles. Sprinkle with cheese and paprika. Bake 25-30 minutes at 350° F. or until heated through. Serves 12-16.

Expensive, but heavenly!

Mrs. James B. Green, Jr. (Betty Brown)

Crabmeat Mornay

1 stick butter
2 tablespoons flour
6 green onions, chopped
2 tablespoons grated onion
½ cup finely chopped parsley
2 cups light cream
3 ounces grated Swiss cheese
¼ pound mushrooms, sliced
½ cup dry white wine

1 tablespoon lemon juice
Salt, cayenne and white
 pepper to taste
1 9-ounce package frozen
 artichoke hearts, cooked
 and drained
1 pound fresh lump crabmeat
3 tablespoons grated Parmesan
 cheese

Melt butter in large, heavy saucepan. Add flour and cook 5 minutes. Do not brown. Add onions and parsley. Cook until onions are translucent. Add cream and Swiss cheese. Cook until thickened. Sauté mushrooms in butter and add to cream sauce. Stir in wine, lemon juice and seasonings. Butter a 2-quart shallow casserole. Layer ½ of cream sauce over bottom. Place artichoke hearts over this. Gently layer crabmeat over artichokes. Cover with remaining sauce. Sprinkle with Parmesan cheese. Bake at 350° F. for about 30-40 minutes. Broil until lightly brown. Serves 6.

Omit artichokes and serve in a chafing dish for an elegant appetizer.
Mrs. Hershel P. Wall (Jean Harrington)

Crabmeat with Vegetables au Gratin

1 cup cooked medium egg
 noodles
1 cup fresh lump crabmeat
½ cup coarsely chopped
 broccoli, cooked al dente
½ cup coarsely chopped
 cauliflower, cooked al dente

1 cup Basic White Sauce (see
 Index)
Salt and pepper to taste
½ cup grated sharp Cheddar
 cheese

Place noodles, crabmeat and vegetables in a 1½-quart casserole. Top with sauce and season to taste. Top with cheese. Brown under broiler for about 5 minutes. Serves 3-4.

Mrs. Charles Schaffler (Mickey Pooley)

Maryland Imperial Crab

½ cup chopped onion
2 tablespoons chopped green
  pepper
2 tablespoons chopped green
  onions, or chives
3 tablespoons butter
1 pound fresh crabmeat
  Salt to taste
  Cayenne pepper to taste

1 teaspoon Colman's English
  prepared mustard
½ teaspoon Worcestershire
  sauce
1½ cups Basic White Sauce (see
  Index)
2 egg yolks, lightly beaten
  Dijon mustard
  Buttered breadcrumbs
  Lemon slices for garnish

Sauté onion, green pepper and green onions in butter for 6 minutes. Add next 6 ingredients and heat for 2 minutes. Remove from heat and blend in yolks. Fill crab shells or ramekins with mixture, spread lightly with Dijon mustard and top with breadcrumbs. Bake at 350° F. until heated. Serve garnished with lemon slices. Serves 4-6.

Mrs. Henry C. Nall, III (Jane Weaver)

Crawfish Pie

2 pounds cooked and peeled
  crawfish tails
½ cup oil
1 cup chopped onions
½ cup chopped celery
1 tablespoon crawfish fat
2 tablespoons cornstarch

1½ cups water
6 green onions, chopped
½ cup chopped parsley
  Cayenne pepper to taste
  Salt to taste
  Basic Pie Crust recipe
  (see index)

Season crawfish tails with salt and pepper and set aside. Sauté onion and celery in oil until tender. Add crawfish and fat and cook for 10-15 minutes. Dissolve cornstarch in water and add to crawfish. Cook until thick, approximately 20 minutes. Stir in remaining ingredients. Butter 10-inch pie pan. Put rolled half of pastry in pan. Pour in crawfish mixture. Top with remaining rolled pastry. Slit top. Bake at 350° F. for 45 minutes, or until pastry lightly browns. Serves 6.

For special dinner, serve as individual pies. Two pounds raw, peeled shrimp may be substituted.

Mrs. Jon K. Thompson (Susan Taylor)

Oysters and Artichokes Justine

4 fresh artichokes, trimmed and washed
3 tablespoons butter
1 tablespoon flour
¼ cup chopped green onions
¾ cup chopped mushrooms
2 cups chicken broth
¼ cup chopped artichoke hearts
¼ cup sherry
Dash Tabasco

1 teaspoon Worcestershire sauce
1 tablespoon finely chopped parsley
Salt and pepper to taste
2 dozen oysters, drained
1 cup flour, seasoned with salt and pepper
1½ sticks butter

Cook artichokes, covered, in 2 inches salted water for 45 minutes, or until leaves pull out easily. Drain well and remove choke. For sauce, melt 3 tablespoons butter until it begins to brown. Add 1 tablespoon flour and cook until it browns. Add green onions and mushrooms and cook, stirring, for 2 minutes. Add next 7 ingredients. Cook until thickened, at least 30 minutes. Dredge oysters on both sides in seasoned flour. Melt butter. When hot and bubbly, fry oysters until brown. Set aside and keep warm. Place artichokes in flat pan. Pour enough hot water to cover bottom of pan and heat artichokes in 325° F. oven for approximately 20-30 minutes. To serve, fill each artichoke with oysters and pour hot sauce over oysters. Serves 4.

Mrs. Dayton Smith (Justine Holloway)

Scalloped Oysters

1 12-ounce jar fresh oysters
6 tablespoons light cream
½ cup dry bread crumbs

1 cup saltine cracker crumbs
1 stick butter, melted
Salt and pepper to taste

Drain oysters, reserving liquid. Mix cream with equal amount oyster liquid. Mix bread, cracker crumbs and melted butter. Grease a 9-inch pie tin. Cover bottom with half of crumb mixture. Place oysters on top. Sprinkle with salt and pepper. Pour cream mixture over oysters. Top with remaining crumbs. Bake at 400° F. for 20 minutes. Serves 3.

A family favorite at holiday meals! Can be doubled or tripled. Use one recipe per pan.

Mrs. Henry H. Hancock (Peggy Fairchild)

Herbed Oysters

2 dozen oysters, in shell, or 2
    jars oysters
1 cup herbed stuffing, crushed
½ cup minced parsley
¼ teaspoon salt
⅛ teaspoon pepper
¼ teaspoon Accent
⅛ teaspoon ground mace

1 teaspoon Worcestershire
    sauce
3-4 drops Tabasco
½ stick butter, melted
3 tablespoons lemon juice
4 slices bacon, cooked and
    crumbled
2 tablespoons pimiento

Shuck oysters, drain and reserve deep shells. Combine next 8 ingredients in a medium saucepan. Gradually add melted butter and stir until moist. Heat until hot. Place oysters in shells in a shallow pan lined with crumpled foil. Spoon lemon juice over each oyster and cover with 1 tablespoon stuffing mix. Sprinkle with crumbled bacon and chopped pimiento. Bake in 500° F. oven for 3-5 minutes. If preparing as a casserole, butter a 1½-quart flat casserole. Add oysters in a single layer. Continue from this point in recipe. Serves 4 as a main course.

As a first course, this makes a plain meal special. Can be doubled or tripled!

Mrs. William C. Harris (Ann Clark Quinlen)

Oysters Bienville

4 tablespoons flour
2 sticks butter
1 cup milk
1 cup oyster liquid
½ cup light cream
½ cup wine (Absinthe, white or
    sherry)
2 pounds shrimp, cooked

2 4-ounce cans mushrooms
5 cloves garlic
1 large onion
48 oysters
Rock salt
Parmesan cheese
Paprika

Make a sauce of flour, butter, milk, oyster liquid, cream and wine. Finely dice shrimp, mushrooms, garlic and onion. This is best done in food processor or blender. Add chopped ingredients to cream sauce and simmer 15 minutes. Put oysters in shells on bed of rock salt and run under broiler for 2 minutes. Drain off water. Pour sauce over each oyster. Sprinkle with Parmesan cheese and paprika. Place under broiler for 5 minutes or until bubbly. Serves 4-8.

Mrs. Michael Lynch (Susan Corcoran)

Oysters Rockefeller

2 10-ounce packages frozen chopped spinach
¼ cup chopped parsley
3 green onions, chopped
½ cup sour cream
2 teaspoons anchovy paste, or more
Salt and pepper to taste
3-4 dashes Tabasco
1 clove garlic, minced

2 teaspoons Worcestershire sauce
2-3 tablespoons lemon juice
¾ stick butter
Herbsaint or anisette to taste (optional)
Parmesan cheese
2 dozen oysters, on the half shell

Thaw spinach and drain in colander, pressing out as much liquid as possible. Combine all ingredients, except oysters and cheese, in blender. Process until thoroughly mixed. Place enough mixture on each oyster to completely cover. Sprinkle with Parmesan cheese. Bake at 450° F. for 5-10 minutes. Serves 6.

Mrs. D. Randolph Ramey (Minje Mitchell)

Grama Truax' Oyster Patties

⅓ cup flour
⅓ cup oil
1 bunch green onions, finely chopped
2 dozen large oysters, or 3 dozen medium oysters, reserving liquid

⅓ bunch parsley, chopped
1 pint oyster water
Salt and pepper to taste
Red pepper flakes to taste

Brown flour in oil until golden brown. Add green onions to flour mixture and sauté until soft. Add oysters and cook until curled, usually about five curls per oysters. Add parsley, oyster water, salt, pepper and red pepper. Cook slowly on low fire about 20 minutes. Serve in patty shells. Serves 4.

This is a very old family recipe.

Mrs. S. R. Pooley, Sr.
Jackson, Mississippi

Deviled Oysters

3 pints oysters, drained and juice reserved
1 cup finely chopped celery
1 cup finely chopped onion
1 cup finely chopped green pepper
½ cup finely chopped parsley
3-4 cloves garlic, finely minced
1 stick butter
2 eggs, well beaten
2 cups saltine cracker crumbs, or more

2 tablespoons Worcestershire sauce
3 tablespoons ketchup
1 teaspoon red pepper
Salt to taste
2 tablespoons lemon juice
Butter
Parsley and lemon slices for garnish

Place oysters in blender or food processor. Turn on and off quickly. Repeat one or two more times, as necessary, being careful not to purée. Sauté celery, onion, green pepper, parsley and garlic in butter until tender. Add chopped oysters and eggs to the sautéed ingredients and mix well. Slowly stir in cracker crumbs and add reserved oyster juice, a little at a time, until you have the consistency of very moist dressing. Cook over slow heat for about 20 minutes, stirring constantly. Remove from heat, add Worcestershire, ketchup, red pepper, salt and lemon juice. If oysters seem too moist, add more cracker crumbs. If too dry, add more oyster liquid. Put mixture into shells or ramekins and sprinkle with cracker crumbs. Dot with butter and brown in 450° F. oven. Garnish with parsley sprigs and lemon slices. Serve 6-8.

Mrs. Michael Lynch (Susan Corcoran)

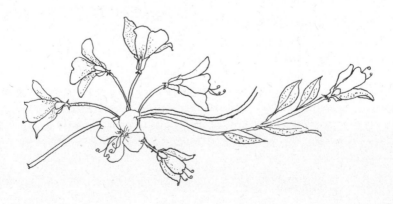

Scallops au Gratin

2 pounds fresh scallops
½ stick butter
2 green peppers, cut in ¾-inch squares
1 cup chopped onion
2 cups celery, cut in ½-inch pieces

3 cups soft bread crumbs
1 teaspoon salt
¼ teaspoon white pepper
2 cups heavy cream
1 cup grated sharp Cheddar cheese

Rinse scallops in cold water. Place in saucepan and add just enough water to cover. Bring to a boil over high heat. Drain immediately. Sauté vegetables in butter until tender. In a large bowl, toss vegetables, scallops, bread crumbs, salt and pepper. Place mixture in greased casserole or 6 ramekins. Pour cream over casserole. If using ramekins, pour ⅓ cup cream per ramekin. Recipe can be frozen at this point. Top with cheese and bake at 350° F. for 45-60 minutes. Serves 6.

Mrs. William E. Denman, III (Julie Moss)

Scampi

2 pounds large raw shrimp
1 stick butter
½ cup olive oil
1 tablespoon lemon juice
2-3 large cloves garlic, split

1 teaspoon salt
Freshly ground black pepper
4 tablespoons finely chopped parsley
Lemon quarters

Shell shrimp, leaving tail segment. Butterfly shrimp and remove vein. Wash under cold water and pat dry. Preheat oven to broil. Melt butter in shallow dish large enough to hold shrimp in one layer. Do not let butter brown. Stir in olive oil, lemon juice, garlic, salt, pepper and shrimp, turning until they are coated with the sauce. Broil 3-4 inches from heat for 5 minutes. Turn over and broil 5 minutes or until lightly browned. Do not overcook. Sprinkle with parsley and garnish with lemon quarters. Serves 6.

Mrs. John Franklin Holmes (Jeanie Hobby)

Shrimp Herman

2 pounds raw shrimp, shelled
   and deveined
2 cups oil
1 tablespoon salt

4 tablespoons ketchup
1 teaspoon paprika
1 small clove garlic, minced

Spread shrimp in single layer in shallow pan. Combine remaining ingredients. Pour sauce over shrimp but do not completely cover. Broil 2-4 minutes per side at 350° F. Serve in bowls with sauce. Serves 4.

Can be served on toothpicks as an appetizer.

Mrs. Rex Amonette (Johnnie Dacus)

Hot and Spicy Baked Shrimp

½ teaspoon cayenne pepper
1 tablespoon thyme
½ teaspoon celery salt
1 tablespoon chopped parsley
⅔ cup Worcestershire sauce
½ teaspoon black pepper

½ teaspoon salt
3 tablespoons olive oil
1 teaspoon crushed rosemary
2 sticks butter
3-4 pounds raw shrimp

Cook all ingredients, except shrimp, for 3-5 minutes. Marinate raw, unpeeled shrimp for 4 hours in this mixture. Bake at 350° F. for 20-30 minutes, or until shrimp are pink and firm. Serves 6-8.

Serve shrimp in bowls with sauce for dipping.

Mrs. Michael Lynch (Susan Corcoran)

Baked Stuffed Jumbo Shrimp

1 pound headless jumbo
  shrimp
1 7½-ounce can minced clams,
  undrained
1 cup fine, dry bread crumbs
¼ cup olive oil
¼ teaspoon powdered garlic

½ teaspoon salt
½ teaspoon freshly ground
  pepper
2 teaspoons finely chopped
  celery
1 stick melted butter
Cayenne pepper to taste

Shell, devein and butterfly shrimp. Do not split completely through. Mix all other ingredients and stuff shrimp. Lightly oil a shallow baking dish and place shrimp stuffed side up. Bake 35 minutes in 350° F. oven. Serves 4.

A really easy gourmet dish.

Mrs. Jon K. Thompson (Susan Taylor)

Szechuan Shrimp

½ cup sliced green onions
½ cup bamboo shoots, cut in
  half
¼ teaspoon minced fresh ginger
  root
3 cloves garlic, minced
¼ teaspoon Tabasco
2 tablespoons sugar
½ cup ketchup
3 tablespoons dry sherry

1 tablespoon soy sauce
1½ teaspoons sesame oil
  or 1 tablespoon toasted
  sesame seeds
1 tablespoon cornstarch
3 tablespoons water
½ cup peanut oil
1½ pounds raw shrimp, shelled
  and deveined

Combine first 5 ingredients in small bowl. In second bowl, combine next 5 ingredients. In third bowl, mix cornstarch and water. Heat oil in wok or large skillet to 400° F. Have ready a large strainer with a bowl underneath. Add shrimp to hot oil, stirring until done, about 2 minutes. Pour oil and shrimp into strainer to drain. Heat 2 tablespoons of the strained oil in same wok over high heat. Add green onion mixture and stir fry for 1 minute. Add drained shrimp and stir fry 30 seconds more. Pour in ketchup mixture. Stir for another 30 seconds. Add cornstarch mixture and cook and stir until slightly thickened. Serves 4.

Szechuan cooking is very hot and spicy. Don't skimp on the pepper sauce. Can be made ahead and reheated in casserole.

Mrs. Mickey Moran (Pat Taylor)

Bombay Shrimp Curry

2 teaspoons paprika
½ teaspoon cayenne pepper
¾ teaspoon turmeric
¾ teaspoon cumin
¼ teaspoon black pepper
½ teaspoon garlic powder
2 tablespoons Worcestershire sauce
2 tablespoons ketchup
1 cup frozen coconut (do not use canned)
1 cup evaporated milk

1-2 tablespoons oil
2 medium onions, sliced
¼ green pepper, sliced
1-2 teaspoons fresh grated ginger root
2 cloves garlic, minced
1 cup water or more
1½ pounds raw shrimp, peeled and salted lightly
1 small fresh cauliflower or 1 10-ounce box frozen cauliflower

Mix first 6 spices. Mix half of the spice mixture with the Worcestershire sauce and ketchup. Heat coconut in milk, strain and reserve milk. Heat oil. Sauté onions, pepper and ginger until onions are translucent. Add both parts of spice mixture to pan. Add garlic and water. Cover and simmer 30-40 minutes, adding more water if necessary. Pour in half of coconut milk, adding more as needed, but avoid having mixture too sweet. Add shrimp and cauliflower. Cook 10 minutes. Serve over rice. Serves 6.

Authentic and unusual—very spicy! Better if prepared one day ahead.

Mrs. Claude Braganza

Shrimp Curry

3 tablespoons butter
¼ cup minced onion
1½ teaspoons curry powder
3 tablespoons flour
¾ teaspoon salt
¾ teaspoon sugar

⅛ teaspoon ground ginger
1 cup milk
1 cup chicken broth
2 cups raw shrimp, cleaned
½ teaspoon lemon juice

Melt butter. Add onions and curry. Blend in flour and seasonings. Cook until thick and smooth. Add milk and broth and bring to boil. Stir until thickened. Add shrimp and cook slowly until shrimp turn pink. Blend in lemon juice. Serves 4-6.

Two cups cooked, boned chicken may be substituted for shrimp. This is delicious served over rice. Serve with condiments such as chopped peanuts, green onions, raisins, hard-boiled egg or coconut.

Mrs. James Bettendorf (Berkeley Blake)

Spicy Shrimp Creole

4 cups water
½ lemon, sliced
4 peppercorns
2 pounds shrimp, shelled and
 deveined
4 slices bacon, cut up
2 tablespoons butter
1 clove garlic, minced
1 cup chopped onion
1½ cups sliced celery
1½ cups chopped green pepper

1 28-ounce can tomato juice
1 6-ounce can tomato paste
1 tablespoon lemon juice
1 tablespoon sugar
1 teaspoon salt
½ teaspoon pepper
1 bay leaf
¼ teaspoon Tabasco
½ teaspoon thyme
¼ teaspoon cayenne pepper
½ teaspoon filé powder

Bring water to boil. Add next 3 ingredients. Reduce heat and simmer 5 minutes. Drain, set shrimp aside and reserve 1 cup liquid. Sauté bacon in large skillet and remove. Add butter, garlic, onion, celery and green pepper. Cook 5 minutes. Add reserved shrimp liquid and remaining ingredients, except filé powder. Bring to a boil and simmer 1½ hours. Add shrimp and filé powder. Heat through but do not boil. Remove bay leaf before serving over rice. Serves 6.

Mrs. Thomas J. Becktold, Jr. (Pamela Stewart)

Shrimp Ramekins

1 cup mayonnaise
⅓ cup chili sauce
¼ teaspoon curry powder
¼ teaspoon dry mustard
4 drops Tabasco
⅛ teaspoon garlic salt
½ teaspoon horseradish
½ teaspoon Worcestershire
 sauce
1 teaspoon lemon-pepper
 seasoning

⅛ teaspoon thyme
1 teaspoon minced parsley
¼ teaspoon Beau Monde, or
 ⅛ teaspoon celery salt and
 ¼ teaspoon Accent
1 teaspoon lemon juice
4 dozen shrimp, cooked,
 cleaned and peeled
 Parmesan cheese

Mix all ingredients except shrimp and cheese. Put shrimp in buttered baking shells or ramekins. Spread sauce over shrimp and sprinkle with Parmesan cheese. Bake in 350° F. oven until hot and bubbly, about 20 minutes. Serves 4-6.

Can be easily doubled or tripled.

Mrs. J. Wesley McKinney (Eleanor Trezevant)

Bea's Artichoke-Shrimp Newburg

1   9-ounce package frozen
    artichoke hearts
1   bay leaf
1   10¾-ounce can cream of
    mushroom soup
2   tablespoons chopped onion

2   tablespoons white wine
½   teaspoon salt
⅛   teaspoon garlic salt
⅛   teaspoon pepper
1   pound cooked, peeled shrimp
½   cup grated Cheddar cheese

Cook artichoke hearts as directed, adding bay leaf during cooking. Drain. Combine soup, onion, wine, salt, garlic and pepper. Mix well. Arrange artichoke hearts and shrimp in casserole. Spread soup mixture over shrimp. Top with cheese and bake at 400° F. for 15 minutes. Serves 4.

Too easy to be so good.

Mrs. Tony M. Parker (Judy Greene)

Shrimp Rockefeller

1   stick butter
½   pound fresh spinach, cut up
½   head lettuce, shredded
6   green onions, chopped
1½ ribs celery, chopped
½   cup chopped parsley
½   cup dry bread crumbs
1   teaspoon salt
⅛   teaspoon freshly ground
    pepper

2   pounds raw shrimp, peeled
    and deveined
½   stick butter
4   heaping tablespoons flour
2   cups milk
2   cups light cream
¼   cup Parmesan cheese
    Salt and pepper to taste
¼   cup buttered bread crumbs

In a large skillet melt 1 stick butter. Add spinach, lettuce, green onions, celery and parsley. Cover and simmer 10 minutes. Add bread crumbs, salt and pepper. Spread mixture in bottom of greased 3-quart casserole. Layer uncooked shrimp over this. Melt ½ stick butter and blend in flour. Slowly add milk and cream. Bring to a boil, stirring constantly. Cook 2 minutes. Stir in cheese and salt and pepper to taste. Pour cream sauce over shrimp, sprinkle with buttered bread crumbs and bake at 350° F. for 45 minutes. Serves 10.

Not only delicious but pretty. This recipe can be done ahead and frozen.

Mrs. Hershel P. Wall (Jean Harrington)

Shrimp and Rice Casserole

2 pounds raw shrimp
1 10¾-ounce package crab boil
2 cans cream of mushroom
  soup
1 cup mayonnaise
1 2-ounce jar chopped
  pimientos
2 cloves garlic, pressed
1½ tablespoons Worcestershire
  sauce

2 tablespoons lemon juice
¼ cup white wine
12 fresh mushrooms, sliced, or
  one 4-ounce can sliced ·
  mushrooms, drained
½ teaspoon lemon-pepper
  seasoning
1½ cups raw rice
  Sliced almonds

Cook shrimp in crab boil and reserve water. Peel shrimp and set aside.
Mix next 9 ingredients. Add shrimp. Cook rice in 3 cups reserved cooking water. Place cooked rice in a casserole. Top with shrimp and sauce.
Sprinkle with sliced almonds and bake at 350° F. for 30 minutes or until
bubbly. Serves 6.

A really great company dish that's so easy to prepare.

Mrs. Jay Eberle

Ben's Shrimp Delight

1 5-ounce package fine noodles
1 pound shrimp
¾ stick butter
1 clove garlic, finely chopped
1½ tablespoons flour
1 cup water

¼ pound fresh mushrooms
12 medium stuffed olives, sliced
1 2-ounce bottle pimientos
1 chicken bouillon cube
⅛ teaspoon each salt and
  pepper

Cook noodles in 2 quarts water for 15 minutes or until tender. Cook
shrimp in boiling water for 2 minutes, peel and set aside. Sauté garlic
in butter 5 minutes. Lower heat and add flour, until blended. Slowly
add water until sauce is smooth. Add remaining ingredients and
shrimp, simmering for 5 minutes. Spoon shrimp and sauce over hot
noodles. Serves 4-6.

Ben Gilliland, Jr.

Creole Shrimp and Eggplant

2 large eggplants, peeled and cubed
1 large red onion, finely chopped
1 medium green pepper, chopped
4 cloves garlic, finely minced
2 tablespoons chopped parsley
2½ pounds raw shrimp, peeled and coarsely chopped

2 tablespoons olive oil
½-1 teaspoon red pepper flakes, or to taste
1 tablespoon basil
1½-2 cups seasoned bread crumbs
2 tablespoons Parmesan cheese
Salt and pepper to taste
Paprika

Boil eggplant until tender in salted water. Drain, reserving liquid, and set aside. Sauté next 5 ingredients in olive oil until wilted and tender. Add ½ cup eggplant juice and simmer for 10 minutes. In large mixing bowl, add eggplant, sautéed vegetables and shrimp, seasonings, bread crumbs and Parmesan cheese. Mix well. Season with salt and black pepper to taste. Pour into casserole or individual ramekins and sprinkle lightly with more bread crumbs and paprika. Bake at 350° F. for 30-40 minutes. Serves 6-8.

This can also be served as a very unusual side dish.

Mrs. Michael Lynch (Susan Corcoran)

Seafood Coquilles

6 tablespoons butter, divided
3 tablespoons flour
1 teaspoon salt
⅛ teaspoon white pepper
2 cups light cream
¼ cup finely chopped onion

1½ pounds scallops, sliced
½ cup fresh sliced mushrooms
½ pound cooked shrimp
¼ pound crabmeat, cleaned
2 tablespoons sherry
3 tablespoons bread crumbs

Melt 4 tablespoons butter in saucepan. Add flour, salt and pepper. Gradually add cream. Stir to boiling point; then reduce heat and cook 5 minutes on low heat. Sauté onion and scallops in remaining butter. Remove after 5 minutes. Add mushrooms. Sauté 3 minutes. Mix sauce, onion, scallops, mushrooms, shrimp and crabmeat. Season with sherry. Pour into 6 buttered scallop shells or individual casseroles. Sprinkle with bread crumbs. Bake at 375° F. for 20-25 minutes, or until delicately browned. Serves 6 as a first course, or 4 as luncheon or supper entrée.

Mrs. Paul Hilt

Baker's Seafood Casserole

½ stick butter
½ cup chopped mushrooms
½ cup chopped green onions
2 cups cream sauce
½ cup diced lobster

½ cup lump crabmeat
½ cup diced boiled shrimp
½ cup diced scallops
¾ cup grated Swiss cheese

Sauté mushrooms and onions in butter. Set aside and make sauce. When sauce is ready, add to mushroom-onion mixture. Add seafood and heat gently for 3 to 4 minutes, shaking pan. Pour in casserole and top with grated cheese. Bake for 20 minutes at 350° F. or until cheese is melted. Serves 4.

Cream Sauce
2 tablespoons butter
2 tablespoons flour

1½ cups hot milk
Salt and pepper to taste

Melt butter in double boiler, add flour and mix. Add milk and stir with whisk over low heat for three minutes, stirring constantly. Replace over hot water and cook 10 minutes stirring frequently. Season to taste with salt and pepper.

The Late Chef F. O. Baker
University Club of Memphis

Gulf Coast Casserole

2 pints oysters, drained
1 stick margarine, divided
1 pound mushrooms, sliced
2 12-ounce packages frozen
   peeled shrimp, thawed in
   boiling water
1 cup cooked and chopped
   chicken

2 10¾-ounce cans mushroom
   soup
1 tablespoon grated onion
½-1 teaspoon pepper
1 teaspoon salt
1 tablespoon chopped parsley
2 tablespoons sherry
Cayenne pepper to taste

Sauté oysters in 4 tablespoons margarine until edges curl, then drain. Sauté mushrooms in other 4 tablespoons margarine and drain. Combine all ingredients. Bake at 350° F. for 30 minutes. Serve over wild rice. Serves 8-10.

Mrs. John D. Glass (Meegie Rogers)

Shrimp and Crabmeat Supreme

1½ gallons water
¾ cup salt
1 box crab boil
  Juice of 2 lemons and rinds
2 pounds large raw shrimp
6 tablespoons butter
½ cup flour
2 cups milk
1 cup heavy cream
½ teaspoon salt

¼ teaspoon cayenne pepper
3 tablespoons ketchup
1 tablespoon Worcestershire
  sauce
1½ tablespoons lemon juice
¼ cup dry sherry
1 cup grated sharp New York
  Cheddar cheese
10 artichoke hearts, sliced
1 pound fresh lump crabmeat
1 cup buttered bread crumbs

Boil shrimp in 1½ gallons water to which ¾ cup salt, crab boil, lemon juice and rind have been added. Boil 6 minutes. Drain and rinse shrimp with cool water. Peel and devein shrimp. Make a cream sauce of butter, flour, milk and cream. When thickened, add seasonings, ketchup, Worcestershire, lemon juice, sherry and cheese. In 2 greased 1½-quart casseroles, place alternate layers of sauce, artichokes, crab and shrimp. Sauce should cover top layer. Cover with bread crumbs. Bake at 350° F. for 20 minutes until bubbly and hot. Serves 8-10.

Mrs. Frank E. Reid (Diana Mann)

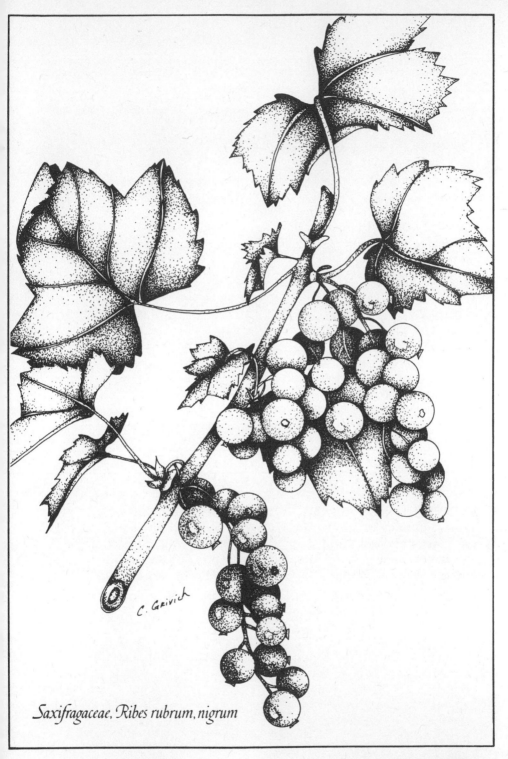

Saxifragaceae, Ribes rubrum, nigrum

Poultry, Game & Stuffing

Lemon-Herb Roast Chicken

Salt, pepper
2 teaspoons oregano and, or, tarragon
2 whole chickens, about 3-3½ pounds each

1 clove garlic, split
2 lemons, quartered
2 small onions

Sprinkle salt, pepper and herbs inside each chicken cavity and on outside. Rub outside with garlic, lemon and onion, then place inside cavities. Place chickens in shallow roasting pan. Bake at 350° F. for 1-1¼ hours, or until tender. Chicken leg should twist easily when done. Serves 8.

Easy and low calorie!

Mrs. James M. Evans (Gayle DuPont)

Twin Roast Chicken

2 whole broiler-fryer chickens, 3 pounds each
2 teaspoons salt, divided
4 tablespoons corn oil, divided
¼ cup chopped onion
½ clove garlic, minced
¼ cup chopped green pepper

2 cups soft bread cubes
½ teaspoon oregano
½ cup chopped black olives
½ cup chopped walnuts
1 tablespoon white wine vinegar

Sprinkle neck and body cavities of chicken with 1 teaspoon salt. Heat 2 tablespoons oil in 10-inch frying pan. Add onion, garlic and green pepper. Sprinkle with remaining salt. Remove from heat. Add last 5 ingredients and mix well. Loosely stuff neck and body cavities of chickens. Hook wing tip onto back to hold neck skin and tie legs together, then to tail. Place chickens in 13x9x2-inch roasting pan lined with foil. Brush chickens with remaining corn oil. Bake at 375° F. for 1 hour and 35 minutes, or until tender. Serves 8.

Mrs. Philip H. Strubing III (Ginny Muller)

Apricot Chicken Bake

8 fryer quarters
Salt and pepper
1 cup chopped onion
1 clove garlic, crushed
1 tablespoon butter
⅓ cup ketchup
¼ cup soy sauce

½ cup apricot preserves
1 cup orange juice
2 teaspoons dry mustard
1 green pepper, cut into strips
4 cups hot, cooked rice, cooked in chicken broth

Season chicken pieces with salt and pepper. Place in greased baking pan. Cover and bake 30 minutes at 350° F. Sauté onions and garlic in butter until tender. Add next 5 ingredients and simmer 15 minutes. Spoon ½ of sauce over chicken. Return to oven and continue baking, uncovered, for 20 minutes. Spoon remaining sauce over chicken. Sprinkle with pepper strips, and cook 20 minutes longer. Serve chicken and sauce over rice. Serves 8.

Mrs. Harry McKee (Larane Wilson)

Crispy Fried Chicken

1 fryer, cut up
1 egg, beaten
2 cups flour

2 teaspoons salt
1 teaspoon pepper
Vegetable oil

Soak chicken pieces in salted water for 2 hours. Rinse and thoroughly dry chicken pieces. Dip each piece into egg, then into flour, which is seasoned with salt and pepper. The best way to apply the flour is to put it into a plastic bag and shake chicken pieces until coated. Set chicken aside; wait 15-20 minutes. Shake in flour a second time. Set aside. Pour at least 2 inches oil into skillet. Heat oil over medium-high heat until smoking. Place chicken into hot oil. Do not crowd. Cover for 5 minutes. Remove top and cook for 10 more minutes or until bottom side is brown. Turn chicken. Replace top for 5 more minutes. Remove top and cook for about 10 minutes, or until brown. Total cooking time should be about 30 minutes. Be sure to turn chicken only once.

A truly Southern dish!

Mrs. D. Randolph Ramey (Minje Mitchell)

111

Buttermilk Pecan Chicken

1 stick butter
1 cup buttermilk
1 egg
1 cup flour
1 cup coarsely chopped pecans
¼ cup sesame seeds

1 tablespoon salt
1 tablespoon paprika
½ teaspoon pepper
2 fryers, cut in pieces
Pecan halves

Melt butter in large baking dish. Mix buttermilk and egg in a shallow bowl. Mix remaining ingredients, except chicken, in another bowl. Dip chicken pieces in buttermilk mixture, then into flour mixture. Place chicken skin side down in butter in baking dish. Turn and coat with butter. Arrange 2 or 3 pecan halves on top of each piece. Bake at 350° F. for 1½ hours. Baste 2 or 3 times. Serves 6-8.

Unusual and tasty.

Mrs. Gus Denton (Candy Stanley)

Health Nut Chicken

2 cups grapefruit juice
¾ cup honey
¾ cup Kikkoman soy sauce
2 cloves garlic, minced

¾ teaspoon powdered ginger
2 chickens, cut in pieces
½ cup chopped walnuts

Mix together first 5 ingredients. Pour over chicken pieces and marinate for one hour. Place marinated chicken skin-side down in shallow baking pan. Cover with half of marinade. Bake 30 minutes. Turn chicken. Pour remaining marinade over chicken, sprinkle with nuts, and bake an additional 30 minutes, or until tender and lightly browned. Serves 6-8.

Tastes like roast duckling!

Mrs. Charles A. Williams III (Elise McDonald)

Chicken Paysan

2 tablespoons butter	1 cup chicken bouillon or broth
2 tablespoons oil	½ cup dry white wine
2½ pounds chicken parts	1 4-ounce can mushrooms
Salt and pepper	8 ounces frozen tiny onions
2 tablespoons flour	½ teaspoon tarragon

Heat butter and oil in large skillet. Brown chicken, sprinkling with salt and pepper. Stir in flour. Stir in bouillon and wine, mixing well. Add mushrooms and liquid, onions and tarragon. Cover and cook over low heat 30-45 minutes. Serves 4.

Mrs. Malcolm McLean, III
Lumberton, North Carolina

Orange Chicken

1 fryer cut up, or 8 chicken breast halves	1 6-ounce can frozen orange juice
½ stick butter	1½ cups water
1 small onion, diced	3 bay leaves
2 ribs celery, chopped	½ teaspoon curry powder
3 tablespoons flour	Salt and pepper, to taste

Brown chicken in butter. Set aside. Add onion and celery to pan and cook until tender, using a bit more butter if needed. Add flour and stir well. Add orange juice and water. Stir and cook until smooth. Add bay leaves, curry powder, salt and pepper and mix well. Return chicken to sauce. Cover and simmer slowly in a 325° F. oven for 1 hour, or until tender. Serves 4-6.

Mrs. Felix Greer
Covington, Tennessee

Chicken in Orange Sauce

1 fryer cut up, or 8 breast halves	⅛ teaspoon cinnamon
Salt	Dash of ginger
½ stick butter	1½ cups orange juice
2 tablespoons flour	½ cup white raisins
½ teaspoon salt	½ cup almonds, slivered
	1 cup fresh orange sections

Salt chicken sparingly and brown in butter in a skillet. Set aside. Add flour and spices to drippings to make a paste. Add orange juice and cook and stir over low heat until thickened. Add chicken, raisins and almonds. Cook covered over low heat for 45 minutes or until tender. Add orange sections and heat lightly. Serve over fluffy white rice. Serves 4.

Mrs. Charles Richard Patterson (Helen Reynolds)

Chicken Tortilla

3 chicken fryers, cooked, or 6 whole breasts, cooked	½ cup sherry
1 medium onion, chopped	1 4-ounce can chopped green chilies
1 green pepper, chopped	1 4½-ounce can chopped black olives
2 stalks celery, chopped	½ package Lawry's Taco Seasoning
2 tablespoons oil	
1 10¾-ounce can cream of mushroom soup	½ cup sour cream
1 10¾-ounce can Cheddar cheese soup	18 flour or corn tortillas
1 10¾-ounce can cream of chicken soup	1 pound Monterey Jack cheese, grated
1 14½-ounce can chicken broth	½ pound Cheddar cheese, grated

Bone chicken and cut into bite-size pieces. Set aside. Sauté onion, pepper and celery in oil. Add next 9 ingredients and chicken to vegetables. Mix well and set aside. Cut tortillas into 1x2-inch pieces. Using 1 greased flat 3-quart casserole and 1 greased flat 1½-quart casserole, layer the ingredients in this order: tortillas, Monterey Jack cheese, chicken mixture. Repeat layers until all is used. Sprinkle Cheddar cheese on top. Refrigerate overnight. Bake at 350° F. for 45 minutes to 1 hour. Serves 10-12.

Must do ahead.

Judy Buffa

Chicken with Thyme

1 fryer cut in pieces, or 8
   chicken breast halves
¼ cup vegetable oil
¼ cup lemon juice
1 clove garlic, chopped

1 tablespoon grated onion
⅛ teaspoon thyme
1 teaspoon salt
1 teaspoon pepper
1 teaspoon celery salt

Place chicken in casserole dish. Mix other ingredients and pour over chicken. Cover tightly with foil. Bake at 500° F. for 15 minutes. Reduce temperature to 325° F. and bake for one hour. Remove foil and cook 15 minutes more to brown chicken. Serves 4.

Tarragon may be substituted for thyme. Delicious either way!

Mrs. Leland Dow, Jr. (Virginia Tayloe)

Baltimore Chicken with Crabmeat

1 10¾-ounce can cream of
   mushroom soup
1 10¾-ounce can cream of
   chicken soup
½ cup milk
1 tablespoon grated onion
½ teaspoon paprika
1½-2 cups diced cooked chicken

1½-2 cups crabmeat
½ cup mushrooms, sliced
1 2-ounce jar chopped
   pimientos
½ cup buttered bread crumbs
   or cornflake crumbs
1 tablespoon parsley

In a saucepan, mix soups, milk, onion and paprika. Heat to just under boiling. Stir in chicken, crab, mushrooms and pimiento. Blend well. Pour into 1½-quart casserole. Top with crumbs and parsley flakes. Bake 20 minutes at 325° F. or until brown and bubbly. Serve in patty shells, over rice or on biscuits. Serves 6.

Mrs. John Wellford Dillard, Jr. (Ann Rogers)

Chicken Puffs

2 cups cooked, cubed chicken
½ teaspoon salt
⅛ teaspoon pepper
3 ounces cream cheese,
softened
2 tablespoons milk
1 tablespoon minced onion
1 tablespoon pimiento

1 8-ounce can Pillsbury
Crescent Dinner Rolls
1 tablespoon butter, melted
¾ cup Parmesan cheese or
crushed seasoned croutons
½ 10¾-ounce can cream of
chicken or cream of celery
soup

Blend first 7 ingredients. Separate rolls into 4 rectangles and seal perforations. Spoon ½ cup chicken mixture into center of each rectangle. Pull up corners and seal. Brush tops with melted butter. Dip in croutons or sprinkle with Parmesan cheese. Bake at 350° F. on ungreased cookie sheet 20-25 minutes, or until golden brown. Heat soup, undiluted or thinned with a little milk, and spoon over top of each puff. Serves 4.

Easy to double and can be made in advance. You may substitute crabmeat, shrimp, tuna or your favorite ground beef mixture for the chicken. You may also substitute a cream sauce for the soup.

Mrs. Harte Thomas, Jr. (Patty Jenkins)

Chicken and Wild Rice

1 6-ounce box Uncle Ben's
Long Grain and Wild Rice
3-4 cups cooked diced chicken
1 4-ounce jar chopped
pimiento, drained
1 16-ounce can French style
green beans, drained
1 medium onion, chopped

1 10¾-ounce can cream of
celery soup
1 8-ounce can water chestnuts,
drained and sliced
1 cup mayonnaise
Salt and pepper, to taste
½ cup grated Cheddar cheese
(optional)

Cook rice according to package directions. Mix together the next 8 ingredients. Place in a greased 3-quart casserole. Top with cheese if desired. Bake at 350° F. for 30 minutes. Serves 8-10.

Great one-dish meal!

Mrs. Harold Webb Jenkins, Jr. (Janice Cochran)

Mrs. Thomas J. Becktold (Pamela Stewart)

"The Best" Chicken Croquettes

3 tablespoons butter
5 tablespoons flour
1 cup milk or chicken stock
4 egg yolks
  Salt and pepper to taste
  Juice of 1 lemon
1 teaspoon Worcestershire
  sauce

3 cups chopped, cooked
  chicken
⅓ cup finely chopped celery
2 tablespoons water
1 cup finely crushed saltine
  crackers
3 cups cooking oil
  Creole Sauce (see Index)

In a double boiler, make thick cream sauce of butter, flour and milk. Beat 2 egg yolks lightly. When sauce begins to thicken, slowly add ½ cup to yolks. Return mixture to sauce and cook slowly for 5 minutes. Remove from heat. Stir in salt, pepper, lemon juice and Worcestershire sauce. Cool. Add enough sauce to chicken and celery to keep mixture soft, but stiff enough to hold its shape. Chill well. Shape into 6 croquettes. Combine remaining yolks with 2 tablespoons water. Dip croquettes in yolks and roll in crumbs. Chill until ready to cook. Fry in oil in heavy skillet over medium-high heat. Serve with Creole Sauce. Serves 6.

You have never eaten croquettes until you've eaten these. Your mouth will water!

Mrs. Frank E. Reid (Diana Morgan Mann)

Chicken Enchilada Casserole

2 cups chopped, cooked
  chicken
1 5⅓-ounce can evaporated
  milk
1 4-ounce can chopped green
  chilies
1 10¾-ounce can cream of
  chicken soup

1 10¾-ounce can cream of
  mushroom soup
1 small onion, chopped
8 corn tortillas, cut into
  1-strips
1 cup Cheddar cheese

Combine first 6 ingredients and warm over low heat. Line a lightly greased, flat, 2-quart baking dish with ½ of the tortilla strips. Pour ½ of sauce over this. Repeat. Sprinkle cheese on top. Refrigerate for 24 hours. Bake at 350° F. for 1 hour. Serves 6.

Mrs. Jon K. Thompson (Susan Taylor)

Chicken Vol-au-Vent

6 chicken thighs
½ stick margarine
2 chicken bouillon cubes
1 cup hot water
6 tablespoons flour
½ teaspoon salt
½ teaspoon paprika
White pepper, to taste
2 cups light cream

12 ounces mushrooms, sliced
   and sautéed
½ cup dry white wine
6 brown and serve link
   sausages, cooked
1 10-ounce package frozen
   patty shells, thawed
2 tablespoons light cream

Brown chicken in margarine in skillet. Dissolve bouillon cubes in water and add to skillet. Cover and simmer 20-30 minutes. Remove chicken from broth; cool and carefully remove bones. Measure broth from skillet and add water to equal 2 cups. Return to skillet. Combine flour, salt, paprika and pepper. Stir in cream. Add to broth and cook, stirring with a whisk until thickened. Stir in mushrooms and wine. Insert sausage in bone cavity of each thigh. On lightly floured surface, roll each patty shell out to a 6-inch square. Place thigh in center and top with 2 tablespoons of mushroom sauce. Fold pastry over and seal center fold. Fold ends to center and seal. Place seam side down in 13x9-inch baking dish. Brush with cream. Bake at 400° F. for 30 minutes or until brown. Heat remaining sauce and pass to serve over chicken. Serves 6.

Mrs. Frank Jemison (Peggy Boyce)

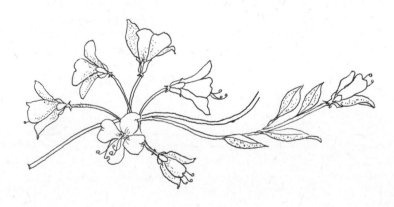

Herbed Chicken Rolls Harris

6 chicken breast halves, boned
   and skinned
Salt and pepper
½ stick butter, melted
2 tablespoons chopped parsley
1 teaspoon marjoram
½ teaspoon thyme

½ stick butter, softened
¼ pound mozzarella cheese
½ cup flour
2 eggs, well beaten
1 cup fresh bread crumbs
½ cup dry white wine

Flatten chicken breasts between waxed paper. Sprinkle with salt and pepper and brush with melted butter. Mix herbs with softened butter, melt and set aside. Cut cheese into 6 strips and place one on each chicken breast. Roll up each breast tucking in ends. Coat with flour, dip in egg and roll in bread crumbs. Arrange in buttered casserole and pour on melted herb butter. Bake 20 minutes at 350° F. Pour wine over chicken. Continue cooking for 15 minutes, basting frequently with pan juices. Serve with sauce. Serves 6.

Mrs. William C. Harris (Ann Clark Quinlen)

Party Chicken

6-8 whole chicken breasts, split
    and boned
2 4-ounce cans mushrooms,
  drained
4 medium tomatoes, peeled
  and quartered
4 bay leaves

1 8-ounce bottle Italian
  dressing
2 envelopes onion soup mix
½ teaspoon oregano
1 5-ounce box chicken flavored
  instant rice

Preheat oven to 350° F. Arrange chicken in one layer in large baking pan or 2 small ones. Place mushrooms, tomatoes and bay leaves on top. Combine dressing, onion soup and oregano and pour over chicken. Bake uncovered 1 hour, basting occasionally. Prepare rice according to directions. To serve, arrange rice on a large platter and top with chicken and sauce. Serves 6-8.

For a luncheon, serve with fresh spinach salad

Mrs. William R. Hackett (Sandy Childress)

Chicken Rochambeau

Mushroom Sauce

½ stick butter
2 cups green onion, including
   3 inches of green tops
2 teaspoons finely chopped
   garlic
4 tablespoons flour
4 cups chicken stock

1 cup chopped fresh
   mushrooms
1 cup dry red wine
2 tablespoons Worcestershire
   sauce
¼ teaspoon red pepper
1 teaspoon salt

Melt butter over moderate heat and stir in onions and garlic. Cook about 5 minutes, until soft but not brown. Add flour. Mix well, stirring constantly with wire whisk. Pour in stock and cook over high heat until sauce boils and thickens slightly. Stir in mushrooms. Reduce heat to low and simmer, partially covered, until mushrooms are tender, about 15 minutes. Add remaining ingredients, stirring over low heat 2 or 3 minutes. Set aside.

Chicken

4 whole chicken breasts, halved
   and boned with skin intact
2 teaspoons salt

1 teaspoon pepper
1 cup flour
1½ sticks butter

Pat chicken dry. Salt, pepper and flour evenly. Melt butter over moderate heat in large skillet and add chicken, skin down. Brown evenly. Cover, reduce heat to low and simmer 20 minutes, or until tender. Baste every 7 or 8 minutes with pan juices.

Ham

2 teaspoons butter
8 slices Canadian bacon or lean
   country ham

8 Holland Rusks

Brown bacon or ham in butter over moderate heat. Drain. Place on rusks and set on baking sheet. Keep warm.

Hollandaise Sauce

4 egg yolks
4 tablespoons fresh lemon juice
2 sticks butter, melted

½ teaspoon salt
⅛ teaspoon cayenne pepper

In top of double boiler, stir egg yolks and lemon until thickened. Remove from heat and add butter, a little bit at a time, stirring constantly with wire whisk. Add seasonings. Do not overheat or it will curdle.

To assemble, spoon 2 or 3 tablespoons Mushroom Sauce over ham, top with half of chicken breast and cover all with Hollandaise Sauce. Serves 8.

Mrs. Taylor Malone (Carey Eckert)

Chicken Breasts with Asparagus Sauce

1 9-ounce package frozen asparagus, thawed
3 green onions, chopped
⅔ cup hollandaise sauce
8 large chicken breast halves, skinned, boned and pounded

Flour with salt and white pepper to taste
½ stick butter
¼ cup dry white wine
½ cup freshly grated Parmesan cheese

Cut asparagus in pieces. Add green onions, cover with salted water and boil for 12 minutes, or until tender but not overcooked. Drain, pressing out all water. Purée in blender or food processor. Combine with hollandaise. Keep warm in double boiler. This may be done ahead.

Dip chicken breasts in flour seasoned with salt and white pepper. Melt butter in skillet. Sauté breasts until golden brown on each side. Cook slowly about 10-15 minutes. Put breasts in shallow greased 9x13-inch casserole. Add wine to skillet and scrape up bits. Pour over chicken. Put large spoonfuls of asparagus sauce on breasts and sprinkle with cheese. Brown lightly in broiler. Serve at once. Do not try to cook chicken ahead and reheat. Serves 8.

Serve with rice pilaf and green or tomato salad.

Mrs. Hershel P. Wall (Jean Harrington)

Chicken with Artichoke Sauce

12   chicken breast halves
4-5 tablespoons butter
½   cup white wine
¾-1 cup chopped shallots
⅓-½ cup sherry

1   cup white wine
½ pound mushrooms, sliced
5-6 artichoke bottoms, thinly
    sliced
Parsley sprigs

Sauté chicken in butter until brown. Add wine and shallots and cook for 3 minutes. Cover and bake at 350° F. for 15 minutes or until chicken is done. Remove chicken and keep warm. Add to the pan, sherry, white wine, mushrooms and artichoke bottoms. Sauté for 3-4 minutes until wine has cooked down and mushrooms are tender. Pour sauce over chicken and add fresh parsley. Serves 10-12.

Mrs. Clyde Patton, Jr. (Leslie Wilsford)

Chicken with Sausage

¼ cup olive oil
2 garlic cloves, quartered
1 green pepper, cut in strips
4 whole chicken breasts, boned
    and cut in half
2 pounds Italian sausage links

2 cups dry white wine
½ pound fresh mushrooms,
    sliced
1 teaspoon salt
¼ cup water
2 tablespoons cornstarch

Heat oil in skillet. Add garlic and cook until golden. Remove garlic and discard. Add pepper strips and cook until softened. Remove from skillet and reserve. Cook chicken pieces and sausage until browned, a few pieces at a time. Remove from skillet. Drain off all but 2 tablespoons drippings. Return chicken, sausage and pepper to skillet. Add wine, mushrooms and salt. Cover skillet and simmer 30 minutes. Place chicken and sausages on warm platter. Blend water and cornstarch until smooth. Stir into liquid in skillet. Cook and stir constantly until thickened. Spoon sauce over meat on platter. Serves 8.

Real man's dish!

Mrs. William E. Denman III (Julie Moss)

Mrs. Marmon's Chicken Jerusalem

4 chicken breast halves, skinned and boned	¼ pound mushrooms
Salt, pepper and paprika to taste	2 tablespoons fresh lemon juice
⅛ teaspoon tarragon	⅓ cup dry white wine
⅛ teaspoon rosemary	1 tablespoon sherry
1½ teaspoons butter	1 8-ounce package frozen artichoke hearts
	2 tablespoons chopped parsley

Season chicken breasts with herbs, salt and pepper. Place in a shallow baking dish and bake at 375° F. for 15 minutes. In a large frying pan, melt butter and sauté mushrooms with lemon juice until lightly glazed. Add wine, sherry, artichoke hearts and heat through. Spoon vegetables over chicken. Quickly boil down remaining juices until reduced by half. Pour over chicken. Sprinkle with parsley. Serves 4.

Only 200 calories per serving!

Mrs. William W. McCrary III (Tancie Lewis)

Chicken Breasts Elena

6 chicken breast halves, boned	3 green onions, chopped
Salt, pepper, flour, butter	6 slices mozzarella cheese
6 large mushrooms, sliced	

Pound breasts until thin. Dust with flour. Sauté in butter in skillet over medium heat until golden. Sprinkle with salt and pepper. Sauté mushrooms and green onions in butter. Put chicken breasts in baking dish, top with mushroom-onion mixture and place slice of cheese over each. Brown under broiler. Serves 6.

Mrs. J. T. Jabbour

Easy Chicken Breasts

Chicken breasts
¼ teaspoon poultry seasoning
¼ teaspoon garlic salt
1 tablespoon Kitchen Bouquet

1-2 tablespoons white wine or
    vermouth
Salt and pepper

Use 1 chicken breast per serving. Rub each chicken breast with poultry seasoning and garlic salt. Rub meaty side with Kitchen Bouquet. Place breasts in foil and add wine or vermouth. Sprinkle with salt and pepper. Wrap tightly and bake at 300° F. for 1 hour.

Easy, non-fattening and children love it!

Mrs. R. Grattan Brown, Jr.

Easy Baked Chicken Breasts

6 chicken breast halves, boned
   Salt, pepper, oregano,
    paprika
3 slices bacon
1 10½-ounce can brown gravy

1 4-ounce can mushrooms,
   drained
1 cup dry white vermouth
Grated Parmesan cheese

Sprinkle chicken breasts with salt, pepper, oregano and paprika. Place bacon slices in bottom of greased 1½-quart flat rectangular baking dish. Place chicken on bacon. Mix gravy, mushrooms and vermouth and pour over chicken. Sprinkle Parmesan over all. Bake covered for 30 minutes at 350° F. Uncover and bake 30 minutes longer. Serve over rice, if desired. Serves 6.

Easy—and has an interesting combination of flavors!

Mrs. Gwin Scott (Wynn Skipper)

Annie's Chicken

8 chicken breast halves, boned
1 bunch green onions, chopped
8 ounces cream cheese,
   softened

8 bacon slices
Toothpicks

Pound chicken breasts flat. Mix cream cheese and onion and shape into walnut-sized balls. Place one on each breast. Roll breasts, tucking in sides. Wrap with bacon slice and secure with toothpick. Broil on lowest oven shelf 30 minutes, or until bacon browns and chicken is done. Reduce heat if necessary. Serves 4.

Mrs. William S. Mitchell

Chicken with Dried Beef

1 2½-ounce jar dried beef
6 chicken breast halves, boned
   and skinned
6 strips bacon
8 ounces sour cream

1 10¾-ounce can cream of
   mushroom soup
1 2¼-ounce package slivered
   almonds

Shred dried beef and place in greased rectangular casserole. Wrap each breast with a slice of bacon and place on beef. Mix sour cream and soup together and pour over chicken. Sprinkle with almonds. Bake uncovered at 250° F. for 4 hours. Serves 6.

Easy and has a wonderful flavor!

Mrs. Jerry B. Martin (Carolyn Cowser)

Pancake Chicken Nuggets

2 whole chicken breasts
1 cup pancake mix
⅔ cup milk

1 teaspoon salt
¼ teaspoon pepper
   Maple syrup

Bone and skin chicken breasts. Cut each breast half into 6-8 chunks, approximately 1½ inches square. Combine pancake mix, milk, salt and pepper. Dip chicken chunks into batter. Drop into deep fat, heated to 340-350° F. Fry until golden, approximately 5 minutes. Serve hot with maple syrup. Serves 4.

Great for a brunch! Can be served with sweet and sour sauce, too.

Mrs. Mickey Moran (Pat Taylor)

Chicken Ah-So

4-6 chicken breast halves, boned
    and skinned
2 tablespoons butter
1 10¾-ounce can Golden
    Mushroom Soup
½ cup water
1 beef bouillon cube
1 tablespoon soy sauce
1 teaspoon Worcestershire
    sauce
½ teaspoon curry powder

½ teaspoon poppy seeds
1 8-ounce can bamboo shoots,
    drained
½ cup sliced celery
1 small onion, sliced
1 4-ounce can sliced
    mushrooms, drained
1 small green pepper, cut in
    strips
3 tablespoons dry white wine
Cooked rice

Cut chicken into 1½-inch pieces and brown in butter until golden brown. Stir in next 7 ingredients and mix well. Cover and simmer for 15 minutes, stirring occasionally. Add next 6 ingredients. Cover and simmer 2-5 minutes longer. Serve over rice. Serves 4-6.

Easy.

Mrs. Neal G. Clement
Florence, Alabama

Oriental Chicken

4-6 chicken breast halves,
    boned, skinned and cut up
6 tablespoons oil
1 medium onion, sliced
1 cup sliced celery
1 8-ounce can bamboo shoots
1 8-ounce can water chestnuts

1 cup bite-size pieces fresh
    broccoli
4 tablespoons soy sauce
1 teaspoon salt
½ teaspoon white pepper
5 ounces chicken broth
1 tablespoon cornstarch

Cook chicken in hot skillet in oil until meat turns white. Stir-fry onion, celery, bamboo shoots, water chestnuts and broccoli. Add soy sauce, salt and pepper. Cook for 5 minutes. Mix broth and cornstarch. Pour into skillet and boil until thickened. Serve over rice. Serves 4.

Mrs. Gwin Scott (Wynn Skipper)

Chicken and Green Bean Oriental

4 whole chicken breasts, cooked, boned and shredded

2 10-ounce packages frozen French style beans, thawed

1 4-ounce can mushrooms, stems and pieces

1 8-ounce can water chestnuts, drained and sliced

1 2½-ounce package slivered almonds, toasted

1 14-ounce can fancy Chinese, or chow mein vegetables

½ cup grated Cheddar cheese

1 10¾-ounce can cream of mushroom soup

¼ cup milk

1 teaspoon soy sauce

¼ teaspoon Tabasco

1 3-ounce can fried onion rings

Butter a 2-quart, or larger, flat Pyrex dish. Layer the first 7 ingredients in order. Mix soup, milk, soy sauce, and Tabasco and pour over chicken and vegetables. Bake at 350° F. for 45 minutes, or until bubbly. Top with onion rings and return to oven for 10 minutes. Serves 6-8.

Can be made ahead and doubled to feed a crowd.

Mrs. Michael A. Stahl
Vienna, Virginia

My Favorite Chicken Casserole

8 chicken breast halves, boiled and torn in pieces

1 cup mayonnaise

1 10¾-ounce can cream of mushroom soup

2½ cups cooked rice

1 cup chopped celery

½ cup chopped onions

1 8-ounce can water chestnuts, sliced

Salt and pepper to taste

1 stack Ritz crackers, finely crumbled

2 tablespoons butter

Combine first 8 ingredients and pour into 3-quart casserole. Melt butter and mix in crumbs. Sprinkle crumb mixture over casserole. Bake at 350° F. for 45 minutes. Can prepare ahead and bake later, or can be frozen. Serves 8.

Unusual contrast of soft and crunchy, bland and nutty textures and tastes.

Mrs. Walker E. Morris, Jr. (Janie Owen)

Pot Luck Chicken Casserole

8 chicken breast halves,
   cooked, boned and cut up
2 10¾-ounce cans cream of
   chicken soup
24 ounces sour cream

1 12-ounce package Ritz
   crackers, containing three
   stacks
Poppy seeds
½ stick butter, melted

Mix soup and sour cream. Crush 2 stacks of crackers; reserve third stack for another use. In a 1½-quart casserole, alternately layer chicken, soup mixture and ½ of cracker crumbs. Sprinkle poppy seeds over crackers until lightly covered. Repeat layering. Drizzle melted butter on top. Bake at 350° F. until it bubbles. Serves 10-12.

Mrs. Harry McKee (Larane Wilson)

Celestial Chicken

4 whole chicken breasts, boned
   and cut into 1½ inch strips
½ cup light cream
1 cup flour
2 teaspoons salt
2 teaspoons paprika

2 teaspoons Accent
¼ teaspoon pepper
¼ cup dried parsley flakes
1 2¾-ounce bottle sesame seeds
Oil for frying

Dip chicken in cream. Mix next 7 ingredients and coat chicken in this mixture. Fry chicken in 2 inches oil until golden brown. Drain on paper towels.

Sauce
½ stick butter
¼ cup flour
1 teaspoon salt
¼ teaspoon cayenne pepper or
   more

2 chicken bouillon cubes
1½ cups light cream
¾ cup water

For sauce, melt butter and add flour, salt, cayenne and bouillon cubes. Cook over moderate heat and add cream and water to make sauce of desired consistency. Serve sauce in individual dishes for dipping chicken. Serves 6-8.

Mrs. Will N. Griffin (Elise Marie Kroell)

Mrs. Clyde L. Patton, Jr. (Leslie Wilsford)

Chicken Paprikas

12-14 crêpes (made from any basic crêpe recipe)
½ cup chopped onion
3 tablespoons butter
2 whole chicken breasts
2 tablespoons Hungarian paprika
½ teaspoon salt
¼ teaspoon pepper
1-1¼ cups chicken stock
½ cup sour cream

Prepare crêpes and set aside. Sauté onion in butter until golden. Add chicken and brown well on both sides. Sprinkle with salt, pepper and paprika. Add stock and bring to boil. Cover, reduce heat and cook very slowly 35-40 minutes or until meat is done. Cool, bone and dice. Boil gravy until reduced to ½ cup. Add chicken and sour cream. Spoon portion of mixture in center of each crêpe and roll up. Place in buttered baking dish and bake at 375° F. for 15 to 20 minutes. Serves 6 to 8.

Mrs. Lee Wardlaw (Mary Linda Lewis)

Chicken Gruyère Casserole

8 whole chicken breasts, boned
4 sticks margarine
1 cup flour
7 cups milk
¼ pound Cheddar cheese, grated
5 ounces Gruyère cheese, grated
1 clove garlic, minced
2 tablespoons Aćcent
1 6-ounce can tomato paste
1 tablespoon salt
5 6-ounce cans whole mushrooms, drained
2 14-ounce cans quartered artichoke hearts, drained

Cook chicken until tender, and cut into large bite-size pieces. Melt margarine in saucepan. Add flour and blend, cooking for 2 minutes. Add milk slowly. Set aside. In another saucepan, melt cheeses and add garlic, Aćcent, tomato paste and salt. Mix well. Blend the 2 sauces together. Scatter chicken in bottom of two greased 3-quart flat casseroles. Put artichokes and mushrooms on top of chicken. Pour sauce over all and bake at 350° F. for 35 minutes. Serves 16.

Can be prepared a day ahead, but do not freeze.

Mrs. Robert M. Williams, Jr. (Julia Gray)

Italian Sautéed Chicken with Italian Mushroom Rice

6 chicken breast halves,
  skinned and boned
½ cup flour
⅛ teaspoon white pepper
1½ sticks butter
1 tablespoon olive oil

1 garlic clove, minced
½ teaspoon crushed rosemary
½ teaspoon sweet basil
½ cup white wine
  Italian Mushroom Rice (see
  Index)

Cut each chicken breast into 3 long strips. Dredge strips with mixture of flour and white pepper. In a heavy skillet, melt 1 stick butter and add olive oil, garlic, rosemary and basil. Sauté chicken in this mixture and lightly brown. Add wine and cook on low heat until ½ of wine has been reduced. This may be done 3 or 4 hours before serving. When ready to serve, reheat on low heat, remove the chicken and add ½ stick butter to remaining gravy. When hot, place chicken pieces on bed of hot Italian mushroom rice and spoon on gravy. Serve immediately. Serves 4.

If you love good Italian food laced with garlic, this is your dish!

Mrs. Frank E. Reid (Diana Mann)

Asparagus-Chicken Casserole

2 whole chicken breasts,
  boned, skinned, and cut
  in chunky pieces
1½ teaspoons Accent
¼ teaspoon pepper
¼ cup vegetable oil
2 10-ounce packages frozen
  asparagus, cooked
  according to package
  directions

1 10¾-ounce can cream of
  chicken soup
½ cup Hellmann's mayonnaise
1 teaspoon lemon juice
½ teaspoon curry powder
1 cup grated sharp Cheddar
  cheese

Sprinkle Accent and pepper over raw chicken pieces. Sauté chicken in oil over medium heat for 6 minutes. Place cooked asparagus in greased 9-inch square pan. Place chicken on top of asparagus. Mix and heat together soup, mayonnaise, lemon juice and curry powder. Pour over chicken and asparagus. Sprinkle cheese on top. Bake at 375° F. for 30 minutes. Serves 4.

Mrs. Gavin M. Gentry (Mary Jane Coleman)

Chiccoli Bake

1   10-ounce package frozen
chopped broccoli, cooked
and drained
2½ cups cooked rice
1   8-ounce jar Cheese Whiz
1   10¾-ounce can cream of
mushroom soup

4   cooked chicken breasts,
boned and chopped
½ cup chopped onion
½ cup chopped celery
½ cup slivered almonds
(optional)

Mix all ingredients together and put into a 2-quart casserole. Bake at 350° F. for 45 minutes. Serves 4-6.

May be prepared without chicken and used as a vegetable dish.

Mrs. Les Hays (Donna Haynes)

Barbecued Chicken

1   medium onion, chopped
2   tablespoons oil
2   tablespoons vinegar
2   tablespoons brown sugar
¼ cup lemon juice
1   cup ketchup
3   tablespoons Worcestershire
sauce

½ tablespoon prepared mustard
1   cup water
½ teaspoon salt
⅛ teaspoon cayenne pepper
½ cup flour
1   fryer, cut in pieces
¼ cup oil

Make sauce by browning onion in 2 tablespoons oil. Add next 7 ingredients and simmer 30 minutes. Combine salt, cayenne pepper and flour in paper bag. Shake chicken in bag until coated. Brown in ¼ cup hot oil. Pour off excess oil. Pour sauce over chicken and bake uncovered in 325° F. oven 1 hour. Serve immediately. Serves 4-6.

Good and easy for family dinners or casual entertaining.

Mrs. Jerry B. Martin (Carolyn Cowser)

Barbecued Chicken in the Oven

3 fryers
Salt
1 stick butter
1 cup ketchup
½ cup Heinz 57 sauce
¼ cup vinegar

¼ cup Worcestershire sauce
1 onion, minced
½ teaspoon granulated garlic
¼ cup sugar
1 teaspoon salt

Cut chicken in pieces, salt and fry in butter until brown. Combine remaining ingredients and bring to a boil. Place chicken pieces in a large casserole. Pour sauce over chicken and cover with foil. Bake in 325° F. oven 1 hour and 15 minutes. Serves 6.

Mrs. Asbury L. Jones, Jr. (Rita Renshaw)

Barbecued Chicken in a Sack

1 teaspoon salt
½ teaspoon pepper
1 tablespoon paprika
1 tablespoon sugar
½ teaspoon garlic salt, or ½ clove garlic
1 cup ketchup
1 medium onion, chopped

½ cup water
⅓ cup lemon juice or vinegar
1 tablespoon Worcestershire sauce
½ stick butter
Salt and pepper
1 fryer, cut up

Mix first 8 ingredients together and heat to boiling. Add next 3 ingredients. Salt and pepper chicken. Place chicken in a large brown paper grocery bag. Pour sauce over chicken and fold down bag. Bake at 350° F. until tender, or about 1 hour. Serves 6.

Good family night dinner.

Mrs. Forrest N. Jenkins (Linda Bauer)

Smoked Chicken

½ cup salad oil
Juice of 2 lemons
1 teaspoon salt
¼ teaspoon freshly ground
pepper

2 garlic cloves, minced, or ½
teaspoon garlic powder
6-8 chicken parts

Mix first 5 ingredients in shallow dish. Mix in chicken pieces, coating well. Refrigerate overnight. Build fire at one end of covered barbecue grill. Add water-soaked hickory chips. Put chicken on rack. Do not place chicken directly over the coals. Cook about 2 hours, basting frequently with marinade. Serves 4.

Mrs. J. T. Jabbour

Cornish Game Hens with Rice Stuffing

2 1-pound Cornish game hens,
thawed
Salt and pepper
2-4 tablespoons slivered
almonds
2 tablespoons finely chopped
onion
⅓ cup uncooked long-grain
rice

3 tablespoons butter
1 cup water
1 chicken bouillon cube
1 teaspoon lemon juice
½ teaspoon salt
Sage (optional)
⅓ cup finely chopped fresh
mushrooms
1 stick melted butter

Season hens with salt and pepper. In a small saucepan, cook almonds, onion and rice in butter for 5-10 minutes. Add water, bouillon cube, lemon juice, salt and sage. Bring mixture to a boil, stirring to dissolve cube. Reduce heat, cover and cook slowly 20-25 minutes, or until liquid is absorbed. Stir in mushrooms. Stuff birds and place breast side up in roasting dish. Brush with melted butter. Bake, covered, at 400° F. for 30 minutes. Uncover and roast 1 hour longer. Brush with melted butter during the last 15 minutes. Serves 2.

Mrs. Harry McKee (Larane Wilson)

Curried Turkey

½	stick butter	1	10¾-ounce can cream of
½	cup sliced almonds		mushroom soup
1	cup sliced fresh mushrooms	⅔	cup milk
1	teaspoon curry powder	2	tablespoons sherry
1	tablespoon grated onion	1½	cups cooked, diced turkey

Lightly brown almonds in butter. Remove almonds and sauté mushrooms. Remove mushrooms. Add curry powder and onion to butter and blend. Stir in soup, milk and sherry. Cook over low heat. Add mushrooms, almonds and turkey. Simmer 10 minutes. Serve over rice. Serves 4-6.

Mrs. Harry McKee (Larane Wilson)

Smoked Turkey or Duck

2	sticks butter	1	teaspoon sage
4	tablespoons lemon-pepper	½	teaspoon garlic salt
	seasoning	1	turkey or duck
1½	tablespoons poultry	3	ribs celery
	seasoning	3	carrots
1½	tablespoons parsley flakes	1	large onion, quartered
1	tablespoon celery salt		

Melt butter. Add next 6 ingredients and simmer 5 minutes. Wash turkey or duck and pat dry. Place celery, carrots and onion in bird cavity. Rub butter mixture all over bird. Insert meat thermometer between thigh and body. Smoke in meat smoker, using charcoal and water-soaked hickory chips. Cook until temperature reaches 185° F.

Mrs. James B. Green, Jr. (Betty Brown)

Doves in Burgundy

12-18	dove breasts or whole birds	½	cup Burgundy
1	medium onion, chopped	¼	teaspoon oregano
1	10¾-ounce can cream of celery soup	¼	teaspoon rosemary
			Salt and pepper to taste
1	4-ounce can sliced mushrooms	½	teaspoon Kitchen Bouquet

Place game loosely in large baking dish. Sauté onions until tender and combine with remaining ingredients. Pour over game and cover lightly with foil. Bake for 1 hour in 325° F. oven, turning occasionally. Bake uncovered for 20 minutes. Serves 6-8.

A quick and easy way to prepare dove.

Mrs. Walter May, Jr. (Helen Fitzhugh)

Doves

4-6	whole doves	1	stick butter
	Salt and pepper to taste	1	cup water, or more
	Garlic powder to taste	3	tablespoons wine

Season doves with salt, pepper and garlic powder. Brown in butter in skillet. Add water, cover, and simmer on low heat for 30 minutes. Add wine and more water, if necessary. Cook 5 more minutes. The gravy may be thickened with a small amount of flour, if preferred. This recipe is recommended for whole doves only. Serves 4.

Wonderful Christmas morning brunch.

Mrs. William T. Black, Jr. (Lida Willey)

Duck à la St. Louis

1 10¾-ounce can cream of
  mushroom soup
4 ounces frozen orange juice
  concentrate, thawed
1 tablespoon soy sauce

2 tablespoons lemon juice
½ cup red wine
2 ducks, split in half, or 1 goose
  Lawry's Seasoned Salt

Mix together first 5 ingredients. Pat ducks or goose dry. Sprinkle with seasoned salt. Place birds in casserole or roaster, breast side up. Pour mixture over. Cover and bake at 300° F. for 3½ hours. Serve pan juices as gravy.

Mrs. Mark R. Loyd

Wild Duck

2 wild ducks
  Salt and pepper
¼ teaspoon thyme
  Celery, quartered
  Onion, quartered
  Orange slices, quartered

½ teaspoon thyme
½ teaspoon rosemary
2-3 strips bacon
1½ cups red wine or consommé
2 bay leaves

Clean ducks well, washing inside thoroughly. Rub inside with salt and pepper and ¼ teaspoon thyme. Stuff birds with pieces of celery, onion and orange. Rub outside of birds with salt and pepper, thyme and rosemary. Lay birds in baking dish, half filled with water. Arrange strips of bacon lengthwise on duck breasts and secure with toothpicks. Bake uncovered at 425° F. until bacon is browned, about 40 minutes. Remove from oven and pour off grease and juices until ½ inch of juice is left in pan. Add wine, or consommé, and bay leaf. Cover with foil. Reduce heat to 300° F. and bake for 1½ hours until tender. Discard stuffing and carve after 10 minutes. Gravy can be made from pan drippings. Serves 4.

Carolyn Mitchell Kittle

Wild Duck Quinlen

3 large wild ducks	2 carrots, quartered
1 stick butter, melted	2 4-ounce cans mushrooms,
6 tablespoons flour	with juice
Fresh pepper	4-5 sprigs fresh parsley
2 small onions, halved	6-8 10½-ounce cans beef
3-4 ribs of celery with leaves,	consommé
halved	3 tablespoons sherry

Split ducks in half and pat dry. Preheat oven to 500° F. Melt butter and stir in flour and pepper to make a paste. Place ducks in bottom of roaster, breast side up. Spread butter-paste on ducks. Place in oven, uncovered, for 20 minutes, or until browned. Remove roaster. Reduce heat to 250° F. Add onion, celery, carrots, mushrooms, with juice, and parsley to pan. Add consommé, using 1 can of water to every 2 cans of consommé. Ducks should be almost covered, so only use what you need. Put top on roaster, close all vents and return to oven. Cook at least 5 more hours. The last ½ hour, add 1 tablespoon sherry per duck. To serve, remove vegetables, leaving mushrooms in juices. Serve each person ½ duck. Thicken pan juices for gravy, if desired. Serves 6.

Mrs. William L. Quinlen, Jr. (Ann Clark Miller)

Bellows' Duck Breasts

1 stick butter	1 teaspoon dry mustard
4 tablespoons Worcestershire	¼ teaspoon cinnamon
sauce	2 garlic cloves, pressed
2 lemons, juiced	1¼ cups cider vinegar, or 1¼
½ teaspoon Tabasco	cups white wine
½ teaspoon salt	4 ducks or 8 duck breasts
½ cup brown sugar	Salt and pepper

Combine first five ingredients and cook over low heat until butter melts. Add next 4 ingredients and cook slowly for 20 minutes. Add vinegar or wine. Season duck breasts and sear on grill. Baste frequently with marinade, turning every few minutes. Cook about 20 minutes, or until pink. Breasts should be crusty and very brown.

May also use doves.

Mrs. Jack Bellows (Lela Hudson)

Diana's Roast Duck Supreme

5 cups orange juice	2 large potatoes, peeled
3 sticks butter	6 slices bacon, halved
6 ducks	1 orange, sliced
Salt and freshly ground	2 cups sherry
pepper	Parsley
2 ribs celery, cut in pieces	
2 onions, quartered	

Place 2½ cups orange juice in bottom of roasting pan. Cut up butter in pats and place in bottom of roaster. Preheat oven and roaster to 500° F. Dry ducks inside and out. Pepper heavily, and salt inside and out of ducks. Rub into ducks. Stuff with pieces of celery, onion and potatoes. Place 2 halves bacon and slice of orange on top of each breast. Remove preheated roaster and put in ducks, breast side up. Cover and bake at 500° F. for 25 minutes. Reduce temperature to 275° F. and baste ducks with juices. Add rest of orange juice and dribble sherry over breasts. Cook for 2½ hours longer. Baste ducks every 30 minutes. Add remaining sherry. To serve, discard bacon. Place ducks and vegetables from duck cavity on platter and decorate with fresh parsley and orange slices. Pour some gravy over sliced ducks and place remainder of gravy in serving bowl. Serves 10-12.

Mrs. Frank E. Reid (Diana Mann)

Cross-Style Duck

2 wild ducks	1 stick butter
1 envelope onion soup mix	

Clean and drain ducks. Place ½ stick butter in cavity of each. Sprinkle soup mix over top of ducks. Wrap birds together in foil. Place in roaster. Bake at 275° F. for 4 hours. Serves 4.

Easy and delicious!

Mrs. James B. Cross (Lynn Woods)

Barbecued Duck

Salted water
3-4 wild ducks
1 stick butter or more
1 large onion, finely chopped
½ cup ketchup
½ cup vinegar

4 tablespoons Worcestershire
   sauce
3-4 drops Tabasco
1 cup water per duck
3 tablespoons flour

Soak ducks for several hours in salted water. Drain and pat dry. Split each duck in half. Brown slowly in butter. Remove ducks and brown onion in drippings. Place ducks and onions in roaster. Make sauce of remaining ingredients, except flour, and pour over ducks. Bake covered at 300° F. for 2½-3 hours, or until tender. Before serving, thicken gravy with flour. Serves 6-8.

Mrs. Dorsey Mathis, Jr. (Margaret Jones)

Fried Wild Duck

Duck breasts, skin removed
Flour
Salt and pepper
Milk

Butter
Wild or long-grain and wild rice
   mixture

Cut breasts in strips, approximately ½ inch x 2 inches. Season flour with salt and pepper. Dip strips into milk and dredge in flour. Fry crisp in butter. To serve, place fried strips over wild or long grain and wild rice mixture. Pour gravy over all.

Gravy
½ cup chopped onion
2 tablespoons butter
1 3-ounce can mushrooms
2 tablespoons flour

½ cup white wine
8 ounces sour cream
   Salt and pepper to taste

Sauté onions and mushrooms in butter. Stir in flour. Add wine slowly. Add sour cream and stir until thickened. Season with salt and pepper. Makes about 1½ cups gravy.

Excellent hors d'oeuvre with sauce served separately.

Mrs. Anne G. Boals (Anne Goodwin)

Smoked Duck

Ducks
Corn oil or peanut oil

Bacon
1 **fifth bottle white wine**

Use as many ducks as your smoker will hold. Rub each duck with corn oil. If you are using whole ducks, split the duck so it will lay flat on the grill. Place bacon criss-cross on each duck. Put wine and enough water to total 7 quarts in water pan. More wine may be used. Smoke 4-5 hours. In cold weather allow 1 extra hour.

This is so good, no sauce is necessary.

Robbie Smith

Max Ostner

Brandied Quail

6 **slices bacon**
4 **tablespoons butter**
8 **green onions, sliced**
1 **garlic clove, minced**
Quail
½ **cup brandy**

2 **cups chicken broth**
1 **teaspoon salt**
½ **teaspoon black pepper**
2 **cups heavy cream**
¼ **cup horseradish**

Fry bacon. When bacon is cooked, remove from skillet. In skillet, with bacon drippings, add butter, onions, garlic and desired number of quail and brown. After browning, place in baking dish with all juices. Pour ¼ cup brandy over quail, ignite and let flame die. Add remaining ¼ cup brandy, ignite and let flame die. Do not add all of the brandy at one time. Add chicken broth, salt and pepper and roast uncovered at 375° F. for ½ hour, basting frequently. Add cream and horseradish to sauce and continue roasting for 15 minutes, basting frequently. Serve on a heated platter. Serves 4-6.

Mrs. Thomas Holloman (Jayne Pressgrove)

Braised Quail

6-8 quail
   Salt and pepper
1 stick butter
½ cup oil
1 onion, sliced
5 mushrooms, chopped

2 tablespoons flour
½ cup white wine
2 cups chicken broth
1 small can seedless white
   grapes, drained

Dry quail. Season with salt and pepper. In a heavy skillet, heat oil and add butter. Sauté onion and mushrooms and remove from skillet. Brown quail. Remove birds and stir flour into pan drippings. Cook, stirring, for 1 minute. Add wine and broth, stirring until well blended. Return quail, onion and mushrooms to skillet. Add grapes. Cover and cook in oven at 300° F. for 1 hour and 15 minutes, turning birds every 25 minutes. Serve over toast points. Serves 3-4.

Try this with chicken breasts.

The late Chef F. O. Baker
University Club of Memphis

Quail Supreme

8 quail
1 10¾-ounce can cream of
   mushroom soup
8 ounces sour cream

½ cup cooking sherry
½ teaspoon salt
1 4-ounce can mushrooms

Place birds in roaster. Mix remaining ingredients. Pour over birds. Bake at 350° F. for 1 hour, covered, and ½ hour, uncovered. Serves 6-8.

Could substitute chicken breasts, but brown in butter before placing in roaster.

Mrs. Anne G. Boals (Anne Goodwin)

Venison, Danish Style

Marinade

1 cup red wine	¼ cup vinegar
1 cup water	3-4 pounds loin of venison

Combine and pour over venison. Marinate for 24-48 hours.

2 tablespoons salt pork, diced	1 heaping tablespoon
1½ teaspoons salt	cornstarch
½ teaspoon pepper	¼ cup cold water
2 sticks butter, melted	½ cup heavy cream
2 cups hot bouillon, divided	¼-½ cup black currant jelly
1 cup red wine, heated	¼ cup sherry

Cut 1 inch wide by ½ inch deep slits in top of venison. Tuck in pieces of salt pork. Rub with salt and pepper. Brush with butter. Place meat on rack in shallow baking pan. Add 1 cup hot bouillon and all wine. Cook at 325° F. Allow 25-30 minutes per pound. Baste often with juices. If necessary, add more hot bouillon and wine. Remove meat to hot platter and keep warm. Use pan juices and measure 1½ cups liquid. Add hot bouillon if needed to make amount. Make paste of cornstarch and water. Heat pan juices and stir in cornstarch paste. Cook, stirring constantly, until thick and smooth. Remove from heat. Stir in cream, currant jelly and sherry. Heat thoroughly but do not boil. Pour over meat. Serves 8.

Jesper Moeller
Lyngby, Denmark

Southern Corn Bread Dressing

2 6½-ounce packages Martha
   White Corn Bread Mix or
   recipe of favorite corn
   bread
1 stick butter
2 medium onions, chopped
1 bunch celery, chopped
2 medium green peppers,
   chopped

2-3 slices day-old white bread
3 tablespoons chopped
   parsley
Salt, pepper and sage to
   taste
2 eggs, beaten
1½-2 10¾-ounce cans chicken
   broth

Prepare corn bread as directed on package, using egg batter recipe. Allow corn bread to sit out overnight. Sauté chopped vegetables in butter until tender. In large bowl, crumble corn bread and white bread. Add vegetables and seasonings. Mix well. Add eggs and broth and blend thoroughly. It will be like thick soup. Allow to stand in refrigerator for several hours or overnight. Pour into greased 2-quart casserole and bake at 350° F. for 30-45 minutes, or until brown and crusty on top.

Two pints whole raw oysters, drained, may be added before baking.

Mrs. Rowe Belcher (Susan Ramsey)

Oyster Dressing

2 sticks butter
2 onions, chopped
3 cups chopped celery
1 cup chopped mushrooms
2 cups chopped oysters
8-9 cups soft bread crumbs
1½ cups stock from boiling
   giblets and neck

1 teaspoon salt and pepper
½ teaspoon poultry seasoning
½ clove garlic
¼ teaspoon thyme
¼ teaspoon sage
¼ teaspoon oregano
3 tablespoons chopped parsley

Melt butter in skillet. Sauté onions and celery until golden. Add mushrooms and oysters. Cook for 1 minute only and remove from heat. Combine bread crumbs, stock and all seasonings and mix well. Fill body and neck cavities of turkey but don't pack. If you prefer, put dressing in a greased casserole and heat uncovered at 350° F. until hot and bubbly.

Mrs. Michael Heffernan (Tracy Plyler)

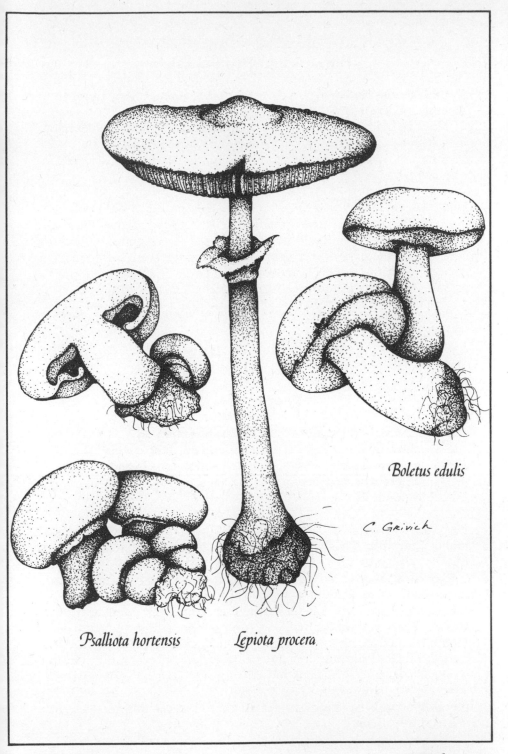

Boletus edulis

C. Grivich

Psalliota hortensis Lepiota procera

Meats

Elegant Pan-Broiled Filets

2 tablespoons butter
1 tablespoon oil
4 6-ounce filets, wrapped in
    bacon
  Salt and freshly ground
    pepper

3 tablespoons chopped green
    onion
3 tablespoons chopped parsley
½ cup canned beef broth
½ cup wine, dry white or red

Heat electric skillet or fry pan on high. Melt butter or oil. Cook filets 3-4 minutes on each side for medium rare. Sprinkle lightly with salt and pepper after turning. Remove meat from pan. Pour off most of fat. Turn heat to medium and cook onions and parsley until softened. Pour in beef broth and wine. Cook over high heat until about ⅓ cup liquid remains. Pour over filets on a warm platter. Serves 4.

A typical French way of cooking meat; even ground beef patties are good this way!

Mrs. Hershel P. Wall (Jean Harrington)

Pepper Steak

1 3-pound sirloin steak, 1¼
    inches thick
1-2 tablespoons black
    peppercorns, crushed
2 tablespoons butter

1 tablespoon oil
½ cup dry white wine
2 tablespoons brandy
1 teaspoon salt

Prepare steak 2 hours before cooking. Wipe steak with a damp cloth and dry carefully. Crush peppercorns by putting in a cloth and pounding. Press pepper firmly into both sides of steak. Pound in with flat side of meat cleaver. Cover steak and let stand at room temperature until ready to cook. Heat a large heavy skillet until very hot. Add 1 tablespoon butter and the oil. As soon as butter is melted, add steak. Brown steak well on each side at high temperature. Reduce heat to medium and cook about 5 minutes on each side for medium rare. Remove to heated platter. Pour fat from skillet. Add remaining butter, wine, brandy and salt. Cook for 3-5 minutes, stirring constantly and scraping all drippings into the mixture. Slice the steak into very thin pieces. Spoon a little sauce over steak. Serve remaining sauce in a heated bowl. Serves 6.

Leftover steak makes a terrific sandwich.

Mrs. Paul Howse

Marinated Steak Drena

4-5 pounds flank or sirloin
    steak, 1½-2 inches thick
½ cup oil
⅓ cup wine vinegar
1 cup dry red wine
2 tablespoons lemon juice

¼ teaspoon salt
⅛ teaspoon pepper
1 teaspoon oregano
2 tablespoons minced onion
1 clove garlic, minced

Place steak in shallow baking pan. Combine remaining ingredients and pour over steak. Cover with plastic wrap and marinate in refrigerator for 12-24 hours, turning once or twice. Cook over charcoal, brushing with marinade during cooking. Serves 6-8.

If using sirloin, marinate 1-2 hours.

Mrs. John Turley, III (Barbara Barham)

Steak Strips Elegant

1½ pounds boneless round steak
1½ tablespoons cooking oil
1 large onion, sliced, separated
    into rings
1 10¾-ounce can cream of
    mushroom soup

1 4-ounce can mushrooms,
    drained, liquid reserved
½ cup beef broth
1 teaspoon garlic salt
2 cups cooked rice or noodles

Cut steak into thin strips. In large skillet, brown meat in oil over high heat; lower heat and add onions. Sauté until tender but not browned. Mix together soup, mushroom liquid, broth and garlic salt. Pour over steak. Add mushrooms. Cover and simmer about 1 hour, or until steak is tender. Serve over rice or noodles. Serves 4.

Good for casual entertaining.

Mrs. Charlie Carr
Chapel Hill, North Carolina

Rouladen

2½ pounds top round steak, sliced horizonally ⅛-inch thick
Salt and pepper
1   6-ounce jar brown mustard
3   large sour pickles, sliced lengthwise

4-5 strips bacon, cut in 2-inch lengths
1   large onion, finely chopped
¼   cup oil
Water

Lay out meat slices. Salt, pepper and spread each slice with mustard. Alternate strips of bacon and pickles on each slice. Sprinkle onion on top of each slice. Beginning with large end, roll each strip of meat and secure with toothpick. Brown on all sides in oil. Place meat in 9x13-inch casserole and bake at 350° F. for 10 minutes. Add 1 cup water to casserole, cover and continue cooking 1 hour. Remove from oven, reserving meat juices.

Sauce
1   cup cold water
1   teaspoon cornstarch

2-3 tablespoons mustard
3-4 tablespoons sour cream

Combine cornstarch and water. In saucepan, heat cornstarch mixture, meat juices and remaining ingredients. Boil 1 minute until thick. Serve over meat. Serves 8-10.

This recipe is from a German friend visiting in the States.

Mrs. Joseph I. McCormack (Cheryl Bobbitt)

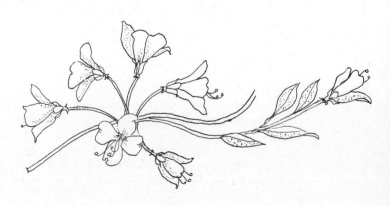

Italian Beef Roulades

½ cup chopped green onions
2 cloves garlic, minced
¼ cup chopped celery
¼ cup minced parsley
1 cup fresh bread crumbs
1 teaspoon salt
¼ teaspoon pepper
¾ cup Parmesan cheese

12 paper-thin slices bottom
   round steak or tenderloin
½ cup olive oil
3 cups beef stock
1½ cups dry red wine
1 bay leaf
1 12-ounce package spinach
   noodles

Mix onions, garlic, celery, parsley and bread crumbs. Add salt, pepper and Parmesan cheese. Blend well. Spread 1-2 tablespoons of filling on each slice of meat and sprinkle with olive oil. Roll up and secure with toothpicks or string. Brown rolls in small amount of olive oil. Add stock, wine and bay leaf. Simmer for 30 minutes. Remove meat and reduce liquid. Serve rolls and sauce over noodles. Garnish with parsley if desired. Serves 6.

Good substitute for beef stock: bouillon simmered with carrot, onion and parsley for 20 minutes.

Mrs. William E. Denman, III (Julie Moss)

Beef Kabobs with Seasoned Rice

1 6-ounce package long-grain
   and wild rice
1 cup Hellmann's mayonnaise
1 pound sirloin beef, cubed
1 cup cherry tomatoes
1 cup mushroom halves
½ cup green pepper chunks

2 tablespoons chopped parsley
2 tablespoons chopped onion
1 tablespoon milk
¼ teaspoon salt
⅛ teaspoon garlic powder
⅛ teaspoon pepper

Prepare rice according to package directions, omitting margarine. When done, combine rice and ½ cup mayonnaise. Toss lightly. Spoon into 8x8x2-inch Pyrex dish. Alternate meat, tomatoes, mushrooms and green pepper on skewers. Arrange over rice. Bake at 350° F. for 40 minutes, turning kabobs once. Combine remaining mayonnaise and ingredients. Mix well. Serve over kabobs. Serves 4.

Mrs. Richard De Saussure (Phyllis Falk)

Teriyaki Kabobs

½ cup salad oil
3 cloves garlic, peeled
½ teaspoon dry mustard
¾ cup soy sauce
1 teaspoon curry powder
6 teaspoons Worcestershire
   sauce
6 teaspoons vinegar

1 cup cooking sherry
¼ cup sugar
2 pounds sirloin steak, cubed
½ pound mushrooms, halved if
   large
3 onions, quartered
3 green peppers, cut in small
   pieces

Blend first 9 ingredients and marinate meat overnight. Add mushrooms four hours before cooking. Blanch onions and peppers 2 minutes, if desired. Alternate meat and vegetables on skewers. Cook over grill or in oven on rack until meat is done according to taste. Serves 4.

Mrs. Jerry B. Martin (Carolyn Cowser)

Oriental Beef and Peapods

1 pound flank or round steak
6 tablespoons soy sauce
1 tablespoon cornstarch
1 teaspoon sugar

1 tablespoon dry sherry
1 6-ounce package frozen
   peapods
Peanut or vegetable oil

Cut steak into very thin strips. Marinate in soy sauce, cornstarch, sugar and sherry for several hours or overnight. Cook peapods 1-2 minutes in small amount of oil in skillet. Remove and drain on paper towels. Sauté meat in skillet, reserving marinade. Add marinade to meat and cook 5-10 minutes more. Return peapods to skillet with meat. Serve over rice or Chinese soft noodles. Serves 4.

Mrs. Gwin Scott (Wynn Skipper)

Marinated Brisket

1   10-ounce can consommé
1   5-ounce bottle soy sauce
¼   cup lemon juice
    Garlic to taste

1   teaspoon liquid smoke
4-5 pounds beef brisket
½   cup barbecue sauce

Combine first 5 ingredients. Pour over brisket and marinate in a non-aluminum pan overnight in refrigerator with fat side up. Bake, covered, in marinade 1 hour per pound at 300° F. Baste each hour. Uncover for last hour. Turn meat. Pour ½ cup barbecue sauce over meat and cook final hour at 350° F. Slice across the grain and serve hot or cold for sandwiches.

Mrs. John A. Stemmler (Marsha Miller)

Beef and Beer

4   pounds lean beef
½   cup flour
½   cup vegetable oil
2   pounds onions, thickly sliced
6   garlic cloves, crushed
¼   cup red wine vinegar
3   tablespoons dark brown
    sugar

2   10¼-ounce cans beef
    bouillon, undiluted
2   12-ounce cans beer
½   cup chopped fresh parsley
2   bay leaves
2   teaspoons ground thyme
1   tablespoon salt (optional)
    Black pepper to taste

Slice beef into ½-inch strips. Flour beef and brown in hot oil in Dutch oven. Remove meat. Add onion and garlic to same pot. Sauté until tender. Return meat to pot and add remaining ingredients. Cover and bake at 325° F. for 2 hours or until meat is tender. Skim off excess grease. Serve with egg noodles. Serves 10.

Can be made early in the day and reheated.

Mrs. James Bettendorf (Berkeley Blake)

French Stew

2 pounds beef stew meat	2 tablespoons bread crumbs
2 cups water	2 beef bouillon cubes
2 tablespoons Worcestershire sauce	2 4-ounce cans mushrooms, undrained
2 tablespoons dry tapioca	½ cup red wine
2 onions, coarsely chopped	

Combine all ingredients and bake 4 hours at 300° F. uncovered. With cover, bake only 3 hours. Add more liquid if needed. Serves 8.

Mrs. Thomas J. Becktold, Jr. (Pamela Stewart)

Farm Style Beef Stew

2 tablespoons shortening	½ teaspoon freshly ground pepper
3 pounds stewing beef, cubed	2½ cups water
2 large onions, sliced	12 small carrots, sliced
1 20-ounce can tomatoes	1 cup English peas
2 cloves garlic, pressed	12 small white onions
1 cup sliced celery	6 potatoes, quartered
¼ cup chopped parsley	½ cup flour
1 bay leaf	¾ cup cold water
½ teaspoon ground thyme	
1 tablespoon salt	

Melt shortening in a 6-quart pot and brown meat. Add next 10 ingredients. Bring to a boil, reduce heat, cover and simmer 2 hours. Add next 4 ingredients and simmer, covered, 1 hour. Blend flour with cold water and stir into stew to thicken. Serves 6-8.

Stew good enough for company.

Mrs. Henry Hancock (Peggy Fairchild)

Easy Beef Stew

2 pounds beef stew meat cut
   into 1-inch cubes
¼ cup flour
1 teaspoon salt
¼ teaspoon pepper
2 tablespoons oil
3 large carrots, cut into
   1-inch pieces

3 medium potatoes, cut into 1-
   inch pieces or 2 1-pound
   cans small whole potatoes,
   drained and rinsed well
1 1-pound 12-ounce can whole
   tomatoes, chopped briefly
   in blender
1 envelope dry onion soup

In 3-quart casserole, toss beef with flour, salt, pepper and oil. Brown uncovered at 400° F. for 30 minutes, stirring once. Add remaining ingredients. If using canned potatoes, add last 15 minutes of cooking. Cover and bake at 375° F. for 2 hours or until meat is tender. Serves 6.

Can be done ahead and reheated. May need more liquid.

Mrs. Malcolm McLean, III
Lumberton, North Carolina

Company Meat Loaf

1 envelope onion soup mix
¾ cup warm milk
1½ cups bread cubes
2 pounds ground chuck
2 tablespoons Parmesan
   cheese

½ cup finely chopped green
   pepper
¼ cup ketchup
4 tablespoons chili sauce
2 eggs, beaten
1 8-ounce can tomato sauce

Add soup mix to milk. Stir well and add bread cubes. Place meat in large bowl. Add next 5 ingredients. Combine thoroughly with hands or fork. Shape into 2 loaves. Cook 40 minutes in 350° F. oven. Cover loaves with tomato sauce and cook 20 minutes longer. Serves 6-8.

May be frozen uncooked.

Mrs. Max Lucas (Ruth Plyler)

Margaret's Meatballs

1½ pounds ground chuck
1 egg
⅔ cup bread crumbs
1 teaspoon rubbed sage
¼ cup milk
2 tablespoons dry onion soup mix

2 tablespoons bacon drippings
2 tablespoons flour
2 tablespoons dry onion soup mix
2 cups water
Salt and pepper to taste

Combine first six ingredients in a bowl and mix well. Shape into large meatballs. Brown in bacon drippings and remove to a platter. Add flour to drippings and cook until flour is dark brown. Add remaining soup mix and water. Season to taste. Return meatballs to gravy and simmer, covered, for 1 hour. Serves 6.

Wonderful family meal.

Mrs. L. Charles Schaffler

Stuffed Peppers

2 pounds ground beef
1 cup chopped celery
1 cup chopped onion
¾ cup long-grain rice
1 16-ounce can tomatoes

1 teaspoon chili powder
Salt and pepper to taste
2 cups Cheddar cheese, shredded
16 green peppers, parboiled

Brown beef in Dutch oven and drain well. Add celery and onion. Sauté until tender. Add rice, tomatoes and spices. Cover and simmer over low heat for 30 minutes, or until all juice is gone. Add cheese and stir until melted. Stuff into peppers. Bake at 350° F. for 30 minutes. Makes 16 peppers.

Can be frozen.

Mrs. John D. Glass (Meegie Rogers)

Microwave Mexican Dish

1 package Doritos
1 10-ounce can Rotel tomatoes
1 10¾-ounce can cream of
  chicken soup

1 pound ground beef, browned
1 onion, chopped
1 cup grated Cheddar cheese

Place layer of Doritos in 2-quart casserole dish. Mix Rotel and soup. Layer ½ of ground beef, ½ of chopped onion, ½ of Rotel mixture and ½ of grated cheese. Repeat layers. Cook 12 minutes, uncovered, on roast or medium heat in microwave, turning dish once. Reduce amount of Rotel if desired. Serves 4-6.

Mrs. Jerry B. Martin (Carolyn Cowser)

Puerto Vallarta Enchiladas

1 10-ounce can Rotel tomatoes
  and green chiles
1 8-ounce can tomato sauce
1 14-ounce package frozen flat
  tortillas

Corn oil for sautéing
1 cup grated sharp Cheddar
  cheese
1 medium onion, chopped
1 pound ground beef, cooked

Mix Rotel and tomato sauce together. Dip each tortilla in mixture before browning lightly in hot oil in skillet. Sprinkle each tortilla with cheese and either beef or onion. Roll up filled tortilla and place side by side in casserole. Sprinkle lightly with cheese and warm in oven at 300° F. Serves 4-6.

A very mild, authentic Mexican enchilada.

Mrs. James A. Breazeale (Beth Baker)

Taco Bake

2 pounds ground beef	1½ teaspoons salt
1½ cups chopped onions	12 taco shells
1 15-ounce can tomato sauce	2 cups grated Cheddar cheese
1 15-ounce can kidney beans, drained	½ small head lettuce, chopped
2 teaspoons chili powder	2 chopped tomatoes
½ teaspoon pepper	8 ounces sour cream (optional)

Brown beef and onions. Stir next 5 ingredients. Break taco shells in half and line bottom and sides of a 13x9x2-inch dish. Spoon meat mixture over shells. Sprinkle with cheese. Bake 15-20 minutes. Top with lettuce and tomatoes. Serve with sour cream. Serves 8.

Top with chopped green onions and sliced black olives for a special treat.

Mrs. William R. Hackett (Sandra Childress)

Mississippi Chili

2-3 large onions, coarsely chopped	2 heaping tablespoons chili powder
4 ribs celery, coarsely chopped	Ground cumin, to taste
2 garlic cloves, minced	1 24-ounce can tomato juice
Oil	2 15-ounce cans kidney beans
1½ pounds coarsely ground beef	Salt and pepper to taste

Sauté onions, celery and garlic in small amount of oil. Transfer to deep pot. Brown meat and add to pot. Add seasonings and tomato juice and mix. Drain kidney beans and reserve liquid. Add bean liquid to pot, and salt and pepper to taste. Simmer 2 hours. Add kidney beans and simmer until thick. Makes about 2 quarts. Serves 6.

This is fantastic served over shredded lettuce and Fritos and topped with grated Cheddar cheese.

Mrs. James Bettendorf (Berkeley Blake)

John Wayne Casserole

2   4-ounce cans chopped green chilies
1   pound, or less, Monterey Jack cheese, coarsely grated
1   pound, or less, Cheddar cheese, grated
1-1½ pounds lean ground beef
4   eggs, separated

⅔   cup evaporated milk, or ⅓ cup milk
1   tablespoon flour
½   teaspoon salt
⅛   teaspoon pepper
2   medium tomatoes, chopped, or one 1-pound can whole tomatoes, drained, chopped and juice reserved

Combine grated cheeses and chilies. Lightly brown beef in skillet, seasoning with salt and pepper. Pour off grease. Put beef in shallow greased 9x13-inch casserole. Place cheese-chili mixture on top. Beat egg yolks in mixer, gradually adding milk, flour, salt and pepper. Pour egg yolk mixture over ingredients in casserole. Top with chopped tomatoes and juice. Beat egg whites until stiff and spread over casserole to edges. Bake at 325° F. for about 1 hour. Serves 6.

Mrs. Burdette Russ (Scottie McCord)

Corned Beef

4-6 pounds corned beef brisket
2   tablespoons pickling spice
1   onion, sliced

1   stalk celery with leaves, sliced
1   carrot, sliced

Line shallow pan with heavy foil. Put corned beef in center of foil and pour ¼ cup water over top. Sprinkle with spices and arrange vegetables over and around meat. Seal meat, bringing foil ends up so juice cannot run out. Bake at 300° F. for 4 hours. Let cool and slice thinly.

Mrs. Burdette Russ (Scottie McCord)

Reuben Casserole

1 27-ounce can sauerkraut, drained
2 medium tomatoes, sliced
2 tablespoons Thousand Island dressing
8 ounces corned beef, shredded

8 ounces Swiss cheese, shredded
1 12-ounce can flakey refrigerated biscuits
¼ teaspoon caraway seed
2 rye crackers, crushed

Spread sauerkraut over bottom of 2-quart casserole. Place sliced tomatoes on top and dot with dressing. Cover evenly with layers of beef and cheese. Bake uncovered for 15 minutes at 425° F. Remove from oven. Separate biscuits into 3 layers each. Place on top of casserole, overlapping slightly, if necessary. Sprinkle with caraway seeds and cracker crumbs. Return to oven for approximately 15 minutes or until biscuits are lightly browned. Serves 6.

Mrs. Mickey Moran (Pat Taylor)

Artichoke Beef

1 14-ounce can artichoke hearts, drained and sliced
6 ounces smoked dried beef, shredded
8 ounces sour cream
1 10¾-ounce can cream of mushroom soup

1 2.2-ounce can sliced ripe olives
2 tablespoons sherry
8 pastry shells, baked

Combine first 6 ingredients and simmer to heat. Serve in pastry shells. Serves 8.

For a less salty taste, pour boiling water over dried beef in colander.

Mrs. Paul Hilt

Scallopini alla Romana

1 stick butter, divided
¾ pound mushrooms, sliced
1 small onion, finely chopped
1 clove garlic, peeled
3 cups coarsely chopped,
   peeled fresh tomatoes
⅔ cup dry white wine

1¼ teaspoons salt, divided
¼ teaspoon dried crushed
   tarragon leaves
12 thin veal scallops, about 1½
   pounds
⅛ teaspoon pepper
Grated Parmesan cheese

In skillet, sauté mushrooms in 5 tablespoons butter until golden brown or about 5 minutes. Add onion and garlic and cook about 5 more minutes. Add tomatoes, wine, ¾ teaspoon salt, tarragon, and blend well. Reduce heat, cover, and simmer for 30 minutes, stirring occasionally. Meanwhile, wipe veal with damp paper towels. Sprinkle with ½ teaspoon salt and the pepper. Heat 3 tablespoons butter in another skillet. Add veal, a few pieces at a time, and cook until lightly browned on both sides, or about 5 minutes. Remove and keep warm. Return veal to skillet. Remove garlic from sauce, and pour sauce over veal. Simmer, covered, for 5 minutes. Sprinkle with Parmesan cheese. Serves 6.

Chicken Variation: Substitute 6 halves chicken breast, boned and skinned, for veal. Half each one again to make 12 pieces. Pound until flattened. Proceed as in veal recipe.

Pork Variation: Substitute 1½ pounds pork tenderloin, sliced and pounded until flattened, for veal. Proceed as in veal recipe up to final cooking. Cook at least 15 minutes longer.

Mrs. Frank Stegbauer

Mrs. Henry Hancock (Peggy Fairchild)

Veal Oscar

8 veal slices, pounded thin
¼ cup flour
1 stick butter, divided
2 tablespoons olive oil
1 clove garlic, crushed

2 pounds fresh asparagus, or
   two 10-ounce packages
   frozen asparagus
1 pound lump crabmeat
2 cups hollandaise sauce

Lightly dust veal slices with flour. Heat 4 tablespoons butter and olive oil in pan and sauté veal, adding crushed garlic for a few minutes until done. Remove veal and keep warm until ready to use. Prepare asparagus, being careful not to over-cook. Melt remaining butter in pan and lightly toss crabmeat until heated. Assemble, first putting veal on plate, then asparagus, crabmeat and hollandaise sauce. Serves 8.

An elegant company dish!

Mrs. J. Franklin Holmes (Jeanie Hobby)

Veal with Artichokes

2 cloves garlic, minced
   Oil
2 pounds veal cutlets
   Flour
   Salt and pepper
1 16-ounce can tomatoes,
   drained

½ cup sherry
¼ teaspoon oregano
2 10-ounce packages frozen
   artichoke hearts

In a heavy skillet, sauté garlic in oil. Dust veal with seasoned flour. Brown in oil. Add tomatoes, wine and oregano. Stir until mixture is hot. Add frozen artichokes. Cover. Simmer 45-60 minutes. Serve with steamed rice. Serves 6.

Mrs. Philip H. Strubing, III (Ginny Muller)

Veal Piccata

1 pound veal cutlets
½ cup flour
1 teaspoon salt
1 stick butter

½ cup chicken broth
2 tablespoons lemon juice
¼ cup chopped parsley
1 lemon, thinly sliced

Pound cutlets until thin and dredge in flour and salt. Sauté in butter about 20 minutes or until done. Add broth and reduce liquid slightly. Add lemon juice, parsley and lemon slices. Shake pan until cutlets are covered and lemon is hot. Serve at once with rice or noodles. Serves 2.

A must for veal lovers! Chicken breasts may be substituted for the veal.

Mrs. Willard G. Logan, Jr. (Hope McCrary)

Jamie's Leg of Lamb

1 6-8 pound leg of lamb
1 stick butter, softened
1 teaspoon garlic powder
1 teaspoon Accent
1 teaspoon salt
1 teaspoon cayenne pepper
3 tablespoons chopped fresh parsley

8 ounces sour cream
¾ teaspoon saffron (optional)
1 teaspoon cornstarch
3 tablespoons cold water
1 2¼-ounce bottle capers, drained (optional)
Paprika

Cut excess fat off lamb. Cream together next 6 ingredients. Spread over roast. Wrap the meat in heavy aluminum foil and refrigerate overnight. Remove from refrigerator 2 hours before cooking, but do not unwrap. Cook in 375° F. oven 35 minutes per pound. One half hour before cooking time ends, remove from oven, unwrap and strain juices into pan. Turn oven to 400° F. Place roast in open pan and brown for 30 minutes. Add sour cream and saffron to strained meat juices. Stir cornstarch into 3 tablespoons cold water. Stir into cream and juices. Add capers and paprika to taste. Cook 1 minute. Serve as accompaniment to meat. Serves 8-10.

Mrs. W. W. Simmons, III

Stuffed Leg of Lamb

1 tablespoon dry mustard
1 tablespoon lemon juice
2 teaspoons salt
½ teaspoon dried thyme
½ teaspoon rosemary
½ teaspoon marjoram
¼ teaspoon pepper

1 clove garlic, crushed
1 6-8 pound leg of lamb, boned
   not tied
¾ pound pork tenderloin
¼ cup water
2 tablespoons flour

Mix first eight ingredients. Brush mixture inside leg of lamb. Place tenderloin inside and wrap lamb around it, tying securely. Insert meat thermometer so that tip is in center of pork tenderloin. Place meat on rack in shallow roasting pan. Do not cover. Bake at 325° F. until thermometer registers 170° F. for 2½-3 hours. Remove roast from oven and let stand while preparing gravy. Skim off fat and add enough water to meat juices to make 1¾ cups. Shake together water and flour until smooth. Stir into drippings gradually. Heat to boiling, stirring constantly, and boil one minute. Serve as accompaniment to meat. Serves 6-8.

Mrs. Mickey Moran (Pat Taylor)

Oven Barbecued Leg of Lamb

1 6-8 pound leg of lamb
   Cooking oil
1 clove garlic, in 4-5 slivers
1 12-ounce bottle ketchup
1 12-ounce bottle chili sauce

Juice of 1 lemon
1 small onion, chopped
1 large plastic Brown 'n Bag
1 tablespoon flour

Cut off all fat from lamb. Rub with oil. Make 4-5 slits in meat and insert garlic slivers. Mix ketchup, chili sauce, lemon juice and onion. Shake flour in baking bag. Put lamb in bag, shake and pour sauce over it. Tie bag. Make 6-7 slits about ½ inch long in bag. Place in large pan with none of bag overlapping. Bake at 350° F. 2 hours for smaller leg, 2½ hours for larger one. Serves 6-8.

Mrs. John C. Patton (Nancy Caradine)

Lamb Chops Niçoise

½ pound fresh green beans
3 tablespoons butter, divided
8 small new potatoes
8 cocktail tomatoes
4 tablespoons olive oil, divided
8 small rib lamb chops

1 clove garlic, pressed
2-3 tablespoons white wine
2-3 tablespoons chicken stock
1 teaspoon tomato paste
½ teaspoon tarragon

Cook beans with 1 tablespoon butter and set aside on warming tray. Boil potatoes until tender. Then brown with remaining butter in skillet. Place on warming tray. Sauté tomatoes in 2 tablespoons olive oil until partly softened. Add to tray. Pan broil chops in remaining olive oil. Add to tray. To juices in pan, add remaining ingredients. Heat sauce, stirring briskly. Arrange chops in center of hot platter. Around chops, arrange beans, potatoes and tomatoes. Pour sauce over. Serves 4.

Mrs. Philip H. Strubing, III (Ginny Muller)

Lamb Chops or Leg of Lamb

½ stick butter
1 clove garlic, pressed
16 center loin chops or 4-5
    pounds leg of lamb

¼ cup vinegar
1 5¾-ounce bottle mint sauce
Dash of A-1 sauce

Melt butter in skillet. Add garlic. Add chops and brown on each side. Add remaining ingredients. Cover and put in 325° F. oven for 20 minutes. Serve on platter with parsley and pan gravy on the side. For leg of lamb, omit butter. Make 3 or 4 small incisions in lamb and insert small slices of garlic clove. Make sauce of remaining ingredients and pour over lamb. Salt and pepper well. Cook in roasting pan with rack, covered, for 2½ hours at 325° F. Serve on platter with parsley and pan gravy on the side. Serves 8-10.

Mrs. Jack Bellows (Lela Hudson)

Tasty Pork Tenders

3 tablespoons flour	2-3 tablespoons oil
1 teaspoon salt	1 cup chicken broth
1 tablespoon dry mustard	½ cup white wine, or more
¼ teaspoon pepper	½ cup water
2 pounds pork tenderloin, cut in 1-inch strips	1 small can mushrooms (optional)

Mix dry ingredients and rub into meat. Melt oil in skillet and brown meat quickly on each side. Pour in liquids and mushrooms and lower heat. Simmer, covered, for 30-45 minutes, stirring occasionally. Serve with rice, if desired. Serves 4.

Mrs. Charles Richard Patterson (Helen Reynolds)

Poor Man's Wiener Schnitzel

1 pound pork tenderloin, thinly sliced	2 eggs, beaten
Salt	Dried bread crumbs
Lemon-pepper seasoning	Cooking oil
¼ cup flour	Lemon wedges

Pound meat between waxed paper until extremely thin. Add salt and lemon-pepper to flour. Dredge meat in flour. Dip in egg and then bread crumbs. Fry on both sides quickly in heated oil. Serve with lemon wedges to be squeezed over meat. Serves 4.

Mrs. Lee L. Wardlaw (Mary Linda Lewis)

Sweet and Sour Pork

Marinade

1 tablespoon white wine
2 tablespoons soy sauce
1 teaspoon minced ginger
1 clove garlic, pressed

½ teaspoon Accent
1 pound pork tenderloin, cut in
  1-inch cubes

Mix first five ingredients and marinate pork 2-3 hours or overnight.

Batter

2 egg yolks, or 1 egg

4 tablespoons cornstarch

Mix ingredients and add more cornstarch if necessary. Drain meat well and combine with batter. Deep fry at 420° F. until crisp and place on platter.

Sauce

6 tablespoons sugar
2 tablespoons soy sauce
1 tablespoon white wine
3 tablespoons vinegar

½ cup pineapple juice
3 tablespoons ketchup
½ cup water
2 tablespoons cornstarch

Combine first 6 ingredients. Bring to a boil. Mix cornstarch and water. Add to boiling ingredients and stir until thickened.

Vegetables

1 small green pepper, cut in
  1-inch squares
2 carrots, diagonally sliced
½ cup pineapple chunks

1 small onion, quartered
6 tablespoons oil
¼ teaspoon salt

Sauté vegetables in hot oil until transparent. Season with salt. Combine sauce, meat and vegetables. Serves 6.

Mrs. James A. Mann (Carol Gates)

Pork Oriental

4 pound boneless, center-cut pork loin, rolled	¼ cup soy sauce
¾ cup sherry or dry white wine	1 tablespoon lemon juice
½ cup chicken bouillon	1 clove garlic, pressed
1 chicken bouillon cube	¼ teaspoon powdered ginger
	1 teaspoon salt

Leave a thin covering of fat on pork. Make a marinade of remaining ingredients. In covered bowl or plastic bag, place pork roast and pour in marinade. Marinate overnight. Turn occasionally. Place roast in shallow pan. Pour marinade over roast and bake 30 minutes per pound at 325° F. If it becomes too brown, reduce heat to 300° F. for the last 30 minutes. Baste with marinade every 20 minutes. This is very important! When roast is done, skim off grease. Reheat liquid to serve as a light gravy. Serves 8.

Good with spoonbread.

Mrs. Lloyd M. Parker
Dyersburg, Tenn.

Sweet and Sour Pork Roast

1 4-5 pound pork roast	1 16-ounce can chunk pineapple
Salt and pepper to taste	1 green pepper, cubed
1 tablespoon oil	
1 12-ounce bottle chili sauce	
1 12-ounce jar apricot preserves	

Season roast with salt and pepper. Brown in oil in Dutch oven. Cover and bake 1 hour at 250° F. Add chili sauce and preserves and bake 5 hours. Add pineapple and green pepper and bake 1 more hour. Serves 8-10.

Mrs. Jere Fones (Ellen Kimbrough)

Crockpot Barbecue

2-3 pound pork roast

1 28-ounce bottle barbecue sauce

Cut roast into chunks. Place in crockpot. Cover with sauce. Cook at least 8-10 hours. Serves 6.

Mrs. Donald Howdeshell (Anne Eastland)

Mrs. Jerry B. Martin (Carolyn Cowser)

Barbecue Seasoning for Ribs

1 tablespoon dry mustard
2 tablespoons chili powder
4 tablespoons paprika
½ teaspoon cayenne pepper
1 teaspoon basil, well crushed

1 tablespoon meat tenderizer
½ teaspoon onion salt
½ teaspoon garlic salt
10-12 pounds pork ribs

Mix all ingredients. Sprinkle over ribs and let stand 30 minutes. Sear over hot fire to seal in juices. Sprinkle more of the seasoning and smoke over low heat for 2 hours, turning every 20 minutes and sprinkling with seasoning. Serves 6-8.

Mrs. Jere Fones (Ellen Kimbrough)

Glazed Pork Chops

6 pork chops, about ½ pound each
2 tablespoons oil
2 cups brown sugar
½ cup pineapple juice
½ cup honey

2 teaspoons dry mustard
3 whole cloves
½ cup orange juice
6 slices each of orange, lemon and lime
6 stemmed cherries

Brown chops in skillet in the heated oil. Place in baking pan. Combine next 6 ingredients to make sauce. Spoon ½ of sauce over chops. Bake uncovered at 350° F. for 1 hour; baste occasionally with remaining sauce. Transfer to serving platter. With a toothpick, peg one slice of orange, lemon, lime and a cherry on top of each chop. Spoon a bit of sauce over each chop as served. Serves 6.

Honeyed Bananas (see Index) are an excellent accompaniment for this dish.

Mrs. Thomas W. Jones (Janice Cox)

Stuffed Pork Chops

1 16-ounce package Pepperidge Farm stuffing mix	4-6 thick pork chops Salt and pepper
1 small onion, chopped	3-5 tablespoons bacon drippings
3-4 stalks celery, chopped	1 10¾-ounce can chicken broth
1 small green pepper, chopped	

Prepare stuffing mix according to package directions. Sauté vegetables and add to stuffing. Slit each chop to form pocket and press as much stuffing as possible into each pocket. Salt and pepper chops and brown 2-3 minutes per side in bacon drippings. Place in 3-quart casserole. Pour chicken broth over chops and seal tightly with foil. Bake at 350° F. for 1½-2 hours.

Mrs. Rowe Belcher (Susan Ramsay)

Tangy Pork Chops

4 pork chops	1 teaspoon salt
8 teaspoons prepared mustard	2 tablespoons oil
¾ cup flour	1 10¾-ounce can chicken with rice soup, undiluted
1 teaspoon pepper	

Spread 1 teaspoon of mustard on each side of chops. Dip chops in flour, seasoned with salt and pepper. Brown in oil in skillet. Remove from pan and place in shallow casserole. Pour soup over chops. Cover and bake at 350° F. for 1 hour. Serves 4.

Variation: This can be done in a crockpot. Pour a little soup into pot before adding browned chops and remainder of soup.

Mrs. Rowlett Wilson Sneed, Jr. (Sarah Gaye Craig)

Mrs. Fletcher Johnson (Jo Ann Hawkes)

Pork Chops and Apples

2 tablespoons oil	1 teaspoon salt
2 cooking apples, cored and thickly sliced	⅛ teaspoon pepper
	1½ cups apple juice
4 ½-inch pork chops	1 tablespoon cornstarch
2 green onions, sliced	¼ cup light cream or milk

In large skillet, heat oil and cook apples until tender, about 5 minutes. Remove and keep warm. Brown chops in skillet about 10 minutes. Add green onions, salt, pepper, and 1¼ cups apple juice. Bring to boil. Reduce heat, cover, simmer 15-20 minutes or until meat is tender. Remove chops and keep warm. In small cup, blend cornstarch and remaining apple juice until smooth. Gradually stir into liquid in skillet. Add cream; stir until gravy is slightly thickened. Return chops and apple slices to skillet and heat. Serves 4.

This gravy is delicious!

Mrs. Bill Summey
Sanford, North Carolina

Sherried Pork Chops

6-8 pork chops, ½-¾-inch thick	4 ounces sour cream
¼ stick butter	½ 10¾-ounce can cream of mushroom soup
Salt and freshly ground pepper	½ cup sherry

Brown chops in butter. Salt and pepper. Place in foil-lined shallow pan. Mix remaining ingredients together. Cover each chop with sauce. Cover pan tightly with foil and bake 1 hour at 350° F. Serves 6-8.

Mrs. Philip Vaiden (Lynda Woodward)

Chalupa

Chalupa Mixture

3½-4 pounds boned and tied
    pork loin
1½-2 pounds dried pinto or
    black beans
2   4-ounce cans chopped
    green chilies

1   teaspoon oregano
1   tablespoon cumin
2-3 tablespoons chili powder
1-3 large cloves garlic, crushed
    Salt to taste
    Tabasco to taste

Place all chalupa ingredients in large pot and cover with water. Cook 6 hours, covered, adding more water as needed. Stir occasionally. Take meat out, cool and shred. Return meat to pot and cook 1 more hour to thicken. This mixture may be done ahead and frozen. Heat before serving.

Chalupa Accompaniments

Small Fritos
Shredded lettuce
Shredded Monterey Jack cheese
Chopped fresh tomatoes

Sliced green onions
Sour cream
Taco sauce, hot, mild or a
    combination of each

Place accompaniments in separate bowls. For each serving, place Fritos on plate topped with chalupa, then accompaniments in order given. Serves 16-20.

A fun way to have a party, and it can be done ahead. Serve with Sangria or icy cold beer.

Mrs. Keith Kays (Jackie Wood)

Country Ham
(Mother's Recipe)

1 whole country ham, aged	pickle juice (optional)
2 stalks celery, with leaves	brown sugar
1 onion	cloves

Place ham in large roasting pan. Fill with water and let sit overnight. Next day, pour off water and scrub ham all over with brush. Rinse. Place back in pan and fill with water. Add celery, onion and pickle juice. Place on top of stove and bring to boil. Lower heat and simmer, covered, for 5-6 hours. Cool. Remove from water. Cut off fat and score. Cover top with brown sugar and cloves. Place in medium oven to brown for 10-15 minutes.

Hint: Grind any leftover scraps and mix with mayonnaise and mustard. Serve on crackers or bread for snacks. Keeps well in refrigerator.

Mrs. William T. Black (Lida Willey)

Tangy Ham Loaf

1½ pounds lean fresh pork	Salt and pepper to taste
1 pound smoked ham	¾ cup brown sugar
2 eggs	½ tablespoon prepared mustard
1 cup milk	¼ cup vinegar
1 cup bread crumbs	¼ cup water

Have butcher grind pork and ham together. Mix first 6 ingredients well and shape into one large loaf or 8 individual loaves. Combine remaining ingredients for sauce. Bake large loaf for 2 hours at 325° F. If using individual loaves, bake for 1 hour at 325° F. Baste often with sauce. Serves 8.

Can be served on pineapple rings.

Mrs. William Mitchell

Southern Hash

1 box Jiffy Corn Bread Mix	½ teaspoon Worcestershire
1 egg, beaten	sauce
⅓ cup milk	1½ cups baked ham, cut in
1 tablespoon bacon drippings	1-inch cubes
½ pound Old English Cheese	1½ cups green beans, cooked
⅓ cup milk	or canned

Preheat oven to 400° F. Mix together muffin mix, egg and milk. Put bacon drippings in cornstick pan and put in oven to heat. When drippings are hot, pour into batter and put batter back into cornstick pan. Bake 15 minutes. In double boiler, cook cheese, milk and Worcestershire sauce, stirring occasionally. When blended into sauce, add ham and beans and cook until warm. Serve over sliced, hot corn sticks. Serves 4.

This dish moves left-overs to the head of the class!

Mrs. John S. Palmer (Nancy Moore)

Ham Supreme

2 tablespoons butter	½ teaspoon Worcestershire
¼ cup chopped green pepper	sauce
2 tablespoons minced onion	1 tablespoon lemon juice
3 tablespoons flour	2 beef bouillon cubes, dissolved
1 cup boiling water	in ¼ cup hot water
1 13-ounce can evaporated	1 3-ounce can sliced
milk	mushrooms, drained
1½ cups diced ham	4 water chestnuts, thinly sliced
¾ teaspoon salt	1 2-ounce jar pimiento
⅛ teaspoon pepper	Slivered almonds (optional)
1 teaspoon prepared mustard	

In large saucepan, melt butter; add green pepper and onion. Cook over low heat until tender, stirring occasionally. Gradually stir in flour and then the boiling water. Cook, stirring constantly, until thickened. Stir in evaporated milk and cook until thickened. Add next 7 ingredients; mix well. Just before serving, add mushrooms, water chestnuts and pimiento. Serve on Holland Rusks and sprinkle with almonds. Serves 4-6.

Freezes well.

Mrs. Max Lucas (Ruth Plyler)

Holiday Casserole

6 tablespoons butter, divided
4 tablespoons flour
2 cups light cream
1 cup sliced fresh mushrooms

1 tablespoon lemon juice
2 cups coarsely chopped ham
1 14-ounce can artichoke hearts
2 tablespoons Parmesan cheese

Melt 4 tablespoons butter, add flour and cook 1 minute. Add cream slowly and simmer, stirring constantly until smooth and thick. Sauté mushrooms in remaining butter and lemon juice. Add mushrooms and ham to cream sauce and blend well. Quarter artichokes and arrange in single layer on bottom of 9x13-inch glass baking dish. Pour ham mixture over artichokes. Sprinkle with Parmesan cheese. Bake at 350° F. until bubbly. Serves 8-10.

Excellent brunch or luncheon dish. Can be served on toast or Holland Rusk.

Mrs. William C. McCrary, III (Tancie Lewis)

Cantonese Ham Casserole

1 10-ounce package frozen
   green beans
1 tablespoon butter
1 tablespoon flour
¾ cup milk
2 tablespoons soy sauce

8 ounces sour cream
2 cups cooked ham, cubed
1 5-ounce can water chestnuts,
   drained and thinly sliced
1 cup buttered bread crumbs
⅛ teaspoon paprika

Pour boiling water over beans to separate. Drain well. In saucepan, melt butter. Blend in flour. Stir in milk and soy sauce. Cook and stir over medium heat until thick and bubbly. Stir in sour cream, ham, beans and water chestnuts. Pour into greased 8-inch square baking dish. Sprinkle with crumbs and paprika. Bake 30 minutes at 350° F. Serves 4-6.

Mrs. Harry McKee (Larane Wilson)

Broccoli and Ham Supreme

1 egg, lightly beaten
1 10-ounce package frozen
   chopped broccoli, partially
   thawed
1 8-ounce can creamed corn
¼ teaspoon salt
1 tablespoon grated onion

Freshly ground pepper to
   taste
2 cups chopped ham, turkey or
   chicken
3 tablespoons butter
1 cup herbed stuffing mix

Combine first 7 ingredients. Melt butter and pour over stuffing mix. Toss until coated. Stir ¾ cup stuffing into meat-vegetable mixture. Pour into buttered casserole. Top with remaining stuffing. Bake 35-40 minutes at 350° F. Serves 4-6.

Mrs. Wallace T. Grogan

Ham and Lima Bean Casserole

1 16-ounce package large dried
   limas
½ stick butter
3-4 tablespoons brown sugar

½ teaspoon freshly ground
   pepper
2-3 cups diced ham
1 clove garlic (optional)

Cover beans with water and soak overnight; drain. Cover with fresh water and cook until firm but done; drain and reserve 3 cups stock. In 1 cup hot stock, melt butter and add brown sugar and pepper. Place ham and beans in large casserole; pour sweetened stock over until almost covered. Use additional stock if necessary. Pierce garlic with toothpick and lay on top. Bake 30-45 minutes at 250° F. to 300° F. Remove garlic. Stir casserole; add more stock if necessary. Return to oven and cook until almost dry. Serves 6-8.

Mrs. William L. Quinlen Jr. (Anne Clark Miller)

Jambalaya

2 tablespoons butter
2 tablespoons oil
1 cup chopped onion
2 green peppers, chopped
2 cloves garlic, minced
1 cup uncooked rice
1 1-pound 3-ounce can
   tomatoes, drained and
   chopped
½ teaspoon thyme

¼ teaspoon basil
¼ teaspoon paprika
1 teaspoon chili powder
1 teaspoon salt
½ teaspoon pepper
½ cup white wine
1½ cups chicken broth
¼ teaspoon saffron
3 cups diced cooked ham
½-1 pint oysters, drained

Heat butter and oil. Sauté onions until limp. Add pepper and garlic. Stir 2 minutes. Add rice and stir until rice is opaque. Add remaining ingredients except oysters. Cover and bake at 350° F. for 35 minutes or until rice is plump and liquid has been absorbed. Add oysters and let steam for 10 minutes more. Serves 8.

Really outstanding!

Mrs. John D. Glass (Meegie Rogers)

Christians and Moors

2 packages dry black beans
1½ cups olive oil
2 large onions, chopped
2 green peppers, chopped
3 bunches celery, chopped
4 cloves garlic, minced
10 ham hocks
6 bay leaves
1½ cups dry red wine
8 10½-ounce cans beef
    bouillon

¼ cup garlic wine vinegar
Lemon pepper to taste
Cayenne pepper to taste
Salt and pepper to taste
2¼ pounds Polish sausage cut
    into 1-inch slices and
    sautéed
1 cup chopped scallions
1 cup chopped parsley

Soak beans overnight in water to cover. Drain. In olive oil, sauté onions, peppers, celery and garlic. Add drained beans to next 5 ingredients. If bouillon does not cover mixture, add enough water to cover. Simmer until beans are tender, approximately 4 hours. If stock becomes too low, add more water. When beans are tender, take out 1 cup of beans and mash. Return to stock for thickening. Add lemon pepper, cayenne, salt and pepper. Remove meat from ham hocks and add to stock. When ready to serve, add Polish sausage and heat. Garnish with chopped parsley and scallions. Serve over rice in a bowl. Serves 20.

Make this ahead of time so the flavors can mellow.

Mrs. Charles W. McCrary (Janie Stone)

New Orleans Red Beans and Rice

1 pound dry red kidney beans
½-1 pound Italian sausage, cut
    into 1-inch slices
1 medium onion, chopped
2 tablespoons chopped
    parsley
    Dash red pepper
2 teaspoons cumin powder
1 teaspoon chili powder

Ham bone with generous
    amount of meat
3-4 cloves garlic, chopped
2 ribs celery, chopped
1 large bay leaf
2 tablespoons Worcestershire
    sauce
1 teaspoon basil
    Salt, to taste

Wash beans well. Cover in cold water and soak overnight. In large kettle, add beans and water in which they have been soaked. To this, add other ingredients and more water to cover, if necessary. Cook slowly until beans are tender, about 1½ hours. Season with salt. Serve over mounds of rice. Serves 8.

Tasty and spicy.

Allison Lynch

Susie's Red Beans and Rice

6 slices bacon
2 15-ounce cans Van Camp's
    New Orleans kidney beans
1 large onion, chopped
½ cup chopped celery
1 small green pepper, chopped
2 tablespoons parsley
⅓ cup green onion tops,
    chopped

2 tablespoons ketchup
1½ teaspoon Worcestershire
    sauce
1 8-ounce can tomato sauce
1-2 teaspoons chili powder
⅛ teaspoon red pepper

Fry bacon and crumble into beans. Sauté vegetables in bacon drippings until wilted. Add beans and remaining ingredients. Cover and simmer about 20-30 minutes. Serve over rice. Serves 6.

Might substitute sausage for bacon.

Mrs. James Martin Greene (Cissy Bell)

Bratwurst Casserole

2 large red potatoes, peeled and
   very thinly sliced
½ onion, thinly sliced

1 pound bratwurst, sliced
1 10¾-ounce can mushroom
   soup.

In greased 9x13 inch casserole, layer half of potatoes, onions and bratwurst. Spread half can of soup over this. Repeat. Cover with foil. Bake at 350° F. for 30-45 minutes. Remove foil and bake for 15 minutes or more until top is browned and vegetables are done. Serves 5.

Mrs. Gavin Gentry (Mary Jane Coleman)

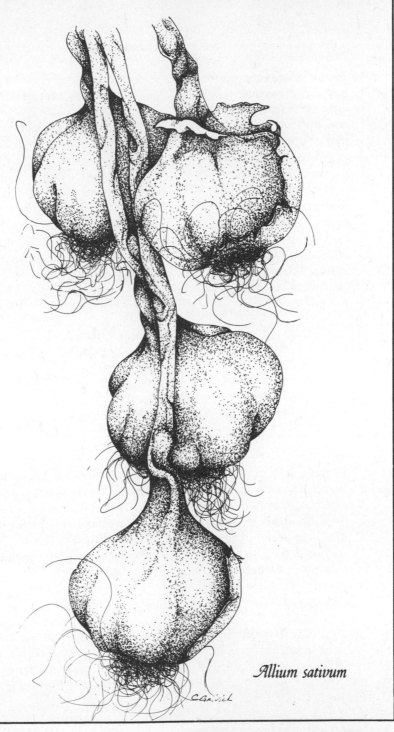

Allium sativum

Pasta and Rice

Sea Shell Surprise

1 pound macaroni shells
⅔ cup cider vinegar
¼ cup vegetable oil
1 cup minced celery
½ cup chopped green pepper
6 green onions, chopped
1 2-ounce jar chopped
   pimiento, drained
3 dashes Worcestershire sauce
3 dashes Tabasco

1 tablespoon canned green
   chilies, chopped
1 teaspoon salt
½ teaspoon pepper
1 15-ounce can blackeyed peas,
   drained
1 17-ounce can whole kernel
   corn, drained
½ cup chopped black olives
½ cup mayonnaise

Cook macaroni until tender and drain. Add vinegar to macaroni and set aside. Mix all other ingredients and add to macaroni. Cover and refrigerate. Serves 12 or more.

This is great to prepare ahead. Good for a buffet in the grove before the game!

Mrs. Gwin Scott (Wynn Skipper)

Mrs. James R. Galyean (Brannan Robbins)

Macaroni Salad

1 7-ounce box macaroni
1½ teaspoons salt
⅛ teaspoon pepper
2 medium carrots, grated
1 medium green pepper,
   chopped
1 cup chopped celery
1 small cucumber, seeded and
   chopped

3 hard-boiled eggs, cut in small
   pieces
1 bunch green onions, chopped
2 tablespoons butter
1 tablespoon flour
¼ cup tarragon vinegar
1 egg, beaten
1 cup mayonnaise

Cook macaroni according to package directions. Drain and rinse in cold water. Combine macaroni and next 8 ingredients. Melt butter in pan. Blend in flour. Combine vinegar and egg. Cook, stirring constantly until thick. Cool. Blend in mayonnaise. Combine with macaroni mixture and chill. Serves 8-10.

Summer Salad

1   16-ounce package spaghetti
1   tablespoon cooking oil
½   cucumber, chopped
1   bunch radishes, sliced
1   bunch green onions, sliced
1½ teaspoons salt
1   teaspoon sugar
¾   teaspoon white pepper
½   teaspoon celery seed
1   large pinch oregano
    Garlic powder to taste
    Cayenne pepper to taste
    Cavender's seasonings to
    taste
4   hard-cooked eggs
3   medium tomatoes, chopped

Break spaghetti into quarters. Cook in amount of water specified on package to which oil has been added. Drain and rinse. Add remaining ingredients. Make dressing. Mix half of dressing with salad. Cover and refrigerate overnight. Serves 8.

Salad Dressing
4   cups mayonnaise
⅔   cup sour cream
1   cup milk or light cream
¼   cup Durkee's sauce
1   teaspoon Dijon mustard
1-2 cloves garlic, minced
    (optional)

Mix all salad dressing ingredients well. Yields about 1½ quarts.

Mrs. Mickey Moran (Pat Taylor)

Mule's Rice Salad

4   cups cooked rice or 4 cups
    cooked chicken Rice-a-
    Roni, prepared according
    to directions
1   cup sliced mushrooms
½   cup chopped green pepper
1   tablespoon chopped parsley
1   teaspoon curry powder
½   cup mayonnaise
½   cup sour cream
2   cups diced chicken or beef
    (optional)
2   6-ounce jars marinated
    artichoke hearts, undrained

Mix all ingredients. Refrigerate overnight. Serve cold. The chicken or beef may be added to make this a main dish. Serves 8-10.

Sliced green onions and stuffed green olives may be added for a different touch.

Mrs. Horace Rainey, III
Columbia, Tennessee

Peggy's Party Loaf

8 ounces elbow macaroni,
  cooked al dente and
  drained
2 cups scalded milk
½ stick butter
½ pound Cheddar cheese,
  shredded
2 cups soft bread crumbs

2 eggs, well beaten
2 tablespoons minced parsley
2 tablespoons minced onion
2 tablespoons minced pimiento
2 teaspoons salt
¼ teaspoon pepper
Peggy's Creamed Mushrooms
  (see Index)

Heat oven to 350° F. Combine all ingredients and pour into well greased 9x5x3-inch loaf pan, 10-inch ring mold or 2-quart casserole. Set in pan with 1-inch water. Bake 30-35 minutes for ring, or 45-60 minutes for loaf pan or casserole. Serve with Peggy's Creamed Mushrooms. Serves 8-10.

Mrs. Henry Hancock (Peggy Fairchild)

Inside Out Ravioli

1½ pounds ground beef
1 medium onion, chopped
1 clove garlic minced, or garlic
  powder or garlic salt
1 tablespoon oil
1 10-ounce package frozen
  chopped spinach
1 15½-ounce jar spaghetti
  sauce with mushrooms
1 8-ounce can tomato sauce

1 6-ounce can tomato paste
½ teaspoon salt
½ teaspoon pepper
1 8-ounce package shell
  macaroni, cooked
1 cup shredded sharp Cheddar
  cheese
½ cup soft bread crumbs
2 well beaten eggs
¼ cup salad oil

Brown first 3 ingredients in oil. Cook spinach according to package directions. Drain spinach and set aside. Reserve liquid. Add water to make 1 cup. Stir spinach liquid and next 5 ingredients into meat mixture. Simmer 10 minutes. Combine spinach with remaining ingredients. Spread in 13x9x2-inch baking dish. Top with meat sauce and little more shredded cheese if desired. Bake at 350° F. for 30 minutes. Serves 6-8.

Mrs. John D. Glass (Meegie Rogers)

Pastitsio

1 large onion, finely chopped
2 sticks butter
3 pounds lean ground beef
½ can tomato paste
½ cup water
  Salt and pepper to taste
½ teaspoon cinnamon
½ teaspoon nutmeg

½ cup white wine
1 16-ounce package elbow
  macaroni, cooked and
  drained
1 pound grated Parmesan
  cheese
2 eggs, well beaten
1 cup milk

Sauté onion in small amount of butter. Add beef and brown. Add next 6 ingredients and simmer until thick. Melt remaining butter and pour over macaroni, mixing well. In a large, flat casserole layer half of macaroni and half of cheese. Top with beef. Spread remaining macaroni and cheese. Mix eggs and milk and pour over casserole. Bake at 350° F. for 45 minutes. Cool slightly and cut into squares. Serves 8-10.

Feeds a bunch. A good change from spaghetti!

Mrs. George Germanos
Athens, Greece

Kirsten's Pasta

4 tablespoon butter
4 ounces cream cheese
1 cup light cream
2 tablespoons tomato paste
  Dash garlic powder

Cayenne pepper, or crushed
  red pepper to taste
3 tablespoons minced parsley
1 16-ounce mostaccioli, or flat
  noodles, cooked al dente

Melt butter and cream cheese. Slowly add cream. Stir in tomato paste and garlic powder. Add cayenne pepper and parsley. Toss with hot drained pasta and serve immediately. Serves 6-8.

A unique pasta combination. The cayenne pepper should create a "bite" to the recipe to assure the authenticity.

Kirsten Christensen
Florence, Italy

Baked Noodles

1   5-ounce package fine noodles
1   cup cottage cheese
8   ounces sour cream
1   clove garlic, minced
1   onion, chopped

1   tablespoon Worcestershire
    sauce
Dash of Tabasco
Salt to taste

Cook noodles in boiling, salted water for 10 minutes. Drain. Mix other ingredients and add noodles. Bake in buttered casserole at 350° F. for 45 minutes. Serves 6.

Mrs. Charles McCrary (Janie Stone)

Fettuccine alla Carbonara

1   12-ounce package noodles
½   cup heavy cream
4   egg yolks
4   ounces Parmesan cheese,
      grated

1-1½ pounds ham, cut in
      julienne strips
1   stick butter

Boil and drain noodles. Mix cream, egg yolks and cheese in small bowl. Sauté ham in butter. Add noodles to ham and blend well. Remove from heat. Add cream mixture and stir well. Serves 4-6.

Use country ham for a very special flavor.

Mrs. Tom C. Henderson (Elizabeth McKee)

Manicotti

1 8-ounce package manicotti noodles	5 tablespoons butter
2 10-ounce packages frozen chopped spinach, thawed	5 tablespoons flour
1 pound ground beef	2½ cups milk
1 pound hot sausage	½ teaspoon salt
1 large onion, chopped	8 ounces mozzarella or sharp Cheddar cheese, grated
½ pound fresh mushrooms	1 cup Romano or Parmesan cheese
2 15-ounce cans tomato sauce	
2 1½-ounce packages dry spaghetti mix	

Cook noodles 8 minutes and drain. Press excess water from spinach and stuff in noodles. Brown meats, onion and mushrooms in skillet. Add tomato sauce and spaghetti mixes. For sauce, melt butter in saucepan. Stir in flour until smooth. Add milk gradually and stir until slightly thickened. Blend in mozzarella cheese and salt. Layer noodles, meat sauce and cheese sauce in greased 2 (2-quart) casseroles and top with Romano or Parmesan cheese. Bake at 350°F. for 45 minutes. Serves 12.

Mrs. Thomas J. Becktold, Jr. (Pamela Stewart)

Lake of Lasagne Casserole

1 5-ounce package medium egg noodles	1 teaspoon salt
½ cup chopped green onion, divided	⅛ teaspoon pepper
2 tablespoons butter	1 cup small curd cottage cheese
1½ pounds ground beef	8 ounces sour cream
2 8-ounce cans tomato sauce	¾ cup, or 3 ounces, shredded sharp cheese

Cook noodles according to package directions. Rinse well and set aside. Sauté ¼ cup onion in butter in large skillet until tender. Add beef and cook until lightly browned. Drain well. Add tomato sauce, salt and pepper. Stir well and simmer 20 minutes. Combine cottage cheese, sour cream and remaining onion. Stir well and set aside. Place noodles in lightly greased 2½-quart casserole. Spoon cottage cheese mixture over noodles. Layer meat over this. Sprinkle with cheese and bake at 350° F. for 25 minutes. Serves 4-6.

Excellent! Appeals to all ages.

Mrs. Mae D. Garner (Mae Dunaway)

Neptune's Favorite

½ pound homemade or
  commercial lasagne
  noodles
1 tablespoon oil
2 10¾-ounce cans cream of
  shrimp soup, or 2½ cups
  medium white sauce
1 pound crabmeat
¼ cup parsley
2 cups small curd cottage
  cheese

8 ounces cream cheese
1 egg, slightly beaten
1 medium onion, chopped
1 teaspoon Worcestershire
  sauce
2 teaspoons basil
½ teaspoon lemon juice
  Salt and pepper to taste
2 tomatoes, thinly sliced
½ cup grated Cheddar cheese

Cook homemade noodles 3 minutes in salted water, adding oil. If using commercial noodles, cook according to package directions. Combine soup, crabmeat and parsley. Combine next 8 ingredients. Butter 3-quart casserole dish. Layer ½ noodles, ½ cheese mixture, all crab mixture, remaining noodles, remaining cheese mixture, and top with tomatoes. Bake 15 minutes at 350° F. Top with Cheddar cheese and continue cooking for 30 minutes. Serves 8.

Lasagne Noodles
3 cups flour
2 teaspoons salt
3 eggs

3 tablespoons oil
¼ cup ice water

Mix all ingredients in order. Knead. Divide into 2 portions and let rest. 1 hour in refrigerator. Remove 1 portion and roll into rectangle 1/16-inch thick on floured board. Cut into 3-inch wide strips. Repeat with second portion. This can be put through pasta machine.

Mrs. John W. McQuiston (Robbie Walker)

Lasagne

1 10-ounce package lasagne
   noodles
4 ounces olive oil

16 ounces ricotta cheese
8 ounces mozzarella cheese
1 cup Parmesan cheese

Cook noodles for 20 minutes in water to which olive oil has been added. Drain. In casserole, make 3 layers each of noodles, ricotta, mozzarella, Marinara sauce and Parmesan cheese. Bake uncovered at 325° F. for 30 minutes.

Marinara Sauce

1 medium onion, minced
2 cloves garlic, minced
2 tablespoons olive oil
1 pound ground beef
1 1-pound, 12-ounce can
   tomatoes, cut up
1 6-ounce can tomato paste
2 cups water

⅛ teaspoon red pepper
1 teaspoon sugar
⅛ teaspoon basil
1 bay leaf
½ cup red wine
1 teaspoon oregano
1 1½-ounce package spaghetti
   sauce mix

For sauce, sauté onions and garlic in oil until tender. Add meat and brown. Add remaining ingredients. Simmer for 1½ hours. Remove bay leaf. Serves 10-12.

Mrs. William David Porter (Alexis De Saussure)

Baked Oysters and Spaghetti

1½ cups saltine cracker crumbs
2 cups cooked spaghetti
1 cup grated sharp Cheddar
   cheese
1 pint oysters, drained

Salt and pepper to taste
Paprika
4 tablespoons butter
½ cup light cream, heated

Grease a 2-quart casserole. Cover bottom of dish with cracker crumbs and then add layer of spaghetti. Sprinkle with grated cheese and top with oysters. Sprinkle with salt, pepper and paprika and dot liberally with butter. Repeat layers ending with layer of oysters. Pour heated cream over casserole. Top with more cracker crumbs and bake, uncovered, for 25 minutes in 400° F. oven. Serves 4-6.

Oyster lovers' delight!

Mrs. John C. Patton (Nancy Caradine)

Creamed Shrimp Spaghetti

1 stick butter
¼ cup heavy cream
½ cup Parmesan cheese
¼ teaspoon minced garlic
(optional)

1 pound mushrooms, sliced
2 tablespoons butter
1 10-ounce package spaghetti
1 pound shrimp cooked, peeled, deveined and kept warm

Cream 1 stick butter and heavy cream with wooden spoon. Blend in cheese. Add garlic to mixture, cover and place in 250° F. oven. Sauté mushrooms in remaining butter. Remove mushrooms and keep warm. Cook spaghetti according to package directions. In large bowl, toss together the cheese mixture, mushrooms, spaghetti and shrimp. Serve immediately. Serves 4.

Rich and delicious.

Mrs. William W. McCrary, III (Tancie Lewis)

Tuna Tetrazzini

4 ounces spaghetti
2 6-ounce cans white albacore tuna, drained
¼ cup diced pimiento
¼ cup chopped celery
¼ cup slivered almonds
1 4-ounce can sliced mushrooms

1 small onion, chopped
½ cup water
1 10¾-ounce can cream of mushroom soup
2 cups shredded Cheddar cheese, divided
Salt and pepper to taste

Break spaghetti into pieces and cook in salted water until tender. Drain. Combine tuna, pimiento, celery, almonds, mushrooms and onion. Mix water and soup and add to tuna mixture. Add 1¼ cups cheese and the spaghetti. Season to taste. Toss lightly until well mixed and coated with sauce. Oil casserole, then add spaghetti mixture. Sprinkle with remaining ¾ cup cheese and bake at 350° F. for 30-40 minutes. Serves 6-8.

This dish tastes more like chicken than tuna.

Mrs. Rowlett Wilson Sneed, Jr. (Sarah Gaye Craig)

Chicken Spaghetti

1 cup milk
½ cup mayonnaise
1 pound Velveeta cheese, cubed
2 cups cooked, cubed chicken
1 8-ounce can tiny green peas, drained

3-4 carrots, sliced and boiled
5 ounces thin spaghetti, cooked
1 tablespoon chopped chives

In double boiler, combine milk and mayonnaise. Add cheese and cook, stirring, until sauce is smooth. Add remaining ingredients, mixing well. Pour into greased 2-quart casserole. Bake at 350° F. for 30-40 minutes or until bubbly. Serves 8.

Mrs. Scott Arnold, III (Anne Dillard)

Chicken Spaghetti Fiesta

1 6-pound hen
2 large onions, chopped
2 large green peppers, chopped
1 stick butter
2 teaspoons Worcestershire sauce
1 2-ounce jar chopped pimientos
1 8½-ounce can English peas, drained

1 10-ounce can Rotel tomatoes, with juice
1 4½-ounce can chopped ripe olives
1 16-ounce package thin spaghetti
2 pounds Velveeta cheese, cubed

Boil hen until tender. Remove meat from bones, and cut into bite-sized pieces. Reserve broth. Sauté onion and pepper in butter. Add Worcestershire sauce, pimientos, peas, tomatoes, olives and chicken to sautéed vegetables. Cook spaghetti in reserved broth. Add spaghetti and cheese to chicken mixture, pouring in enough broth to make it moist. Mix well. Place in 2 greased 3-quart casseroles and bake uncovered at 350° F. until hot and bubbly. Serves 16.

A spicy version. Different and very good.

Mrs. K. William Chandler (Gee Gee Taylor)

Mrs. John D. Glass (Meegie Rogers)

Chicken Tetrazzini

1 6-pound hen
   Water, celery leaves, small
   onion, salt and pepper for
   broth
1 12-ounce package thin
   spaghetti
1 pound fresh sliced
   mushrooms, or 1 8-ounce
   can
2 green peppers, chopped
1 stick butter
5 tablespoons flour
2 cups milk

2 10¾-ounce cans cream of
   mushroom soup
1 4-ounce jar pimientos,
   drained and chopped
½ teaspoon garlic salt
1 clove garlic, minced
1 teaspoon Worcestershire
   sauce
½ cup dry white wine
¾ cup Parmesan cheese
6 cups grated sharp Cheddar
   cheese, divided
   Slivered almonds

Place hen in large pot with water to cover and other broth ingredients. Simmer until tender. Remove hen, strain broth and reserve. Cool meat, remove from bones and chop. Cook spaghetti in reserved broth. Drain. Sauté mushrooms and peppers in butter for 1 minute. Stir in flour. Add milk gradually and stir until thickened. Add next 8 ingredients, 4 cups cheese and chicken. In two 3-quart flat Pyrex casseroles layer spaghetti and sauce, starting with spaghetti and ending with sauce. Sprinkle remaining 2 cups cheese on top of casseroles. Sprinkle with almonds. Bake at 350° F. until hot. Serves 8-10.

Mrs. James B. Cross (Lynn Woods)

Spaghetti Superb

2 tablespoons olive oil
4 cloves garlic, minced
1 green pepper, chopped
1 onion, chopped
1 pound fresh mushrooms, sliced
1 pound hot sausage
1 pound ground chuck
1 32-ounce can Italian plum tomatoes

2 6-ounce cans tomato paste
2 tablespoons minced parsley
1 teaspoon oregano
1 tablespoon salt
1 teaspoon pepper
¾ cup red wine
1 12-ounce package spaghetti

In oil, sauté garlic, green pepper, onion and mushrooms. Cook sausage and ground chuck until browned and drain. Add meats to vegetables and add remaining ingredients except spaghetti. Cover and simmer about 2 hours. Serve over noodles. Serves 6-8.

Mrs. Thomas J. Becktold, Jr. (Pamela Stewart)

Sicilian Pork Spaghetti

1½ pounds boneless pork tenderloin, cut in bite size pieces
Oil
2 cloves garlic, minced
1 15-ounce can tomato sauce

2 6-ounce cans tomato paste
2-3 teaspoons oregano
2-3 teaspoons basil
¼ teaspoon salt
1 7-ounce package spaghetti or vermicelli

Brown meat in oil on all sides. Remove. Cook garlic until yellow, not brown. Drain off oil. Replace pork and cover with water. Add tomato sauce and paste. Cook 1 hour. Add seasonings and cook another hour or until pork is done. Serve over spaghetti or vermicelli noodles. Serves 6.

Serve Parmesan cheese as garnish.

Mrs. John C. Patton (Nancy Caradine)

Italian Mushroom Rice

1 gallon water	½ stick butter
1 teaspoon salt	½ cup red wine
2 cups white rice	Salt and white pepper to
¼ pound fresh mushrooms,	taste
sliced	¼ cup chopped fresh parsley

In large container, bring water to a boil. Add salt and rice and stir. Boil uncovered for 15 minutes. Pour rice into colander and drain. In separate saucepan, sauté mushrooms in butter and wine. Season with salt and pepper. Add chopped parsley and let wilt slightly. Toss drained rice with wine-mushroom mixture. Put in greased 1-quart flat Pyrex dish. Cover with foil. Heat thoroughly in 350° F. oven about 20-25 minutes. Serves 4.

May be done ahead and refrigerated. Bring to room temperature before placing in oven. Serve with Italian Sautéed Chicken. (see Index)

Mrs. Frank E. Reid (Diana Mann)

Rice Pilaf

20 raw spaghetti noodles,	1 cup rice
broken in 2-inch pieces	3 tablespoons butter
3 beef bouillon cubes	Salt and pepper
2 cups boiling water	

Melt butter in skillet. Add spaghetti noodles and brown, stirring constantly. Dissolve bouillon cubes in water. Add bouillon water, rice, salt and pepper to spaghetti in skillet. Cover and simmer 15-20 minutes. Remove from heat and let stand 8-10 minutes for fluffier rice. Serves 4-6.

Mrs. William S. Mitchell

Dirty Rice

1 pound pork sausage, mild
   or hot
1 medium-large onion,
   chopped
1 green pepper, chopped
1-2 cloves garlic, chopped
½ pound fresh mushrooms,
   chopped

4-5 chicken livers, chopped
4 green onions, chopped
2 cups cooked rice
½ cup chopped parsley
   Salt to taste

Brown sausage in skillet about 5 minutes. Add other ingredients except rice. Cook over medium low heat until vegetables are very soft and lightly browned. Add cooked rice, and stir well. Place in covered casserole and bake 20-30 minutes at 350° F. Serves 6-8.

Mrs. Michael Lynch (Susan Corcoran)

Rice in the Oven

2 cups converted rice
1¼ teaspoons salt

2 tablespoons butter
4 cups boiling water

Place rice, salt and butter in a pan with tight lid. Pour boiling water in pan, stir and cover. Bake 40 minutes in 350° F. oven without raising lid. Fluff with a fork before serving. Makes 6 cups.

Mrs. James G. Hughes (Jane Barker)

Rice Royale

1 stick butter
4 green onions, chopped
2 10¾-ounce cans cream of
   mushroom soup
1 4-ounce can mushrooms

4 cups cooked rice
10 ounces grated sharp cheese
1 cup chopped toasted almonds

Sauté onions in butter until lightly brown. Add onions, soup and liquid from mushrooms to cooked rice. Put in casserole. Add layer of grated cheese. Next add mushrooms and almonds. Bake at 350° F. until heated through. Serves 10.

Mrs. Winford Clark
Covington, Tennessee

Oyster and Wild Rice Casserole

6 cups beef broth	2 pints raw oysters with juice
1½ cups raw wild or brown rice	1 stick butter

Bring broth to boil in a large saucepan. Add rice and simmer for 1 hour. Broth will be absorbed by rice. Drain oysters and reserve 1 cup liquid for sauce. Place oysters in skillet and sauté until edges just begin to curl. Drain well and set oysters aside. To make casserole, combine rice with butter and mix well. Place ½ of the rice over bottom of 2-quart casserole. Layer oysters over rice and top with remaining rice. Spoon mushroom sauce over all and bake in 325° F. oven for 30 minutes.

Mushroom Oyster Sauce

½ onion, finely chopped	⅛ teaspoon salt
4 shallots, peeled and finely minced	⅛ teaspoon pepper
	⅛ teaspoon thyme
2½ tablespoons butter	¼ teaspoon curry powder
1½ tablespoons flour	¾ cup heavy cream
¼ pound fresh mushrooms	

Chop onions and shallots and set aside. Heat 1½ tablespoons butter in heavy skillet. Stir in flour and cook until it bubbles. Add the reserved cup of oyster liquid and cook, beating with wire whisk, until the sauce thickens. Set aside. Melt remaining 1 tablespoon of butter and sauté onions and shallots until soft. Add mushrooms to onion mixture and cook until liquid evaporates. Add salt, pepper, curry, thyme, oyster-flour mixture and cream. Cook, stirring constantly, for 5 minutes. This casserole serves 6 as a main course or 10 as a dinner side dish.

Shrimp may be substituted for oysters, or a combination of oysters and shrimp may be used.

Mrs. Thomas Dunn (Carol Samples)

Wild Rice Casserole

2 10¾-cans consommé
8 ounces wild rice
1 stick butter
½ cup chopped onion
½ cup chopped green pepper

1 cup mushrooms, pieces and
   stems, drained
7-8 chicken livers
1 cup evaporated milk
½ cup Parmesan cheese

Add consommé and 2 cans water to rice. Cook slowly until liquid is almost gone. Set aside. Sauté onions in 1 tablespoon butter until transparent. Add to rice. Sauté green pepper in 1 tablespoon butter until tender and add to rice. Sauté livers in 1 tablespoon butter, cool and cut into pieces. Add to rice. Sauté mushrooms in 1 tablespoon butter and add to rice. Mix, then add remaining butter, melted. Add milk and ¼ cup Parmesan cheese and stir. Sprinkle ¼ cup cheese on top of casserole. Bake at 350° F. for 30 minutes. May be made a day ahead. Serves 6-8.

Mrs. Fletcher Johnson (Jo Ann Hawkes)

Phaseolus vulgaris

C. Grivich

Vegetables

Asparagus-Tomato Casserole

3 slices bacon
¼ cup sliced green onions
3 tablespoons vinegar
1 tablespoon water
2 teaspoons sugar
¼ teaspoon salt
1½ pounds fresh asparagus, cut diagonally into 1½-inch pieces

2 medium tomatoes, cut into eighths, or one 14½-ounce can of tomatoes drained and cut up
¾ cup bread crumbs
¼ cup Parmesan or Romano cheese, grated

Cook bacon until crisp. Drain and crumble. Sauté onions in bacon drippings until tender. Add bacon, vinegar, water, sugar and salt. Bring to a boil. Add asparagus. Cover and cook 5 minutes. Add tomatoes. Cover, and cook 3 more minutes. Serve as is or place in flat casserole and top with breadcrumbs and cheese. Heat at 350° F. until bubbly. Serves 6.

Mrs. Ann H. Roy
Florence, Alabama

Green Bean Casserole

13 slices bacon
3 tablespoons vinegar or vermouth
3 tablespoons sugar
1 onion, minced

1 16-ounce can French style green beans, drained
1 2½-ounce package slivered almonds

Fry bacon until crisp. Crumble. Reserve drippings. Dissolve vinegar or vermouth, sugar and onion in 2 tablespoons bacon drippings. Layer beans and almonds in casserole. Pour vinegar-onion mixture over top. Bake at 350° F. for 20 minutes. Add crumbled bacon. Bake 10 minutes. Serves 6.

Mrs. Anne G. Boals (Anne Goodwin)

Chinese Green Bean Casserole

2 10-ounce packages frozen
   green beans, French style
1 cup sliced water chestnuts
½ pound fresh mushrooms,
   sliced
1 14-ounce can bean sprouts,
   drained

1 medium onion, chopped
2 cups medium cream sauce
1 cup grated Cheddar cheese
1 3-ounce can French fried
   onions, crumbled

In a greased 2-quart casserole, layer the following: ½ the beans, ½ the water chestnuts, ½ the mushrooms, ½ the bean sprouts, ½ the onions, ½ the cream sauce and ½ the cheese. Repeat layering. Bake at 400° F. for 30 minutes. Top with fried onions and bake 10 more minutes. Serves 6.

Cream Sauce
2 tablespoons butter
2 tablespoons flour
2 cups milk

1 teaspoon salt
¼ teaspoon pepper

Melt butter over low heat. Stir in flour. Add milk gradually while stirring. Cook and stir until thickened. Add salt and pepper.

Mrs. John Parsons (Frances Urquart)

Very French Green Beans

3 16-ounce cans French style
   green beans
2 slices bacon

1 cup sour cream
   Basil, to taste
1 3-ounce can fried onion rings

Drain beans, reserving liquid. Simmer liquid and bacon in uncovered saucepan until liquid is reduced by ⅔. Add beans and continue simmering until all liquid has been absorbed. Place beans in a 1½-2-quart casserole. Add sour cream. Sprinkle generously with basil. Mix and top with onion rings. Bake uncovered at 350° F. until onions are brown and beans are hot. Serves 8-10.

Mrs. Harte Thomas (Patty Jenkins)

Green Beans in Spring Sauce

3 teaspoons olive oil
¾ cup chopped onion
2 cloves garlic, minced
2 tomatoes, peeled and
  chopped
1 teaspoon grated lemon rind

½ teaspoon salt
½ teaspoon Tabasco
½ teaspoon sugar
¾ cup light cream
2 pounds French style green
  beans, fresh or frozen

Heat oil in saucepan. Sauté onion, garlic and tomatoes for 3 minutes, stirring. Add remaining ingredients. Bring to a boil, then lower heat. Cover loosely and cook until just tender. May be served hot or cold. Serves 6.

An unusual green bean dish.

Mrs. Kay K. Butler (Kay Kendall)

Swiss Green Beans

2 10-ounce packages French
  style green beans
2 tablespoons grated onion
3 tablespoons butter
2 tablespoons flour
8 ounces sour cream

1 teaspoon salt
1 teaspoon sugar
3 cups (about 8 ounces) grated
  Swiss cheese, divided
2 cups cornflakes, crushed

Thaw green beans and place in buttered 2-quart flat casserole. Sprinkle onions over beans. Melt butter and stir in flour. Remove from heat and stir in sour cream, salt, sugar, and 1 cup of the cheese. Spread over beans. Top with remaining cheese and cornflakes. Bake at 350° F. for 30 minutes. Serves 8.

Men love this.

Mrs. John D. Glass (Meegie Rogers)

Party Bean Casserole

7 16-ounce cans kidney beans,
   drained
½ stick butter
3 cups thinly sliced onion
2 cups diced green pepper
3 cloves garlic, crushed
1 28-ounce can tomatoes,
   chopped
¼ cup cider vinegar

¾ cup dark molasses
1 tablespoon salt
½ teaspoon salt
½ teaspoon pepper
1 bay leaf
1 tablespoon sugar
1 tablespoon dry mustard
2 teaspoons sweet basil
1 teaspoon thyme

Place drained beans in 4-quart baking dish. Sauté onion, pepper and garlic in butter until tender. Add tomatoes and remaining ingredients. Bring to boil and boil for 1 minute. Pour sauce over beans and mix well. Cover and bake at 350° F. for 1½ hours, stirring beans after 1 hour. Serves 10-12.

Mrs. Neal G. Clement
Florence, Alabama

Hopping John

4 slices bacon
½ cup chopped onion
1 15-ounce can black-eyed
   peas, drained

½ cup rice, uncooked
2 cups boiling water
½ cup sliced mushrooms
   Salt and pepper to taste

Sauté bacon and onion. Reduce grease to 2 tablespoons. Add peas, rice, mushrooms, water, salt and pepper. Cook over low heat for 35 minutes. Serves 4-6.

Serve with ham.

Mrs. Robert Chapman

Minnesota Baked Beans

½ pound bacon
4 green onions, chopped, or
    1 small onion, chopped
½ cup vinegar
¾ cup brown sugar
½-1 teaspoon garlic powder
1 teaspoon salt
½ teaspoon dry mustard
1 teaspoon chili powder

3-4 drops Tabasco
1 16-ounce can green beans,
    drained
1 16-ounce can lima beans,
    drained
1 16-ounce can red kidney
    beans, drained
1 16-ounce can pork and beans

Cut bacon in pieces and brown. Remove bacon and sauté onion in drippings. Add the next 7 ingredients to onions and simmer 20 minutes. Combine bacon and beans with onion mixture. Place in large covered casserole and bake at 350° F. for 1½-2 hours. Serves 12.

Really different!

Mrs. Richard Williamson (Norma Buffington)

Mexican Baked Beans

1 16-ounce can pork and beans
1 15-ounce can chili (without
    beans)
1 15-ounce can kidney beans
1 12-ounce can whole kernel
    yellow corn

⅓ cup ketchup
2 tablespoons Worcestershire
    sauce

Drain all vegetables, except chili. Mix all ingredients together and bake in 350° F. oven for 30 minutes. Serves 8.

Easy, easy.

Mrs. Asbury L. Jones (Rita Renshaw)

Broccoli Elizabeth

2 bunches fresh broccoli, or
two 10-ounce packages
frozen broccoli spears
2 tablespoons butter
2 tablespoons flour
2 cups milk
1 cup grated Cheddar cheese

1 teaspoon salt
¼ teaspoon pepper
¼ cup chopped almonds
½ cup bread crumbs
4 slices bacon, cooked crisp
and crumbled

Cook broccoli, drain, and place in greased 1½-quart casserole. Melt butter over low heat and stir in flour. Add milk gradually while stirring. Continue cooking and stirring until thickened. Add cheese, salt and pepper. Remove from heat. Sprinkle broccoli with almonds. Pour sauce over all. Sprinkle crumbs and bacon on top. Bake at 350° F. for 20 minutes. Serves 6-8.

Mrs. Clyde L. Patton, Jr. (Leslie Wilsford)

Broccoli Parmesan

2 10-ounce packages frozen
broccoli spears, or 1 large
bunch fresh broccoli
3 tablespoons butter
2 tablespoons minced onion
¾ teaspoon salt
¼ teaspoon pepper
⅛ teaspoon marjoram

½ teaspoon dry mustard
3 tablespoons flour
1 chicken bouillon cube
2½ cups milk
½ cup plus 2 tablespoons
grated Parmesan cheese
Paprika

Cook broccoli, drain and place in greased 1½-quart casserole. Sauté onion in butter and blend all seasonings and flour. Add bouillon cube and milk. Cook until thick, stirring constantly. Remove from heat, add ½ cup cheese, and stir until melted. Pour over broccoli. Garnish with 2 tablespoons cheese and paprika. Bake at 375° F. for 20-25 minutes. Serves 6.

Mrs. Robert A. Stebner (Martha McLaughlin)

Broccoli Puff with Curried Mayonnaise

1 10-ounce package frozen
   broccoli spears
3 tablespoons butter
3 tablespoons flour
1 teaspoon salt

1 cup milk
⅛ teaspoon nutmeg
1 teaspoon lemon juice
4 eggs, separated

Cook broccoli according to package directions, drain, and chop finely. Melt butter, add flour and salt and cook until bubbly. Add milk. When thick, add nutmeg, lemon juice, and broccoli. Cool slightly and add beaten egg yolks. Cool mixture completely and fold in stiffly beaten egg whites. Pour into buttered 1½-quart soufflé dish. Place dish in pan containing 1 inch of hot water and bake at 325° F. for 1 hour. Mix together topping ingredients and serve with casserole. Serves 6.

Topping
½ cup sour cream
½ cup Hellmann's mayonnaise

¼ teaspoon curry powder

Mrs. Willard Parks Dixon, Jr. (Beth Cartwright)

Broccoli Casserole

3 tablespoons butter
1 medium onion, chopped
2 10-ounce packages chopped
   broccoli, cooked and
   drained
1 10¾-ounce can cream of
   mushroom soup
1 cup grated sharp Cheddar
   cheese
1 cup mayonnaise

2 eggs
½ teaspoon garlic salt
¼ teaspoon pepper
1½ teaspoons Worcestershire
   sauce
½ teaspoon seasoned salt
1½ teaspoons lemon juice
½ cup seasoned bread crumbs
2 tablespoons butter

Sauté onion in 3 tablespoons butter and mix with broccoli and all ingredients except crumbs and 2 tablespoons butter. Place in greased 2-quart casserole. Top with crumbs and dot with butter. Bake at 350° F. for 45 minutes. Serves 8.

Mrs. Raymond Cobb

Company Broccoli Casserole

2 10-ounce packages chopped broccoli, or 3 cups fresh chopped broccoli
1 10¾-ounce can cream of chicken soup
1 tablespoon flour
1 teaspoon Aćcent
5 drops Tabasco

½ cup sour cream
1 small carrot, grated
2 tablespoons grated onion
¼ teaspoon salt
⅛ teaspoon pepper
¾ cup herbed stuffing mix
2 tablespoons butter, melted

Cook and drain broccoli. Blend soup and flour. Add Tabasco, Aćcent, sour cream, carrot, onion, salt and pepper. Mix well and stir in broccoli. Place in 2-quart casserole. Combine stuffing mix with melted butter and sprinkle over top. Bake at 350° F. for 30-40 minutes or until bubbly. Serves 6-8

Can be easily doubled. A crowd pleaser!

Mrs. Ann H. Roy
Florence, Alabama

Cajun Style Cabbage

4 slices bacon
6-8 green onions chopped
2 14½-ounce cans tomatoes
1 small to medium cabbage, coarsely shredded

⅛-¼ teaspoon cayenne pepper
2 tablespoons vinegar
½ teaspoon salt
⅛ teaspoon black pepper

Cook bacon until crisp. Remove. Sauté onion in drippings until soft. Squeeze tomatoes through fingers to break up. Add tomatoes and remaining ingredients to skillet. Cover and simmer for 45 minutes. Serves 8-10.

Mrs. Patricia Taylor

Cabbage and Sausage

2½ pounds green cabbage	2 eggs
1 pound sausage, crumbled	2 cups milk
1 large onion, chopped	Cracker crumbs

Shred cabbage and cook 15 minutes in salted water. Cook sausage and remove from skillet. In same skillet, cook onion until clear. Set onion aside and save the drippings. Beat eggs and add to milk. Layer cabbage, sausage and onions in casserole. Repeat layers and pour egg mixture over all. Top with crumbs and drizzle with 2 or 3 tablespoons of sausage drippings. Cover and cook in 350° F. oven for 45 minutes. Serves 6.

Mrs. Max Lucas (Ruth Plyler)

Cabbage Stroganoff

1 large head green cabbage, cored and slivered	1 tablespoon sugar
	1 tablespoon vinegar
3 tablespoons butter	8 ounces sour cream

Boil cabbage in small amount of salted water, tightly covered, for 5 minutes only. Drain in colander. Butter casserole. Put hot cabbage in casserole, add butter and toss. Add sugar, vinegar and sour cream. Toss well. Bake uncovered at 350° F. for 20 minutes. Serves 6-8.

As a variation, add 1 clove minced garlic and ¼ teaspoon caraway seeds.

Mrs. William McCrary III (Tancie Lewis)

Celery Casserole

3-4 cups diagonally sliced celery	2 tablespoons chopped pimiento
1 10¾-ounce can cream of chicken soup, undiluted	½ cup sliced almonds
2 tablespoons diced green pepper	1 cup sliced water chestnuts
	1 cup buttered bread crumbs

Boil celery in salted water for 3 minutes and drain. Mix celery with remaining ingredients, except bread crumbs, and place in greased 1-quart casserole. Top with buttered bread crumbs and bake for 15-20 minutes at 350° F. Serves 6-8.

Mrs. William Bryant Nobles (Peggy Hall)

Unique Corn on the Cob

1 stick butter, softened
1 tablespoon prepared mustard
1 teaspoon horseradish
1 teaspoon salt

Fresh pepper and chopped
  parsley
8 ears fresh corn

Combine all ingredients except corn. When corn has been boiled tender-crisp, spread with mixture and serve. Serves 8.

Mrs. Bob Phlegar

Curried Corn Pudding

½ cup minced green pepper
½ cup minced onion
3 tablespoons butter
¾ tablespoon curry powder
2 cups cooked corn

2 cups light cream
3 eggs, slightly beaten
1 teaspoon salt
½ teaspoon sugar
Parsley sprigs

In heavy skillet, sauté pepper and onion in butter until vegetables are tender. Stir in curry powder and transfer to bowl. To vegetables, add corn, cream, eggs, salt and sugar and mix together. Pour into well buttered 1¼-quart soufflé dish and bake at 350° F. for 45 minutes or until puffed and golden. Garnish with parsley sprigs. Serves 8.

Mrs. Frank E. Reid (Diana Mann)

Kentucky Corn Pudding

½ stick butter
4 eggs
2 tablespoons flour
3 tablespoons sugar

1 teaspoon salt
1¾ cups milk
2 cups corn, frozen, fresh or
  canned

Grease 2-quart casserole, using 2 tablespoons butter. Cut up remaining butter and place in blender with all ingredients except corn. Blend well. Add corn and blend at low speed, turning on and off twice. Hand mixer may be used instead of blender. Bake at 325° F. for 45 minutes. In microwave, cook 15 minutes, turning dish often. Serves 6-8.

Mrs. Walter Broadfoot (Anne Uhlhorn)

Ritzy Corn Casserole

4 tablespoons flour
3 tablespoons butter
1 cup milk
1 can cream of chicken soup

2 cups corn, drained
½ teaspoon salt
1 stick butter, melted
36 Ritz crackers, crushed

Make white sauce, using 3 tablespoons butter, flour and milk. Add soup and corn. Cook until thickened. Pour into buttered casserole. Mix remaining butter and Ritz crackers and spread on top. Bake at 350° F. for 30 minutes or until brown and bubbling. Serves 6-8.

Mrs. William S. Mitchell

Stuffed Creamed Eggplant

2 ¾-pound long eggplants,
   trimmed and halved
   lengthwise
Flour
⅓ cup oil
¾ cup minced onion
½ stick butter
3 tablespoons flour
⅔ cup milk

¼ cup heavy cream
5½ tablespoons Parmesan
   cheese
5½ tablespoons grated Swiss
   cheese
1 teaspoon dry mustard
   Cayenne pepper, salt, and
   white pepper to taste
Butter

Score eggplants in several places. Salt and lay on paper towels for 30 minutes. Squeeze out water. Dust cut sides of eggplant with flour. Heat oil in skillet. Put in eggplant, cut side down. Cover. Cook over low heat for 15 minutes. Turn. Cook 15 minutes. In saucepan, sauté onion in butter and stir in flour. Cook 5 minutes. Add milk and cream. Bring to a boil, stirring constantly. Cook 2 minutes. Add 1½ tablespoons of each of cheeses, mustard, salt and pepper. Remove pulp from eggplant; chop and stir into sauce. Pack into reserved eggplant shells. Place in greased shallow casserole. Sprinkle each half with 1 tablespoon of each cheese. Dot with butter. Brown under broiler. Recipe can be done ahead and reheated in 350° F. oven for 20 minutes. Serves 4.

Mrs. Hershel P. Wall (Jean Harrington)

Melanzane alla Noce

1 large eggplant, peeled and
  sliced
1 small onion, finely chopped
2 tablespoons butter
½ teaspoon salt
¼ teaspoon pepper
1 16-ounce can tomatoes,
  drained

1 cup grated sharp cheese
¾ cup cashew nuts, crushed
  (optional)
1 cup cracker crumbs
1 egg, beaten

Soak eggplant for 30 minutes in heavily salted water. Drain and wash twice in clear water. Cook in clear water until tender, about 15-20 minutes. Drain and add butter, onion, salt, pepper, tomatoes, ½ cup cheese, ½ cup cracker crumbs and egg. Mix thoroughly. Put in 2-quart casserole and sprinkle with remaining cheese, nuts and cracker crumbs. Bake at 350° F. for 30 minutes or until light brown. Serves 6.

Mrs. Marion W. Fore, Jr. (Louise Livaudais)
Greenville, South Carolina

Ratatouille

2 medium onions, sliced
2 cloves garlic, chopped
¼ cup olive oil
2 small zucchini, cut in
  ½-inch slices
3 tomatoes, peeled and diced
1 small eggplant, peeled and
  cubed

1 green pepper, cut in strips
2 tablespoons chopped parsley
2 teaspoons salt
½ teaspoon basil
½ teaspoon rosemary
⅛ teaspoon pepper

Sauté onion and garlic in olive oil in Dutch oven. Add remaining ingredients. Cover and cook 15 minutes. Uncover and continue cooking until vegetables are tender but not mushy and juice is thickened. Stir occasionally. Serves 8.

Mrs. Lee L. Wardlaw (Mary Linda Lewis)

Vegetables Parmigiana

1	eggplant, peeled and sliced	½	teaspoon salt
2	zucchini, sliced	⅛	teaspoon pepper
1	green pepper, cut in squares	¼	teaspoon oregano
2	large onions, sliced	2-3	tablespoons grated sharp
2	tablespoons olive oil		cheese
2	cups tomato sauce		
½-1	pound mozzarella cheese, sliced		

Heat oil in large skillet; add eggplant, zucchini, green pepper and onions. Cook until barely tender. Layer ½ vegetables, cheese and sauce in greased baking dish, seasoning layers with salt, pepper and oregano. Repeat. Sprinkle with grated sharp cheese. Bake at 350° F. for 20-30 minutes, or until cheese is melted. Serves 6-8

Great meatless main dish!

Mrs. Huey L. Holden (Barbara Hopper)

Stacked Eggplant Parmesan

1 eggplant	Margarine
1 large onion	Salt
1 large tomato	Grated Parmesan cheese

Cut ends off eggplant and slice into ½-inch thicknesses. Peel tomato and onion and slice into ¼-inch slices. Stack eggplant, tomato, and onion, salting each layer very lightly, in a greased flat baking dish. Add small pat of margarine to top of each stack. Cover tightly wtih foil. Bake 1 hour at 350° F. Remove foil and sprinkle with Parmesan cheese. Bake uncovered 10 minutes prior to serving.

Mrs. John W. Dillard, Jr. (Ann Rogers)

Stuffed Mushrooms

20-30 whole fresh mushrooms
4 slices bacon, chopped
1 onion, chopped
1 teaspoon salt
⅛ teaspoon pepper
1 teaspoon butter

8 ounces cream cheese
½ cup buttered breadcrumbs
Paprika
Garlic salt
Parmesan cheese

Sauté bacon, onion, salt, pepper and chopped mushroom stems in butter until lightly brown. Remove from heat and stir in cream cheese. Stuff mushrooms with mixture and top with crumbs. Sprinkle with paprika, garlic salt and Parmesan cheese. Refrigerate 2 days. Add ¼ cup hot water to baking dish or pan. Bake 15 minutes at 375° F.

Mrs. Anne G. Boals (Anne Goodwin)

Wheat Germ Stuffed Mushrooms

12 large or 24 small mushrooms
1 tablespoon butter
2 tablespoons olive oil
1 clove garlic, minced
1 tablespoon parsley, minced
¼ cup wheat germ

½ teaspoon salt
¼ teaspoon pepper
½-1 teaspoon vermouth
2 tablespoons grated Romano
   or Parmesan cheese

Remove mushroom stems and mince finely. Heat butter and 1 tablespoon of oil in skillet. Add minced mushrooms, garlic and parsley. Cook until lightly browned. Stir in wheat germ, salt, pepper and enough vermouth to make mixture cling together. Arrange mushroom caps, cup side up, in a greased shallow baking dish. Fill with crumb mixture. Brush with remaining oil and sprinkle with cheese. Bake at 400° F. for 10-15 minutes. Serves 6.

Serve as vegetable, or as appetizer if using small mushrooms.

Mrs. Huey L. Holden (Barbara Hopper)

Mushrooms Imperiale

12 large fresh whole mushrooms
¼ cup minced onions
¼ cup minced ham
¾ teaspoon salt
⅛ teaspoon pepper
⅛ teaspoon oregano
⅛ teaspoon thyme

¼ teaspoon Worcestershire
   sauce
2 tablespoons bread crumbs
4 tablespoons butter
1½ ounces Burgundy wine
   Hollandaise sauce (see
   Index)

Remove mushroom stems from caps, wash, chop and set aside. Sauté onions, ham, mushrooms stems, salt, pepper, oregano, thyme, Worcestershire sauce and bread crumbs in butter. Add wine and simmer 5-10 minutes. Fill caps with mixture and sauté in 2 tablespoons butter for 1 minute. Top with hollandaise sauce.

These may be served on melba rounds as an appetizer.

Mrs. Frank O. Oakes, Jr. (Judy Broemmelsick)

Mushroom Casserole

4 slices bread
  Butter
2 pounds fresh mushrooms
2 cups light cream

Freshly ground pepper
1 tablespoon lemon juice
3 tablespoons butter

Dry bread at 200° F. Butter when warm, and break into small pieces. Chop mushroom stems and slice caps. Layer mushrooms and bread in casserole. Sprinkle with lemon juice and fresh pepper. Add cream until dish is ⅔ full. Dot with butter. Bake at 350° F. for 30-45 minutes or until most of liquid is absorbed. Serves 6 as side dish.

Try this dish with beef instead of potatoes.

Mrs. William L. Quinlen Jr. (Ann Clark Miller)

Scalloped Mushrooms

6 cups whole fresh mushrooms, approximately 1½ pounds
1 cup Pepperidge Farm stuffing mix

¾ cup heavy cream
½ cup chicken stock
2 tablespoons butter
2 tablespoons dry sherry

Remove and slice stems. Place layer of mushrooms, caps and stems, in a buttered shallow casserole. Sprinkle half of stuffing mix. Repeat layer of mushrooms and then stuffing mix. Combine cream and stock; pour over top. Dot with butter. Sprinkle sherry on top. Bake 45 minutes at 350° F. Serves 8.

Mrs. James Bettendorf (Berkeley Blake)

Peggy's Creamed Mushrooms

1 pound mushrooms, sliced
4 tablespoons butter
2 tablespoons oil
¼ cup minced shallots or green onions

4 tablespoons flour
2 cups milk
¼ teaspoon salt
Pinch of pepper
½ cup Madeira (optional)

Sauté mushrooms in butter and oil for 4-5 minutes, browning as little as possible. Add shallots and toss over moderate heat for 2 minutes, or until moisture has evaporated. Stir in flour and cook, stirring, 2 more minutes. Remove from heat and blend in milk, seasonings, and Madeira. Return to moderate heat and boil down, stirring, until desired thickness, about 5 minutes. Makes approximately 3 cups.

Mrs. Henry Hancock (Peggy Fairchild)

East India Okra

Small amount of cooking oil
2 medium onions, finely
   chopped
1 green pepper, finely chopped
3 fresh tomatoes, peeled and
   chopped

10-12 pods okra, cut ¼-inch
   thick
¾-1 cup water
¼ teaspoon salt
   Cayenne pepper to taste

In cooking oil, brown onions and pepper. Add tomatoes, okra, ¾-1 cup water, salt and pepper. Reduce heat to simmer and cook until water is gone and mixture is thick. Serves 6.

Mrs. William V. Lawson, Jr. (Carolyn Townes)

Red Onion Pie

1 9-inch pie crust, unbaked
1 egg white, lightly beaten
4 large red onions, chopped
1 stick butter

4 tablespoons flour
1 cup heavy cream
   Salt and pepper to taste
2 egg yolks, beaten

Brush pie crust with egg white to seal crust. Slowly cook onions in butter until golden and soft. Stir in flour and cream. Season with salt and pepper. Add yolks and remove from heat. Pour into pie crust. Bake for 30 minutes at 400° F.

Mrs. Charles McCrary (Janie Stone)

Fabulous Fried Onion Rings

1½ cups flour
1½ cups beer, active or flat,
   cold or warm

3 large yellow onions, or other
   vegetables
3-4 cups shortening

Mix flour and beer in large bowl with whisk. Cover and allow to sit at room temperature for at least 3 hours. Peel and cut onions into ¼-inch thick slices. Separate into rings. Melt enough shortening in pan to be 2 inches deep. Heat to 375° F. on a deep frying thermometer. Dip a few rings into batter with metal tongs, then fry in hot fat until golden brown. Remove to cookie sheets that have been lined with paper towels and keep in 200° F. oven until serving time. Can be frozen and reheated in 400° F. oven for 4-6 minutes.

Try this recipe using other vegetables instead of onions.

Mrs. Dennis Higdon (Joanna Coss)

Company English Peas

½ pound mushrooms, sliced
2 tablespoons butter
2 10-ounce packages frozen
   baby English peas
1 3¼-ounce jar cocktail onions,
   drained

1 2-ounce jar chopped
   pimiento, drained
Salt, pepper and sugar to
   taste

Sauté mushrooms in butter. Cook peas until tender. Combine all ingredients and heat. Serves 8.

Mrs. Frank E. Reid (Diana Mann)

Orange-Mint Peas

1 10-ounce package frozen
   peas
2-3 tablespoons fresh orange
   juice
1 tablespoon finely grated
   orange rind
1 teaspoon lemon juice

1 teaspoon sugar
1 teaspoon dried mint or 1
   tablespoon fresh crushed
   mint
1 tablespoon butter
Salt and white pepper to
   taste

Cook peas according to package directions. Do not overcook. Drain. Add orange juice and rind, lemon juice, sugar and mint. Stir to blend. Add butter. Season to taste with salt and pepper. Serves 3-4.

Mrs. Charles Richard Patterson (Helen Reynolds)

Lucerne Potatoes

2 medium baking potatoes
⅓ pound Swiss cheese, grated
1 teaspoon salt
⅛ teaspoon pepper

⅛ teaspoon nutmeg
2 eggs, beaten
1½ cups milk, scalded

Peel and grate potatoes. Set aside ½ cup cheese and mix potatoes with all other ingredients. Pour into buttered 1½-quart casserole and sprinkle with remaining cheese. Bake at 350° F. for 1 hour. Serves 6.

Mrs. Bill Summey
Sanford, North Carolina

Spuds in a Blanket

Baking potatoes   Bacon

Peel potatoes and wrap each with 1 slice of bacon. Cover with foil. Puncture with a fork. Bake at 375° F. for 1¼ hours. Serve 1 potato per person.

Serve with sour cream and chives.

Mrs. David Rawles Hurt (Becky Bell)

Beef's Best Friend

9 medium red potatoes   Onion powder to taste
1 stick butter, melted   ¼-½ pound Cheddar cheese,
1 tablespoon salt   grated
2 cups light cream

Boil potatoes in their skins. Cool, refrigerate overnight and then peel and grate. Heat butter, salt, cream and onion powder until hot. Do not boil. Stir in cheese. Pour over potatoes and mix well. May be prepared a day or more ahead. Bake in buttered casserole for 1 hour at 350° F. Serves 8-12.

Mrs. Dennis Higdon (Joanna Coss)

Harriette's Potatoes

1 32-ounce package frozen hash   1 small onion, chopped
   brown potatoes   Salt and pepper
1 10¾-ounce can cream of   2 sticks butter
   chicken soup   2 cups corn flakes, crushed
8 ounces sour cream
12 ounces Cheddar cheese,
   grated

Mix first 6 ingredients and pour in 3-quart casserole. Pour 1 stick butter, melted, over potatoes. Coat corn flakes with remaining stick butter, melted, and sprinkle over casserole. Bake at 350° F. for 1¼ hours, or until bubbly. Serves 12.

For a variation, substitute one 12-ounce package medium-wide egg noodles for potatoes.

Mrs. O. B. Quin
Columbia, Tennessee

Brandied Sweet Potato Soufflé

1 pound sweet potatoes, uncooked	1 teaspoon cinnamon
2 cups milk	1 teaspoon grated lemon peel
3 eggs	1 teaspoon salt
1 cup sugar	4 tablespoons butter
1 teaspoon allspice	¼ cup brandy
	¼ cup chopped black walnuts

Peel and dice potatoes. Blend half of milk and potatoes and 2 eggs in a blender or food processor. Pour into greased 3-quart casserole. Blend remaining ingredients except walnuts. Stir into casserole. Add walnuts. Bake at 350° F. for 1½ hours or until knife comes out clean. Serves 8.

For an elegant touch, pour ¼ cup brandy over soufflé before serving and ignite.

Mrs. Richard Reynolds, Jr. (Anne Tuthill)

South Carolina Sweet Potatoes

3 large sweet potatoes	2 eggs, beaten
¼ cup sugar	½ cup brown sugar
1 tablespoon cinnamon	3 tablespoons flour
1 teaspoon nutmeg	3 tablespoons butter
1 stick butter	½ cup chopped pecans

Cut sweet potatoes in quarters and boil until tender. Remove skins and mash. Combine hot sweet potatoes, approximately 3 cups, with next 5 ingredients and beat well. Put potatoes in 1½-quart casserole. Mix remaining ingredients and sprinkle over top. Bake at 350° F. for 30 minutes. Serves 8.

Mrs. Burr K. Hughes, Jr. (Sue Cheek Smith)

Creamed Spinach

2 cups chopped, cooked fresh
  spinach
2 heaping tablespoons medium
  cream sauce
Dash Worcestershire sauce
Dash Tabasco

Salt and pepper to taste
4 thick slices toasted French
  bread
¼ cup hollandaise sauce
  (see Index)

Mix together first 5 ingredients and heat. Lay a toast slice in bottom of 4 individual casseroles. Top each casserole with spinach and hollandaise sauce. Lightly brown in 450° F. oven. Serves 4.

Mrs. Dayton Smith (Justine Holloway)

Spinach Surprise

2 12-ounce packages frozen
  spinach soufflé
1 14-ounce can artichoke
  bottoms

Lemon juice
1-2 cups hollandaise sauce (see
  Index)

Cook soufflé according to package directions. Heat artichokes. Drain. Sprinkle with lemon juice. Mound spinach on artichoke bottoms. Spoon hollandaise over each. This is pretty topped with snipped parsley or slivered almonds. Serves 5-7.

Elegant and easy!

Mrs. James C. Blackburn

Oregano Spinach

1 10-ounce package chopped
  spinach, cooked and
  drained
1 tablespoon butter
¼ cup bread crumbs

1 egg, lightly beaten
Salt
Pepper
½ teaspoon oregano

Mix all ingredients in skillet. Stir over medium heat until egg is cooked. Serves 4.

Mrs. John A. Stemmler (Marsha Miller)

Pat's Creamed Spinach

2 10-ounce packages frozen leaf
   spinach
1 4-ounce package whipped
   cream cheese with chives

½ teaspoon garlic salt

Cook spinach and drain well. Add cream cheese and garlic salt. Bake at 350° F. in buttered casserole until hot.

Mrs. Patricia Taylor

Brother's Favorite Spinach

2 10-ounce packages frozen
   chopped spinach
1 stick butter
½ cup finely chopped onion
1 14-ounce can artichoke
   hearts, drained and
   chopped

16 ounces sour cream
½ cup Parmesan cheese, grated
Salt and pepper to taste

Cook spinach; drain well. Sauté onion in butter. Mix all ingredients and place in buttered casserole. Stir in ¼ cup cheese; sprinkle remainder on top. Bake at 350° F. for 20-30 minutes. Serves 8.

Mrs. John W. Dillard (Ann Rogers)

Spinach and Artichoke Casserole

4 10-ounce packages frozen
   chopped spinach
16 ounces sour cream
1 teaspoon Lawry's seasoned
   salt
1 teaspoon garlic salt

1 14-ounce can artichoke
   hearts, cut in quarters
8 3-part Waverly Wafers,
   crumbled
1 stick margarine, melted

Cook and drain spinach. Season sour cream with Lawry's salt and garlic salt. Combine sour cream, spinach and artichokes in buttered casserole. Mix crumbs with margarine; spread on top of casserole. Cover and bake at 350° F. for 30 minutes. Serves 12.

Mrs. James M. Crews, Jr. (Elaine Elliot)

Stuffed White Squash

12 large or 15 small white
    squash
1 large white onion, chopped
1 green pepper, chopped
½ cup chopped parsley
1 stick butter
1 cup grated Cheddar cheese

1 egg
2 scant teaspoons sugar
Salt and pepper to taste
1 tablespoon lemon juice
¾ cup dry bread crumbs
Cherry tomatoes

Boil squash in salted water just until tender. Drain on paper towels with flat side down. Scoop out squash using a knife and a spoon and drain pulp. Put shells in a buttered pan. Press out as much water from pulp as possible. Sauté onion, green pepper and parsley in butter until onion is translucent. Combine with the mashed pulp. Add remaining ingredients, except tomatoes, and mix thoroughly. Lightly stuff mixture into shells and top with a tomato half. Bake at 350° F. for 35-40 minutes, depending on the size of the squash. These may be placed on a baking pan and cooked on a covered grill. Serves 12.

Mrs. Palmer K. Bartlett (Martha Williams)

Click's Stuffed Squash

12 medium-sized yellow squash
6 green onions, minced
4 ribs celery, finely chopped
2 tablespoons minced parsley
1 clove garlic, minced or
    pressed
2 sticks butter
2 10-ounce packages frozen
    chopped spinach, cooked
    and drained

1½ cups Italian bread crumbs
1 tablespoon Worcestershire
    sauce
4 dashes Tabasco
Salt and freshly ground
    pepper to taste
Freshly grated Parmesan or
    Romano cheese

Cut squash in half lengthwise. Scoop out seeds and drop shells in boiling salted water until just tender, about 2-3 minutes. Drain and cool. Sauté onions, celery, parsley and garlic in butter for 5 minutes. Add spinach, bread crumbs and seasonings and mix well. Butter enough flat Pyrex dishes to hold all the squash halves. Stuff each half and top with cheese. Bake at 350° F. for 20 minutes, or until heated through. Serves 12-24.

Make this ahead and cover until ready to heat.

Mrs. William C. Harris (Ann Clark Quinlen)

Maysie's Skillet Squash

1 onion, sliced
½ green pepper, chopped
½ stick butter
1 tomato, peeled and quartered

2 cups sliced yellow squash
Salt and pepper to taste
¼ cup shredded Cheddar or Parmesan cheese

Sauté onion and green pepper in butter. Add the rest of the ingredients, except cheese, and cook until squash is tender. Stir in the cheese and cook until cheese melts. Serves 2-4.

Mrs. Scott May (Linda Morse)

Herbed Squash Casserole

2-3 cups sliced squash
1 10¾-ounce can cream of chicken soup
2 carrots, shredded
1 onion, finely chopped

1 2-ounce jar pimiento
8 ounces sour cream
1 8-ounce package Pepperidge Farm Herb Stuffing Mix
1 stick margarine

Cook squash and drain thoroughly. Mix all ingredients except stuffing. Melt margarine and mix well with stuffing. Line bottom of casserole with half of stuffing. Top with squash mixture, then remaining stuffing. Bake at 350° F. for 30-40 minutes. Can be frozen. Serves 6.

Mrs. John D. Hughes (Nell Jones)

Sailor's Squash

2½ pounds yellow squash, about 10 medium
2 onions, chopped
½ cup chopped green pepper
2 cups Pepperidge Farm Herb Dressing, prepared according to directions
Salt and pepper to taste

Cayenne pepper to taste
½ stick margarine
2 eggs, beaten
1 pound fresh shrimp, cooked, shelled and coarsely chopped
Breadcrumbs for topping

Slice squash and boil with green pepper and onion until tender. Drain well and mash. Add dressing, salt, pepper and lots of cayenne pepper. Stir in margarine until melted. Fold in eggs, then shrimp. Pour in 2-quart casserole and top with buttered breadcrumbs. Bake at 350° F. for 30-45 minutes. Serves 8.

Mrs. Seymour R. Pooley, Sr.
Jackson, Mississippi

Squash Tunica

2 pounds yellow squash, sliced	8 ounces sour cream
1 cup water	½ cup chopped onion
1 teaspoon salt	½ cup Parmesan cheese
⅛ teaspoon sugar	Salt and pepper to taste
½ stick butter	1 cup bread crumbs
1 cup grated Cheddar cheese	3 tablespoons butter

Boil squash in water with salt and sugar. Turn to low, cover and cook about 15 minutes. Drain, return to pan and add ½ stick butter. Mash until well blended. Add rest of ingredients, except bread crumbs and 3 tablespoons butter. Pour into 2-quart casserole and top with the bread crumbs. Cut butter into small pieces and put on top of casserole. Bake at 350° F. for 30 minutes. Serves 6-8.

Mrs. Scott Arnold, III (Anne Dillard)

Baked Summer Tomatoes

4 medium ripe tomatoes	½ cup chopped parsley
Salt and pepper	⅓ cup dry bread crumbs
2 green onions, minced	½ teaspoon salt
1 clove garlic, pressed	2 tablespoons olive oil

Cut tops off tomatoes. Gently squeeze out some of juice and seeds. Salt and pepper inside. Combine remaining ingredients and spoon into tomatoes. Place in greased baking dish. Bake at 400° F. for 15 minutes or until lightly browned. Serves 4.

Use only summer's best tomatoes.

Mrs. Charlie Carr
Chapel Hill, North Carolina

Mushroom-Stuffed Tomatoes

6 medium tomatoes
1 pint mushrooms, chopped
2 tablespoons butter
½ cup sour cream
2 egg yolks, beaten
¼ cup Italian bread crumbs

½ teaspoon salt
4 drops Tabasco
⅛ teaspoon thyme
Pepper to taste
1 tablespoon butter, melted
3 tablespoons bread crumbs

Cut out stems of tomatoes, scoop out pulp, and invert to drain. Finely chop 1 cup of pulp. Sauté mushrooms in butter until tender. Combine sour cream and egg yolks; add mushrooms, tomato pulp, crumbs, and spices. Mix well. Cook, stirring until thick. Place tomato shells in buttered baking dish and fill with mushroom mixture. Combine butter and remaining bread crumbs; sprinkle over tomatoes. Bake at 375° F. for 25 minutes. Serves 6.

Great with steak

Mrs. William C. Harris (Ann Clark Quinlen)

Pomodóri Ripieni

6 medium tomatoes
5 tablespoons soft bread
  crumbs
¼ cup milk
2-3 sprigs parsley, finely
  chopped

1 clove garlic, finely chopped
2 egg yolks, beaten
¼ cup grated Parmesan cheese
Salt and pepper to taste
½ cup olive oil

Cut tomatoes in ½ horizontally. Remove seeds and discard. Scoop out pulp and chop finely. Soak bread crumbs in milk; mix with pulp, parsley and garlic. Add egg yolks, cheese, salt and pepper. Stuff tomatoes with mixture and place in large baking dish greased with olive oil. Drizzle remaining olive oil over tomatoes. Bake at 375° F. for 30 minutes. Serves 6-12.

Delicious hot or cold!

Mrs. Harold D. Walker, Jr. (Foxy Von Lackum)

Sautéed Cocktail Tomatoes

1 pint cocktail tomatoes	4 green onions, finely chopped
2 cloves garlic, crushed	¼ cup green pepper, finely
½ stick butter, ¼ cup olive oil,	chopped
or a combination of both	1 tablespoon sugar

Heat butter or oil in skillet. Add garlic and heat, do not brown. Add vegetables and sugar. Stir with wooden spoon over high heat for 3 minutes. Serves 4.

Carolyn Mitchell Kittle

Tomato Pudding

2 cups canned tomatoes	¼ teaspoon Tabasco
⅛ teaspoon pepper	1 teaspoon lemon juice
⅛ teaspoon salt	1 loaf Pepperidge Farm very
1 stick butter	thin bread, crusts removed
½-1 cup dark brown sugar	
1 teaspoon Worcestershire	
sauce	

Heat tomatoes for 5 minutes. Add butter, sugar and all seasonings. Mix well. Butter 2-quart casserole and fill with loosely torn pieces of bread. Pour tomato mixture over bread and mix well. Cover and bake at 350° F. for 30 minutes. Serves 8-10.

Mrs. Thomas W. Jones (Janice Cox)

Tomato Casserole

1 1-pound can stewed tomatoes	1 tablespoon grated onion
1 8-ounce package mozzarella	¾ teaspoon pepper
cheese, cubed	½ stick butter, melted
3 slices bread, toasted and	
cubed	

Mix all ingredients together, saving some cheese to garnish top. Pour into casserole. Bake at 375° F. for 20 minutes. Serves 4-6.

Mrs. Martin McNamara
Nashville, Tennessee

Zucchini Bravo

3 large zucchini	½-⅔ cup bread crumbs
¼ cup finely minced onions	½ cup grated Swiss cheese
1½ tablespoons olive oil	1 large egg
½ cup ground blanched almonds	Salt and pepper to taste
	⅛ teaspoon powdered cloves
½ cup heavy cream	3 tablespoons butter, melted

Blanch zucchini 10 minutes in boiling salted water. Cut in half lengthwise. Hollow out, leaving ⅜-inch thick shell. Salt lightly and drain. Chop pulp and drain. Sauté onion in oil until transparent. Stir in pulp and sauté until tender. Combine pulp mixture, almonds, cream and ⅓ cup bread crumbs. Set aside 3 tablespoons of cheese. Add remaining cheese, egg, salt, pepper and cloves to mixture. Stuff zucchini shells and top with reserved cheese, bread crumbs and butter. Bake at 350° F. for 25-30 minutes. Serves 6.

Baked Zucchini Boats

Zucchini	Bread crumbs made from
Onion, finely chopped	seasoned croutons
Salt and pepper to taste	Parmesan cheese
Butter	

Cut zucchini in half. Split each half through the middle lengthwise, then cut across several times being careful not to cut through the outside skin. Stuff as much onion as possible into zucchini where it has been cut. Sprinkle more onion on top. Sprinkle with salt and pepper and dot generously with butter. Cover with bread crumbs and sprinkle with Parmesan cheese. Bake at 350° F. for 1 hour.

Mrs. Leland Dow (Virginia Tayloe)

Cheesy Zucchini Casserole

6-10 medium zucchini	½ teaspoon salt
1 stick butter	¼ teaspoon paprika
¾ cup grated Cheddar cheese	¼ cup chopped green onions
¼ cup grated Swiss cheese	1 cup bread crumbs
8 ounces sour cream	¼ cup Parmesan cheese

Boil whole zucchini for 10 minutes. Cut ends off, slice lengthwise and arrange in buttered casserole. Melt butter and mix in Cheddar cheese, Swiss cheese and sour cream. Add salt, paprika and onions. Pour over zucchini and sprinkle crumbs and Parmesan cheese on top. Dot with butter. Bake at 350° F. for 45 minutes. Serves 6-8.

This cheese sauce would be good on any vegetable.

Mrs. Michael Heffernan (Tracy Plyler)

Zucchini Mexicali

2 pounds zucchini, unpeeled and sliced	3 tablespoons flour
	1 teaspoon salt
½ cup milk	4 eggs, beaten
1 pound Monterey Jack cheese, grated	1 teaspoon baking powder
	1 tablespoon butter or margarine
¼ cup chopped parsley	
1 4-ounce can chopped green chilies	1 cup fresh bread crumbs

Drop zucchini into boiling water and cook until barely tender, approximately 3-5 minutes. Drain well. Mix together all ingredients except butter and crumbs. Grease sides and bottom of 8-inch square dish with butter. Sprinkle with ½ cup bread crumbs. Add squash mixture and top with remaining crumbs. Bake in 325° F. oven for 40 minutes, or until firm. Serves 6-8.

Spicy and different.

Mrs. William E. Denman, III (Julie Moss)

Zucchini in Salsa Verde

1½ pounds small zucchini
½ cup flour
1¾ teaspoons salt
  Oil
¼ cup olive oil
¼ cup minced parsley

3 tablespoons white wine
  vinegar
3 anchovies, minced
½ clove garlic, minced
½ teaspoon black pepper
1 lemon, very thinly sliced

Cut zucchini into ⅛-inch slices. Mix flour and salt in paper bag. Toss zucchini slices in flour a little at a time. Cook in 1 inch of oil in electric skillet to brown lightly. Drain and cool. Mix remaining ingredients except lemon. Arrange zucchini in serving dish. Pour sauce over. Garnish with lemon slices. Let mixture marinate 1-2 hours before serving. Serve at room temperature. Serves 6-8.

Mrs. Kay K. Butler (Kay Kendall)

C. Grivich

Citrus monachello

Fruit Salads & Sidedishes

Apricot Salad

1 large can apricots, drained, reserving juice
¼ pound Cheddar cheese, grated
2-3 tablespoons toasted coconut

1 cup chopped pecans
½ cup sugar
2 tablespoons flour
1 egg

In a large flat dish, layer apricots, cheese, coconut and pecans. Combine juice from apricots with sugar, flour and egg. Cook until thick. Pour over apricot mixture. Chill thoroughly. Serves 8-10.

Mrs. Max Lucas (Ruth Plyler)

Cheese-Filled Apples

4 medium apples
½ lemon
3 ounces cream cheese, softened

1⅓ ounces Camembert cheese
1 tablespoon white wine

Core apples and sprinkle with lemon. Beat cream cheese, Camembert and wine until smooth. Stuff centers of apples. Chill for several hours. Cut in wedges and serve. Serves 4.

Great as an appetizer with white wine.

Mrs. Burdette Russ (Scottie McCord)

Cinnamon Apples

2 cups water
½ cup sugar
½ cup red hot cinnamon candies
6 large tart cooking apples, pared and cored

3 ounces cream cheese, softened
1 tablespoon mayonnaise
2 tablespoon pecans, finely chopped

In a large saucepan, mix water and sugar. Bring to a boil and boil for 5 minutes. Add candies, stirring until melted. Add apples, cover and simmer until tender, about 10 minutes. Turn apples occasionally. Let stand in syrup until they turn a deep red. Remove from liquid and drain. Combine cream cheese, mayonnaise and pecans and stuff in apple centers. Chill well. Serves 6.

Apples can be cut in half for luncheon-size serving.

Mrs. Rowe Belcher (Susan Ramsey)

Spiced Peaches

1 28-ounce can peach halves
1 3-inch stick cinnamon
1 teaspoon whole cloves

1 teaspoon whole allspice
¼ cup white vinegar

Drain syrup from peaches into saucepan. Add spices and vinegar. Simmer 5 minutes. Pour over peaches and refrigerate overnight. The sauce can be re-used; just add more drained peaches and chill. Serves 4-5.

This is much better than "store-bought." Keeps a long time in refrigerator and gets better with age!

Mrs. William R. Hackett (Sandy Childress)

Burgundy Pears

6 winter pears
4 whole cloves
2 cups Burgundy
1 2-inch stick cinnamon

2 cups water
1 cup sugar
1 lemon, sliced

Select firm pears with stems. Pare. Combine all ingredients in glass or enamel saucepan. Cover and cook over low heat for 30 minutes, or until tender. One hour may be necessary. Remove pears. Reduce juice to ½. Pour over pears and chill. Serve plain or with whipped cream.

Good as dessert or salad.

Mrs. L. Draper Hill
Grosse Pointe, Michigan

Winter Fruit Bowl

4 medium grapefruits
1 cup sugar
½ cup orange marmalade

2 cups fresh cranberries
3 medium bananas

Pare and section grapefruit, reserving juice. Set grapefruit sections aside. Add enough water to reserved juice to measure one cup. Combine with sugar and marmalade. Heat to boiling, stirring to dissolve sugar. Add cranberries. Cook and stir until skins pop, 5-8 minutes. Remove from heat and cool. Add grapefruit. Cover and chill. Just before serving, slice bananas and stir into chilled grapefruit mixture. Serves 10-12.

Great for Christmas brunch.

Mrs. Rowlett W. Sneed, Jr. (Sarah Gaye Craig)

Congealed Blueberry Salad

2 3-ounce packages blackberry
    gelatin
2 cups boiling water

1 15-ounce can blueberries
1 8¼-ounce can crushed
    pineapple

Dissolve gelatin in boiling water. Combine juices of berries and pineapple. If necessary, add enough water to make 1 cup. Add cup of juices to gelatin mixture. Stir in drained fruit and pour into 2-quart flat pan. Refrigerate until firm.

Dressing
8 ounces cream cheese,
    softened
½ cup sugar
8 ounces sour cream

½ teaspoon vanilla
½ cup chopped pecans

Combine all ingredients except pecans. Spread over gelatin and garnish with chopped pecans. Serves 10-12.

Mrs. James M. Graham, Jr. (Catherine Couch)

Raspberry-Applesauce Salad

1 cup applesauce
1 3-ounce package raspberry
   gelatin
1 10-ounce package frozen
   raspberries, thawed

8 tablespoons sour cream
4 tablespoons mayonnaise

Heat applesauce just to boil. Add gelatin and mix well. Stir in raspberries. Pour into 8 or 9-inch ring mold and chill until set. Serve with sour cream dressing, using 8 tablespoons sour cream to 4 tablespoons mayonnaise. Serves 6.

Mrs. Bailey Wiener (Marilyn McGee)

Raspberry Salad

1 10-ounce package frozen
   raspberries, thawed
2 3-ounce packages raspberry
   gelatin
2 cups boiling water

1 pint vanilla ice cream
1 6-ounce can frozen lemonade,
   thawed
½ cup chopped pecans

Drain raspberries. Reserve syrup. Dissolve gelatin in boiling water. Add ice cream and stir until melted. Stir in lemonade and reserved syrup. Chill until slightly set. Add raspberries and chopped pecans. Turn into a 6-cup ring mold or serve in individual molds. Serves 8-10.

Mrs. Larry H. Formby (Tlitha Stone)
Rome, Georgia

Rhubarb Salad

1 10-ounce package frozen
   rhubarb
1 cup orange juice
1 6-ounce box strawberry
   gelatin
1 8¼-ounce can crushed
   pineapple, undrained

1 cup chopped celery
1 large apple, peeled and diced
½ cup chopped pecans
   Mayonnaise and fresh
   strawberries for garnish

Cook rhubarb with orange juice until tender. To 1¼ cups hot rhubarb, add gelatin and stir to dissolve. Add remaining ingredients and mix well. Pour into oiled mold or oiled 8x8-inch pan. Chill until firm. To serve, cut into squares or unmold on lettuce. Garnish with mayonnaise and fresh strawberries. Serves 6-8.

Mrs. Kemper Durand

Congealed Strawberry Salad

1 6-ounce box strawberry
   gelatin
1 cup boiling water
2 10-ounce packages frozen
   strawberries, thawed

1 20-ounce can crushed
   pineapple, drained
1 cup chopped pecans
½ teaspoon lemon juice
8 ounces sour cream

Melt gelatin in boiling water. Add next 4 ingredients. Pour half of mixture into 6-cup mold and congeal. When set, spread with sour cream. Top with remaining salad mixture. Refrigerate until firm. Serves 6-8.

You may use any variation of fruits and gelatin.

Mrs. Kemmons Wilson, Jr. (Norma Thompson)

Cranberry Delight

1 16-ounce can whole berry
   cranberry sauce
8 ounces sour cream

1 cup whole pecans
1 15½-ounce can crushed
   pineapple, well drained

Combine all ingredients. Freeze for 5-7 hours in 8-inch square pan or ring mold. Unmold 15 minutes before serving. Serves 8-10.

Lynley Scott

Salad for the Holidays

1 20-ounce can unsweetened
  crushed pineapple
1 envelope unflavored gelatin
2 3-ounce packages raspberry
  gelatin
1 cup boiling water
1 16-ounce can whole
  cranberry sauce
1 cup port wine
1 cup chopped walnuts
8 ounces cream cheese,
  softened
8 ounces sour cream
Pineapple slices or mandarin
  oranges for garnish

Drain ½ cup syrup from pineapple. Sprinkle unflavored gelatin over syrup to soften. Place softened gelatin over low heat, stirring constantly until dissolved. Dissolve raspberry gelatin in boiling water. Add unflavored gelatin to raspberry gelatin. Stir in remaining undrained pineapple, cranberry sauce and port wine and chill until mixture begins to thicken. Stir in walnuts and pour into mold or 9x12-inch dish. Chill until firm. Mix sour cream and cream cheese and spread on top. Garnish with pineapple or oranges, if desired. Serves 12.

An inexpensive, pretty salad—especially good for a ladies' luncheon or brunch.

Mrs. William D. Evans (Maxey Carter)

Frozen Caribbean Salad

1 large banana, sliced
1 tablespoon lime juice
1 cup mayonnaise
8 ounces heavy cream, whipped
1 13¼-ounce can crushed
  pineapple
1 cup miniature marshmallows
  (optional)
¼ cup powdered sugar
3 tablespoons rum or ¾
  teaspoon rum flavoring
1 teaspoon grated lime rind
Fresh mint leaves for garnish
  (optional)

Toss banana slices in lime juice. Fold mayonnaise into whipped cream. Add remaining ingredients, except mint leaves, and mix well. Pour into lightly oiled pie pan and freeze. Top with mint leaves before serving. Serve in wedges. Serves 6-8.

Mrs. Ann H. Roy
Florence, Alabama

Apples Burgundy

8 cooking apples, preferably
    York, peeled and quartered
⅔ cup Burgundy
⅔ cup sugar
½ stick cinnamon

4 whole cloves
⅛ teaspoon salt
½ lemon or lime, thinly sliced
    and seeded

Place apples in baking dish. Combine and heat remaining ingredients. Do *not* boil. Pour over fruit. Bake covered at 350° F. for 1 hour or until tender, stirring every 15 minutes. Flavor enhanced if made a day or 2 ahead. Can be served cold. Serves 6-8.

Mrs. John Turley, III (Barbara Barham)

Dottie's Hot Apple-Cranberry Salad

3 cups chopped apples
2 cups washed cranberries
1 cup sugar
1 cup quick oats

½ cup brown sugar
½ cup chopped pecans
½ stick butter

In an 8 to 10-inch Pyrex pie pan, mix together apples, cranberries and sugar. Cover with a mixture of oats, brown sugar and nuts. Cut pats of butter to dot over top. Bake 1 hour in 325° F. oven. Watch so it doesn't get too dry. Serves 12.

This is very easy and a little different from the congealed salads of the holiday season.

Mrs. A. H. Johnson
Mobile, Alabama

Apricot Casserole

2 28-ounce cans apricots
1 pound light brown sugar

1 12-ounce box Ritz crackers,
    crushed

Place half of apricots in greased 3-quart flat casserole. Sprinkle with sugar and then crackers. Dot with butter. Repeat. Bake at 300° F. for 1 hour. Serves 12.

Mrs. William T. Black, Jr. (Lida Willey)

Banana Fritters

1 cup flour
1 egg *plus* enough milk to
   make 1 cup
2 tablespoons sugar
½ teaspoon salt
⅓ teaspoon baking powder

3 bananas, thinly sliced in
   rounds
Vegetable oil
Butter
Cinnamon sugar

Mix first six ingredients. Heat 1 inch of oil in skillet. Spoon fritters into oil. Cook 10 minutes, or until brown. Drain on paper towel. Butter each fritter and sprinkle with cinnamon sugar. Serves 4-6.

Fun breakfast dish for family or weekend company.

Mrs. Scott A. Arnold, III (Anne Dillard)

Honeyed Bananas

6 bananas, peeled and cut in
   half
½ cup lemon juice

2 tablespoons butter
¼ cup honey

Dip bananas in lemon juice. Melt butter in saucepan and stir in honey. Add bananas, turning until glazed. Use care not to overcook. Takes 3-5 minutes.

Goes well with glazed pork chops.

Mrs. Thomas W. Jones (Janice Cox)

Peach Baskets

3-4 30-ounce cans peach halves
2 cups Total cereal, crushed
½ cup dark brown sugar,
   packed
½ teaspoon salt
3 tablespoons flour

¼ cup white corn syrup
¼ cup peach juice
½ teaspoon lemon juice
3 tablespoons butter
½ cup chopped pecans

Drain peach halves on paper towels. Mix together next 4 ingredients, add remaining ingredients and mix well. Fill center of each peach half with mixture and bake in Pyrex dish at 350° F. for 25-30 minutes. Serves 18-24.

Best when made ahead. Store covered in refrigerator. Bring to room temperature before reheating.

Mrs. Rowe Belcher (Susan Ramsay)

Stuffed Baked Pears

Fresh pears
Lemon juice
2 tablespoons mincemeat per
   pear

Butter
1 teaspoon brandy per pear

Cut unpeeled fresh pears in half lengthwise. Core and dip in lemon juice. Fill each pear with 2 tablespoons mincemeat. Dot with butter and place in a buttered baking dish. Add water to fill ¼ inch and bake in a 350° F. oven for 30 minutes, or until tender. Drizzle a teaspoon of brandy over each pear. Canned pears may be used. Bake only 15 minutes.

Good with duck and pork.

Mrs. Max B. Ostner, Jr. (Mary Margaret Buffa)

Baked Pineapple

4 cups fresh bread cubes
1 cup sugar
3 eggs, beaten
1 stick butter, melted

1 cup milk
1 15¼-ounce can pineapple
   chunks, drained

Mix bread cubes, sugar, eggs and butter together. Add milk and mix; then add pineapple. Mix and pour into 1-quart buttered casserole. Bake at 350° F. for 1 hour. Serves 6-8.

Good dessert with whipped cream.

Mrs. William S. Mitchell

Gretchen's Pineapples

½ cup sugar
½ cup flour
1 20-ounce can crushed
   pineapple and juice

1 20-ounce can pineapple
   chunks and juice
1 pound Velveeta cheese, cubed

Mix together all ingredients and pour into casserole. Bake, uncovered, at 250° F. for 1 hour. This may be mixed ahead and baked later. Reheats well. Serves 8.

Mrs. Bill Bobbitt (Janie Wade)

Curried Fruit for 60

4   gallons salad fruit
2-3 15-ounce cans Bing cherries
4   tablespoons curry powder
4   1-pound boxes dark brown
    sugar

4   sticks butter, melted
8-9 bananas

Drain fruit well for 24 hours the day before serving. Blend curry, sugar and butter. Pour over fruit mixture and mix. Marinate 24 hours. Add bananas last. Heat on top of stove or in oven until warm.

Recipe may be divided by 4 for 10-15.

Mrs. Robert G. Allen (Sally Ball)

Hot Fruit Casserole

1   28-ounce can peach halves
1   28-ounce can peach slices
1   15¼-ounce can pineapple
    chunks
1   17-ounce can apricot halves
1   28-ounce can pear halves
1   17-ounce can pitted dark
    cherries
1   17-ounce can Kadota figs, or
    figs packed in light syrup
6   dozen almond macaroons, or
    Nabisco coconut
    macaroons

3-4 bananas
    Lemon juice
    Brown sugar
    Butter
2   2-ounce packages slivered
    almonds
⅔ cup banana liqueur or
    Cointreau

The day before serving, drain fruit dry and crumble macaroons. The day of serving, slice bananas and sprinkle with lemon juice to keep from turning brown. Mix all fruits together. Layer macaroons and fruits in two 2-quart casseroles. Sprinkle liberally with brown sugar and dot with butter. Sprinkle almonds on top. Pour liqueur over top. Bake at 300° F. for 20-30 minutes. Serves 12-14.

Mrs. Michael Heffernan (Tracy Plyler)

Citrus medica

C. Grivich

Salads and Salad Dressings

Caesar Salad à la Romanoff

2 cloves garlic, pressed
⅔ 2-ounce tin of anchovies
1 teaspoon Worcestershire
   sauce
10 tablespoons olive oil, divided
   Freshly ground pepper

3 tablespoons wine vinegar
2 eggs, boiled 1 minute
1 large head romaine lettuce,
   broken into pieces
1 cup croutons
½ cup Parmesan cheese, freshly
   grated

In a wooden bowl, mash garlic, anchovies, Worcestershire, 1 table-spoon olive oil and pepper until well mixed. Add remaining olive oil and vinegar and blend well. Just before serving, toss dressing with romaine. Break eggs into salad and toss again. Add liberal amount of Parmesan and toss again. Add croutons and toss for final time. Serves 6.

Mrs. William Quinlen, Jr. (Ann Clark Miller)

Fancy Salad

2 pounds fresh spinach
4-5 heads Bibb lettuce
1 11-ounce can mandarin
   orange sections, drained
1 14-ounce can hearts of palm,
   sliced

1 small purple onion, thinly
   sliced (optional)
Poppy seed Dressing (see
Index)

Wash, pick and break up greens. Wrap in a towel or paper towel and chill. When ready to serve, add oranges, hearts of palm and onion. Add about ½ of dressing and toss.

If serving after the main course, eliminate the onion.

Edwina Theresa Thomas

Wilted Spinach Salad

3 bunches fresh spinach
4 strips bacon
2 tablespoons vinegar
2 tablespoons water

Salt and freshly ground
  pepper to taste
1 tablespoon sugar
3 hard-boiled eggs, sliced

Wash and thoroughly dry spinach. Fry bacon until crisp. Drain on paper towel and cool to crumble. Mix next 4 ingredients into bacon fat and stir. Heat to boiling point. Add crumbled bacon pieces. Pour over greens mixed with hard cooked eggs. Toss lightly and serve. Serves 4.

Mrs. J. Logan Morgan

Coleslaw Salad

½ head lettuce, shredded
½ head cabbage, shredded
⅔ cup chopped dill pickle
½ cup chopped onion
1 teaspoon sugar

½ teaspoon garlic powder
⅔ cup Hellmann's mayonnaise
1 teaspoon Durkee's or
  prepared mustard
Salt and pepper to taste

Mix together all ingredients and chill. Serves 8.

Mrs. Henry B. Turner (Anne Doughten)

Ann's Coleslaw

1 large head cabbage, finely
  shredded
1 large onion, sliced and
  separated into rings
¾ cup sugar
1 cup vinegar

1 teaspoon prepared
  mustard
1 tablespoon sugar
1 teaspoon celery seed
1½ teaspoons salt
1 cup oil

Mix cabbage and onion rings. Sprinkle evenly with sugar. Combine remaining ingredients and bring to a boil. Pour liquid over cabbage and onion. Let stand for 12 hours. Refrigerate. Serves 8-10.

Mrs. Ed Tillman

Do-Ahead Slaw

1 large head cabbage	1 teaspoon turmeric
1-2 small onions	1 cup sugar
3-4 stalks celery	1 cup vinegar
1 green pepper	1 teaspoon mustard seed

Finely chop all vegetables. Add turmeric. Combine remaining ingredients and bring to a boil. Pour hot mixture over vegetables. Cover and refrigerate. Best after 2-3 days. Serves 6-8.

Keeps a week or longer.

Mrs. Max B. Ostner, Jr. (Mary Margaret Buffa)

Salad Olé

Dressing

½ cup mayonnaise	1 teaspoon vinegar
½ cup chili sauce	Few drops Tabasco
½-1 teaspoon chili powder	
1 teaspoon Beau Monde seasoning	

Early in the day, prepare dressing and chill.

Salad

1 medium head lettuce, cut up	1 large avocado, cut in chunks
½ cup sliced olives	2 cups crumbled corn chips
1 cup grated sharp cheese	Salt and pepper to taste
1 small red onion, thinly sliced	

About 30 minutes before serving time, mix salad. Add dressing and toss. Serves 6-8.

Mrs. William R. Hackett (Sandy Childress)

Taco Salad

1 head romaine lettuce
½ head red cabbage
2 30-ounce cans kidney beans, drained
2 1¼-ounce packages taco seasoning
2 pounds lean ground round
5 tomatoes, chopped but not peeled

1 cucumber, chopped
1 onion, chopped
1 pound Cheddar cheese, grated
2 8-ounce bottles 1000 Island dressing
1 cup light cream
1 9-ounce package tortilla chips

The day before serving, sauté meat and drain. Add taco seasoning. About 15 minutes before serving, break up tortilla chips and mix with meat, dressing and other vegetables. Serves 20.

Mrs. Gavin Gentry (Mary Jane Coleman)

Beef Salad

1 head romaine
3 cups cooked roast beef, cubed
6 new potatoes, cooked, cooled and sliced
20 cherry tomatoes, quartered
1 small onion, thinly sliced in rings
¾ cup thinly sliced fresh mushrooms

1 tablespoon capers
2 tablespoons chopped parsley
6 tablespoons olive oil
2 tablespoons wine vinegar
1 teaspoon horseradish
1 teaspoon dry mustard
⅛ teaspoon pepper
4 hard-boiled eggs, sliced

Break romaine into pieces in large bowl. Top with next 7 ingredients. Chill. Mix next 5 ingredients in a jar and shake well. Pour over all and toss well. Garnish with eggs and serve immediately. Serves 4-6.

Mrs. William L. Quinlen III

Different Chicken Salad

½ pound vermicelli, cooked al dente and drained
⅓ cup garlic salad dressing
Salt, to taste
3 cups cubed cooked chicken
1 9-ounce package frozen artichoke hearts, cooked according to directions

1 2.2-ounce can sliced black olives
1 tablespoon grated onion
1 cup homemade mayonnaise
4 tablespoons snipped parsley
½ cup sliced green onions
Cherry tomatoes for garnish
Avocado slices for garnish

Put warm pasta in bowl and toss well with dressing. Let cool and refrigerate several hours or overnight. When ready to serve, add chicken, artichokes and black olives to pasta. Toss this mixture gently with mayonnaise. Serve topped with parsley and green onions. Garnish with cherry tomatoes and avocado slices that have been marinated in small amount of garlic salad dressing. Serves 6-8.

Garlic Salad Dressing

¼ cup wine vinegar
2 teaspoons Dijon mustard
4 cloves garlic, split
1 teaspoon paprika

Salt
Ground Pepper
1 cup olive oil

Combine all ingredients except olive oil. Add oil slowly while whisking. This must be done at least one day ahead of time. Yields 1¼ cups.

Mrs. Charles D. Schaffler (Mickey Pooley)

California Cobb Salad

1 head each romaine and
  iceberg lettuce
2 medium tomatoes, or 1 box
  cherry tomatoes, cut in half
1 ripe avocado, sliced
¼ pound Roquefort cheese,
  crumbled

6 slices crisp bacon
2 hard-cooked eggs
2 tablespoons minced chives, or
  ¼ red onion, thinly sliced
2 cups cooked and slivered
  chicken

Slice lettuce in food processor or shred by hand. Toss with other salad
ingredients. Pour half of dressing over salad. Pass remaining dressing.
Serves 6.

Dressing
¼ cup red wine vinegar
1 teaspoon salt
¼ teaspoon pepper
½ teaspoon sugar

½ teaspoon Worcestershire
  sauce
⅔ cup oil

Combine all dressing ingredients.

*This recipe was named for Sally Cobb, whose father started the famous
Brown Derby Restaurant in Los Angeles.*

Mrs. David Alexander
Claremont Calif.

Calcutta Luncheon Salad

1 cup sliced water chestnuts
1 4-ounce can mushrooms,
   drained
1½ cups cooked and diced
   chicken, turkey or duck
¼ cup bottled French dressing
1 cup chopped celery

½ cup chopped green onions
¼ cup mayonnaise
1 teaspoon celery salt
⅛ teaspoon curry powder
½ cup shredded coconut
1 cup mandarin orange
   sections

Combine first three ingredients. Add French dressing and mix well. Cover and let stand in refrigerator 3-4 hours. When ready to serve, drain off excess dressing and add next 5 ingredients. Mix well with folding motion. Mound mixture on bed of lettuce. Sprinkle coconut over top and garnish with orange sections. Serves 6.

Better made a day ahead!

Mrs. Phillip H. McNeill (Mabel McCall)

Crab-Sprout Salad

1 cup fresh crabmeat
1 hard-boiled egg, finely
   chopped
1 cup alfalfa sprouts

3-4 artichoke hearts, thinly
   sliced
2 teaspoons mayonnaise
2 teaspoons La Martinique
   Salad Dressing

Combine first 4 ingredients. Mix mayonnaise and salad dressing and pour over salad. Serves 4.

Mrs. Clyde L. Patton, Jr. (Leslie Wilsford)

Shrimp Horcher

1 cup mayonnaise
2 tablespoons chili sauce or
   ketchup
1-2 tablespoons horseradish
2 tablespoons sherry
   White pepper to taste
   Lemon juice to taste

½ cup heavy cream, whipped
1 pineapple
1 pound shrimp
Water
Salt
Slice of lemon

Make sauce of first 6 ingredients. Fold in whipped cream. Set aside. Cut pineapple into quarters lengthwise. Core, remove meat and cut into bite-size pieces, leaving shells intact. Bring salted water to a boil; add shrimp and lemon slice. Turn off heat and allow shrimp to cool in water. Peel. Mix with sauce and pieces of pineapple. Heap into shells and serve chilled. Serves 4.

Dr. Richard J. Reynolds, Jr.

Shrimp Divine

2 pounds cooked shrimp,
   shelled and deveined
1 large onion, thinly sliced
3 tablespoons capers, drained

⅛ teaspoon caper juice
Juice of 4-5 lemons
1½ cups Hellmann's mayonnaise

Combine all ingredients and refrigerate overnight. Serve on lettuce leaves for an elegant salad course. Serves 6-8.

Serve with toothpicks for an appetizer.

Mrs. James Bettendorf (Berkeley Blake)

Salade Niçoise

2 large red potatoes
3 tablespoons red wine vinegar
1 teaspoon salt
½ teaspoon dry mustard
  Freshly ground pepper to taste
½ cup salad oil
3 tablespoons chopped parsley
3 green onions, chopped
  Salad greens

2 7-ounce cans tuna, chilled and drained
4 hard-boiled eggs, quartered
4 medium tomatoes, quartered
1 10-ounce package frozen whole green beans, cooked and chilled
1 cucumber sliced
  Anchovies and black olives (optional)

Peel, quarter and boil potatoes until barely tender. Drain, cool and cube. Mix next 5 ingredients. Toss potatoes with ¼ cup vinegar mixture, parsley and green onion. Chill. Line serving bowl with salad greens. Spoon in potato salad. Attractively arrange remaining ingredients on top. Drizzle remaining salad dressing over all. Serves 4.

Makes a great meal on hot summer days!

Mrs. Hershel P. Wall (Jean Harrington)

Baby Clark's Salad

1 12½-ounce can tuna in water, drained and flaked
2 16-ounce cans mixed vegetables, drained
1 10-ounce carton frozen peas, thawed and drained
6 stalks celery, finely chopped
1 medium onion, finely chopped
1 green pepper, finely chopped
6 eggs, hard-boiled and chopped

2 cups Creamettes or small elbow macaroni, cooked
1½-2 cups mayonnaise
1 tablespoon white vinegar
2 teaspoons prepared mustard
  Salt, pepper and paprika to taste

Mix all ingredients together. Serves 10-12.

Better if prepared a day before serving.

Mrs. Van Shapard, Jr.
Columbia, Tennessee

Hearty Tuna Salad

1   10-ounce package frozen
     green beans
1   7-ounce can tuna, drained
     and flaked
1   cup thinly sliced celery
½   cup mayonnaise or salad
     dressing

1   tablespoon freshly squeezed
     lemon juice
1½ teaspoons soy sauce
⅛   teaspoon garlic powder
1   cup chow mein noodles
     Lettuce

Cook green beans according to package directions, drain and cool. Combine green beans with next six ingredients. Chill. Before serving, add chow mein noodles to tuna mixture. Toss lightly. Serve on bed of lettuce. Serves 4.

Even better made a day ahead!

Mrs. Eugene Callicott (Mildred Morgan)

Salmon Mousse

1   envelope unflavored gelatin
¼   cup dry vermouth
½   cup boiling water
3   thin slices onion
2   teaspoons lemon juice
½   cup mayonnaise
1   teaspoon dry dill weed

1   tablespoon capers
½   teaspoon paprika
1   tablespoon Tabasco
1   teaspoon salt
1   15½-ounce can salmon,
     cleaned and drained
1   cup heavy cream, whipped

Dissolve gelatin in vermouth and boiling water. Add onion. Put in food processor with steel blade for 3-4 seconds. Add next 7 ingredients. Add salmon. Process 10 seconds. Fold whipped cream into mixture. Pour into greased 1-quart mold and chill. Serves 6-8.

Sour Cream Dill Sauce

1   egg
1   teaspoon salt
     Pinch of sugar
     Pinch of freshly ground black
     pepper
4   teaspoons lemon juice

1   teaspoon grated onion
2   tablespoons dill weed, fresh
     if possible, or 2 teaspoons
     dry
1½ cups sour cream

Blend all ingredients together in food processor. Chill and serve over mousse.

Mr. Haskins Ridens

Mother's Vegetable Salad

1½ cups water
1   3-ounce package lemon
    gelatin
½   cup vinegar
1   8-ounce can green peas,
    drained

1   8-ounce can French style
    green beans, drained
1   14-ounce can quartered
    artichokes, drained
½   cup black olives (optional)

Boil water and mix with gelatin until it is dissolved. Add vinegar. Pour into mold or 8-inch square pan. Chill until it begins to thicken. Add vegetables and chill until set. Serves 8-12.

Sauce
   Horseradish to taste
8 ounces sour cream

1   tablespoon mayonnaise

Mix small amount of horseradish with sour cream and mayonnaise. Refrigerate. Top each serving with sauce.

This is a nice change from the usual green salad, and would be pretty done in a mold and garnished with parsley and tomatoes.

Mrs. James B. Cross (Lynn Woods)

Gazpacho Aspic

4   cups V-8 juice, divided
1   rib celery
1   small onion, sliced
1   lemon, sliced
1   bay leaf
1   teaspoon salt
3   envelopes unflavored gelatin
¼   cup red wine vinegar
2   teaspoons lemon juice

2   teaspoons Worcestershire
    sauce
2   dashes Tabasco
¼   cup finely chopped celery
¼   cup finely chopped carrots
6   green onions, finely chopped
¼   cup finely chopped and
    seeded cucumber

Combine 3 cups V-8 juice with next 5 ingredients. Bring to a boil and simmer 10 minutes. Meanwhile, soften gelatin in remaining 1 cup V-8 juice and vinegar in a large bowl. When soft, pour in hot, strained V-8 and stir until gelatin is dissolved. Add lemon juice, Worcestershire and Tabasco. Refrigerate, stirring occasionally, until mixture thickens. When thickened, fold in chopped vegetables. Pour into oiled 6-cup mold or individual molds and refrigerate until firm. Unmold on lettuce and serve with mayonnaise. Serves 8-10.

Mrs. William C. Harris (Ann Clark Quinlen)

Congealed Asparagus Salad

½ tablespoon unflavored gelatin
¼ cup cold water
1 cup boiling water
1 3-ounce package lime gelatin
¼ cup grated Cheddar cheese

1 tablespoon grated onion
1 tablespoon vinegar
1 teaspoon salt
½ cup mashed asparagus
1 cup mayonnaise

Soften unflavored gelatin in cold water. Pour boiling water over lime gelatin. Add softened gelatin and remaining ingredients, except mayonnaise, to lime gelatin. Mix well. Add mayonnaise. Pour into an 8-inch square pan or 8 small individual molds. Cut into squares or unmold on lettuce. Serves 8.

Mrs. J. Michael Gregory

Mrs. William B. Nobles (Peggy Hall)

Cold Broccoli Mold

1 3-ounce package cream cheese
2 10-ounce packages frozen chopped broccoli, cooked and drained
1 10¾-ounce can condensed chicken broth

1 envelope unflavored gelatin
1 cup mayonnaise
2 hard-cooked eggs, chopped
⅛ teaspoon Tabasco sauce
Salad greens and radish roses
8 ounces sour cream

Dice cream cheese and let stand at room temperature to soften. To hot broccoli, add cream cheese and stir until melted. Pour half of chicken broth into small pan. Sprinkle gelatin into broth and allow to soften, about 5 minutes. Stir over low heat until gelatin is dissolved. Use a rubber spatula and scrape down sides. Stir gelatin into broccoli. One at a time, stir in mayonnaise, eggs, Tabasco and remaining cold broth. Refrigerate, stirring often, until chilled and partly thickened. Turn into a 6-cup mold and chill until set. Unmold onto lettuce greens and garnish with radish roses. Top with sour cream. Serves 10-12.

You may substitute spinach or asparagus for the broccoli.

Mrs. Lucian Wadlington (Patsy Mullins)

Cucumber Salad Mold

1 3-ounce package lime gelatin
¾ cup hot water
2 3-ounce packages cream
   cheese, softened
1 cup mayonnaise
1 tablespoon prepared
   horseradish
¼ teaspoon salt

2 tablespoons lemon juice
¾ cup drained, shredded
   cucumber
¼ cup finely sliced green onions
   Cottage cheese
   Sliced cucumber
   Watercress

Dissolve gelatin in hot water. Add cream cheese, mayonnaise, salt and horseradish. Beat with electric beater until smooth. Add lemon juice. Chill until partially set. Stir in onion and cucumber. Turn into 3-cup mold or individual molds. Chill until set. Unmold and garnish with cottage cheese, sliced cucumber and watercress. Serves 6.

Mrs. William B. Nobles (Peggy Hall)

Tomato Aspic

1 46-ounce can V-8 juice
4 envelopes gelatin
1 onion, grated
1 cup chopped celery
1 green pepper, grated
2 bay leaves

1 tablespoon Worcestershire
   sauce
1 14-ounce can artichoke hearts
   Seasoned salt and pepper to
   taste

Dissolve gelatin in 2 cups V-8 juice. Put remaining juice in pan and bring to a boil. Add gelatin and remaining ingredients to juice. Boil about 15 minutes and pour into oiled mold or 9x13-inch Pyrex dish. Refrigerate overnight. Serves 8-10.

Mrs. Charles H. Davis, Jr. (Mary O'Ryan)

Frozen Tomato Salad

3 8-ounce cans tomato sauce
1 cup Hellmann's mayonnaise
3 tablespoons strained lemon
   juice

4 drops Tabasco
1 tablespoon grated onion
1 tablespoon celery seed
   Salt to taste

Mix all ingredients with a wire whisk and pour into an oiled 9-inch square pan. Cover and freeze. This will keep one month. Cut into squares when ready to serve. Makes 9 squares.

This is delicious with roast and is an easy company dish.

Mrs. Gus Denton (Candy Stanley)

Frozen Tomato Surprise

1 envelope unflavored gelatin
1 28-ounce can tomatoes,
   reserving juice
1½ cups mayonnaise
   Juice of 1 lemon

1 teaspoon Worcestershire
   sauce
2 teaspoons chopped onion
1 teaspoon salt
   Dash of pepper

Dissolve gelatin in ⅓ cup juice from tomatoes. Put all in blender. Freeze overnight, stirring 2 or 3 times as it freezes. Serves 8.

Mrs. Jon K. Thompson (Susan Taylor)

Dieter's Delight

12 ounces cottage cheese
2 green onions, chopped
½ green pepper, chopped
½ carrot, chopped

½ tomato, chopped
½ cucumber, chopped
   Salt to taste
   Pepper to taste

Combine all ingredients. Prepare ahead of time to bring out the flavor. Serves 2-4.

Mrs. Gwin Scott (Wynn Skipper)

Creamy Marinated Vegetables

1 10-ounce package frozen
  broccoli
1 10-ounce package frozen
  French style green beans
1 10-ounce package frozen
  asparagus
1 small onion, thinly sliced
1 14-ounce can artichokes,
  quartered

1 small cucumber, thinly sliced
8 ounces fresh mushrooms,
  sliced
1 cup light cream
¼ cup mayonnaise
⅛ cup garlic wine vinegar
⅛ cup lemon juice
  Parsley
  Salt and pepper

Cook frozen vegetables until tender, but do not overcook. Put cooked vegetables, onion, artichokes, cucumber and mushrooms in a 3-quart Pyrex dish. Mix the rest of the ingredients in a small bowl and pour over vegetables. Marinate for at least 24 hours in refrigerator, stirring several times. Serves 10.

A different way to serve vegetables!

Mrs. Thomas Shipmon, III (Brokke Bilbrey)

Seven-Layer Salad

1 head iceberg lettuce
1 10-ounce package English
  peas, unthawed
½ head cauliflower, chopped
4-6 green onions, chopped
1-1½ cups mayonnaise
2 tablespoons McCormick's
  Salad Supreme

½ cup Parmesan cheese
6 slices bacon, cooked and
  crumbled
1 8-ounce can water chestnuts,
  sliced

Layer ingredients in order given. Cover tightly and chill overnight. When ready to serve, toss lightly. Serves 8-10.

Mrs. Forrest N. Jenkins (Linda Bauer)

Layered Gazpacho Salad

1 6-ounce box seasoned
   croutons
4 fresh tomatoes, diced
1 cucumber, peeled and thinly
   sliced
½ cup chopped onion
½ cup chopped green pepper
½ cup chopped celery

1 quart Hellmann's
   mayonnaise
3 tablespoons lemon juice
½ teaspoon Lawry's seasoned
   salt
Pepper, freshly ground
   (optional)

Sprinkle ⅓ of croutons over the bottom of a 2-quart casserole. Layer ½ of the following ingredients: tomatoes, cucumbers, onions, green pepper and celery. Mix mayonnaise, lemon juice and Lawry's salt and spread ½ of mixture over top. Repeat layers ending with last ⅓ of croutons. Refrigerate for 24 hours. Serves 8-10.

Prepare day ahead. Great with roast beef sandwiches for a casual supper!

Mrs. Burdette Russ (Scottie McCord)

Winter Salad

⅓ cup white vinegar
1 cup salad oil
1½ tablespoons sugar
½ small onion, coarsely
   chopped
2 teaspoons paprika
¼ teaspoon garlic powder

Salt and pepper to taste
Salad greens
2 avocados, peeled and sliced
3 small yellow squash, thinly
   sliced
½ cup sliced black olives

Make dressing by blending first 7 ingredients in blender or food processor. At serving time, arrange greens, avocado slices and squash on salad plates. Sprinkle with black olive slices and drizzle salad dressing on top. Serves 6.

Mrs. Hershel P. Wall (Jean Harrington)

Pickled Green Beans

2 28-ounce cans cut green
   beans, drained
2 cups sugar
2 cups vinegar
1 large onion, sliced

3 tablespoons oil
2 cloves garlic, chopped
1 teaspoon each salt and
   pepper

Mix and chill at least 24 hours before serving. Keeps indefinitely in refrigerator.

Delicious in a tossed salad or served alone.

Mrs. Floyd James, Jr. (Tempe Walker)

Salad Sutherland

2 16-ounce cans French style
   green beans
1 8-ounce bottle Wishbone
   Italian dressing
½ cup mayonnaise
½ cup sour cream
1 teaspoon lemon juice

Salt and pepper to taste
1 tablespoon Old Shedd's
   Sauce
Lettuce
4 firm ripe tomatoes
Dill weed

Marinate green beans in Wishbone dressing overnight. Make sauce of mayonnaise, sour cream, lemon juice and Old Shedd's. On lettuce leaf, place 2 slices of tomato and ½ cup of beans. Sprinkle with dill and top with sauce. Serves 8.

Mrs. Art Sutherland

Bean-Sprout Salad

1 cup vinegar
1 cup sugar
1 teaspoon soy sauce
3 tablespoons oil
1 16-ounce can bean sprouts,
   drained

1 16-ounce can French style
   green beans, drained
¼ cup chopped pimiento
½ cup chopped celery
⅓ cup chopped green onion

In a small saucepan, heat vinegar and sugar to a boil until sugar is dissolved. Remove from heat and add soy sauce and oil. Cool. In a medium bowl combine vegetables. Pour vinegar over and toss. Cover and chill. Serves 6.

Will keep for 2 weeks.

Mrs. Jere Fones (Ellen Kimbrough)

Chinese Wonder Salad

1 16-ounce can Chinese
vegetables
1 16-ounce can French style
green beans
1 17-ounce can tiny English
peas
1 8½-ounce can water
chestnuts, sliced

2 cups diced celery
1 onion, thinly sliced and
separated into rings
1 cup sugar
¾ cup cider vinegar
2 tablespoons tarragon vinegar
Salt and pepper to taste

Mix all ingredients together. Marinate overnight in refrigerator. Serves 10-12.

Mrs. Marshall Criss (Mary Jane Irvine)

Broccoli Salad

1 bunch fresh broccoli
2 tablespoons chopped red
onion
6-8 mushrooms, sliced

1 envelope Good Seasons Mild
Italian dressing
4 slices bacon, fried crisp and
crumbled

Put fresh vegetables in bowl. Prepare Good Seasons dressing according to directions and pour over vegetables. This may be made a day ahead. Sprinkle crumbled bacon over salad before serving. Serves 6-8.

Easy but fancy enough for your next dinner party.

Mrs. Will Hergenrader

Broccoli and Cauliflower Marinade

1 garlic clove
½ cup cider vinegar
½ cup white vinegar
1½ cups olive oil
1 tablespoon dill weed
1 tablespoon sugar
1 tablespoon Accent

1 teaspoon salt
1 teaspoon pepper
1 teaspoon garlic powder
1 head cauliflower, broken into
flowerets
2 bunches broccoli, broken into
flowerets

Rub glass salad bowl with garlic. Mix next 9 ingredients. Marinate cauliflower and broccoli for 12 hours in mixture. Stir occasionally. Drain and serve. Serves 12.

Mrs. James Green (Betty Brown)

Cauliflower Salad

1 medium head cauliflower
1 small head iceberg lettuce, shredded
1 pound bacon, cooked and crumbled

2-4 tablespoons sugar
¼ cup Parmesan cheese, grated
1 cup mayonnaise

Wash cauliflower, remove green leaves and break into flowerets. In a large bowl, layer all ingredients in order given. Toss lightly before serving. Serves 10-12

Wonderful crunchy substitute for potato salad.

Mrs. Dennis Higdon (Joanna Coss)

Cauliflower Salad Denman

1 cauliflower, separated into flowerets and sliced
2 ribs celery, chopped
1 green pepper, chopped
¾ cup sliced stuffed olives
3 tablespoons olive juice

½ pound Cheddar cheese, cut in tiny cubes
1 8-ounce bottle Caesar salad dressing
8 ounces sour cream

Combine all ingredients. Refrigerate several hours or overnight. Serves 6-8.

Even children love it!

Mrs. William E. Denman, III (Julie Moss)

Kraut Salad

1 28-ounce can sauerkraut, drained
2 tomatoes, peeled and diced
2 small green onions, finely sliced

2 tablespoons chopped parsley
¼ green pepper, diced
4 tablespoons oil
1½ tablespoons wine vinegar
½ teaspoon fresh pepper

Toss and chill. Serves 6-8.

Mrs. Thomas Holloman (Jayne Pressgrove)

Sauerkraut Ambrosia

1 28-ounce can sauerkraut,
   undrained
1 cup chopped celery
1 large onion, chopped

1 2-ounce jar chopped
   pimientos
1 cup sugar
1 cup chopped green pepper

Mix and marinate overnight. Serves 6-8.

Very unusual!

Mrs. Thomas F. Gaines, III (Layne Beaumont)

Spinach-Cottage Cheese Salad

1 10-ounce package frozen
   chopped spinach, cooked,
   drained and cooled
12 ounces small curd cottage
   cheese
3 green onions, finely chopped

1 tablespoon mayonnaise
   Salt and pepper to taste
1 pimiento, drained and finely
   chopped

Mix all ingredients together. Serve as salad in whole tomato or lettuce leaf. Can also be served as spread on saltines or Triscuits. Serves 4-6.

Great for lunch and very low-cal.

Mrs. John Klettner (Virginia Hays)

French Potato Salad

12 or more new potatoes
1 cup finely chopped green
   onion
1½ teaspoons salt
½ teaspoon ground black
   pepper

4 tablespoons olive oil
1 tablespoon wine vinegar
¼ cup chopped parsley
1 teaspoon chopped chives

Cook new potatoes in jackets and peel while warm. Cut into bite-sized pieces. Toss while warm with onions, salt, pepper and olive oil. Add vinegar. Toss again and cool at room temperature, not in refrigerator. Just before serving, toss again and add parsley and chives. Serves 4.

Mrs. Sam A. Gassaway, Jr. (Barbara Billings)

Fire and Ice Tomatoes

¾ cup vinegar
1½ teaspoons celery salt
1½ teaspoons mustard seed
½ teaspoon salt
5 teaspoons sugar
⅛ teaspoon black pepper

¼ cup cold water
6 large ripe tomatoes, peeled
    and quartered
1 green pepper, sliced in rings
1 medium onion, sliced in rings
1 cucumber, peeled and sliced

Mix first 7 ingredients in saucepan. Bring to boil and simmer for 1 minute. Pour hot mixture over tomatoes, green pepper and onion. Cover and place in refrigerator to chill. Before serving, add cucumber. Serve very cold on lettuce. Serves 8-10.

Mrs. Harte Thomas, Jr. (Patty Jenkins)

Lynette's Tomato Salad

6 ripe tomatoes, peeled and
    cored
¼ cup chopped parsley
1 clove garlic, crushed
1 teaspoon salt
1 teaspoon sugar

¼ teaspoon pepper
¼ cup oil
2 tablespoons tarragon or cider
    vinegar
2 teaspoons prepared mustard

Put tomatoes in glass dish with sides. Shake together remaining ingredients. Pour over tomatoes and into cores. Let sit at least 20 minutes. Before serving, slice and salt tomatoes. Serves 6.

Mrs. Earle Wrenn

French Tomato Salad

4   medium-sized ripe tomatoes,
     sliced vertically
3   tablespoons chopped green
     onion
3   tablespoons chopped parsley
1   pinch sugar
     Salt and pepper to taste

     Salad greens
2   tablespoons red wine vinegar
⅛   teaspoon salt
¼   teaspoon dry mustard
6   tablespoons salad oil
     Pepper, freshly ground

Line plate with salad greens and arrange tomato slices on top. Sprinkle with green onions, parsley, sugar, salt and pepper. Shake together last 5 ingredients and pour over tomatoes. Refrigerate for 30 minutes before serving. Serves 4.

Easy and delicious.

Mrs. Charlie Carr
Chapel Hill, North Carolina

Tomato-Corn Salad

2   large tomatoes, peeled and
     diced
1   12-ounce can Niblets corn,
     drained
2   green onions, chopped, using
     only white parts

     A grind or 2 of fresh pepper
¼   cup Hellmann's mayonnaise
4   lettuce cups

Add drained corn to diced tomatoes. Add green onions, pepper and enough mayonnaise to hold it together. Chill and serve in lettuce cups with a dollop of mayonnaise on top. Serves 4.

Different way to serve homegrown tomatoes.

Mrs. Robert Khayat
Oxford, Mississippi

Stuffed Tomato Salad

Firm, ripe tomatoes, cored with
  pulp scooped out
Salt, pepper and dill weed
Tomato pulp
Celery
Onion

Cucumber
Green pepper
Mayonnaise
Lemon
Parsley

Season tomatoes with salt, pepper and dill. Chop equal amounts of vegetables and mix with tomato pulp. Add mayonnaise and lemon juice to taste. Stuff tomatoes with vegetable mixture and top with snipped parsley.

Great luncheon salad!

Mrs. L. Charles Schaffler

Zucchini Salad Toss

1 head iceberg lettuce, cut in
    bite-sized pieces
1 head romaine lettuce, cut in
    bite-sized pieces
2 medium zucchini, thinly
    sliced

2 tablespoons sliced green
    onions
3 tablespoons salad oil

Toss vegetables in oil until leaves glisten. Toss again with garlic dressing. Serves 6-8.

Dressing
2 tablespoons tarragon vinegar
1½ teaspoons salt

1 crushed garlic clove
    Dash of pepper
    Dash of Accent

Combine dressing ingredients.

Mrs. Robert M. Williams, (Julia Gray)

Blender "Homemade" Mayonnaise

2 eggs
1 teaspoon dry mustard
1 teaspoon salt
½ teaspoon sugar
½ teaspoon paprika

2 dashes cayenne pepper
4 tablespoons lemon juice
2 tablespoons vinegar
2 cups salad oil, chilled

Place all ingredients, except oil, in blender. Add ¼ cup of chilled oil and blend on "chop" for 5 seconds. Stop blender. Then start blender again, pouring remainder of chilled oil in a fine stream. Makes approximately 3 cups.

Simple, foolproof, and very good!

Mrs. J. R. Mann
Montgomery, Alabama

Blue Goddess Salad Dressing

1 cup mayonnaise
½ cup sour cream
¼ cup minced fresh parsley
1 tablespoon lemon juice
1½ tablespoons anchovy paste

1 clove garlic, crushed
1 teaspoon minced green onion
3 ounces Roquefort or blue
   cheese, crumbled

Mix all ingredients together and refrigerate. Best made day before serving or very early on day of serving. Makes 1 pint.

Mrs. William E. Denman, III (Julie Moss)

Dill Salad Dressing

⅔ cup oil
¼ cup red wine vinegar
1 teaspoon sugar
1 teaspoon salt
   Freshly ground pepper

1 teaspoon Dijon mustard
1 garlic clove, split
¼ teaspoon dill weed
¼ teaspoon oregano

Shake all ingredients together. Remove garlic before serving. Makes about 1 cup.

Mrs. Malcolm McLean, III
Lumberton, North Carolina

Divine Dressing

1 teaspoon garlic powder	¼ teaspoon Accent
1½ tablespoons salt	1 teaspoon oregano
1½ tablespoons dry mustard	6 tablespoons cider vinegar
1 egg	2 cups oil
⅛ teaspoon pepper	½ cup water

Mix together first 7 ingredients with a rotary beater. Add vinegar and beat until egg foams on top. Add salad oil, ½ cup at a time, and beat. Add water and beat. Refrigerate 1 hour before serving. Makes 1 quart.

Even easier with a blender.

Mrs. Jackson Watts Moore (Betty Wilson)

Honey French Salad Dressing

1 small onion, diced	1 teaspoon salt
1 cup salad oil	¼ teaspoon pepper
½ cup sugar	¼ teaspoon paprika
½ cup vinegar	Juice of 1 lemon
½ cup ketchup	

Put all ingredients in jar and shake. Will keep in refrigerator indefinitely. Makes approximately 3 cups.

Mrs. J. Logan Morgan

Honey-Rum Cream Dressing or Dip

1 cup heavy cream	2 tablespoons honey
Juice of 1 lemon	2 tablespoons dark rum
Grated rind of 1 lemon	

Whip cream. Mix with other ingredients and chill. Makes approximately 1 cup.

Delicious over fruit salads or as a dip for fresh fruits.

Mrs. Frank E. Reid (Diana Mann)

Le Ruth's Italian Dressing

3-4 garlic cloves, chopped
¼ teaspoon oregano
⅛ teaspoon red pepper flakes
¼ cup white vinegar

½ cup plus 2 tablespoons corn oil
1½ teaspoons salt
1½ teaspoons sugar
3 tablespoons water

Place in bottle and shake well. Make a day in advance and refrigerate.

For Italian Gorgonzola Dressing, add 2 ounces crumbled Gorgonzola cheese to above recipe.

Le Ruth's Restaurant
Gretna, Louisiana

Peggy's Salad Dressing

1 cup salad oil
1 cup sugar
1 cup white vinegar
1 medium green pepper, chopped
1 2-ounce jar chopped pimientos

1 medium white onion, chopped
3 teaspoons salt
3 teaspoons Worcestershire sauce
3 teaspoons prepared mustard

Mix all ingredients together. Chill and serve over lettuce. Best made the day before. Makes 1 quart.

Mrs. William T. Reid

Poppy Seed Dressing

1½ cups sugar
2 teaspoons dry mustard
2 teaspoons salt
⅔ cup vinegar

3 tablespoons onion juice
1¾ cups salad oil
3 tablespoons poppy seeds

Mix first 4 ingredients. Add onion juice and stir thoroughly. Add oil slowly, beating constantly, and continue to beat until thick. Add poppy seeds and beat a few minutes. The secret is fresh onion juice, obtained by grating a large white onion and straining out the juice. Serves 8-10.

Mrs. Stephen L. Gammill (Mary Ann Perich)

Mrs. W. Jeffries Mann

Red, White and Blue Dressing

½ onion, finely chopped
½ green pepper, finely chopped
1½ cups ketchup
1 cup mayonnaise
1 teaspoon paprika

¼ teaspoon Worcestershire
   sauce
⅛ teaspoon garlic powder
   Cayenne pepper to taste
4 ounces blue cheese, crumbled

Mix together all ingredients. This will be lumpy. Keeps refrigerated for several weeks. Makes one quart.

Great as dip with fresh vegetables. Can be made in blender. Don't process after adding cheese.

Mrs. Charles D. Schaffler (Mickey Pooley)

Sour Cream Dressing

2 tablespoons minced green
   onion, including green top
1 tablespoon anchovy paste
2 tablespoons lemon juice
2 tablespoons white wine
   vinegar

⅛ teaspoon dried, crushed
   tarragon
8 ounces sour cream
½ cup mayonnaise

Mix all ingredients together. Cover and chill. Makes 1½ cups.

Mrs. Lucian Wadlington (Patsy Mullins)

Thousand Island Dressing

1 cup mayonnaise
½ cup ketchup
¾ cup sweet pickle relish

½ teaspoon Worcestershire
   sauce
2 hard-boiled eggs, chopped

Mix well and refrigerate. Makes 1 pint.

So easy to be so good.

Le Ruth's Restaurant
Gretna, Louisiana

Sweet and Sour Dressing for Potato Salad

5 slices bacon
⅓ teaspoon salt
½ teaspoon paprika
¼ teaspoon pepper

¼ teaspoon dry mustard
3 tablespoons cider vinegar
⅓ cup water
1 teaspoon sugar

Chop bacon finely and fry in skillet on low heat until brown. Stir in next 4 ingredients. Mix vinegar with water and sugar. Add bacon. Cook and stir over low heat 5 minutes. Let dressing cool. Makes 1 cup.

Mrs. George Long (Rosa Nelle Ransom)

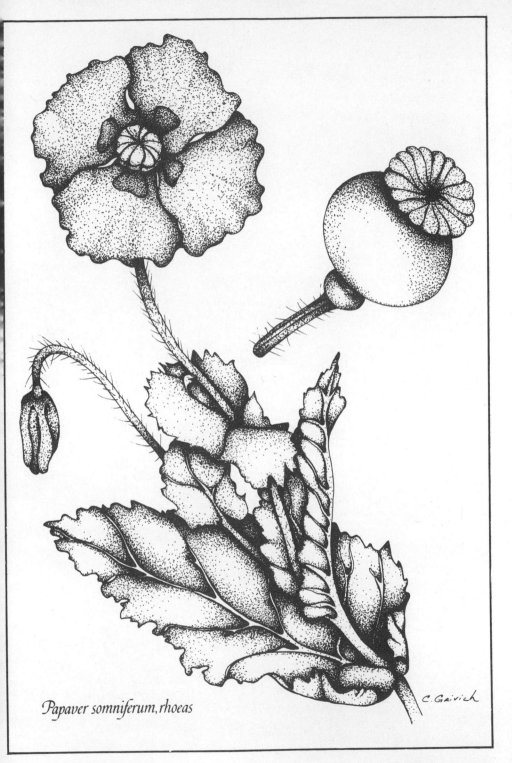

Papaver somniferum, rhoeas

C. Grivich

Breads

Company Pancake for Two

½ cup flour
½ cup milk
¼ teaspoon salt
2 eggs
1 cup blueberries, thoroughly
   drained

4 tablespoons butter
1 lemon
Powdered sugar

Preheat oven to 450° F. Blend flour, milk, salt and eggs. Fold in blue-berries very carefully. In black iron skillet, pour batter into sizzling butter. Bake 15 minutes. Remove from heat and squeeze lemon over the pancake. Sprinkle liberally with powdered sugar. This should be served in the skillet. Recipe may be doubled.

Any fruit may be substituted for the blueberries.

Mrs. Kay K. Butler (Kay Kendall)

Popovers

2 eggs
1 cup milk
1 tablespoon butter, melted

1 cup flour
¼ teaspoon salt

Beat eggs until light. Add remaining ingredients and beat until blended. Batter should be like heavy cream. Fill well-greased muffin tins or custard cups ½ full. Bake at 450° F. for 20 minutes; reduce heat to 350° F. and bake 20 minutes longer. Yields 12 popovers.

Mrs. R. Franklin Adams (Corinne Ridolphi)

Beignets I

2½ cups flour
1 tablespoon sugar
1 teaspoon salt
3 teaspoons baking powder

3 eggs, beaten
1 cup milk
Oil
Powdered sugar

Blend together all ingredients except oil and powdered sugar. Have oil hot enough so beignets will sizzle when cooked. Drop mixture by ta-blespoons into hot oil and fry until golden. They will become light and rise to the top of the oil. Drain on paper towels and sprinkle with pow-dered sugar. They must be eaten while hot. Serves 6-8.

Julia Dupuis Huval
Cecilia, Louisiana

Beignets II

1 8-ounce package crescent Powdered sugar
   rolls
   Oil

Divide and cut crescent triangles in half. Deep fry in hot oil, turning to get both sides golden brown. Drain on paper towels and sprinkle with lots of powdered sugar. Oil should be deep enough to cover beignets. A heavy sauce pan may be used. Makes 16 beignets.

Easy French donuts.

Mrs. Charles Frankum (Linda Lacey)

Applesauce Puffs

2 cups biscuit mix   ¼ cup milk
½ cup sugar, divided   1 egg, lightly beaten
1¼ teaspoons cinnamon, divided   2 tablespoons oil
½ cup applesauce   2 tablespoons butter, melted

Combine biscuit mix, ¼ cup sugar and 1 teaspoon cinnamon. Add next 4 ingredients and beat well for 30 seconds. Fill greased muffin pans ⅔ full. Bake at 400° F. for 12 minutes or until lightly browned. Cool slightly. Combine ¼ cup sugar and ¼ teaspoon cinnamon. Dip tops of muffins into melted butter, then sugar-cinnamon mixture.

Great for breakfast or brunch.

Mrs. Jack Moran

Biscuit Coffee Cake

¾ cup sugar
1 teaspoon cinnamon
½ cup chopped nuts

4 large cans Hungry Jack Biscuits

Sauce
1 cup sugar
1½ sticks margarine

1 teaspoon cinnamon

Combine sugar, cinnamon, and nuts in a baggie. Cut each biscuit into quarters. Put quartered biscuits into baggie and shake to coat. Place coated biscuits in a greased bundt pan, sprinkling remainder of sugar mixture over biscuits. Pour sauce over biscuits. Bake at 350° F. for 40-45 minutes. Let stand 15 minutes before serving. Serves 12.

Boil sauce until it reaches pouring consistency.

Mrs. James A. Breazeale (Beth Baker)

Inverted Coffee Cake

Topping
5½ tablespoons butter
½ cup brown sugar, firmly
  packed

½ cup chopped nuts
1 teaspoon cinnamon
1 teaspoon nutmeg

Melt butter in 8-inch pan in oven. Mix together remaining ingredients and sprinkle evenly over butter. Set aside.

Cake
½ stick butter
1 cup brown sugar
2 eggs
1 tablespoon orange rind,
  grated
½ teaspoon vanilla

1½ cups sifted flour
1 teaspoon baking powder
½ teaspoon soda
¼ teaspoon salt
¾ cup buttermilk

In mixing bowl, cream butter, gradually adding sugar. Beat until light and fluffy. Beat in eggs, one at a time. Blend in orange rind and vanilla. Sift together next 4 ingredients. Add to creamed mixture, alternating with buttermilk. Spread batter over topping in 8-inch pan. Bake 45-50 minutes at 350° F. Invert onto plate. Serves 9.

Mrs. William Watson (Pattie Walker)

Streusel Coffee Cake

Cake

1 cup sugar	1 teaspoon soda
2 sticks butter	1 teaspoon baking powder
3 eggs	8 ounces sour cream
2 cups flour	

Cream sugar and butter. Add eggs, one at a time, beating well after each. Sift next 3 ingredients into mixture. Add sour cream and blend all together.

Filling

1 cup brown sugar	2 tablespoons cinnamon
1 cup chopped pecans	2 tablespoons butter, melted
2 tablespoons flour	

Blend all filling ingredients together. Pour half the batter into buttered tube pan. Add half the filling. Repeat. Bake at 350° F. for 45 minutes.

Makes a lovely Christmas present.

Mrs. Robert Norton

Texas Coffee Cake

2 sticks butter	1 teaspoon baking powder
2 cups sugar	8 ounces sour cream
2 eggs	½ teaspoon vanilla
2 cups flour	¼ teaspoon salt

Cream butter, sugar and eggs. Sift flour and baking powder and add to batter. Add sour cream and vanilla and beat 4-5 minutes. Pour ½ of batter into bundt pan and sprinkle ½ topping onto batter. Spread remaining batter, then remaining topping. Bake at 350° F. for 45 minutes.

Cinnamon Topping

½ teaspoon cinnamon	2 tablespoons sugar
1 cup chopped pecans	

Combine topping ingredients.

Wonderful!

Mrs. John Albritton (Patsy Thomas)

Party Coffee Cake

½ cup shortening
½ cup sugar
½ teaspoon vanilla
1 egg
½ cup flour

½ teaspoon salt
1½ teaspoons baking powder
½ cup milk
¼ cup chopped nuts

Cream shortening, sugar and vanilla. Add egg and beat thoroughly. Add sifted dry ingredients alternately with milk. Spread ½ of batter in greased 8-inch square pan. Cover with date filling. Add remaining batter. Bake at 350° F. for 45 minutes. Top with nuts.

Date Filling
½ cup brown sugar
1 tablespoon flour
1 tablespoon cinnamon

½ stick butter, melted
¼ cup chopped dates

Combine all filling ingredients.

Tasty and different!

Mrs Fletcher Johnson (Jo Ann Hawkes)

Quick Buttermilk Drop Biscuits

2 cups flour
3 teaspoons baking powder
½ teaspoon salt
½ teaspoon soda

4 tablespoons shortening
1 tablespoon bacon drippings
1 cup buttermilk

Mix dry ingredients. Cut in shortening and bacon drippings. Add buttermilk and mix well. Drop on lightly greased cookie sheet by teaspoon and bake at 375° F. until golden brown. Makes 20 biscuits. Can be frozen before baking.

Mrs. Raymond E. Henley (Kim Baxter)

Pecan Party Biscuits

2 cups flour
3 teaspoons baking powder
3 tablespoons sugar
1 stick margarine

½ cup broken pecans
½ cup milk
1 egg, lightly beaten

Sift dry ingredients together. Cut margarine into flour mixture with pastry blender or fork until mixture is the consistency of cornmeal. Add pecans. Combine milk and egg. Add to flour mixture and stir with a fork. Turn dough onto lightly floured board and knead two or three times. Roll dough ⅓-inch thick. Cut into 1-inch rounds with floured cutter. Bake on cookie sheet 12-15 minutes in 425° F. oven. Yields 3-4 dozen.

Great for luncheons!

Mrs. George M. Klepper, Jr. (Gladys Dye)

Sanksy's Corn Bread

2 cups self-rising corn meal
1 cup flour
¼ cup sugar
2 eggs

1¾ cups buttermilk
1 teaspoon salt
½ cup shortening

Mix first 6 ingredients well. Melt ¼ cup shortening in each of 2 bread pans or 1 large iron skillet. After pans are very hot, pour in batter and bake at 425° F. for 25-30 minutes. This can easily be divided in half. Makes two loaves or 1 large skillet of corn bread.

The best! If made in loaf pans, it is great sliced cool for sandwiches.

Mrs. Carl H. Langschmidt, Jr. (Paula Rainey)

Bea's Light Corn Bread

2 cups white corn meal
½ cup flour
¾ cup sugar or molasses
½ teaspoon soda

1 teaspoon salt
1 teaspoon dry yeast
2 cups buttermilk
3 tablespoons melted shortening

Sift together first 5 ingredients. Add yeast, buttermilk and shortening. Stir until just mixed. Bake in greased loaf pan at 350° F. for 1 hour. Let cool for 15 minutes before turning out. Serves 10-12.

Easy to make! Great "down home" cooking.

Mrs. Dudley Bridgforth (Donna Kay Byrd)

Cheese Corn Bread

1 cup yellow corn meal
1 cup sifted flour
¼ cup sugar
½ teaspoon salt
4 teaspoons baking powder

1½ cups grated sharp cheese
1 egg
1 cup milk
¼ cup shortening

Sift together dry ingredients. Add remaining ingredients and beat until smooth. Pour in greased 8-inch square pan. Bake 30 minutes at 375° F. Serves 8.

Mrs. Walter P. Wills, Jr. (Dorothy Kirby)

Good Corn Bread

1½ cups self-rising corn meal
¾ cup oil
½ cup finely chopped onion

2 eggs
8 ounces sour cream
1 8-ounce can cream-style corn

Mix all ingredients together well. Heat a 10-inch iron skillet in 400° F. oven until hot. Put 1 tablespoon oil in skillet until heated. Pour off hot oil into cornbread and stir quickly. Pour batter into skillet. Bake 20 minutes or until brown.

Mrs. Scott Arnold, III (Anne Dillard)

Hush Puppies

1 cup pancake mix	¼ teaspoon black pepper
⅓ cup plain corn meal	1 cup finely chopped onion
½ teaspoon garlic salt	1 egg, beaten
½ teaspoon baking powder	⅓ cup buttermilk

Sift first 5 ingredients. When ready to fry, mix in last 3 ingredients. Drop by teaspoon into deep fat heated to 325° F. Fry hushpuppies on all sides until golden brown. Drain on paper towels. If serving with fish, fry in grease used for fish. One batch serves 6 people.

You will like these as much as the fish!

Mr. Frank H. Reid

Spoon Bread

1 cup corn meal	1 cup milk
2 cups milk	3 egg yolks, well beaten
1 teaspoon salt	3 egg whites, beaten until stiff
2 teaspoons baking powder	but not dry
2 tablespoons oil	

Preheat oven to 325° F. Cook cornmeal in 2 cups milk until mushy. Remove from heat and add salt, baking powder, oil and milk. Mix well. Add egg yolks and mix. Fold in egg whites. Pour into a well greased 2½-quart casserole and bake at 325° F. for 1½ hours.

Mrs. Henry B. Gotten

Sour Cream Tidbits

1 stick margarine	8 ounces sour cream
2 cups self-rising flour	

Melt margarine. Add to flour and sour cream and mix. Put in tiny muffin tins. Bake at 350° F. about 30 minutes. Do not use large muffin tins because it will not work. For a brunch, add approximately 8 teaspoons sugar and 4 teaspoons cinnamon. Makes about 3 dozen muffins.

For variations, add ½ cup grated sharp Cheddar cheese to flour mixture, or ½ teaspoon dill weed, or ½ teaspoon fine herbs or shake of onion powder. For a sweet treat, add ¼ cup sugar, 1 egg and ½ cup blueberries, raisins or dates.

Mrs. Larry Beech
Mendenhall, Mississippi

Mrs. Richard J. Reynolds (Anne Tuthill)

Beer Muffins

4 cups Bisquick	12 ounces beer, room
3-4 teaspoons sugar	temperature.

Grease muffin tins and warm slightly in 400° F. oven. Mix all ingredients and fill muffin tins ⅔ full. Bake 20-25 minutes or until brown. Makes about 2 dozen.

Quick and easy.

Mrs. Palmer K. Bartlett (Martha Williams)

Delicious Blueberry Muffins

2 cups flour
3 teaspoons baking powder
½ teaspoon salt
½ cup sugar
1 cup milk

1 egg, lightly beaten
½ stick melted butter
1 cup blueberries, fresh or
  frozen

Sift first four ingredients twice. Add milk and beaten egg to melted butter. Combine with dry ingredients, mixing just enough to moisten. Lightly fold in blueberries and fill well greased muffin tins no more than ⅔ full. Bake at 400° F. about 20 minutes or until lightly brown. Makes 12 muffins.

These rise high and are pretty!

Mrs. Julia Taylor

Bran Muffins

1 cup boiling water
1 cup Nabisco 100% Bran
  Cereal
½ cup shortening, rounded
1-1¼ cup sugar
2 eggs, room temperature
2 cups buttermilk, room
  temperature

2½ cups flour
2½ teaspoons soda
1 teaspoon salt
2 cups Kellogg's All-Bran
  Cereal
½ cup raisins (optional)
½ cup pecans (optional)

Pour boiling water over 100% Bran. Cream shortening and sugar. Add eggs, one at a time and cream well. Beat in cereal mixture and add buttermilk. Sift flour, soda and salt together. Add all at once to Kellogg's All-Bran Cereal. Mix well. Add raisins and nuts, if desired. Fill well-greased muffin pan ¾ full. Bake at 375° F. for 15 minutes. If covered, batter will keep indefinitely in refrigerator. Try storing in a pitcher—it will pour!

Delicious for the whole family.

Mrs. J. R. Mann
Montgomery, Alabama

Mrs. John McCallen (Ann Henderson)

281

Cheese Muffins

2 cups flour
4 teaspoons baking powder
1 teaspoon salt
¾ cup grated cheese

3 tablespoons butter, melted
⅞ cup milk
½ teaspoon dill weed (optional)

Sift dry ingredients. Stir in remaining ingredients and mix well. Bake in greased muffin tins for 15 minutes at 375° F. Makes about 18 medium-sized muffins.

Mrs. Fletcher Johnson (Jo Ann Hawkes)

Orange Muffins

2 orange rinds, grated
1 cup sugar
1 teaspoon soda
2 eggs
1 stick butter, melted

1 cup buttermilk
2 cups flour
1 cup chopped raisins
1 cup brown sugar
1 cup orange juice

Mix first 8 ingredients together and bake in muffin tins for 15 minutes at 400° F. Boil sugar and juice for 2-5 minutes. Use for dipping or pour over muffins.

Wonderful every time. If using a food processor to chop raisins, freeze slightly before chopping.

Mrs. J. Cash King (Mary Nance)

Vegetable Pull Apart Bread

1 stick butter
1 cup chopped zucchini
1 cup chopped onion
½ cup chopped green pepper
4 cans refrigerated biscuits, 8
   biscuits each, cut in half

½ cup crisply fried, crumbled
   bacon
¾ cup Parmesan cheese

Melt butter in skillet and sauté next three ingredients. Grease bundt pan. Put one layer of biscuits in bottom of pan. Follow with layers of ½ of the vegetables, bacon and cheese. Repeat these four layers and top with one layer of biscuits. Bake at 350° F. for 30-45 minutes.

Mrs. Jon K. Thompson (Susan Taylor)

Apricot Bread

1 cup dried apricots
1 cup sugar
2 tablespoons butter
1 egg
¼ cup water
½ cup orange juice

2 cups sifted flour
1½ teaspoons baking powder
½ teaspoon soda
1 teaspoon salt
½ cup chopped walnuts

Soak 1 cup of dried apricots in warm water for 30 minutes. Drain and dice. Can be put in a food processor. Set aside. Beat together sugar, butter and egg thoroughly. Stir in water and orange juice. Sift dry ingredients together and beat into sugar mixture. Blend in nuts and apricots. Pour batter in thoroughly greased 9x5-inch loaf pan. Allow to stand 20 minutes. Bake in 350° F. oven for 50-60 minutes. Remove and cool on wire rack for 5 minutes. Makes 1 loaf.

Wonderful with cream cheese.

Mrs. Huey L. Holden (Barbara Hopper)

Fresh Apple Bread

1 stick margarine
1 cup sugar
1 egg
2 cups flour
1 teaspoon soda

½ teaspoon ground cloves
1 teaspoon ground cinnamon
½ teaspoon salt
2 cups pared, chopped apples
⅔ cup chopped pecans

Cream together margarine and sugar. Add egg and beat well. Sift together dry ingredients and add to sugar mixture. Stir in apples and nuts. Pour into 9x5-inch greased loaf pan. Bake at 350° F. for 1 hour. Sprinkle with powdered sugar and slice. Makes 1 loaf.

Heat with butter for breakfast or serve with ice cream for dessert.

Mrs. Charles A. Williams III (Elise McDonald)

Applesauce Raisin Bread

1 stick butter
1 cup packed brown sugar
1 egg
1¾ cups flour
½ teaspoon salt
1 teaspoon cinnamon
½ teaspoon ground cloves

1 teaspoon soda
1 cup applesauce
1 cup raisins
8 ounces heavy cream,
    whipped, or 3 ounces
    cream cheese, softened

Cream butter and sugar. Add egg and mix. Add flour, salt and spices, mixing well. Stir in applesauce and raisins. Pour into two 1½-quart loaf pans and bake at 350° F. for 45-50 minutes. Top with whipped cream or cream cheese. Makes 2 loaves.

Can be done in a food processor.

Mrs. Jon K. Thompson (Susan Taylor)

Banana Nut Bread

1½ sticks butter
1½ cups sugar
3 eggs, separated
5 large bananas, mashed,
    about 1½ cups
½ cup milk

½ cup sour cream
3 cups flour
1½ teaspoons soda
¾ teaspoon salt
¾ cup finely chopped pecans

Grease and flour 4 small loaf pans or two 9x5-inch loaf pans. Cream butter and sugar. Add egg yolks, mixing well. Mix in bananas. Measure ½ cup milk and add sour cream to fill cup. Sift together flour, soda and salt. Add flour and milk mixture alternately to the banana mixture. Mix in pecans. Beat egg whites until stiff and fold into batter. Divide among loaf pans. Bake at 300° F. for 45-50 minutes. Cool on rack.

Mrs. Ernest Skipper
Jackson, Mississippi

Blueberry Bread

2 eggs
1 cup sugar
1 cup milk
½ stick butter, melted
3 cups flour

1 teaspoon salt
2½ teaspoons baking powder
2 cups blueberries, fresh,
   frozen or canned, without
   syrup

Beat eggs and sugar until well mixed. Add milk and butter. Sift together dry ingredients and add to sugar mixture just until combined. Toss berries in a little flour and add to batter. Pour into 2 small, or 1 large, well greased loaf pans. Bake at 350° F. for 30-40 minutes.

Mrs. Max Ostner, Jr. (Mary Margaret Buffa)

Lemon Tea Loaf

1 stick butter, softened
1 cup sugar
2 eggs, beaten
   Grated lemon peel

1½ cups flour
1 teaspoon baking powder
½ cup milk
½ cup chopped pecans

Cream butter with sugar until light and fluffy. Stir in eggs and lemon peel. Sift together flour and baking powder and add alternately with milk to egg mixture. Fold in pecans. Pour in greased 9x5-inch loaf pan and bake 45 minutes at 375° F. or until golden.

Glaze
¼ cup sugar
½ cup lemon juice

1 tablespoon grated lemon peel

Heat all glaze ingredients. After removing loaf from oven, make holes in loaf with toothpicks. Spread glaze over loaf and cool 10 minutes before removing from pan.

Mrs. Charles D. Schaffler (Mickey Pooley)

Carrot Bread

2 cups flour	1½ cups oil
2 teaspoons soda	2 tablespoons vanilla
½ teaspoon salt	3 eggs
2 teaspoons cinnamon	2 cups grated carrots
1½ cups sugar	

Sift dry ingredients in bowl. Add all other ingredients except carrots. Beat on medium speed until well blended. Fold in carrots. Turn into 2 greased and floured loaf pans. Bake at 300° F. for 1 hour.

Straight from the heart of Texas. Good with cream cheese.

Mrs. E. O. Edwards

Orange Nut Bread

3 cups flour, sifted	1½ teaspoons salt
1½ cups coarsely chopped pecans	Grated peel of large orange
1¼ cups sugar	3 eggs, lightly beaten
5 teaspoons baking powder	1½ cups milk
	⅓ cup salad oil

Preheat oven to 350° F. Grease 9x5-inch loaf pan. In large bowl, mix first 6 ingredients with a fork. In medium bowl, whisk together eggs, milk and salad oil. Stir into flour mixture just until moist. Pour batter evenly into loaf pan and bake 30-40 minutes, or until bread pulls away from pan. Cool in pan, then completely cool on rack. Makes 1 loaf.

Mrs. Alan Carey (Nancy Brunson)

Pumpkin Bread

2⅔ cups sugar
⅔ cup oil
4 eggs
2 cups pumpkin
3⅓ cups flour
½ teaspoon baking powder
2 teaspoons soda
1½ teaspoons salt

1 teaspoon cinnamon
½ teaspoon ground cloves
⅔ cup water
⅔ cup chopped pecans (optional)
⅔ cup chopped dates (optional)

Cream oil and sugar in large bowl. Add eggs one at a time, beating after each addition. Stir in pumpkin. Sift dry ingredients and beat into creamed mixture. Beat in water. Toss dates and nuts lightly with flour and add to batter. Place in 2 greased 9x5-inch loaf pans and bake at 350° F. for 1 hour. Makes 2 loaves.

Soften cream cheese in orange juice for a yummy spread.

Mrs. James B. Cross (Lynn Woods)

Strawberry Bread

3 cups flour
1 teaspoon soda
1 teaspoon salt
3 teaspoons cinnamon
2 cups sugar

1¼ cups oil
3 eggs, well beaten
2 10-ounce packages, frozen strawberries, thawed
1¼ cups chopped pecans

Sift dry ingredients in large bowl. Mix oil into eggs and add to flour mixture. Fold in strawberries and pecans and pour into 2 greased and floured 9x5-inch loaf pans. Bake at 350° F. for 1 hour and 20 minutes. Cool in pans for 15 minutes. Makes 2 loaves.

Mrs. Max B. Ostner, Jr. (Mary Margaret Buffa)

Zucchini Bread

3 eggs
2 cups sugar
1 cup oil
1 tablespoon vanilla
2 cups coarsely grated
   zucchini, unpeeled
2 cups flour

1 teaspoon cinnamon
2 teaspoons baking powder
1 teaspoon salt
¼ teaspoon soda
1 cup chopped pecans
8 ounces cream cheese
   (optional)

Beat eggs until frothy. Beat in sugar. Add oil and vanilla and beat until thick and lemon colored. Add loosely packed, grated zucchini. Sift together dry ingredients and add to egg mixture. Fold in pecans. Pour into 8x4-inch greased and floured loaf pan, or 3 small loaf pans. Bake at 350° F. for 1 hour. Bake 45 minutes for small loaves. Cool in pan 10 minutes. Serve plain or with cream cheese.

Mrs. Allen Carey (Nancy Brunson)

Rolls

2 cups milk
½ cup shortening
½ cup sugar
4 cups sifted flour
1½ teaspoons salt

½ teaspoon soda
1 teaspoon baking powder
1 package dry yeast
¼ cup lukewarm water

Combine first three ingredients and heat in saucepan but do not boil. Cool. Sift dry ingredients. Add to milk mixture mixing well. Dissolve yeast in water. Add yeast to dough, mix and let rise until double. Punch down and roll out, adding more flour if necessary. Cut with 2-inch biscuit cutter, dipping both sides of roll in melted butter. Fold over and let rise 2 hours. Bake at 400° F. 12-15 minutes. Dough is easier to work with if refrigerated after first rise. Makes approximately 4 dozen rolls.

Mrs. William M. Vaughan (Carmine Baker)

Mother's Refrigerator Rolls

1 cup hot water
1 teaspoon salt
6 tablespoons shortening
¼ cup sugar
1 package yeast

2 tablespoons lukewarm
   water
1 egg, beaten
3½-4 cups sifted flour

Combine hot water, salt, shortening and sugar in a large bowl. Cool to lukewarm. Add yeast, softened in 2 tablespoons of lukewarm water. Add egg and ½ the flour. Beat well. Stir in enough of remaining flour to make dough easily handled. Grease top of dough with oil. Cover and store in refrigerator. It keeps 4-5 days. Roll out on board. Cut into rolls with cutter. Place in greased pan and cover with towel. Let rise about 1½ hours. Bake at 425° F. for 15-20 minutes. Makes 2-2½ dozen.

Mrs. John Turley, III (Barbara Barham)

Whole Wheat Rolls

¾ cup boiling water
1 cup shortening
¾ cup sugar
3 cups flour
2 eggs
2 packages yeast

¼ cup lukewarm water
1 tablespoon salt
1 cup water
3 cups whole wheat flour
Melted butter

Boil water, shortening and sugar, stirring constantly. Let cool. Add plain flour, well-beaten eggs and yeast, which has been dissolved in ¼ cup lukewarm water. Beat well. Add salt and remaining water. Beat well. Add whole wheat flour. Refrigerate several hours or overnight. Roll out dough using as little white flour as possible. Cut with biscuit cutter and dip in melted butter. Fold over and pinch edge. Let rise about 1½ hours. Bake at 350° F. until golden brown. Makes 50-75 rolls.

Mary Clark
Mason, Tennessee

Mort's Bread

2 teaspoons salt	½ cup warm water
2 tablespoons sugar	4 cups flour, divided
2½ cups heated milk	1 stick butter, melted
2 packages dry yeast	

Mix salt, sugar and milk in large bowl. Dissolve yeast in warm water and add to bowl. Add 2 cups flour. Mix in butter and add 2 more cups flour. Lay out on flour-covered board with bowl over it for 5-10 minutes. Take bowl off and knead bread, adding flour until dough doesn't stick. Place in buttered bowl, cover with wet dish towel and let rise approximately ½ hour. Knock down, cut in half and put in 2 buttered loaf pans. Cover with wet towel and let rise, approximately ½ hour. Put in oven at 400° F. and reduce heat to 375° F. Bake for ½ hour. Makes 2 loaves.

Mortimer Cushman
LaPointe, Wisconsin

French Canadian Bread

1 package dry yeast	2 cups lukewarm water
¼ cup lukewarm water	1 teaspoon salt
¾ cup flour	5 cups flour

Dissolve yeast in a generous ¼ cup of lukewarm water. Stir in ¾ cup flour and knead until smooth and elastic. Form into ball. Cut an X in the top and drop into a bowl filled with 2 cups lukewarm water. It will sink at first but, in 15 minutes or so, it will rise and be light and puffy. Turn bread and water into large bowl and add salt and remaining flour, one cup at a time until all mixed. Knead until smooth. Form into a ball. Put in a buttered bowl, turning once to get butter all over. Cover and let rise until double in bulk. Turn dough onto floured board and cut in half. Roll each piece into a long loaf. Make furrow down center of each loaf. Set on an oiled baking sheet, cover and let rise until double. Bake at 450° F. for 30 minutes. Makes 2 loaves.

Almost like sour-dough bread.

Mrs. William C. Harris (Ann Clark Quinlen)

Grama's Swedish Rye Bread

4 cups milk
¼ cup shortening
3 tablespoons salt
½ cup dark molasses
½ cup brown sugar

2 packages dry yeast
¼ cup lukewarm water
2 cups rye flour
4 cups white flour, or more as needed

Scald milk. Add next 4 ingredients. Cool to lukewarm. Stir in yeast which has been dissolved in warm water. Beat both flours in well. Add more white flour until dough is stiff enough to turn out on floured board. Knead in more white flour until dough is fairly stiff. Place in greased bowl and cover. Let rise until doubled. Divide into 3 parts and place in loaf pans. Let rise again until doubled. Bake at 375° F. for 1 hour. Cover with brown paper if loaves brown too quickly.

Mrs. Jon K. Thompson (Susan Taylor)

Dill Flowerpot Bread

2 4-inch clay flowerpots
1 package dry yeast
½ cup warm water
3 tablespoons sugar
1 tablespoon dried dill weed

1 cup evaporated milk
2 tablespons melted butter
1 teaspon salt
3-3½ cups flour
Melted butter

Wash clay pots. Line completely with foil. Dissolve yeast in warm water in a large bowl. Stir in 1 tablespoon of sugar and all dill. Let mixture stand at room temperature until bubbly, about 15 minutes. Stir in remaining sugar, milk, butter and salt. Stir in flour to make dough. This will be sticky. Divide dough in half and place in pots. Cover with buttered wax paper. Let stand about 30 minutes in warm place until dough rises 1-1½ inches above rim of pots. Heat oven to 350° F. Place pots on cookie sheet. Bake until brown, about 35 minutes. Brush tops with melted butter. Let cool in pots 5-10 minutes. Remove bread and cool on wire rack. To give as gifts, return to clay pots, wrap in plastic and decorate. Makes 2 loaves.

Mrs. Mickey Moran (Pat Taylor)

Bread Sticks

2 sticks butter
8 hot dog buns
1 teaspoon poppy seeds

1 teaspoon seasoned salt
1 teaspoon garlic salt
1 tablespoon Parmesan cheese

Melt butter and pour into shallow bowl. Quarter bread lengthwise and dip edges into bowl of butter. Place on cookie sheet with buttered edge up. Sprinkle top of sticks with seasonings and bake 1½-2 hours in a 225° F. oven or until crisp. Cool and store in air-tight containers. Can substitute or eliminate seasonings as desired. Makes 32 bread sticks.

Wonderful as snacks or substitute for dinner rolls. Keeps for weeks.

Mrs. Edward M. Priest

Herbed Garlic Bread

1 stick butter
½ teaspoon thyme
½ teaspoon rosemary
½ teaspoon oregano

½ teaspoon basil
1 large loaf French bread
4 cloves garlic, minced
   Grated Parmesan cheese
   Fresh minced parsley

Place first five ingredients in a small saucepan and warm over low heat until butter is melted. Slice bread. Generously brush herbed butter on each slice. Sprinkle with minced garlic, Parmesan cheese and parsley. Place in a very hot oven or in broiler for a few minutes until lightly browned. Makes 1 loaf.

Good with any meal!

Adrian Lynch

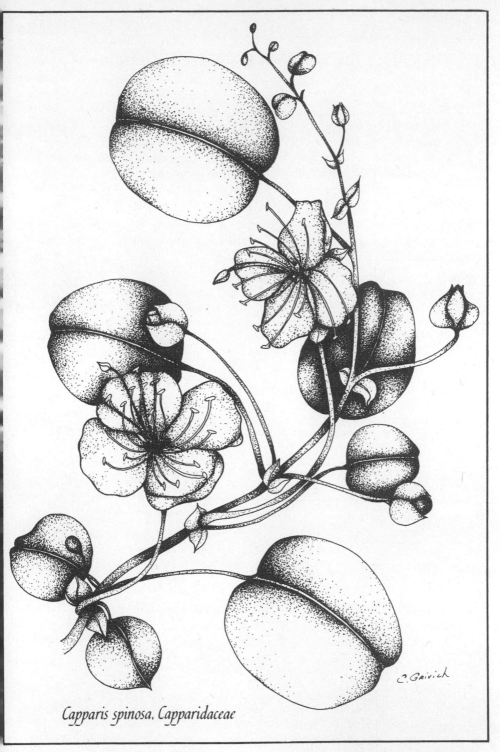

Capparis spinosa, Capparidaceae

Sandwiches

Mary Boxley's Vegetable Sandwich Mix

1 cup chopped celery	1 cup chopped cucumber
1 medium onion, chopped	2 cups mayonnaise
1 medium green pepper, chopped	1 teaspoon salt
	¼ teaspoon pepper
2 tomatoes, peeled and chopped	1 envelope unflavored gelatin
	3 tablespoons water

Combine first 5 ingredients. Let stand for 2-3 hours in a bowl and pour off accumulated water. Mix in mayonnaise. Soften gelatin in 3 tablespoons water in small saucepan. Add softened gelatin to vegetable mixture. Makes 2½ loaves of sandwiches.

For a slightly different taste, add 1 tablespoon lemon juice, ¼ teaspoon Tabasco, and 1 teaspoon Worcestershire sauce to mixture.

Mrs. John Franklin Holmes (Jeanie Hobby)

Herbed Cheese and Sprout Sandwiches

8 ounces cream cheese, softened	½ teaspoon pepper
⅓ cup snipped chives	16 thin slices pumpernickel bread
1 teaspoon thyme	1½ cups alfalfa sprouts
¾ teaspoon salt	

Blend first 5 ingredients in bowl. Cover and let stand for 1 hour. Spread about 2 tablespoons of mixture on each of 8 slices of bread. Top each slice with about 2 tablespoons of sprouts and another slice of bread. Makes 8 sandwiches or 16 finger sandwiches.

Mrs. William E. Denman, III (Julie Moss)

Party Cheese Fingers

32 slices white or whole wheat
    bread
2 cups grated sharp Cheddar
    cheese
⅓ cup chili sauce

¾ cup mayonnaise
½ cup chopped stuffed olives
½ cup pecans, chopped
1 teaspoon Worcestershire
    sauce

Mix all ingredients together except bread. Trim bread crusts. Spread mixture on 16 slices of bread. Top with remaining bread slices. Cut each slice into 3 strips. Cover sandwiches with damp dish towel and refrigerate. Makes 4 dozen finger sandwiches.

Cheese mixture can be molded into a ball and served with crackers as an appetizer.

Mrs. J. Logan Morgan

Frosted Chicken Salad Sandwiches

1 loaf extra-thin sliced bread
2 5-ounce cans boned chicken,
    drained
4 eggs, hard-boiled and
    chopped

½ cup chopped black olives
⅔ cup mayonnaise
Salt and pepper to taste

Cut circles from each slice of bread with chicken can. Combine eggs, chicken, olive and mayonnaise, mixing well. Spread filling on 1 slice of bread, top with second slice and spread filling again. Top with third slice of bread.

Frosting
2 5-ounce jars Old English
    Cheese Spread

1 egg
1 stick margarine, softened

Combine ingredients and beat until fluffy. Frost top and sides of sandices. Let sandwiches stand in refrigerator overnight or at least 6-8 hours. Bake at 375° F. for 15 minutes. Serve hot.

Mrs. Jerry Nations
Brookhaven, Mississippi

Ranch Style Cucumber Sandwiches

1-2 cucumbers
½ cup white tarragon vinegar
1 1½-ounce package Hidden
   Valley Ranch Party Dip

2 cups sour cream
1-2 loaves thin sliced Pepperidge
   Farm bread

Trim cucumbers and slice thinly. Place in bowl, add vinegar, cover and refrigerate 1 hour. Drain for 15 minutes. Mix party dip with sour cream. Cover and refrigerate for 1 hour. Trim breadcrusts. Cut into rounds. Spread bread with party dip and top with cucumber slice.

Mrs. Lucian Dent (Phoebe Paxton)

Stacked Sandwich

1 loaf unsliced butter bread
1 cup pimiento cheese
1½ cups chicken salad

16 ounces cream cheese
½ cup mayonnaise

Trim crusts from loaf with electric knife. Horizontally cut equal slices as thin as possible. Five will be used. Freeze remainder for later use. Place one slice of bread on platter. Spread with pimiento cheese. Cover with another slice of bread. Spread with chicken salad. Repeat these two layers ending with bread slice. Beat cream cheese and mayonnaise until spreading consistency, using more mayonnaise if necessary. Ice the loaf completely with cream cheese mixture. Slice and serve. Serves 6.

Mrs. John Glass (Meegie Rogers)

French Onion Dip Sandwiches

2-4 pounds chuck roast
2 cups water
1 package Lipton's dry onion
   soup mix

1 tablespoon Worcestershire
   sauce
Salt & pepper to taste
Small French bread loaves

Brown roast quickly on both sides. Cover with water. Add onion soup mix, Worcestershire sauce, salt and pepper. Cook several hours, covered, until tender. Slice bread and generously butter. Wrap in foil and heat 15-20 minutes until butter is melted and bread is hot. Slice roast and put on hot French bread. Put gravy in ramekins or lotus bowls for dipping sandwiches. Serves 8-10 people.

Add ¼ cup of red wine to the gravy for a different taste.

Mrs. Burdette Russ (Scottie McCord)

Teenage Delight

1 pound ground beef	1 cup ketchup
1½ stalks celery, chopped	1 tablespoon vinegar
1 onion	1 tablespoon chili powder
1 green pepper, chopped	1 teaspoon sugar
¼ stick margarine	1 package hamburger buns
½ teaspoon prepared mustard	

Sauté ground beef, celery, onions and green pepper in margarine. Do not brown completely. Add remaining ingredients. Simmer 30 minutes or until vegetables are tender. Serve on toasted hamburger buns. Makes 8 buns.

Freezes well.

Mrs. Lucian Wadlington (Patsy Mullins)

Hot Goddess Sandwiches

12 ounces sharp cheese, grated	4 teaspoons grated onion
1 cup mayonnaise	Salt & pepper to taste
1 tablespoon Worcestershire sauce	8 slices white or whole wheat bread
1 tablespoon Green Goddess Salad Dressing	1 cup cheese, grated
1 teaspoon prepared mustard	Stuffed olives, for garnish

Mix first 7 ingredients together. Trim crusts from bread. Place cheese mixture on four slices of bread. Top with remaining slices of bread and sprinkle ¼ cup of cheese on top of each sandwich.

Place in oven at 400° F. until cheese starts to melt and bubble. Then put under broiler until brown. Serve hot with olive on top. Serves 4.

This can be served on toast rounds as an appetizer.

Mrs. Julia Taylor

Cheese Soufflé Sandwiches

8 slices white bread	1½ cups milk
Dijon mustard	Salt & pepper
4-6 ounces sharp Cheddar	4 slices bacon, fried and
cheese, sliced	crumbled
3 eggs	

Trim bread crusts. Spread mustard on 1 side of 4 slices. Top with cheese and remaining bread slices. Place in greased Pyrex dish with sides touching. Beat eggs, milk and seasonings; pour over sandwiches. Let stand 2 hours. Bake at 325° F. for 35 minutes until brown. Sprinkle with bacon. Serves 4.

Mrs. Thomas J. Becktold, Jr. (Pamela Stewart)

Curried Cheese Sandwiches

1 cup chopped ripe olives	½ cup mayonnaise
½ cup chopped scallions or	½ teaspoon curry powder
onions	½ teaspoon salt
1½ cups grated Cheddar cheese	6 English muffins

Mix together all ingredients except muffins. Split muffins in half. Spread with mixture. Bake at 350° F. until bubbly, about 10-15 minutes. Makes 12 open faced sandwiches.

Good with soup or salad. Be prepared to give this recipe to everyone!

Mrs. Donald Howdeshell (Anne Eastland)

Mrs. Walker Uhlhorn (Ann Taylor)

Ida's Hot Cluckers

12 slices white bread
¼ cup margarine, softened
4 chicken breasts, cooked and
   chopped
½ cup stuffed sliced olives

2 tablespoons grated onion
¾ cup Hellmann's mayonnaise
¼ cup margarine, softened
1 5-ounce jar Old English sharp
   cheese spread

Trim crust from bread. Spread 6 slices with softened margarine. Place on cookie sheet. Top with mixture of chicken, olives, onions and mayonnaise. Put other 6 slices of bread on top. Blend last 2 ingredients and spread over top of sandwich. May be stored in refrigerator until ready to use. Bake at 400° F. until hot and bubbly. Serves 6.

Mrs. E. O. Edwards

Hot Browns

2 slices toast
2 slices cooked turkey or
   chicken
1 package McCormick's cheese
   sauce, prepared according
   to directions

2 strips bacon, cooked
2 slices tomato
Dots of butter
Parmesan cheese

Place toast on cookie sheet. Arrange turkey or chicken on top. Cover with cheese sauce, bacon and tomato. Dot with butter and sprinkle with cheese. Broil until it bubbles. Serves 1.

Mrs. R. W. James

Carla's Ham Sandwiches

¼ cup chopped onion	1 tablespoon poppy seeds
½ stick butter, melted	6 slices ham
¼ cup prepared mustard	6 slices Swiss cheese
¼ cup mayonnaise	6 egg bread buns

Sauté onion in butter until golden. Combine mustard, mayonnaise and poppy seeds. Add to onion. Arrange ham slice and cheese slice on bottom half of bun. Spread a generous amount of mixture over ham and cheese. Cover with top half of bun. Wrap in foil and bake 15-20 minutes at 350° F. Serves 6.

Mrs. William W. McCrary, III (Tancie Lewis)

Ham Sandwich Supreme

Sauce

1 8-ounce can sliced mushrooms, reserving liquid	2 tablespoons butter
	2 tablespoons flour
	1 cup grated Swiss cheese
Milk	

Drain mushrooms, reserving liquid in can. Add milk to fill can. In saucepan, heat butter, flour and milk-mushroom liquid mixture. Add Swiss cheese and cook until thickened. Keep warm.

Sandwich

2 slices ham	2 tablespoons butter
4 slices bread	

Make ham sandwiches, buttering both sides of bread. Grill in hot skillet. Place on plate and cover with sauce. Serve hot. Makes 2 sandwiches.

Mrs. Clyde Patton, Jr. (Leslie Wilsford)

Hot Ham and Cheese Sandwiches

6 ounces Danish ham
½ pound Swiss cheese
½ stick margarine
1 tablespoon chives

1 tablespoon chopped parsley
1 teaspoon prepared mustard
8 round buns

Shred ham and then cheese in a food processor and mix together. Mix next four ingredients well. Spread both halves of buns with this mixture. Place generous amount of ham mixture on each. Wrap sandwiches in foil and bake at 350° F. for 25 minutes. Makes 8 sandwiches.

Great use for leftover ham!

Mrs. Max B. Ostner, Jr. (Mary Margaret Buffa)

Martini Mushroom Sandwiches

8 green onions, finely sliced
½ stick butter
1½ pounds fresh mushrooms, sliced

Vermouth to taste
8 slices thin whole wheat bread
2 tablespoons butter

Sauté onions in butter for 2 minutes. Add mushrooms and sauté for another 2 minutes. Add vermouth to taste. Drain mushroom mixture and spread on 4 slices of bread. Top with remaining slices of bread and grill on both sides in skillet using remaining butter. Serves 4.

Mrs. Jack Bellows (Lela Hudson)

Jeanette's Hot Crab Sandwiches

6 ounces crabmeat
2 ounces mushroom pieces, drained
4 hard-boiled eggs, chopped

¼ cup chopped green onion
¼ cup mayonnaise
8 slices bread, crusts trimmed
Butter

Combine first 5 ingredients. Spread both sides of bread with butter. Put filling between 2 slices of bread. Bake 20 minutes on cookie sheet at 350° F.

Sauce
1 10¾-ounce can cream of chicken soup

8 ounces sour cream

Heat sauce ingredients and pour over hot sandwiches. Serves 4.

Mrs. Thomas Holloman (Jayne Pressgrove)

Golden Crabmeat

½ stick butter
¼ cup green onions, sliced
⅓ cup fresh mushrooms
½ pound crabmeat, or one 7¾-ounce can crabmeat, drained

⅛ teaspoon garlic salt
⅛ teaspoon cayenne pepper
4 slices toast or Holland Rusk
1 teaspoon lemon juice
hollandaise sauce (see Index)

Sauté onion in butter. Add mushrooms and sauté slightly. Add crabmeat, garlic salt, cayenne and lemon juice. Serve over toast and top with hollandaise. Serves 4.

Mrs. Charles D. Schaffler (Mickey Pooley)

Broiled Tuna Sandwiches

6 hamburger bun halves
Soft margarine
1 7-ounce can tuna, drained and flaked
1 cup shredded sharp cheese

¼ cup minced green pepper
2 tablespoons minced onion (optional)
½ cup mayonnaise

Spread buns with margarine. Mix remaining ingredients well and place on buns, making open-faced sandwiches. Place under broiler 5 minutes or until lightly browned. Serves 6.

Freezes well. If frozen, thaw one hour in wrapper before broiling.

Mrs. Malcolm McLean, III
Lumberton, North Carolina

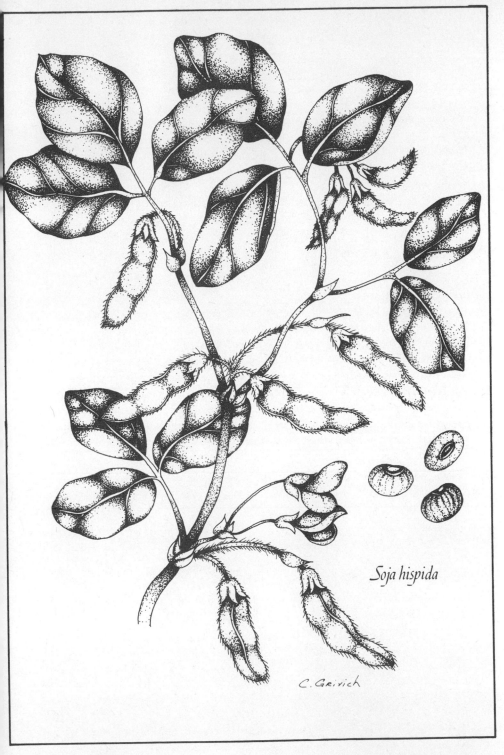

Soja hispida

C. Grivich

Sauces and Accompaniments

Basic White Sauce

3 tablespoons butter
5 tablespoons flour
2 cups milk

Salt
Freshly ground pepper
Cayenne pepper to taste

Melt butter over moderate heat. Add flour and mix well. Cook mixture for 2 minutes. Remove pan from heat and stir in milk. Return to heat and cook, stirring constantly, until thickened. Season with salt and pepper. Add cayenne pepper if desired. Makes approximately 2 cups.

Mimi Dossett

Béarnaise Sauce

1½ teaspoons tarragon
1½ teaspoons chervil
1 tablespoon chopped shallot, or white part of green onion
¼ cup tarragon vinegar
¼ cup dry vermouth

Salt
Freshly ground pepper
4 egg yolks, beaten
1 tablespoon water
1½ sticks melted butter
1 teaspoon lemon juice
Cayenne pepper

Boil first 7 ingredients together in an enamel saucepan until reduced to 2 tablespoons. Add egg yolks and water. Whisk over very low heat until thickened. Remove from heat. Very gradually, add melted butter, whisking constantly until thickened. Season with lemon juice and cayenne pepper. Makes about 1 cup.

Mrs. Malcolm McLean, III
Lumberton, North Carolina

Lynch's Hollandaise

3 egg yolks
1½-2 tablespoons lemon juice
¼ teaspoon salt

Pinch of cayenne pepper
1 stick butter

Place all ingredients, except butter, in blender. Heat butter in a small saucepan until foaming hot. Cover blender and run at top speed for 2-3 seconds. Uncover. Still blending at top speed, start pouring in hot butter in a slow thin stream of droplets. Omit milky residue at bottom of butter pan. Taste sauce and adjust seasonings if necessary. If not used immediately, set jar in tepid water. Makes about ¾ cup.

Mrs. Michael Lynch (Susan Corcoran)

Hollandaise Sauce for Fish

2 egg yolks
¼ teaspoon dry mustard
1 tablespoon tarragon vinegar
1 stick butter, melted

Salt to taste
Cayenne pepper to taste
Paprika for garnish

Combine egg yolks, mustard and vinegar and beat well. Continue beating and gradually add butter. Cook and stir over medium heat until sauce thickens. Add seasonings. Spoon over fish and sprinkle with paprika. Especially good on smoked fish. Serves 4-6, depending on size of fish.

Mrs. Phillip H. McNeill (Mabel McCall)

Creole Sauce

1 lemon
¾ cup chopped mushrooms
½ cup chopped green pepper

1 tablespoon Worcestershire
  sauce
2 cups chili sauce

Peel lemon. Chop lemon pulp very fine and cut rind into thin strips. Put all ingredients in double boiler and cook over low heat for 20-30 minutes.

This is terrific with Chicken Croquettes.

Mrs. Frank E. Reid (Diana Morgan Mann)

Dijon Sauce

½ stick butter
1 teaspoon Dijon mustard
3 tablespoons lemon juice
2 tablespoons chopped parsley

1 teaspoon grated onion
¼ teaspoon ground mace
4 egg yolks, well beaten

Combine first 6 ingredients in top of double boiler set over hot water. Stir with wire whisk until butter is melted. Stir egg yolks into butter mixture and beat briskly until mixture thickens to the consistency of mayonnaise. If it thickens too much, thin with cream. Keeps an hour or so over warm water. Makes about 1 cup.

Wonderful with salmon mousse!

Mrs. Leo J. Fairchild
Monroe, Michigan

Marchand de Vin Sauce

8 medium shallots
1½ cups dry red wine
2 teaspoons meat glaze
1 stick unsalted butter
1 teaspoon flour

1 teaspoon fresh lemon juice
2 tablespoons chopped chives
   or parsley
Salt and freshly ground
   pepper

Cook shallots and wine in a large skillet over high heat until liquid has cooked down to about ¾ cup. Stir in meat glaze and simmer until dissolved. Strain mixture through a sieve, pressing down hard on the shallots to extract all juices before discarding. Beat butter in a bowl until creamy. Beat flour into butter. Add lemon juice, drop by drop, and chives and parsley. Set aside. Just before serving, bring wine to a simmer. Whisk butter mixture into wine. Simmer sauce a minute or 2 until it thickens slightly. Taste for seasoning. Serves 6.

Serve with eggs, steak or hamburger.

Mimi Dossett

Mushroom Sauce

4 pounds fresh mushrooms
2 10¾-ounce cans beef
   consommé, undiluted
2 10¾-ounce cans cream of
   mushroom soup, undiluted

1 cup red wine
Salt and pepper to taste

Remove stems from mushrooms and slice. Combine all ingredients and simmer, covered, for 20 minutes.

Can be used as a light sauce for beef or as an appetizer.

Mrs. L. P. Daniel (Betty Hurt)

Mushroom Wine Sauce for Steak

3 tablespoons butter	1 cup red wine or water
Small strip of fat from steak	2 beef bouillon cubes, crushed
½ pound fresh mushrooms, sliced	

Melt 2 tablespoons butter in heavy skillet. Add steak fat. Sauté mushrooms over medium heat for 1 minute. Remove mushrooms to serving bowl. Pour off grease. Over high heat, add wine and bouillon cubes to skillet and cook for 3 minutes. Remove from heat and add mushrooms to skillet. Add 1 tablespoon butter and stir until blended. Serves 4.

Delicious over broiled steak.

Mrs. James McCormick

Minje's Mushroom Sauce

2 cloves garlic, minced	2 egg yolks, lightly beaten
6 tablespoons butter, divided	1 cup light cream
½ pound mushrooms, sliced	4 teaspoons fresh lemon juice
3 tablespoons whole wheat flour	Salt and pepper to taste
	Soy sauce to taste

Sauté garlic in 3 tablespoons butter in saucepan. Add mushrooms and cook briefly, keeping firm. Remove and reserve. Blend remaining 3 tablespoons butter with flour over low heat. Combine eggs and cream; add to flour and butter, stirring until mixture starts to thicken. Add lemon juice, a little at a time. Add seasonings and cooked mushrooms and serve. Makes about 2 cups.

Good with meat or pasta or as a dip with Melba rounds.

Mrs. D. Randolph Ramey (Minje Mitchell)

Tomato Sauce

¼ cup oil
1 onion sliced
1 carrot, sliced
1 rib celery, sliced
2 tablespoons minced parsley
1 tablespoon dried marjoram
2-3 cloves garlic, crushed
¼ cup mushrooms, chopped

½ teaspoon honey
½ cup dry white or red wine
3½ cups chopped, peeled, seeded
and drained tomatoes
1 teaspoon salt
¼ teaspoon pepper

Heat oil in large saucepan. Add next 8 ingredients. Sauté until vegetables are pale golden color. Add wine and boil uncovered until most of wine is evaporated. Add tomatoes, salt and pepper. Cover and simmer 1 hour, adding hot water if mixture becomes too thick. Purée in food processor or strain and reheat. If sauce is too thin, simmer until thick as desired. Serve over pasta or meats, or use in recipes which call for canned tomato sauce. Makes 2½ cups.

Mrs. Huey L. Holden (Barbara Hopper)

Two-Day Italian Spaghetti Sauce

2 large white onions, diced
2 cloves garlic, diced
8 6-ounce cans tomato paste
8 6-ounce cans water
1 teaspoon each salt, pepper
and sugar

1 cup chopped fresh parsley
¼ cup crushed oregano
4 pork chops
½ cup olive oil
1 pound ground beef
1 3-ounce jar Romano cheese

Sauté onions and garlic. Blend next 5 ingredients. Fry pork chops in olive oil until brown. Add to sauce. Add onions and garlic to sauce. Lightly brown ground beef. Drain and add to sauce. Cook over low temperature for 4 hours. Refrigerate overnight. Skim off oil. Add Romano cheese and simmer 4-6 more hours. Serves 10.

Mrs. Michael Heffernan (Tracy Plyler)

Special Southern Barbecue Sauce

½ cup oil
¾ cup chopped onion
¾ cup ketchup
¾ cup water
⅓ cup fresh lemon juice
3 tablespoons sugar

3 tablespoons Worcestershire
   sauce
2 tablespoons prepared
   mustard
2 teaspoons salt
½ teaspoon pepper

Sauté onion in oil until soft and clear. Add remaining ingredients. Simmer for 30 minutes. Use for basting when barbecuing or smoking on a charcoal grill. Makes about 3 cups.

Fabulous on chicken, pork or even steaks.

Mrs. Frank H. Reid

Mother's Barbecue Sauce

2 sticks butter
1 tablespoon prepared
   mustard
3 tablespoons salt
½ teaspoon Tabasco
½ tablespoon Worcestershire
   sauce
2½ teaspoons black pepper

1½ teaspoons sugar
2 teaspoons chili powder
¼ cup mild pepper sauce
1¾ cups water
1 cup vinegar
1 onion, chopped
1 clove garlic, minced

Mix all ingredients in saucepan. Simmer for 30-45 minutes. Can be stored in refrigerator for 2-3 weeks. Makes 1 quart.

Delicious with chicken.

Mrs. Lucian R. Wadlington, Jr. (Patsy Mullins)

Sparerib Sauce

¼ cup cider vinegar
1 cup water
½ cup ketchup
3 tablespoons lemon juice
2 tablespoons brown sugar
1 teaspoon celery salt
1 teaspoon onion powder
¼ teaspoon cayenne pepper

1½ teaspoons chili powder
¼ teaspoon instant minced
  garlic, or 1 clove garlic,
  minced
1 teaspoon freshly ground
  pepper
1 teaspoon Kitchen Bouquet

Mix all ingredients in saucepan. Bring to a boil and boil 3 minutes.
Makes about 2 cups.

Mrs. Tony M. Parker (Judy Greene)

Teriyaki Sauce

¼ cup soy sauce
¼ cup white wine or white wine
  vinegar
1 clove garlic minced, or ⅛
  teaspoon instant minced
  garlic

2 tablespoons brown sugar
2 tablespoons Worcestershire
  sauce

Combine all ingredients. Marinate meat or vegetables. Baste while
cooking.

Very versatile. Use for steak, chicken, chops or vegetables.

Mrs. Grover Lee Walker, III (Susan Whittenberg)

Cocktail Sauce

½ cup ketchup
½ cup chili sauce
3-4 tablespoons horseradish
½ teaspoon Worcestershire
   sauce

¼ teaspoon Tabasco
Juice of 1 lime
Juice of 1 lemon
1 tablespoon olive oil

Mix well and refrigerate. Makes about 2 cups.

Le Ruth's Restaurant
Gretna, Louisiana

Chili Cocktail Sauce

⅔ cup chili sauce
1 tablespoon horseradish
2 tablespoons lemon juice
½ teaspoon grated lemon rind

1 teaspoon Worcestershire
   sauce
3-4 drops Tabasco
¼ teaspoon salt

Mix well and chill. Serve with seafood. Makes ¾ cup.

The best ever.

Mrs. Scott Allison Arnold, III (Anne Dillard)

Creamy Cocktail Sauce

1 cup mayonnaise
3 tablespoons ketchup
1 tablespoon Worcestershire
   sauce
1 clove garlic, crushed

1 teaspoon Tabasco
1 teaspoon salt
Pepper to taste
2 tablespoons grated onion
Juice of 1 lemon

Mix all together. Makes 1½ cups.

Easy and different. Wonderful with shrimp or crab.

Mrs. J. R. Mann
Montgomery, Alabama

Rémoulade Sauce

2   cups mayonnaise
½ cup Dijon mustard
¼ cup ketchup
4   teaspoons horseradish
2   teaspoons Worcestershire
     sauce

3   tablespoons lemon juice
1   teaspoon pepper sauce
¾ cup chopped parsley
½ cup chopped green onion
1   cup minced celery
¼ cup capers, drained

Combine all ingredients together and chill. Serve with crab claws, shrimp, as a dip or as a dressing over seafood salad.

Mrs. Neal G. Clement
Florence, Alabama

Le Ruth's Tartar Sauce

1   cup mayonnaise, homemade
     or Hellmann's preferred
½ cup chopped dill pickle

¼ cup chopped onion
2   tablespoons chopped parsley
     Tabasco, to taste

Mix well and refrigerate. Makes 1¾ cups.

LeRuth's Restaurant
Gretna, Louisiana

Cambridge Sauce for Cold Turkey

½ cup heavy cream, whipped
3   tablespoons mayonnaise
1   tablespoon tarragon vinegar
1   teaspoon prepared mustard
1   tablespoon drained
     horseradish

3   tablespoons Durkee's sauce
½ teaspoon salt
     Paprika

Fold all ingredients into whipped cream. Sprinkle with paprika and chill.

Delicious with roasted or smoked turkey.

Mrs. George William Albright (Barbara Marks)

Sauce for Vegetables

1 cup mayonnaise
2½ teaspoons Worcestershire
sauce
2 tablespoons olive oil

¼ teaspoon dry mustard
1 small onion, grated
2 hard-boiled eggs, chopped

Mix all ingredients and refrigerate.

May be served cold over fresh raw vegetables or hot over steamed vegetables.

Mrs. Robert O. Carloss Johnson (Brenda Evans)

Click's Cajun Seasoning

4 tablespoons salt
2 tablespoons black pepper
1 tablespoon cayenne pepper

2 tablespoons garlic powder
1 tablespoon chili powder
1 2-ounce can Accent

Mix all together and store in jar. Makes 1 cup.

Great in soups, gumbos, casseroles, meats and vegetables. Wonderful Christmas gift.

Mrs. William C. Harris, Jr. (Ann Clark Quinlen)

Artichoke Pickles

1 pint cider vinegar
½ cup water
1 teaspoon salt, per jar
Jerusalem artichokes or
sunchokes, well scrubbed

1 hot red pepper per jar, or 1
teaspoon crushed red
pepper

For 2 pints of pickles, bring vinegar, water and salt to boil. Put artichokes, cut in half if necessary, and red peppers in jars. Pour boiling liquid over hearts and seal. Do not open for at least 2 weeks. Makes 2 pints.

A "crunchy" treat.

Mrs. John Franklin Holmes (Jeanie Hobby)

Bread and Butter Pickles

Salted ice water
4 cups thinly sliced cucumbers
6 white onions, thinly sliced
3 cloves garlic, thinly sliced
⅓ cup salt

3 cups sugar
1½ teaspoons turmeric
1½ teaspoons celery seed
2 tablespoons dry mustard
3 cups white vinegar

Soak cucumbers, onions and garlic for 3 hours in ice water mixed with salt. In enamel roaster pan, bring remaining ingredients to boil. After solution boils, place drained cucumbers, onions and garlic in solution and cook for 15 minutes, or until tender. Transfer pickles to sterilized canning jars and cover with liquid. Wipe lip of jar clean and seal with sterilized lids. Makes 4-6 pints.

Mrs. James B. Green, Jr. (Betty Brown)

Garlic Sweet Pickles

Iced water
2 tablespoons powdered alum
1 gallon sour pickles cut in
   1-inch rounds
5 pounds sugar minus 1 cup

8 cloves garlic
1 1½-ounce can pickling spice
1 cup white vinegar
½ cup tarragon vinegar

Soak pickles in iced water and alum for 2 hours. Make sure the water mixture covers the pickles. Drain off water and rinse pickles. Layer sugar, pickles, garlic and spices. Pour vinegar over this mixture. Store in large bowl in refrigerator for 36 hours, stirring occasionally. Put in sterile jars and seal. Makes 8 pints.

This is the best crunchy sweet pickle you will ever eat.

Mrs. Palmer K. Bartlett (Martha Williams)

Lulu's Pickled Beets

8 medium beets
2 teaspoons salt
1 cup vinegar

4 tablespoons water
1 teaspoon caraway seeds

Boil unpeeled beets in salted water until barely tender. Remove skins and slice. Put in pint jars. Boil vinegar and water. Pour over beets. Add caraway seeds to jars. Cool and refrigerate overnight. This keeps indefinitely. Makes 2 pints.

Beet lover's treat.

Mrs. James Bettendorf (Berkeley Blake)

Marie's Carrots

5 cups sliced carrots
1 2-ounce jar pimiento, chopped
1 red onion, cut in rings

1 green pepper, cut in bite-sized pieces
1 3¼-ounce can black olives

Pour boiling water over carrots. Let sit for 1-2 minutes and drain. Mix carrots, pimiento, onion and green pepper in large salad bowl. Pour marinade over carrots. Refrigerate for 12 hours. Serves 6.

Marinade
1 10½-ounce can tomato bisque soup
1 cup sugar
¼ cup red wine vinegar
¼ cup white vinegar

1 teaspoon dry mustard
1 teaspoon salt
1 teaspoon white pepper
Cayenne pepper to taste

Heat all ingredients.

Serve this as a side dish, or garnish with black olives and serve as an appetizer.

Mrs. Philip B. White

Pickled Okra

1 pint small okra, cleaned
1 whole pod fresh red pepper
1 clove garlic
1 teaspoon dill seed
½ teaspoon mustard seed

1 tablespoon powdered alum
1 quart white vinegar
½ cup salt
1 cup water

Pack first 6 ingredients in sterilized pint jars. Bring vinegar, salt and water to full boil. Pour boiling mixture over contents in jar. Seal promptly. Let age at least 2 weeks.

Good with cocktails. Makes a great Christmas gift with the red and green colors.

Mrs. William V. Lawson, Jr. (Carolyn Townes)

Kim's Pickled Onions

9 pounds small onions, peeled
 and sliced or quartered
1 garlic clove, split
¼ teaspoon dill seed
 Dash turmeric
 Dash celery salt, or 2-inch
 celery rib

¼ teaspoon whole cloves
¼ teaspoon whole allspice
1 teaspoon pickling spice
1 quart vinegar
2 quarts water
1 cup salt

Pack prepared onions into clean jars. To each 16-ounce jar, add listed amount of seasonings. Combine vinegar, water and salt and boil 5 minutes. Cover onions with hot brine and seal. Pickles will be ready in 3 weeks. Makes approximately 9 pints.

Mrs. Raymond E. Henley (Kim Baxter)

Squash Pickle

8 cups thinly sliced yellow
   squash
2 cups thinly sliced white
   onions
4 large green peppers, thinly
   sliced
1 cup kosher salt

2-3 trays ice
3 cups sugar
3 cups white vinegar
2 tablespoons celery seed
2 tablespoons mustard seed
2 tablespoons turmeric
1 teaspoon alum

Combine first 5 ingredients and let stand for 2-3 hours. Stir often, about every 15 to 20 minutes. Combine remaining ingredients and bring to a boil. Drain squash mixture and add to boiling mixture. Boil 3 minutes. Pack in sterile jars and seal. Makes about 7 to 8 pints.

Mrs. Harte Thomas, Jr. (Patty Jenkins)

Mrs. James Bettendorf (Berkeley Blake)

Mock Watermelon Pickles

7 pounds very large cucumbers
3 cups lime
5 pounds sugar

6 cups cider vinegar
3 sticks cinnamon

Wash, peel and cut cucumbers into 3-inch strips, removing all seeds. Place in large glass dish. Sprinkle with lime and add enough water to cover. Let mixture soak overnight. The next day, rinse well and soak several hours in clean water. Drain well. Make a hot syrup of sugar, vinegar and cinnamon. Pour over cucumbers and let stand for 2 hours. Cook slowly for 1 hour. Pickles will turn clear. Seal in pint jars and process in hot water bath for 15 minutes. Makes 7 pints.

Mrs. Dorsey Mathis, Jr. (Margaret Jones)

Jane's Garden Relish

1 gallon green tomatoes	5 cups sugar
1 gallon cabbage	2 teaspoons turmeric
1 quart white onions	1 teaspoon cloves
6 green peppers	1 teaspoon celery seed
3 jalapeño peppers	¼ teaspoon cinnamon
1 cup salt	1 quart cider vinegar

Coarsely chop vegetables. Sprinkle salt over all, cover with ice and let stand 2 hours. Bring remaining ingredients to a boil and add vegetables. Boil 10 minutes. Pack in sterilized jars and seal. Makes 15 pints.

Easily prepared in a food processor.

Mrs. Lorenzo Adams (Mary Lou Wittenberg)

Vegetable Relish

6 large onions, finely chopped	½ cup salt
6 large green peppers, finely chopped	5 cups sugar
1 extra-large head cabbage, finely chopped	4 tablespoons mustard seed
	1 tablespoon turmeric
	1 tablespoon ground ginger
2 quarts green tomatoes, finely chopped	3 tablespoons celery seed
	2½ quarts white vinegar
6 large carrots, grated or finely chopped	

Mix first 6 ingredients in a bowl and let stand covered overnight. Drain well. Combine sugar, spices and vinegar in large enamel pot and bring to a boil. Simmer about 20 minutes. Add vegetables and simmer for about 15 more minutes. Pack in hot, sterile jars and seal. Makes 6-8 pints.

Great with meats, hotdogs or other sandwiches.

Mrs. William C. Harris (Ann Clark Quinlen)

Marie's Kraut Relish

1 16-ounce can chopped
   sauerkraut, drained
¾ cup chopped celery
¼ cup chopped white onion
1 green pepper, chopped

1-2 carrots, chopped
1 2-ounce jar pimiento
¾ cup sugar
¾ cup vinegar

Mix first 6 ingredients. Place sugar and vinegar in pan and bring to a boil. Stir and pour over vegetable mixture. Fill jars and refrigerate for 24 hours. If canning, seal jars according to standard canning procedures.

Mrs. Phillip B. White

Cranberry-Orange Relish

1 pound fresh cranberries
2 cups sugar
2 cups water
1 11-ounce can mandarin
   oranges
1 teaspoon vanilla extract

1 teaspoon orange extract
1 teaspoon ground cinnamon
1 teaspoon ground allspice
1 cup chopped pecans or
   walnuts (optional)

Combine berries, sugar and water. Boil for 5 minutes. Reduce heat and skim off foam. Add oranges, extracts and spices. Simmer, stirring occasionally, 3-5 minutes. Remove from heat and cool. Yields 1½ quarts.

Carolyn Mitchell Kittle

Pepper Jelly

⅔ cup hot red or green peppers
1 cup chopped green bell
   peppers
6½ cups sugar

1½ cups wine or cider vinegar
3 ounces Certo
   Green food coloring
   Paraffin

Chop hot peppers. Do not seed. Seed and chop green peppers. Mix all peppers with sugar and vinegar and bring to a boil for 1 minute. Cook about 5 minutes. Remove from heat. Add Certo and food coloring and fill sterilized jars. Seal with paraffin. Makes 3 pints.

Mrs. Charles D. Schaffler (Mickey Pooley)

Apple Cinnamon Jelly

1   quart apple juice
1   1¾-ounce package Sure Jell
4½ cups sugar

1   2⅜-ounce box red hots
    Paraffin

Combine juice and Sure Jell in large pan. Bring to rolling boil. Add sugar and candy, stirring constantly. Boil 2 minutes. Remove from heat and skim off foam. Fill sterilized, hot jelly glasses to within ½-inch of top. Seal with thin layer of paraffin poured over hot jelly. Yields 7 half-pint jars.

Mrs. William R. Hackett (Sandra Childress)

Melinda's Strawberry Fig Preserves

3   cups mashed figs
3   cups sugar

1   6-ounce package strawberry
    gelatin

Remove stems from figs but do not peel. Mix all ingredients. Boil 3-5 minutes. Seal and sterilize in hot jars. Makes 3 pints.

A cinch to make.

Mrs. Michael Rauscher

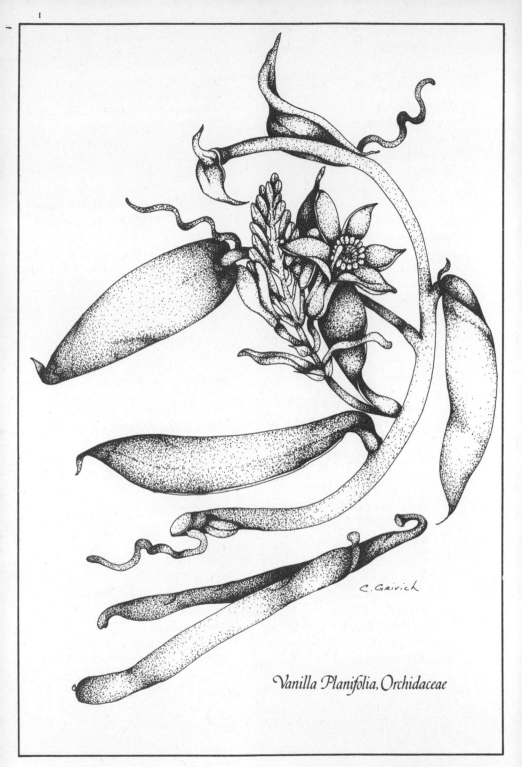

Vanilla Planifolia, Orchidaceae

Desserts

Basic Pie Crust

1½ cups flour
½ teaspoon salt
1 tablespoon shortening
7 tablespoons chilled butter,
   cut into chunks

4 tablespoons ice water
1 teaspoon white vinegar

Blend first 4 ingredients in food processor until crumbly. Add remaining ingredients and blend for a few seconds until dough begins to form a ball. Divide and chill for 1-2 hours. Roll out on floured board.

This recipe makes two 9-inch pie crusts.

Mrs. Charles D. Schaffler (Mickey Pooley)

Buttermilk Coconut Pie

1 stick butter
2 cups sugar
¾ cup buttermilk
1 cup flaked coconut

1 teaspoon vanilla
Pinch of salt
5 eggs
1 deep-dish pie crust, unbaked

Melt butter. Add next 5 ingredients. Beat eggs lightly and add to first mixture. Pour into pie crust. Bake at 350° F. for 50-60 minutes. Serves 6-8.

Mrs. John Bassi

Classic Karo Pecan Pie

1 cup sugar
4 tablespoons butter
3 eggs
1 cup Karo syrup

1 teaspoon vanilla
Pinch of salt
1 cup chopped or whole pecans
1 deep-dish pie crust, unbaked

Cream sugar and butter. Beat in eggs by hand. Add Karo syrup, vanilla and salt. Stir and add pecans. Put in pie crust and bake for 10 minutes at 425° F. Reduce heat to 325° F. and bake until pie is firm, about 40 minutes. Serves 6-8.

Add 2 tablespoons of dark rum for a different twist.

Mrs. William West (Carole Wilson)

Chocolate Pecan Pie

½ cup sugar
1 cup dark Karo syrup
¼ teaspoon salt
1 tablespoon flour
2 eggs
1 tablespoon butter

2 squares unsweetened
   chocolate
1 teaspoon vanilla
1¼ cups pecan halves
1 9-inch pie crust, unbaked

Beat together first 5 ingredients. Melt butter and chocolate together. Add vanilla and pecans to first mixture. Add chocolate mixture. Pour into pie crust. Bake at 300° F. for 50-60 minutes or until filling is set. Serves 8.

Mrs. Charles S. Wilson

French Raisin Pie

1 cup seedless raisins
1 stick butter
1½ cups sugar
3 eggs
1 cup pecans, chopped

½ teaspoon cinnamon
½ teaspoon allspice
½ teaspoon cloves
2 tablespoons vinegar
2 9-inch pie crusts, unbaked

Boil raisins in water until tender. Drain. Cream butter and add sugar slowly, beating constantly. Add eggs, one at a time, and beat just until blended. Stir in raisins and pecans. Mix spices and vinegar and add to mixture. Spoon mixture into pie crusts. Bake at 350° F. for 30-40 minutes or until pies are set, but not firm in center. Cool before serving. Serves 12-16.

French raisin tarts melt in your mouth too. Recipe makes sixteen 3-inch tarts.

Mrs. Gilbert McSpadden, Jr. (Jane Ridens)

Mrs. Cash King (Mary Nance)

Ora May's Chess Pie

2 cups sugar
1 stick butter
5 egg yolks
1 heaping tablespoon flour

1 cup milk
1 rounded tablespoon cornmeal
1 teaspoon vanilla
1 8 or 9-inch pie crust, unbaked

Cream sugar and butter. Add remaining ingredients and mix well. Pour into pie crust and bake at 425° F. for 10 minutes. Reduce oven to 325° F. and bake about 45 minutes, or until set. Serves 6.

Mrs. Anne G. Boals (Anne Goodwin)

Lemon Chess Pie

2 cups sugar
4 eggs, beaten
½ stick butter, melted
¼ cup lemon juice

1 tablespoon flour
1 tablespoon corn meal
1 9-inch pie crust, unbaked

Mix first 6 ingredients well and pour into pie crust. Bake at 375° F. for 35-45 minutes. Serves 6.

Mrs. R. Franklin Adams (Corinne Ridolphi)

Peaches and Cream Pie

6-8 fresh peaches
1 cup sugar
¼ cup flour
¼ teaspoon salt

1 cup heavy cream
½ teaspoon vanilla
¼ teaspoon almond extract
1 9-inch pie crust, unbaked

Peel and slice peaches. Sprinkle with ⅓ cup sugar. Mix together ⅔ cup sugar, flour and salt. Stir in cream and flavorings. Place peaches in pie crust and pour cream mixture over fruit. Bake at 400° F. for 40 minutes or until almost set. Serve slightly warm. Serves 6-8.

Delicious and different.

Mrs. J. R. Mann
Montgomery, Alabama

Sour Cream Apple Pie

½ cup sugar
2 tablespoons flour
¼ teaspoon salt
8 ounces sour cream
1 egg

1½ teaspoons vanilla
2 cups chopped, pared cooking apples
1 9-inch pie crust, unbaked

Preheat oven to 425° F. Combine sugar, flour, and salt in a bowl. Beat in sour cream, egg and vanilla. Stir in chopped apples. Pour in pie crust. Bake 15 minutes, reduce oven to 350° F. and bake for 30 minutes longer. Remove pie from oven when done and turn oven to 400° F. Sprinkle topping on pie and return to 400° F. oven for 10 minutes. Serves 6.

Topping
⅓ cup flour
⅓ cup sugar

1½ teaspoons cinnamon
½ stick butter

Blend all topping ingredients together.

Mrs. John Bassi

Divinity Lemon Pie

3 eggs, separated
2 lemons
3 tablespoons hot water

1 cup sugar
⅛ teaspoon salt
1 cup heavy cream, whipped

Beat egg yolks very lightly. Add juice of one lemon, rind of two lemons, hot water, salt and ½ cup sugar. Cook in double boiler until thick. Beat egg whites until stiff. Add remainder of sugar to egg whites and fold into cooked mixture. Put in pre-baked pie crust. Bake at 350° F. until brown. Top with whipped cream.

Pie Crust
1 cup flour
½ cup shortening

¼ teaspoon salt

Mix all ingredients well. Add just enough ice water to soften. Line pie plate and bake at 350°F. for 20 minutes.

Mrs. Gavin M. Gentry (Mary Jane Coleman)

Peach Chiffon Pie

1½ cups thinly sliced fresh
    peaches
1 tablespoon Grand Marnier
    liqueur
1 cup sugar
1 tablespoon unflavored
    gelatin

1 tablespoon cold water
¼ cup hot water
1 cup heavy cream, whipped
1 9-inch pie crust, baked

Combine peaches, Grand Marnier and sugar. Dissolve gelatin in cold water. Add hot water and stir until clear. Add peaches, fold in whipped cream and pour in pie crust. Chill 4-6 hours. Serves 6.

Mrs. Malcolm McLean, III
Lumberton, North Carolina

Pumpkin Pie

2 8-inch pie crusts, or 1 9-inch
    deep-dish pie crust, baked
1½ cups cooked pumpkin
1¼ cups sugar
¾ teaspoon nutmeg
¾ teaspoon cinnamon
¼ teaspoon ginger
¼ teaspoon cloves

½ teaspoon salt
2 teaspoons vanilla
½ stick butter, melted
4 eggs, lightly beaten
2 cups evaporated milk, scalded
1 cup heavy cream, whipped
    Chopped candied ginger for
      garnish

Preheat oven to 450° F. Mix all ingredients together. Pour into crust and bake for 10 minutes. Reduce heat to 350° F. and bake 25-30 minutes longer, until almost set in center. Serve slightly warm. Top with lightly sweetened whipped cream and candied ginger. Serves 6-8.

Mrs. J. R. Mann
Montgomery, Alabama

Fresh Strawberry Pie

1 9-inch pie crust, baked	3 tablespoons cornstarch
1½ pints strawberries	1 cup water
3 tablespoons strawberry or	1 cup sugar
raspberry gelatin	1 cup heavy cream, whipped

Cut strawberries and place in shell. Combine the next 4 ingredients and cook until thick, stirring constantly. Pour mixture over strawberries and refrigerate to congeal. Top with whipped cream. Serves 8.

Mrs. James Crews, Jr. (Elaine Elliot)

Strawberry Cheese Pie

1¼ cups sugar	3 ounces cream cheese
3 rounded tablespoons	1 tablespoon milk
cornstarch	4 cups fresh strawberries,
Juice of 1 lemon	sliced
1½ cups water	1 cup heavy cream
¼ teaspoon salt	¼ cup sugar
Red food coloring	1 tablespoon lemon juice
1 9-inch pie crust, baked	

To make sauce, combine first 6 ingredients. Cook until thick, stirring constantly. Remove from heat and cool. Line pie crust with cream cheese that has been softened with milk. Mix sauce and berries and pour over cream cheese. Whip cream, ¼ cup sugar and lemon juice. Spread over strawberry mixture. Garnish with sliced strawberries and chill. Serves 8.

Mrs. Stephen W. Keltner (Jane Farrimond)

Fudge Pie

2 sticks butter, melted
2 cups sugar
½ cup flour
½ cup cocoa

4 eggs
½ teaspoon vanilla
½ cup pecans, chopped

Sift sugar, flour and cocoa together. Add melted butter and mix well. Add eggs and vanilla and beat with mixer on low speed, just until blended. Do not overbeat! Stir in pecans. Pour into greased, floured 9-inch square pan or 9-inch pie pan. Bake at 375° F. for 25-30 minutes. Serves 8-12.

Carolyn Mitchell Kittle

Pâte Sablée

Sugar Crust
2 cups flour, sifted
½ cup sugar, sifted
¼ teaspoon baking powder

2 sticks butter, chilled
1 egg yolk
½ teaspoon vanilla

Place dry ingredients in bowl and cut butter into flour mixture until size of oatmeal flakes. Add egg yolk and vanilla. Knead with hand until smooth. Place dough in quiche pan and press to fit. Prick well with fork and bake at 375° F. for 15-20 minutes.

Mock Cream Patissière
2 3¾-ounce packages French
   vanilla instant pudding
3 cups light cream

½ teaspoon almond extract
Sliced fruit in season, for
   garnish

Mix first three ingredients together and allow to set partially. Pour into sugar crust. Decorate with favorite fruit of season and glaze.

Glaze
½ cup red currant jelly

1 tablespoon kirsch or water

Heat jelly until melted. Add the kirsch or water and glaze the Pâte Sablée.

Mrs. John G. Albritton (Patsy Thomas)

Frozen Raspberry Pie

Almond Crust
1¼ cups flour
1 stick butter, softened
¼ cup toasted almonds, finely
    chopped

3 tablespoons sugar
¼ teaspoon salt

Mix ingredients well and press evenly into a 9-inch pie plate. Prick bottom of crust in several places. Bake 10-12 minutes at 400° F. Cool.

Filling
2 egg whites
1 10-ounce package frozen
    raspberries, thawed
¾ cup sugar

1 tablespoon lemon juice
½ teaspoon almond extract
1 cup heavy cream

In a large bowl, combine first 5 ingredients. Beat 5 minutes with mixer at medium speed. Increase speed of mixer and beat approximately 10 minutes, or until stiff peaks form. In a small bowl, beat cream until soft peaks form. Gently fold cream into raspberry mixture. Spoon into crust and freeze until firm. Let pie stand at room temperature for 10 minutes before cutting. Serves 8.

Make the day before for a great company dessert.

Mrs. John A. Stemmler (Marsha Miller)

Frozen Peach Pie

Coconut macaroon cookies
1 cup fresh peaches, mashed

1 cup sugar
1 cup heavy cream

Crush macaroon cookies and line pie plate with crumbs. Add sugar to peaches. Whip cream and fold into peaches. Pour in pie crust and freeze. Serves 8.

Mrs. Anne G. Boals (Anne Goodwin)

Baker's Grasshopper Pie

20 large marshmallows
½ cup milk
1-2 ounces crème de menthe
1-2 ounces crème de cocoa
2 cups heavy cream, whipped
and divided

1 package thin chocolate
wafers
Shaved chocolate (optional)

Melt marshmallows in milk and cool. Add liqueurs and mix. Fold in ½ the whipped cream. Pour into a pie pan lined with chocolate wafers. Freeze. When ready to serve, top with remaining whipped cream and garnish with shaved chocolate. Serves 6.

The late Chef F. O. Baker
The University Club of Memphis

Frozen Crème de Menthe Pie

2 cups crushed chocolate
wafers
5½ tablespoons butter, softened
½ gallon vanilla ice cream
7 tablespoons green crème de
menthe
2 1-ounce squares
unsweetened chocolate

6 tablespoons light cream
½ cup sugar
Dash of salt
3 tablespoons butter
1 teaspoon vanilla

Combine wafer crumbs with softened butter. Press into a 9-inch springform pan. Refrigerate at least one hour. Turn ice cream into large bowl to soften. Stir crème de menthe into ice cream. Fill wafer shell with ice cream mixture and freeze. Melt chocolate squares in cream over low heat. Add sugar and salt. Remove from heat and add butter and vanilla. Stir until cooled. Let stand until cooled thoroughly. When pie is frozen, spread chocolate sauce over top. Return to freezer until firm. Serves 10.

Delicious and easy. Men love it.

Mrs. Robert J. Hussey, Jr.

Easy Rum Pie

1 cup evaporated milk
25 regular size marshmallows
4 tablespoons light rum
1 4-ounce container Cool Whip

1 prepared chocolate crumb pie
  crust
1 Hershey bar

Heat evaporated milk and marshmallows until all are melted. Add rum. Fold in Cool Whip and stir thoroughly. Turn into pie crust and chill in refrigerator until firmly set. Shave one Hershey bar on top at serving time. Serves 6.

Easy and always gets compliments

Mrs. William V. Lawson, Jr. (Carolyn Townes)

Rum Chiffon Pie

Crust
2½ cups graham cracker crumbs
1 stick butter, melted

2 tablespoons sugar
½ teaspoon cinnamon
2 9-inch pie pans

Combine all crust ingredients and press into pie pans. Chill.

Pie Filling
2 envelopes unflavored gelatin
½ cup water
2 cups milk
1 cup sugar
6 egg yolks
½ cup rum

4 egg whites
⅓ cup sugar
1 cup heavy cream
2 tablespoons sugar
Nutmeg

Soften gelatin in ½ cup water. Set aside. Bring milk and sugar to boil. Beat egg yolks. Add small amount of hot milk mixture to yolks. Add to remaining milk mixture. Cook until mixture coats metal spoon. Stir in gelatin and rum. Cool in refrigerator until mixture begins to set. Beat egg whites with ⅓ cup sugar. Fold into custard. Divide between crumb crusts. Beat heavy cream with 2 tablespoons sugar. Spread over pies. Sprinkle nutmeg over pies and chill until ready to serve. These freeze well. Remove from freezer about ½ hour before serving. Serves 10-12.

Mrs. Hershel P. Wall (Jean Harrington)

Kahlua Pie

Crust

15 gingersnaps

5 tablespoons margarine, melted

Crush gingersnaps and add margarine. Form crust in pie pan and bake at 300° F. for 10 minutes.

Filling

21 marshmallows
1   13-ounce can evaporated milk
1   tablespoon unflavored gelatin
¼ cup cold water

2   cups heavy cream, ½ for pie and ½ for topping, whipped
7   tablespoons Kahlua, or to taste
Grated chocolate, for garnish

Melt marshmallows in evaporated milk in saucepan. Do not boil. Remove from heat and add gelatin that has been dissolved in cold water. Chill. Fold ½ of whipped cream into chilled marshmallow mixture. Add Kahlua. Pour marshmallow mixture into cooled crust and chill overnight. Top with remaining whipped cream and grated chocolate.

Mrs. Charles W. McCrary (Janie Stone)

French Silk Chocolate Pie

Meringue Pie Crust

2   egg whites
⅛ teaspoon salt
⅛ teaspoon cream of tartar

½ cup sugar
½ cup chopped pecans
1   teaspoon vanilla

Beat egg whites, salt and cream of tartar until foamy. Add sugar gradually and beat until stiff. Fold in pecans and vanilla. Place in greased 9-inch pie plate, building up sides ½ inch. Bake 1 hour at 300° F. Cool.

Filling

1   stick butter, softened
¾ cup sugar
2   squares unsweetened
    chocolate, melted

1½ teaspoons vanilla
2   egg yolks
2   whole eggs
1   cup heavy cream, whipped

Cream butter and sugar. Blend in chocolate and vanilla. Add eggs and yolks, one at a time, beating 5 minutes between each one. Do not underbeat! Pour into cooled crust and refrigerate. Decorate with whipped cream and shaved chocolate if desired. Serves 8.

Mrs. William Mitchell

Mocha Meringue

4   egg whites
⅔ cup sugar
1   cup chopped pecans
¼ cup light corn syrup
1   tablespoon instant coffee
1   6-ounce package semi-sweet
    chocolate chips

⅔ cup condensed milk
1½ cups heavy cream, divided
1   teaspoon vanilla
    Shaved chocolate

Beat egg whites until soft peaks form. Add sugar, beating until stiff peaks form. Fold in pecans. Mold around sides and bottom of a greased and floured 9-inch pie plate, forming a high edge. Bake at 275° F. for 1 hour. Turn off oven. Cool in oven 2 hours. Mix syrup, coffee and 1 tablespoon water in saucepan. Bring to a boil. Reduce heat and add chocolate. Stir until melted. Remove from heat and stir in milk, 1 cup of cream and vanilla. Cover and chill 1 hour. Whip mixture until soft peaks form. Fill meringue shell with mixture and freeze overnight. Whip remaining ½ cup cream. Spread over dessert. Decorate with shaved chocolate, if desired. Serves 8.

Mrs. Rowe Belcher (Susan Ramsey)

Sinful Sundae Pie

Vanilla wafers
1 cup evaporated milk
1 cup small marshmallows
1 6-ounce package chocolate
  chips

⅛ teaspoon salt
2 pints vanilla ice cream,
  softened in refrigerator

Line bottom and sides of greased 9-inch pie pan with whole vanilla wafers. Combine next 4 ingredients in saucepan. Cook and stir until blended and thick. Cool slightly. Spoon 1 pint ice cream into wafer crust. Drizzle half of sauce over ice cream. Repeat layers of ice cream and sauce. Return to freezer and chill 4 hours. Serves 8-10.

Mrs. Mickey Moran (Pat Taylor)

Banana Split Pie

Crust
¾ stick margarine
2 cups vanilla wafer crumbs

¼ cup sugar

Melt margarine and mix well with vanilla wafer crumbs and sugar. Cover bottom of 3-quart rectangular casserole with crumb mixture. Bake for 10 minutes at 350° F. and cool.

Filling
1½ sticks margarine, softened
2 eggs
2 cups powdered sugar
6 bananas, sliced

1 20-ounce can crushed
  pineapple, drained
1 cup heavy cream, whipped
1 cup chopped pecans

Beat margarine and eggs together. Slowly add powdered sugar, beating at least 15 minutes with electric mixer. Spread mixture over crust and cover with layers of sliced bananas, drained pineapple and whipped cream. Sprinkle chopped pecans on top. Serves 15.

Mrs. R. Franklin Adams (Corinne Ridolphi)

English Lemon Tarts

½ stick butter
3 eggs, beaten
1 cup sugar

Juice of 2 large lemons
6-8 3-inch tart shells, baked
1 cup heavy cream, whipped

Melt butter and sugar in double boiler. Stir well and add eggs slowly, beating continuously. Add lemon juice and stir well. Cook over low heat. Stir constantly until custard is thick. Refrigerate until ready to serve in baked shells. Top with whipped cream. Serves 6-8.

Mrs. Rowe Belcher (Susan Ramsey)

Southern Blackberry Cobbler

4 cups fresh blackberries or
   two 16-ounce packages
   frozen blackberries,
   thawed
¾ cup sugar

3 tablespoons flour
1½ cups water
1 tablespoon lemon juice
2 tablespoons butter, melted

Place berries in greased 2-quart baking dish. Mix sugar and flour. Add water and lemon juice. Pour this mixture over berries. Bake at 350° F. for 15 minutes while preparing crust. Place crust over hot berries. Brush with butter. Bake at 425° F. for 20-30 minutes.

Crust
1¾ cups flour
2-3 tablespoons sugar
2 teaspoons baking powder
1 teaspoon salt

¼ cup shortening
6 tablespoons heavy cream
6 tablespoons buttermilk or
   sour cream

Mix first 4 ingredients. Cut in shortening until mixture resembles coarse crumbs. Stir in cream and buttermilk. Knead dough 4 or 5 times. Roll to ¼ inch thickness on floured board and cut to fit dish. Serves 8.

Mrs. Nick Agneta

Amaretto Cheesecake

1½ cups chocolate wafer crumbs
1 cup blanched almonds, lightly toasted and chopped
⅓ cup sugar
¾ stick butter, softened
24 ounces cream cheese softened
1 cup sugar
4 eggs
⅓ cup heavy cream
⅓ cup Amaretto
2 teaspoons vanilla
16 ounces sour cream
1 tablespoon sugar

In a bowl, combine wafer crumbs, almonds, ⅓ cup sugar and butter. Pat the mixture into the bottom and sides of a buttered 10-inch spring-form pan. In a large bowl, blend cream cheese, 1 cup sugar and beat in 4 eggs, one at a time. Add heavy cream, Amaretto and 1 teaspoon vanilla. Beat this mixture until light. Pour batter into crumb-lined pan. Bake cake at 375° F. for about 30 minutes. Center may be shaky. To use a 9-inch pan, bake 10-15 minutes longer. Transfer cake to a rack and let stand for 5 minutes. In bowl, combine 1 teaspoon vanilla, sour cream and 1 tablespoon sugar. Spread mixture evenly on cake and bake 5 more minutes. Transfer cake to a rake and let cool completely. Serves 12-16.

One 8½-ounce box of chocolate wafers equals 2½ cups of chocolate wafer crumbs.

Mrs. Max B. Ostner, Jr. (Mary Margaret Buffa)

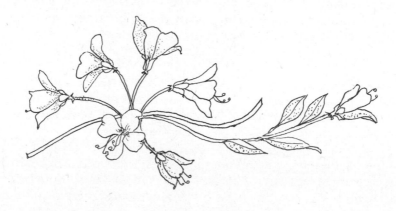

Cheesecake for All Seasons

½ stick butter, melted
1 cup graham cracker crumbs
6 eggs, separated
1 teaspoon cream of tartar
3 tablespoons sugar
19 ounces cream cheese

1½ cups sugar
3 tablespoons flour
½ teaspoon salt
16 ounces sour cream
1 teaspoon vanilla

Have all ingredients at room temperature. Mix butter and crumbs. Set aside ¼ cup and press remainder firmly on bottom of well greased 9-inch springform or tube pan. Add cream of tartar to egg whites. Beat until foamy. Gradually add 3 tablespoons sugar. Beat until stiff. Set aside. Beat cream cheese until soft. Mix sugar, flour and salt and gradually beat into cheese. Add egg yolks one at a time, beating well after each. Mix in sour cream and vanilla. Fold in egg whites and pour batter into prepared pan. If cake is to be served without fruit topping, sprinkle reserved ¼ cup crumbs over batter. Bake at 325° F. for 1¼ hours, turn off heat, open oven door and let sit for 10 minutes. Remove and let stand on rack out of drafts until cool. Chill. Cake will shrink as it cools. Serves 12.

Decorate with pie cherries and holly, blueberries and violets, strawberries and roses, or mandarin oranges and autumn leaves.

Mrs. William T. Satterfield (Janet Reid)

Miniature Cheesecakes

24 ounces cream cheese, softened
1¼ cups sugar, divided
5 eggs
2 teaspoons vanilla, divided

1 cup sour cream
Canned blueberries or peaches, or strawberry or cherry preserves

Mix cream cheese, 1 cup sugar, eggs and 1 teaspoon vanilla with electric mixer. Fill midget foil cups ¾ full. Bake on cookie sheet for 30-40 minutes at 300° F. Mix sour cream, ¼ cup sugar and remaining vanilla. Spoon on top of each cupcake. Dot with preserves. Bake 5 minutes longer. If using blueberries or peaches, spoon on top after final baking. Cheesecakes may be frozen. If using canned fruit, add after thawing. Makes about 50.

Mrs. James B. Chase, Jr. (Barbara Ruth Duncan)

Mrs. William McCrary, III (Tancie Lewis)

Chocolate Cheesecake

Crust

1 cup graham cracker crumbs	3 tablespoons sugar
3 tablespoons butter, melted	3 tablespoons cocoa

Combine crust ingredients and mix well. Press evenly over bottom and sides of 9-inch springform pan. Refrigerate while preparing filling.

Filling

3 eggs	1 teaspoon vanilla
1 cup sugar	⅛ teaspoon salt
24 ounces cream cheese, softened	1 cup sour cream
2 6-ounce packages chocolate chips, melted	

Combine eggs and sugar. Beat cream cheese with electric mixer until smooth. Add egg-sugar mixture and beat. Add chocolate, vanilla, salt and sour cream. Beat until smooth. Pour into crust. Bake at 350° F. for 1 hour. Remove cheesecake from oven. Cool in pan on wire rack. Cover, then refrigerate overnight.

Topping

1 cup heavy cream, whipped	2 tablespoons powdered sugar

Mix together whipped cream and sugar. Remove sides of springform pan. Decorate with sweet whipped cream. Serves 16.

Variation: Also delicious made with the crust for Amaretto cheesecake.

Mrs. Harry McKee (Larane Wilson)

Yummy Apple Cake

3 cups flour	2 eggs, well beaten
2 cups sugar	2 teaspoons vanilla
2 teaspoons soda	3 cups peeled, cored and
2 teaspoons cinnamon	chopped apples
1 teaspoon salt	1 cup raisins
1 teaspoon nutmeg	2 tablespoons butter
2 sticks butter, melted	2 tablespoons sugar

Sift first six ingredients together. Add next five ingredients. Mix well and pour into greased 9 x 13-inch pan. Bake at 350° F. for 40 minutes. Spread warm cake with butter and sprinkle with sugar. Serve warm or cold. Store cake in refrigerator. Serves 12.

This is good topped with whipped cream.

Mrs. Scott Allison Arnold, III (Anne Dillard)

Delia's Applesauce Cake

1 stick margarine	½ teaspoon cloves
1½ cups sugar	2 teaspoons soda
1 egg	1½ cups applesauce
3 cups flour	1 cup chopped dates
½ teaspoon nutmeg	1 cup chopped pecans
½ teaspoon salt	Powdered sugar
1 teaspoon cinnamon	

Cream margarine, sugar and egg together until fluffy. Sift next 6 ingredients together. Add alternately with applesauce to creamed mixture. Mix thoroughly. Add dates and pecans. Pour into greased and floured tube pan. Bake at 350° F. for 45 minutes or until done.

Mrs. Gilbert McSpadden, Jr. (Jane Ridens)

Carrot Cake

2 cups sugar	2 teaspoons baking powder
4 eggs	1½ teaspoons cinnamon
1⅓ cups oil	1 teaspoon salt
2 cups flour, presifted	4 cups grated carrots
2 teaspoons baking soda	

Preheat oven to 350° F. Grease and flour three 9-inch cake pans. Beat sugar and eggs until thickened. Stir in oil. Sift flour, soda, baking powder, cinnamon and salt. Stir into egg mixture. Fold in carrots. Spoon batter into pans. Bake for 35-40 minutes until cake tests done. Turn onto wire racks and cool.

Cream Cheese Frosting

8 ounces cream cheese, softened	2 cups powdered sugar
1 stick butter	1 8-ounce can crushed pineapple (optional)
1 teaspoon vanilla	

Mix together all frosting ingredients. Beat until smooth and frost cake.

This is really moist. It should be kept in the refrigerator. Vary cake by baking in a tube pan, as cupcakes or sheet cake.
Tube pan—1 hour
Cupcakes—25-30 minutes
Sheetcake—45-50 minutes

Mrs. Scott Allison Arnold, III (Anne Dillard)

Grandmother's Jam Cake

1½ sticks butter
1 cup sugar
3 eggs, separated
2 cups flour
1 teaspoon cinnamon
½ teaspoon nutmeg
½ teaspoon allspice
½ teaspoon ground cloves

¼ teaspoon salt
½ cup buttermilk
1 teaspoon soda
1 cup blackberry jam
1 cup mincemeat
1 cup chopped pecans
Carol's Glaze (see Index)

Have all ingredients at room temperature. Cream butter and sugar. Add egg yolks and beat well. Combine flour, spices and salt. Mix buttermilk and soda. Add flour mixture and buttermilk alternately to creamed mixture. Stir in jam, mincemeat and pecans. Fold in stiffly beaten egg whites. Pour into greased and floured tube or bundt pan. Bake at 350° F. for 15 minutes. Reduce heat to 325° F. and bake approximately 1 hour longer. While cake is hot, pour on Carol's Glaze, if desired. Cool in pan.

This recipe is over 100 years old and is really different. Stays moist.

Mrs. J. R. Mann
Montgomery, Alabama

Becky's Pumpkin Cake

Cake
2 cups sugar
1¼ cups oil
4 eggs
1 teaspoon soda

2 teaspoons cinnamon
2 cups self-rising flour
1 16-ounce can pumpkin

Beat ingredients together with mixer in order given. Bake in greased and floured bundt pan at 350° F. for 1 hour. Let cool for 5 minutes and remove from pan. Serves 14-16.

Icing
3 ounces cream cheese
½ stick butter, melted
1 cup powdered sugar

1 tablespoon milk
1 teaspoon vanilla

Beat icing ingredients together until smooth. While cake is still warm, pour icing over top, allowing to drip down sides.

Mrs. James B. Cross (Lynn Woods)

Peach Cake

Cake

1 box yellow cake mix
4 tablespoons flour
1 3-ounce package peach
   gelatin
4 eggs

1 cup cooking oil
1 cup mashed peaches, fresh or
   canned, with juice

In a large bowl, sift cake mix, flour and gelatin together. Add eggs, beating after each addition. Add oil and beat well. Mix in peaches and juice. Bake in greased tube pan for 40-60 minutes at 350° F. Cool 15 minutes and remove from pan.

Icing

2 cups powdered sugar
1 stick butter, softened

½ cup mashed peaches and
   juice

Cream sugar and butter together until blended. Mix in peaches. Ice cooled cake. Serves 15-20.

The moistest cake ever! For strawberry cake, use white cake mix and strawberry gelatin. Substitute strawberries for peaches and add 1 cup chopped pecans to cake batter for special touch.

Mrs. Joel W. Brown (Lisa McBurney)

Mrs. Richard A. Miller, Jr. (Shelley Ann Brodnax)

Prune Cake

3 eggs
1 cup oil
1½ cups sugar
2 cups sifted flour
1 teaspoon soda
1 teaspoon cinnamon
1 teaspoon nutmeg
1 teaspoon allspice
1 teaspoon salt
1 cup buttermilk
1 cup cooked, seeded, chopped
  prunes
1 teaspoon vanilla
½ cup chopped pecans

Mix together eggs, oil and sugar, and beat until light. Sift together flour, soda, cinnamon, nutmeg, allspice, salt and add to sugar mixture. Mix buttermilk, prunes, vanilla and pecans and add to first mixture. Mix well by hand and pour into a tube pan lined on bottom with waxed paper. Bake 1 hour at 300° F. or until cake tests done.

Sauce
1 cup sugar
½ cup buttermilk
1 stick butter
½ teaspoon soda
1 tablespoon white corn syrup
½ teaspoon vanilla

Boil sauce ingredients 2 minutes. Pour over cake as soon as cake is taken from oven. Leave in pan until thoroughly cold. Serves 16.

Mrs. George M. Klepper, Jr. (Gladys Dye)

Apricot Brandy Pound Cake

2 sticks butter
3 cups sugar
6 eggs
3 cups flour
1 teaspoon salt
¼ teaspoon soda
8 ounces sour cream
¼ teaspoon rum flavoring
1 teaspoon vanilla
1 teaspoon orange extract
½ teaspoon lemon extract
¼ teaspoon almond extract
½ cup apricot brandy

Grease and flour tube or bundt cake pan. Cream butter and sugar well. Add eggs one at a time, beating well after each addition. Sift together dry ingredients. Combine sour cream, flavorings, and brandy. Add dry ingredients to egg mixture alternately with liquid. Bake at 325° F. for 70-90 minutes. Cool before removing from pan. Serves 10-20.

Cake keeps in refrigerator for several weeks and freezes well.

Mrs. William C. Lewis

Brown Sugar Pound Cake

2 sticks plus 3 tablespoons
    butter
5 tablespoons shortening
2 cups light brown sugar
1 cup sugar
5 eggs
3 cups sifted flour

½ teaspoon salt
1 teaspoon baking powder
1 cup milk
1 teaspoon vanilla
1 cup chopped walnuts or
    pecans (optional)

Cream butter and shortening. Gradually add sugars, creaming until mixture is light and fluffy. Beat in eggs one at a time. Sift dry ingredients and add alternately with milk and vanilla to the creamed mixture. Begin and end with dry ingredients. Fold in nuts. Pour batter into greased and floured 10-inch tube pan. Bake at 350° F. for 1 hour and 15 minutes. Cool 10 minutes, then remove from pan. Pour Walnut Glaze over hot cake. Serves 12-14.

Walnut Glaze
1 cup powdered sugar
2 tablespoons butter
6 tablespoons light cream

½ teaspoon vanilla
½ cup chopped walnuts or
    pecans

To make glaze, cream sugar and butter. Add cream, vanilla and nuts and blend well.

Mrs. Richard Rossie

Double Chocolate Pound Cake

1   8-ounce Hershey bar
2   sticks butter
4   eggs
2   cups sugar
1   16-ounce can Hershey syrup
2½ cups flour, sifted

¼   teaspoon salt
½   teaspoon soda
1   cup buttermilk
1   cup chopped pecans
     (optional)

Melt Hershey bar over boiling water, adding 2 tablespoons water to smooth if necessary. Cream butter, add sugar and eggs; beat well. Add melted Hershey bar and remaining ingredients, mixing well after each addition. Fold in pecans. Pour batter into greased and floured tube or bundt pan. Bake at 350° F. for 1¼-1½ hours. Cool on rack before removing cake from pan. Sprinkle with powdered sugar. Serves 12-16.

For a special treat, top with chocolate glaze!

Mrs. Richard S. Dickerson

Five Flavor Pound Cake

2   sticks butter
½   cup shortening
3   cups sugar
5   eggs
3   cups flour
½   teaspoon baking powder

1   cup milk
1   teaspoon lemon flavoring
1   teaspoon butter flavoring
1   teaspoon vanilla flavoring
1   teaspoon rum flavoring
1   teaspoon coconut flavoring

Mix butter, shortening and sugar. Add eggs one at a time. Mix baking powder with flour. Add this alternately with milk to butter-sugar mixture. Add the five flavorings. Grease and flour tube pan. Bake for 1 hour and 20 minutes at 325° F.

Mrs. Frank H. Reid (Diana Mann)

Seven-Up Pound Cake

2 sticks butter, softened
½ cup shortening
3 cups sugar
5 eggs

3 cups flour
1 teaspoon vanilla extract
1 teaspoon lemon extract
1 cup 7-Up or Sprite

Cream butter, shortening and sugar. Add eggs and flour alternately, beating well between additions. Fold in remaining ingredients. Bake in well-greased and floured bundt or tube pan for approximately 1¼ hours at 325° F. Cool before removing from pan. Dust with powdered sugar. Serves 15.

This cake is moist and freezes well.

Mrs. William S. Mitchell

Dr. Bird's Cake

2¾ cups flour
1 teaspoon cinnamon
1 teaspoon salt
1 teaspoon soda
2 cups sugar
3 eggs, lightly beaten
2 medium bananas, diced

1 8-ounce can crushed
   pineapple, drained
1 7-ounce can coconut
1 cup chopped pecans
1½ teaspoons vanilla
1½ cups oil

Sift dry ingredients into bowl. Add remaining ingredients. Mix well but do not beat. Pour into greased and floured bundt pan. Bake approximately 1-1½ hours at 325° F., or until done. Serves 12-15.

This cake freezes well and stays moist for 2 weeks.

Mrs. Dorsey Mathis, Jr. (Margaret Jones)

"Almond Cake" from Albufeira

1 cup flour
¾ cup sugar
½ teaspoon baking powder
½ teaspoon soda
¼ teaspoon salt
1 egg

½ cup buttermilk
½ teaspoon vanilla
5½ tablespoons butter, melted
    and cooled to room
    temperature
⅔ cup sliced almonds

Sift together flour, sugar, baking powder, soda and salt. Beat egg, buttermilk and vanilla until smooth; stir in butter. Add flour mixture, stirring until nearly smooth. Pour batter into greased 9-inch springform pan. Bake at 350° F. until center of cake springs back when lightly touched, approximately 35 minutes. While cake is hot, cover top with almonds and Hot Almond Syrup, letting syrup soak into cake. Broil about 6 inches from heat until almonds are lightly toasted. Cool for 10 minutes on rack. Loosen sides between pan and cake. Cool completely before releasing springform.

Hot Almond Syrup
¾ cup sugar
6 tablespoons water

½ teaspoon almond extract

In a 1-quart saucepan, combine sugar and water. Boil until mixture reaches 220° F. on candy thermometer. Remove from heat and stir in almond extract. Serves 8-10.

This cake was served in the late 17th and early 18th centuries by convent nuns of Portugal to visiting religious dignitaries, royalty and other travelers of importance!

Mrs. James B. Green, Jr. (Betty Brown)

Orange Oatmeal Cake

1¼ cups boiling water
1 cup quick-cooking oats
1 stick butter
1 cup sugar
½ cup dark brown sugar
2 eggs
¼ cup frozen orange juice
concentrate, thawed but
not diluted

1 teaspoon vanilla
1¾ cups flour
1 teaspoon baking powder
1 teaspoon soda
½ teaspoon salt
½ teaspoon ground cinnamon
¾ cup chopped walnuts

Pour boiling water over oats and set aside. Cream butter with sugars. Beat in eggs one at a time. Add orange juice concentrate and vanilla. Sift together flour, baking powder, soda, salt and cinnamon; blend into creamed mixture alternately with oats, beginning and ending with flour mixture. Fold in walnuts. Bake in greased 13 x 9 x 2-inch pan at 350° F. for 30 minutes, or until cake is done. Cool before adding topping.

Topping
½ cup packed dark brown sugar
4 tablespoons butter
2 tablespoons frozen orange
juice concentrate, thawed
but not diluted

1 cup flaked coconut
¾ cup chopped walnuts

In a small saucepan, combine brown sugar, butter and orange juice. Bring to a boil and cook for 1 minute, stirring constantly. Add coconut and walnuts. Spread cake with topping. Place cake under broiler until topping is golden brown and bubbly. Watch carefully to avoid burning.

This makes 18-20 small squares for pick-up servings. It serves 12 cut into larger squares for dessert. Top with whipped cream and dust with grated orange peel.

Mrs. John S. Palmer (Nancy Moore)

Dorothy Mann's Pecan Cake

1½ pounds golden raisins
    Bourbon for soaking raisins
3 sticks butter
2 cups sugar
6 eggs
½ cup unsulfured molasses
1 teaspoon soda

4 cups sifted flour
½ teaspoon salt
2 teaspoons nutmeg
2 teaspoons cinnamon
1 cup good bourbon
5 cups broken pecans

Soak raisins overnight in bourbon and then drain well. Have all ingredients at room temperature. Cream butter and sugar. Add eggs, one at a time, beating well. Stir in molasses mixed with soda. Sift flour, salt and spices. Add alternately with bourbon. Fold in raisins and nuts. Grease tube pan and line with 4 layers of waxed paper, sticking paper together with shortening. Bake at 275° F. about 2½ hours. Check after 2 hours. Cool thoroughly in pan.

This cake will keep indefinitely if wrapped in cloth dampened with bourbon and covered with heavy aluminum foil.

Mrs. J. R. Mann

Layered Coconut Floss Cake

16 ounces sour cream
2 cups sugar
2 packages frozen coconut

1 package Duncan Hines
    Deluxe II yellow cake mix

Mix sour cream, sugar and coconut and let stand overnight. Bake cake in two round cake pans according to package directions and let sit overnight. Next day, cut the layers in half with dental floss. Ice one layer at a time, putting cut side up. Let icing begin to soak in before putting on the next layer. When finished, refrigerate until serving time. May sprinkle coconut on top.

*May be made a day or two in advance. This is a **must** for coconut lovers!*

Mrs. Harold Jenkins, Jr. (Janice Cochran)

Etta Mae's Yellow Cake

2 cups sugar
2 sticks butter
3 eggs
¼ cup lemon juice

3 cups flour, sifted
2 teaspoons soda
1 cup buttermilk
2 teaspoons vanilla

Cream sugar and butter. Add eggs and mix. Add lemon juice, flour, soda and buttermilk, mixing after each addition. Add vanilla. Bake at 350° F. for one hour in greased bundt pan, or until done.

Etta Mae Jones

One More Chocolate Cake

Cake
1 cup sugar
1 cup flour
½ stick butter
¼ cup shortening
2 tablespoons cocoa
½ cup water
½ teaspoon soda

¼ cup buttermilk
1 teaspoon cinnamon
1 tablespoon instant coffee
   crystals
1 teaspoon vanilla
1 egg
⅛ teaspoon salt

Combine sugar and flour in mixing bowl. Blend next 4 ingredients in saucepan, bring to a boil and add to flour and sugar. Mix well. Add remaining ingredients and blend thoroughly. Pour into greased 8 x 8-inch pan and bake at 400° F. for 20 minutes. Top with following icing.

Icing
½ stick butter
2 tablespoons cocoa
3 tablespoons buttermilk
1 tablespoon instant coffee
   crystals

1 cup powdered sugar
½ cup chopped pecans

Prepare icing while cake bakes. Combine first 4 ingredients and heat until melted. Add to sugar and mix well. Stir in pecans. Pour over hot cake. Serves 12.

Mrs. Russell G. Henley (Suzanne Smith)

My Mother's Shortcakes

¼ cup shortening
1 cup flour
⅛ teaspoon salt
2 level teaspoons baking
  powder

¼ cup sugar
1 egg, lightly beaten
1 teaspoon vanilla
¼-½ cup milk

Grease muffin pan with shortening. Mix together all remaining ingredients. Blend in extra milk, if necessary. The less milk used, the shorter the cakes. Spoon batter into pan and bake at 375° F. for 15 minutes Makes 6-8 cakes.

A real treat served split and topped with ice cream and fresh fruit. These may be baked ahead and reheated.

Mrs. Rowlett W. Sneed, Jr. (Sarah Gaye Craig)

Date Torte

4 egg whites
½ cup sugar
1 teaspoon vanilla
¼ teaspoon salt

1 cup chopped pecans
1 cup chopped dates
½ cup vanilla wafer crumbs
1 cup heavy cream, whipped

Beat egg whites until stiff; fold in sugar gradually. Add flavoring and salt. Fold in pecans and dates. Pour into greased 8-inch pan lined with cookie crumbs. Bake at 325° F. for 45 minutes. Top with whipped cream. Serves 6.

Mrs. John Parsons (Frances Urquart)

Meringue Torte

6 egg whites
2 teaspoons vanilla
½ teaspoon cream of tartar
2 cups sugar

4 1⅛-ounce or six ¾-ounce
  Heath bars, frozen
2 cups heavy cream, whipped

Beat egg whites, vanilla and cream of tartar to soft peaks. Very gradually beat in sugar until very stiff peaks form. Cover 2 cookie sheets with brown paper. Draw a 9-inch circle on each and spread meringue evenly within the lines. Bake at 275° F. for 1 hour. Turn off heat and let dry at least 2 hours. Break up the Heath bars and fold gently into the whipped cream. Spread ⅓ of Heath bar mixture between layers of meringue. Frost top and sides with remaining mixture. Chill overnight. Garnish with more candy. Serves 12-15.

Mrs. William R. Hackett (Sandra Childress)

Pineapple Torte

Cake
1 cup sugar
1 stick butter, melted
2 egg yolks
1 cup milk
2 teaspoons baking powder

1 teaspoon vanilla
1 cup chopped pecans
2 cups crushed graham
  crackers
2 egg whites, stiffly beaten

Mix cake ingredients as listed. Bake at 300° F. for 30 minutes in a 9 x 13-inch pan.

Topping
1 cup sugar

1 cup crushed pineapple

Cook topping ingredients in saucepan until thick. Spread on cake as soon as it is removed from the oven. Cut into squares. Top with whipped cream if desired. Serves 10-12.

Mrs. Dennis Higdon (Joanna Coss)

Addie's Divinity

3 cups sugar, divided
⅓ cup boiling water
3 egg whites, stiffly beaten
1 cup white corn syrup
½ cup chopped pecans
1 teaspoon vanilla

Combine 1 cup sugar with water and boil, without stirring, until mixture spins a thread, 230° F. on candy thermometer. Slowly pour over egg whites, beating constantly. Combine remaining sugar and syrup and begin cooking on medium-low heat when first mixture is removed from heat. Beat egg mixture until the sugar-syrup mixture reaches the crack stage, 300° F., or until small drops form brittle mass in cup of cold water. Remove from heat and cool until bubbles disappear; pour over egg mixture and beat continuously until stiff. Add pecans and vanilla. Drop from spoon onto waxed paper.

This must be made on cool, dry day to be completely successful.

Mrs. D. Randolph Ramey (Minje Mitchell)

Caramel Candy

1 teaspoon soda
1 cup buttermilk
2 tablespoons white corn syrup
2 cups sugar
1 cup chopped pecans
1 teaspoon vanilla
⅛ teaspoon salt
1 tablespoon butter

Add soda to buttermilk in heavy iron skillet. Add corn syrup and sugar and mix thoroughly. Cook, stirring constantly, until soft ball forms in water. Set aside to cool. Add pecans, vanilla, salt and butter. Drop by teaspoon on waxed paper.

Mrs. Max Lucas (Ruth Plyler)

Corena Lewis's Chocolate Marvels

2 6-ounce packages
   butterscotch morsels
1 4-ounce package German
   sweet chocolate
1 1-inch square paraffin
2 cups chopped pecans

Melt first three ingredients in top of double boiler. Stir well and mix in pecans. Drop by tablespoon on waxed paper. Let cool. Makes 2 dozen.

Mrs. Lee L. Wardlaw (Mary Linda Lewis)

Kay's Candy

2   sticks butter
1⅓ cups sugar
3   tablespoons water
1   tablespoon light corn syrup
1   cup coarsely chopped,
     blanched almonds, toasted

4   4½-ounce milk chocolate
     candy bars, melted
1   cup finely chopped blanched
     almonds, toasted

In large saucepan, melt butter. Add sugar, water and corn syrup. Cook over medium heat, stirring occasionally. When mixture reaches the hard crack stage, 300° F. on candy thermometer, quickly stir in the coarsely chopped almonds. Spread in well-greased 13x9x2-inch baking pan. Cool thoroughly. Turn out on waxed paper. Spread with chocolate and sprinkle with remaining almonds. If necessary, chill to firm chocolate. Break in pieces. Makes about 50 pieces.

Mrs. Kay K. Butler (Kay Kendall)

Pecan Goodies

½ cup evaporated milk
½ cup sugar
1 tablespoon corn syrup

1 cup semi-sweet chocolate
   chips
1 cup coarsely chopped pecans
1-inch square paraffin, grated

Mix milk, sugar and syrup in a heavy 2-quart pan. Cook, stirring constantly, over medium heat until mixture boils. Boil and stir two minutes more. Remove from heat. Stir in chips until melted. Stir in pecans and paraffin. Drop mixture by teaspoon onto waxed paper. Chill until firm. Makes 36-40 clusters.

Mrs. William R. Hackett (Sandy Childress)

Orange Pecans

1 cup sugar
1 orange, juice and rind

1 pound pecan halves

Bring sugar, juice and rind of orange to quick boil. Remove from heat and stir in pecans. Let cool 10 minutes and stir again. Cool 10 more minutes, stir and pour onto waxed paper.

A very special Christmas gift.

Mrs. L. P. Daniel (Betty Hurt)

Spiced Pecans

2 tablespoons cold water	¼ teaspoon cinnamon
1 lightly beaten egg white	¼ teaspoon crushed cloves
½ cup sugar	¼ teaspoon allspice
¼ teaspoon salt	1 cup pecan halves

Add water to egg white. Dissolve sugar in water and egg mixture. Add salt and spices and mix well. Dip nuts in mixture. Place on greased cookie sheet, flat side down. Bake at 250° F. until golden brown, about one hour.

Can be frozen and reheated.

Mrs. John Lawo, Jr. (Paula Domke)

Mudballs

½ cup powdered carob	½ cup sesame seeds
½ cup honey	½ cup wheat germ
½ cup crunchy peanut butter	1 cup coconut
½ cup sunflower seeds	

Mix all ingredients except coconut. Shape into ¾-inch balls and roll in coconut. Makes about 4-5 dozen.

Healthy snack!

Mrs. Gavin M. Gentry (Mary Jane Coleman)

Peanut Butter Surprises

½ cup peanut butter	Powdered sugar
1 cup dry powdered milk	Peanuts or M & M candies
½ cup honey	

Mix peanut butter, dry powdered milk and honey into stiff batter. Form into small balls and roll in sugar or dry powdered milk. Top each with peanut or M & M candy. Refrigerate to keep firm.

Nutritious treat children can make for themselves.

Mrs. Ned E. Turner (Cathy Carberry)

Our Christmas Cookies

5 sticks butter	6 cups flour
4 cups light brown sugar	3 eggs, separated and divided

Cream together butter and sugar. Beat together 3 egg yolks and 1 egg white. Add flour alternately with beaten eggs. Roll out to desired thickness and cut with cookie cutter. Beat remaining egg whites and brush tops of cookies. Bake at 350° F. until edges of cookies are barely brown.

This is a good recipe for children because the dough does not toughen from the attentions of too many bakers.

Mrs. Raymond H. Larson (Carol Edmunds)

Bran Crisps

2 sticks butter	½ teaspoon soda
1½ cups sugar	½ teaspoon salt
2 eggs	2 cups 40% bran flakes
1 teaspoon vanilla	⅓ cup wheat germ
2 cups flour	

Cream butter and sugar until light and fluffy. Add eggs and vanilla. Sift next 3 ingredients together, add to creamed mixture and blend well. Stir in bran flakes and wheat germ. Drop by teaspoon onto ungreased baking sheets and bake for 12 minutes at 375° F. Makes 5½ dozen.

Mrs. William Denman (Julie Moss)

Cashew Oatmeal Cookies

1 stick butter	¾ teaspoon baking powder
1 cup brown sugar, packed	½ teaspoon soda
¼ cup sour cream	1½ cups oats
1 egg	1 cup salted cashews, coarsely
1 teaspoon vanilla	chopped
1 cup flour	

Beat butter and sugar together until creamy. Add next 3 ingredients. Sift together next 3 ingredients. Add to creamed mixture and mix well. Stir in oats and cashews. Drop by rounded teaspoon onto greased cookie sheets. Bake at 400° F. about 8 minutes.

Frosting

½ stick butter	½ teaspoon vanilla
3 tablespoons milk	2 cups powdered sugar

Heat butter in medium saucepan and brown lightly. Remove from heat and cool 5 minutes. Add milk and vanilla. Beat in sugar until smooth and thick enough to spread. Frost cooled cookies. Makes 4 dozen.

Mrs. Dennis Higdon (Joanna Coss)

Cream Wafers

Wafers

2 sticks butter, softened	2 cups sifted flour
⅓ cup heavy cream	½ cup sugar

Mix first three wafer ingredients well and chill at least 1 hour. Roll out ⅛-inch thick on floured board. Cut with 1½-inch cookie cutter. Coat each round with sugar and place on ungreased baking sheet. Prick with fork several times and bake 7-9 minutes at 375° F.

Filling

½ stick butter, softened	1 egg yolk
¾ cup powdered sugar	1 teaspoon vanilla

Mix filling ingredients well and put wafers together with filling. Makes about 5 dozen.

Mrs. Donald Howdeshell (Ann Eastland)

Divine Cookies

1   stick margarine
1   cup sugar
3   tablespoons water
1   teaspoon vanilla
8   ounces chopped dates

2½ cups Rice Krispies cereal
1   cup chopped pecans
1   3½-ounce can flaked coconut

Boil margarine, sugar, water, vanilla and dates for 5 minutes. Remove from heat. Stir in Rice Krispies and pecans. Spread in flat, greased 6x9-inch pan. Sprinkle with coconut and cut into squares.

Instead of pressing flat, may form into small bite-sized balls. Then shake balls in powdered sugar in paper bag until coated.

Mrs. Rad Daniel (Ann Gill)

Holiday Treats

1½ cups brown sugar
2   sticks butter
3   eggs
2   squares unsweetened
      chocolate, melted
3   cups flour
1   teaspoon cinnamon
1   teaspoon nutmeg
1   teaspoon allspice

1   teaspoon soda
1   cup raisins
1   pound candied pineapple,
      chopped
1   pound candied cherries,
      chopped
1   pound dates, chopped
1   pound pecans, chopped
¼   cup bourbon

Cream sugar and butter. Add eggs, one at a time, mixing well. Cream in chocolate. In separate bowl, mix next 5 ingredients. Blend flour mixture into creamed mixture. Fold in remaining ingredients. Drop from teaspoon onto greased cookie sheet. Bake at 325° F. for 20 minutes, or until done. Makes about 12 dozen cookies.

Really nice Christmas present.

Mrs. Lucian Wadlington (Patsy Mullins)

Kolachki (Russian Cookies)

Dough

8 ounces cream cheese
2 sticks butter

2 cups flour

Mix dough ingredients well and form into ball. Wrap in waxed paper and chill overnight.

Filling

2 egg whites
½ cup sugar
¼ teaspoon vanilla

½ pound ground walnuts
Powdered sugar

Mix filling ingredients together. Roll dough ⅛-inch flat in powdered sugar. Cut dough into 2-inch squares. Fill squares by placing some filling mixture top to bottom in a line off-center of square and roll up. Bake at 350° F. for 12-15 minutes. Roll in powdered sugar. Makes 3 dozen cookies.

Great holiday cookies, and they freeze well.

Mrs. Keith S. Kays (Jackie Wood)

Lemonade Cookies

2 sticks butter
1½ cups sugar
2 eggs
3 cups flour

1 teaspoon soda
1 6-ounce can frozen lemonade
   concentrate, thawed

Cream together butter and 1 cup sugar. Add eggs and beat until light and fluffy. Sift together flour and soda. Add alternately to creamed mixture with ½ cup of lemonade concentrate. Drop dough by teaspoon 2 inches apart onto ungreased cookie sheet. Bake cookies in 400° F. oven about 8 minutes, or until lightly browned around edges. Brush hot cookies lightly with remaining lemonade concentrate. Sprinkle with remaining sugar. Remove cookies to cooling rack. Makes about 4 dozen small cookies.

Children love them!

Mrs. John Klettner (Virginia Hays)

Poppy Seed Cookies

1 cup shortening
1 cup sugar
3 eggs
¼ cup orange juice

3½ cups flour
1 tablespoon baking powder
½ cup poppy seeds

Cream shortening and sugar. Add eggs and orange juice. Sift flour and baking powder together and add to creamed mixture. Add poppy seeds. Dough will be soft. Refrigerate 30 minutes. Drop by teaspoon onto well-greased cookie sheets. Bake at 375° F. for 10 minutes. Makes 3-3½ dozen cookies.

Unusual!

Mrs. Dan Turley, Jr.

Pecan Butter Cookies

2 sticks butter
½ cup brown sugar
¼ cup sugar
1 egg yolk

2 cups flour
1 teaspoon vanilla
1 cup chopped pecans

Cream butter and sugars well. Add egg yolk, flour and vanilla. Stir in pecans. Form dough into small balls and refrigerate at least 2 hours. Place balls on a cookie sheet. Press with fork and bake at 350°F. for 10 minutes. Makes 5 dozen.

Mrs. Jimmy Haskins
Union City, Tennessee

Pumpkin Cookies

1 cup dark brown sugar
1 cup canned pumpkin
½ cup oil
1 teaspoon vanilla
2 cups flour
½ teaspoon salt
½ teaspoon ginger

1 teaspoon baking powder
1 teaspoon soda
1 teaspoon cinnamon
1 teaspoon cloves
1 teaspoon nutmeg
1 cup raisins
½ cup chopped pecans

Beat brown sugar, pumpkin, oil and vanilla. Sift together dry ingredients and add to pumpkin mixture. Blend in raisins and pecans. Drop by teaspoon onto greased cookie sheet. Bake at 350° F. for 12-15 minutes. Cool and frost.

Frosting

1 tablespoon shortening
1 tablespoon butter
¾ teaspoon vanilla

¼ teaspoon salt
2 cups powdered sugar
3 tablespoons scalded milk

Combine shortening, butter, vanilla and salt. Blend. Beat in ½ cup sugar. Add scalded milk alternately with remaining sugar, beating well after each addition. Makes 3-4 dozen cookies.

Mrs. Roy Stauffer (Melanie Province)

Snickerdoodles

1 cup shortening	1 teaspoon soda
1½ cups sugar	½ teaspoon salt
2 eggs	2 tablespoons sugar
2¾ cups flour	2 teaspoons cinnamon
2 teaspoons cream of tartar	Pecan halves (optional)

Cream shortening and sugar. Beat in eggs. Sift together the next 4 ingredients and mix into creamed mixture. Chill dough. Mix together sugar and cinnamon. Shape dough into walnut-sized balls. Roll in cinnamon-sugar mixture. Place 2 inches apart on ungreased cookie sheet. Bake at 400° F. for 8-10 minutes. For a really special looking and tasting cookie, press a pecan half into each ball before baking. Makes 5 dozen.

Mrs. John A. Stemmler (Marsha Miller)

Frosted Brownies

Brownies

1 stick butter, softened	1 tablespoon milk
1 cup sugar	1 teaspoon vanilla
2 eggs	1 cup chopped pecans
2 squares unsweetened chocolate, melted	¾ cup flour

Cream butter and sugar. Add eggs and beat until frothy. Blend in next 4 ingredients and fold in flour. Bake at 325° F. for 25 minutes in greased and floured 9x13-inch pan. Frost when cooled and cut in small squares.

Frosting

1 stick butter, softened	4 squares unsweetened chocolate, melted
2 cups powdered sugar	2 tablespoons butter
1 teaspoon vanilla	
1 tablespoon heavy cream	

Blend together first 4 ingredients and frost brownies. Combine chocolate and butter and spread evenly. Cut and store in refrigerator. Must be refrigerated. Yields 3-5 dozen.

Very rich!

Mrs. Max B. Ostner, Jr. (Mary Margaret Buffa)

Brownies That Brag!

1 4-ounce package German
   Sweet Chocolate
5 tablespoons butter
3 ounces cream cheese
1 cup sugar
3 eggs

1 tablespoon flour
1½ teaspoons vanilla
½ teaspoon baking powder
¼ teaspoon salt
½ cup flour
½ cup chopped pecans

Melt chocolate and 3 tablespoons butter and cool. Blend rest of butter with cream cheese, ¼ cup sugar, 1 egg, 1 tablespoon flour and ½ teaspoon vanilla. Set aside. Beat remaining eggs with ¾ cup sugar, baking powder, salt and ½ cup flour. Add cooled chocolate mixture. Add pecans and 1 teaspoon vanilla. Spread ½ chocolate mixture in an 8 or 9-inch square pan. Spread cheese mixture over chocolate. Then spread rest of chocolate mixture over top. Swirl to marbleize. Bake at 350° F. for 35-40 minutes. Makes 16 brownies.

Mrs. Jay Eberle

Coconut-Chocolate Meringue Bars

1½ sticks margarine
½ cup packed brown sugar
½ cup granulated sugar
3 eggs, separated
1 teaspoon vanilla
2 cups flour
1 teaspoon baking powder

¼ teaspoon soda
¼ teaspoon salt
1 6-ounce package semi-sweet
   chocolate pieces
1 cup coconut
¾ cup chopped pecans
1 cup brown sugar

Grease a 13x9x2-inch pan. Mix margarine, ½ cup brown sugar, granulated sugar, egg yolks and vanilla. Beat 2 minutes at medium speed. Sift flour, baking powder, soda and salt together. Combine thoroughly with first mixture. Pat dough in pan and sprinkle with chocolate pieces, coconut and pecans. Beat egg whites until frothy. Add 1 cup brown sugar and beat until stiff. Spread over nuts. Bake at 350°F. for 35-40 minutes. Cool. Cut into bars. Makes 3 dozen.

Mrs. John D. Glass (Meegie Rogers)

Mrs. W. Jacques Schuler, Jr. (Gayle Worthingham)

Nannie's Nut Bars

2 sticks butter, softened
1 cup sugar
1 egg, separated
2-3 teaspoons cinnamon

1½ teaspoons nutmeg
2 cups flour
1½ cups chopped pecans

Cream butter and sugar until light and fluffy. Add egg yolk and mix well. Stir in spices and slowly work in flour. Mixture will become a very stiff dough. Last of flour may have to be worked in by hand. On ungreased cookie sheet, press dough in layer ¼-inch thick. Glaze top of dough with unbeaten egg white. Pour off excess white. Cover dough with chopped pecans and gently pat into dough. Bake at 325° F. for 20-30 minutes, or until golden brown. Cool 5 minutes. Cut into bars. Makes 3 dozen.

Mrs. Rowe Belcher (Susan Ramsay)

Pecan Turtle Bars

2 cups flour
2⅓ sticks butter, divided
1½ cups light brown sugar,
    firmly packed, divided

1 cup pecan halves
1 cup milk chocolate morsels

Combine flour, 1 stick butter and 1 cup brown sugar. This is easily done in a food processor. Pat into a 9x13-inch ungreased aluminum pan. Cover with pecans. Combine remaining butter and brown sugar in heavy saucepan. Boil 1 full minute. Pour over pecans. Bake 18-20 minutes at 350°F. until bubbly and brown. Remove from oven and scatter with chocolate morsels. Swirl slightly with a knife. Cool and cut into bars or squares. Makes 3-4 dozen.

Tastes like Heath bars—very rich!

Mrs. Dorsey Mathis, Jr. (Margaret Jones)

Toffee Bars

2 sticks butter
1 cup light brown sugar
1 egg yolk, lightly beaten
1 cup flour

¼ teaspoon salt
1 teaspoon vanilla
6 Hershey bars
Chopped pecans

Cream butter and sugar. Add egg yolk, flour, salt and vanilla. Cream well and spread evenly in a 9x15x2-inch aluminum pan. Bake for 20 minutes in a 350° oven. Remove from oven and immediately spread Hershey bars over top. Sprinkle chopped pecans over chocolate. Chill until hard enough to cut into squares. Freezes well. Makes 4 dozen.

Mrs. Fletcher Johnson (Jo Ann Hawkes)

B & B Chess Squares

1 cup sugar
2 cups light brown sugar
2 sticks butter, softened
4 eggs, separated
2 cups flour, sifted

2 teaspoons baking powder
1 cup chopped pecans
1 teaspoon vanilla
½ teaspoon salt

Cream sugars and butter. Add lightly beaten egg yolks. Add dry ingredients and mix well. Beat egg whites until stiff and fold into mixture along with pecans. Bake in a well-greased 13x9x2-inch pan at 350° F. for 40 minutes. Cool and cut into very small pieces. Makes 45 squares.

Mrs. Fielding Williams
Richmond, Virginia

Cheesecake Squares

1 box yellow cake mix
1 stick butter, melted and
cooled
1 egg

2 cups powdered sugar
8 ounces cream cheese,
softened
2 eggs

Mix cake mix, butter and egg. Press into 9x12-inch pan. Mix sugar, cream cheese and eggs. Spread on crust and bake at 350° F. for 40 minutes. Cut into squares.

Mrs. Thomas J. Becktold (Pamela Stewart)

Catulla Squares

2 sticks butter
1 cup brown sugar
1 teaspoon vanilla
1½ cups chopped pecans

14-16 graham cracker squares or
Town House Crackers

Melt butter and stir in brown sugar. Bring to a boil, stirring constantly, for 2 minutes. Remove from heat and add vanilla and pecans. Place graham crackers on a 13x9-inch cookie sheet with sides. Spoon hot mixture evenly over crackers. Bake at 350° F. for 10-12 minutes. Watch carefully because they brown quickly. Allow to cool completely so they become crispy. Cut into squares.

Mrs. Dennis Higdon (Joanna Coss)

Mrs. Henry T. V. Miller (Alice Ann Bolling)

Holiday Pecan Squares

1½ sticks butter
¾ cup sugar
2 eggs
½ teaspoon lemon extract
3 cups flour
½ teaspoon baking powder

2 sticks butter
1 cup packed dark brown sugar
1 cup honey
¼ cup cream
3 cups pecans, chopped

Cream butter and sugar. Add eggs and lemon extract. Add flour and baking powder. Chill dough ½ hour. Press into bottom and sides of greased and floured 13x9-inch pan and prick with fork. Bake 12-15 minutes at 375°F. Combine butter, sugar and honey in deep saucepan. Boil 5 minutes. Add cream and chopped pecans. Spread mixture evenly over partially baked crust. Reduce heat to 350°F. and bake 30 minutes. Cut into bars or squares when cool. Freezes well. Makes about 36 squares.

Mrs. Charlie Carr
Chapel Hill, North Carolina

Carly's Deadlies

Cakes

1½ squares unsweetened chocolate	⅔ cup flour
1 stick butter	1 teaspoon vanilla
1 cup sugar	2 eggs, beaten

Melt chocolate and butter and add rest of cake ingredients. Fill midget muffin tins ½ full and bake at 350°F. for 15 minutes. While baking, make icing.

Icing

5 tablespoons butter	2 cups powdered sugar, sifted
1 square unsweetened chocolate	¼ cup cold coffee
	Pecan halves

Melt butter and chocolate in a double boiler. Add powdered sugar and coffee. Stir to dissolve, but do not cook. Make an X on top of hot cakes and pour on icing. Decorate with pecan halves. Makes about 24 cakes.

Freezes well.

Mrs. Thomas Holloman (Jayne Pressgrove)

Laurie's Fudge Cupcakes

4 squares semi-sweet chocolate	1¾ cups sugar
1 stick butter	4 eggs
1 stick margarine	2 teaspoons vanilla
1 cup flour	2 cups chopped pecans
	2 dozen paper baking cups

Melt chocolate, butter and margarine over hot water in top of double boiler. In a large bowl, sift flour and sugar together. Add eggs, one at a time, mixing with spoon. Stir as little as possible. Add chocolate mixture, vanilla and pecans. Bake at 325° F. for 25 minutes in muffin tins lined with paper baking cups. Do not overbake. Yields 2 dozen cupcakes.

Super picnic dessert! For children's birthday parties, cut off top, fill center with ice cream, replace top, cover with Cool Whip and add birthday candle.

Mrs. Gus B. Denton (Candy Stanley)

367

Jonnie's Peppermint Cupcakes

2 sticks butter
2 cups sifted powdered sugar
4 squares unsweetened
   chocolate, melted
4 eggs
1 teaspoon peppermint
   flavoring

2 teaspoons vanilla
18 paper baking cups
18 vanilla wafers
1 cup heavy cream, whipped
½ cup chopped pecans
   Maraschino cherries

Cream butter and sugar. Blend in unsweetened chocolate. Add eggs and flavorings and beat until smooth. Line muffin tins with paper baking cups and in each put 1 vanilla wafer. Fill ¾ full with chocolate mixture and top with whipped cream, pecans and cherry. Put immediately in freezer, muffin tins and all. When frozen, store cupcakes in plastic bag. Remove from freezer a few minutes before serving. Serves 18.

Mrs. James Bettendorf (Berkeley Blake)

Chocolate Muffins

4 ounces semi-sweet chocolate
2 sticks margarine
4 eggs

1½ cups sugar
1 cup flour

Melt chocolate and margarine in double boiler. Mix eggs, sugar and flour well; add chocolate mixture. Line muffin tins with paper cups. Fill ⅔ full. Bake at 325° F. for 20-25 minutes. Makes 18 muffins.

Easy enough for children to do.

Mrs. Scott Allison Arnold, III (Anne Dillard)

Dessert Puffs

1 cup water
1 stick margarine
1 cup flour

3 eggs
1 teaspoon vanilla

Heat water and margarine to rolling boil. Reduce heat and stir in flour. Mixture will form a ball. Remove from heat and beat in eggs and vanilla until batter is smooth. Drop by scant teaspoon 1-inch apart on ungreased baking sheet. Bake at 400° F. for 20-25 minutes, or until puffed and golden. Yields 4 dozen puffs.

Puffs may be topped with chocolate glaze or strawberry preserves. They can also be filled with custard.

Mrs. Pat Seale (Pat McKay)

Dessert Crêpes

¾ cup milk
¾ cup flour
¼ cup water
2 tablespoons sugar

3 eggs
2 tablespoons butter, melted
    and cooled

Combine first 5 ingredients in blender for 30 seconds. Add butter and blend 5 seconds. Allow to rest 45 minutes. For small dessert crêpes use ¼ cup batter in 6-inch crêpe pan. Crêpes may be made ahead, stacked and covered with damp towel. Yields 24 dessert crêpes.

Mrs. Michael Hewgley (Canon Thomas)

Apricot Crêpes

1 stick butter, no substitute
1 8-ounce jar apricot preserves

¼ cup bourbon or cognac
Dessert Crêpes (see above)

Melt butter in heavy skillet. Add preserves and blend well; do not scorch. When well blended, remove from heat and add bourbon or cognac. Drop crêpes into hot sauce. Fold in half and again in fourths, coating well. Place in buttered baking dish or chafing dish. Pour remaining sauce over all crêpes and serve warm with a dollop of ice cream, sour cream or whipped cream. May be made ahead and heated. If served in chafing dish, pour 2 warmed tablespoons additional bourbon or cognac over surface and ignite. Serves 8-12.

Mrs. Doug Averitt (Mary Francis Keenan)

Crêpes Fitzgerald

Filling

12 ounces cream cheese
8 ounces sour cream

4 tablespoons cream
Dessert Crêpes (see Index)

Whip filling ingredients together until fluffy. Spoon generous amount on each crêpe and roll. Yields 24 dessert crêpes.

Sauce

4 pints fresh strawberries
1 cup sugar
1 stick butter
2 ounces kirsch

2 ounces strawberry liqueur
   (optional)
4 ounces rum, warmed

Wash and slice strawberries. Place berries and all ingredients for sauce, except rum, in saucepan. Let cook over medium heat until mixture thickens very slightly. Pour on warm rum and ignite. Stir carefully until flame dies. Ladle over crêpes. Serve 2-3 per person.

This sauce is delicious served over ice cream.

Mrs. Michael Lynch (Susan Corcoran)

Cheese Blintzes

1½ cups cottage cheese
4 ounces cream cheese
¼ cup sugar
1 egg, beaten
1 teaspoon vanilla

½ teaspoon grated lemon or
   orange rind
2 tablespoons butter
Powdered sugar
Dessert Crêpes (see Index)

Mix first 6 ingredients. Put 1 tablespoon mixture on a crêpe and roll up. Brown in butter on both sides. Sprinkle with powdered sugar. Serves 10-12.

Top with fresh fruit or preserves and sour cream.

Mrs. Robert Knapp (Barbara Robertson)

Caramel Soufflé

6 eggs
1 pound superfine granulated
   sugar

English Custard Sauce (see
   Index)

Separate eggs. Place whites into largest bowl of electric mixer. Save yolks for custard sauce. Allow whites to warm to room temperature for 1 hour. Meanwhile, place ¾ cup sugar in 6-inch heavy skillet. Caramelize by stirring over high heat with wooden spoon until melted and beginning to boil. Syrup will be medium brown. Pour into 1½-quart rounded, deep Pyrex bowl, tilting to cover entire surface with caramel. Hold bowl with a hot pad. Set on wire rack to cool. When egg whites have warmed, beat at high speed for 8 minutes, until very stiff. While whites are beating, measure 6 tablespoons of sugar into small skillet and set aside. When 8 minutes are up, begin pouring remaining sugar slowly into still beating egg whites. This should take 1-1½ minutes. Beat 15 minutes more. After 10 of the 15 minutes, caramelize the 6 tablespoons sugar in skillet. When caramelized, remove from heat and place skillet in cold water for 1 second, stirring constantly. Immediately reduce mixer speed to medium and beat syrup into egg white. Scrape bowl. Beat 12 minutes on high speed. Preheat oven to 250°F. Turn mixture into caramel-lined bowl. Spread evenly. Set in large baking pan and pour boiling water 1-inch deep into baking pan. Bake 1 hour, until firm when gently shaken and rises about 1 inch above edge of bowl. Remove from oven and cool on rack. Refrigerate overnight. To unmold, hold bowl in pan of very hot water at least one minute. Invert on serving dish. Spoon caramel over soufflé. Serve with English Custard Sauce. Serves 8.

Specified beating time in this recipe is essential!

Mrs. Henry Hancock (Peggy Fairchild)

Mississippi Mock Mousse

6 regular-sized Hershey Bars
8 ounces Cool Whip
3 tablespoons Hershey's Syrup

1 small package slivered
   almonds

Melt chocolate bars in double boiler. Fold melted chocolate into Cool Whip and add syrup. Top with almonds which have been slightly toasted. Chill. Serves 4-6.

Even better with a dash of brandy.

Mrs. Tom Caldwell Henderson (Elizabeth Ann McKee)

Cold Chocolate Soufflé

1 envelope unflavored gelatin
3 tablespoons cold water
1 cup milk
2 squares unsweetened
  chocolate

½ cup powdered sugar
¾ cup sugar
1 teaspoon vanilla
¼ teaspoon salt
2 cups heavy cream, divided

Soften gelatin in 3 tablespoons water and set aside. Melt chocolate over hot water. Do not boil. Heat milk and stir in chocolate. Slowly add powdered sugar and beat with a whisk until smooth. Over low, direct heat, cook until simmering, stirring constantly. Remove from heat. Stir in softened gelatin. Add sugar, vanilla, salt and mix with whisk. Refrigerate until slightly thick. Beat until light and airy. Beat 1 cup heavy cream until stiff. Using a whisk, combine the two mixtures. Pour into a 2-quart soufflé dish. Chill 2-3 hours. Garnish with remaining cream, which has been whipped and sweetened. Serves 6-8.

Mrs. Neal G. Clement
Florence, Alabama

Crème Amaretto

1 tablespoon unflavored
  gelatin
1½ cups milk
3 egg yolks
¼ cup sugar

4 tablespoons Amaretto
½ teaspoon almond extract
2 cups heavy cream, divided
6 macaroons, crumbled
  Slivered almonds, toasted

Soak gelatin in ¼ cup milk. Scald rest of milk and add gelatin. Pour over egg yolks which have been beaten with sugar. Place over boiling water and cook until thickened. Remove from heat and chill. When cold, beat. Add Amaretto and beat. Add almond extract. Fold in 1 cup cream, whipped. Pour into macaroon-lined soufflé dish. Chill. When ready to serve, garnish with remaining 1 cup cream, whipped, and toasted almonds. Serves 6-8.

Mrs. William C. Harris (Ann Clark Quinlen)

Grand Marnier Soufflé

1 3-quart soufflé dish	5 eggs
Brown paper or foil,	3 egg whites
30x6 inches	1 cup sugar
5½ tablespoons butter	2 tablespoons lemon juice
4 tablespoons flour	1 teaspoon grated lemon rind
½ teaspoon salt	½ cup Grand Marnier
1½ cups milk	

Lightly butter and sugar soufflé dish. Butter and sugar one side of paper which has been folded in half lengthwise. Attach collar to dish with string and pins, sugar side in, 2 inches above top. Melt butter over low heat. Remove from flame and add flour and salt. Stir with whisk to make smooth. Add milk a little at a time. Return to heat and cook, stirring constantly, until thick. Set aside. Separate eggs. Put 8 egg whites in large mixing bowl. Put 5 yolks in a small bowl. Beat yolks until thick and lemon colored. Continue beating while adding cream sauce by the spoonful. Cover and set aside. Beat egg whites until almost stiff. Add sugar, a little at a time, beating constantly. Stir lemon juice, rind and Grand Marnier into custard. Pour custard into whites and fold in. Pour into prepared soufflé dish. Bake in preheated 350° F. oven for 1 hour or a little longer, until firm but a bit wiggly. Serve immediately. If desired, make a boiled custard out of 3 remaining yolks and flavor with Grand Marnier. Pour warm custard over serving of soufflé. Serves 6-8.

Mrs. Henry Hancock (Peggy Fairchild)

Caramel Custard Cups

4 tablespoons brown sugar	⅓ cup sugar
2 eggs	1½ teaspoons vanilla
1 cup evaporated milk	Pinch salt
⅔ cup water	

Press 1 tablespoon brown sugar into each of 4 custard cups. Beat eggs lightly, and add remaining ingredients. Mix thoroughly and pour carefully over brown sugar in cups. Set custard cups in a shallow pan holding 1 inch of hot water. Bake at 350° F. for 50 minutes or until knife inserted near edge of custard comes out clean. Cool. Loosen edges with knife and unmold. Serves 4.

Mrs. Dudley Bridgforth (Donna Kay Byrd)

Old South Bread Pudding

1 5.33-ounce can evaporated
   milk
1⅓ cups milk or light cream
1 stick margarine
3 eggs

½ teaspoon salt
1½ teaspoons vanilla
1 cup sugar
2-6 slices white bread, crumbled

Put evaporated milk in 16-ounce measuring cup. Add milk or cream to measure 16 ounces and pour into double boiler. Scald. Add margarine and let melt. Add eggs, salt, vanilla and sugar. Mix well. Add bread and mix. Put in loaf pan. Set in pan containing 1 inch of water. Bake at 325° F. for 45 minutes. Serves 6-8.

The more bread that is added, the firmer the pudding will be.

Mrs. William C. Lewis
Tallahassee, Florida

Rice Pudding

1 cup rice
6 cups light cream
½ cup sugar
1 teaspoon salt

3 eggs, beaten
Stick of cinnamon
Butter
Ground cinnamon

Wash rice until free of all starch. Place in double boiler with cream, sugar, salt and cinnamon stick, and steam rice until done, 1-1½ hours. Remove from heat and mix with eggs. Remove cinnamon. Put in well-greased baking dish, dot with butter and sprinkle with cinnamon. Bake at 350° F. for 15-20 minutes, or until pudding is set and brown on top.

Traditional Swedish Christmas Eve dessert.

Mrs. Fletcher Johnson (Jo Ann Hawkes)

Lemon Baskets

2 tablespoons butter, melted
1 cup sugar
½ teaspoon salt
¼ cup flour
6-7 tablespoons fresh lemon
   juice, or more to taste

Grated peel from one lemon
1½ cups milk
3 egg yolks, well beaten
3 egg whites, stiffly beaten

Thoroughly mix first 6 ingredients. Add milk, heated to point just before boiling, to the egg yolks very slowly; then add this to the above mixture. Fold in egg whites. Grease ramekins and fill with mixture. Place ramekins in pan with at least 1-inch of hot water and bake at 350° F. for 45 minutes. Serves 8.

This recipe layers during cooking to form cake plus custard.

Mrs. Lee Wardlaw (Mary Linda Lewis)

Peach Almond Trifle

1 3¼-ounce package vanilla
   pudding
¼ cup sherry, divided
⅛ teaspoon nutmeg
¼ teaspoon vanilla
1 cup crumbled pound cake

8 ounces cream cheese,
   softened
2 cups heavy cream, whipped
   and divided
1 cup sliced peaches
1 cup toasted almonds, divided

According to package directions, make pudding and add 1 tablespoon sherry and all of cinnamon, nutmeg and vanilla. Soak pound cake in remaining sherry. Blend cream cheese and 1 cup whipped cream. In glass bowl, layer in the following order: cream cheese mixture, pound cake, peaches, pudding, ¾ cup almonds, remaining whipped cream, remaining almonds. Serves 6-8.

Mrs. Jackie Nichols

Roulade au Grand Marnier

5½ tablespoons butter
6 eggs
1 teaspoon vanilla
¾ cup super-fine granulated
    sugar
1 cup cake flour, sifted
¼ teaspoon salt

½ cup ground blanched
    almonds
1½ teaspoons grated orange
    rind
Powdered sugar
Whole almonds

Melt butter and set aside. Combine eggs and vanilla and beat at high speed until eggs are very thick and lemon colored. Gradually add sugar, beating well after each addition. Fold in flour, salt, almonds and orange rind. Add melted butter and fold in quickly and thoroughly. Pour into well buttered and lightly floured 15x10x1-inch pan. Bake at 350° F. for 18-20 minutes. Loosen edges and turn out immediately onto tea towel sprinkled with powdered sugar. Roll cake immediately in towel, starting along 15-inch edge. Cool, unroll, spread with Grand Marnier Butter Cream, re-roll and frost with Chocolate Icing. Garnish with whole almonds.

Grand Marnier Butter Cream

½ cup sugar
3 tablespoons flour
½ cup milk
1½ sticks butter, softened to
    room temperature

2⅓ tablespoons Grand Marnier
1½ teaspoons grated orange rind

Combine sugar and flour in saucepan, add milk and cook over moderate heat, stirring constantly, until mixture comes to boiling point. Cook for 2 minutes, stirring constantly. Remove from heat and cool thoroughly. Gradually add butter, about 1 tablespoon at a time, beating well after each addition. Beat in Grand Marnier and orange rind.

Chocolate Icing

1 5½-ounce can evaporated
    milk
⅛ teaspoon salt

1½ cups semi-sweet chocolate
    bits
1 teaspoon vanilla

Combine evaporated milk and salt in pan. Bring to boil over moderate heat, stirring constantly. Remove from heat, add chocolate bits and stir until chocolate is melted and smooth. Add vanilla and cool until thick enough to spread.

This cake can be made ahead for the Yule Log at Christmas. Freezes well. This dessert is expensive, rich, time consuming, calorie laden and worth every bit of it!

Mrs. John S. Palmer (Nancy Moore)

Chocolate Log

Cake

5 eggs, separated	Powdered sugar
1 cup powdered sugar	1 cup heavy cream, whipped
¼ cup flour	and sweetened
½ teaspoon salt	2 cups miniature
3 tablespoons cocoa	marshmallows
1 teaspoon vanilla	

Beat egg yolks until thick. Sift next 4 ingredients together 3 times and beat into egg yolks until well blended. Add vanilla. Beat egg whites until stiff and fold into batter. Bake at 375° F. for 15-20 minutes in 15½x10½x1-inch jelly-roll pan lined with aluminum foil and greased. Lightly dust dish towel with powdered sugar. Loosen cake around edges, invert onto towel; lift off pan and carefully remove foil. On long side roll up gently in towel and cool. Combine whipped cream and marshmallows. Unroll cake and spread with cream/marshmallow mixture. Roll again and sprinkle with powdered sugar. Serve with Hot Fudge Sauce. Serves 8-10.

Hot Fudge Sauce

4 squares unsweetened	⅛ teaspoon salt
chocolate	1 15-ounce can evaporated
1 stick butter	milk
3 cups sugar	

Melt chocolate and butter in top of double boiler, adding sugar and salt. Gradually add milk. Stir and cook until smooth. Yields 6 cups.

Mrs. Bruce Taylor (Senter Crook)

Apple Crisp

6 apples, thinly sliced
⅓ cup sugar
¼ teaspoon cinnamon

3 tablespoons water
Dots of butter

Place apples in buttered 8-inch square pan or 9-inch pie pan. Sprinkle with sugar and cinnamon. Pour water over top and dot with butter. Spread topping ingredients over apples. Bake at 350° F. for 1 hour. Serve with whipped cream or ice cream. Serves 6-8.

Topping
1 cup flour
½ cup brown sugar

1 stick butter

Blend all topping ingredients.

Mrs. Walter Wills, Jr. (Dorothy Kirby)

Apple Rings

1½ cups flour
½ teaspoon salt
½ cup shortening
4-5 tablespoons ice water
4 cups grated apples

Cinnamon
1 cup white sugar
½ cup brown sugar
1 stick butter
2 cups water

Combine first 4 ingredients into a dough and roll out thinly. Place apples on dough and sprinkle with cinnamon. Roll up like a jelly roll. Cut in slices 1-2 inches thick. Combine sugars, butter, and water in baking dish in 400° F. oven. When liquid is hot, place apple rings in dish. Bake until brown, about 1 hour. Top with ice cream. Serves 6.

Mrs. Dennis Higdon (Joanna Coss)

Bananas Foster

2 tablespoons butter	1/8 teaspoon cinnamon
4 tablespoons brown sugar	1 tablespoon banana liqueur
2 bananas, cut lengthwise in quarters	1 ounce rum or brandy
	Vanilla ice cream

Mix butter and sugar in saucepan. Cook over medium heat until caramelized. Add bananas and cook until tender. Add cinnamon and liqueur. Stir. Heat rum or brandy, but do not boil. Pour over top of fruit mixture. Do not stir. Ignite. Spoon over vanilla ice cream while still flaming. Serves 6.

Allison Lynch

Blueberry Dessert

Crust

2 cups flour	1 teaspoon vanilla
3/4 cup oil	1/4 cup chopped pecans
1/4 cup ice water	

Mix all ingredients except pecans. Press into 13x9-inch pan on bottom and sides. Sprinkle with chopped pecans. Prick crust and bake at 350° F. for 30 minutes.

Filling

8 ounces cream cheese	1 1-pound, 6-ounce can
2 cups powdered sugar	blueberry pie filling
1 envelope Dream Whip	

Mix cheese and sugar. Prepare Dream Whip according to package directions. Add Dream Whip to cheese mixture. Spread 1/2 mixture on cooled crust. Evenly top with blueberry pie filling. Top with remaining cheese mixture and freeze. Remove 1/2 hour before serving. Serves 10.

Excellent party dessert!

Mrs. Jack Horner

Fruit Cake Roll

1 pound candied cherries
1 pound raisins
1 pound pecans
½ cup bourbon
1 12-ounce package vanilla
    wafers, crushed

1 14-ounce can sweetened
    condensed milk
Coconut

Soak cherries, raisins and pecans in ½ cup bourbon overnight. Pour milk over vanilla wafers, mixing well. Add undrained cherries, pecans and raisins. Divide into 2 parts. Shape into rolls and roll in coconut. Keep in refrigerator at least 3 hours before slicing.

Mrs. Dennis Higdon (Joanna Coss)

Baked Alaska with Fluffy Bourbon Sauce

1 8 to 10-ounce angel food cake
1 quart mocha ice cream,
    softened
⅛ teaspoon salt

6 egg whites
⅛ teaspoon cream of tartar
¾ cup sugar

Slice cake into 6 slices, ¾-inch thick. Arrange slices 4 inches apart on cookie sheet. Put layer of ice cream 1 inch thick on each slice. Freeze while preparing meringue. Add salt to egg whites and beat until frothy. Add cream of tartar and beat until stiff. Gradually beat in sugar. Completely cover ice cream-cake slices with meringue. Return to freezer. This may be done early in the day. At serving time, bake frozen Alaska at 450° F. for 5 minutes, or until meringue is lightly brown. Serve immediately with Fluffy Bourbon Sauce. Serves 6.

Fluffy Bourbon Sauce
3 egg yolks
6 tablespoons powdered sugar

4-5 tablespoons bourbon
1 cup heavy cream

Beat egg yolks; stir in powdered sugar and bourbon. Whip cream; fold into mixture. This may be done ahead.

Mrs. Scott May (Linda Morse)

Lemon Parfait Alaska

½ stick butter
1 cup sugar
2 tablespoons cornstarch,
   or 4 tablespoons flour
¼ teaspoon salt
1 tablespoon grated lemon rind

⅓ cup lemon juice, about 1½
   lemons
3 egg yolks
1 quart vanilla ice cream
1 9-inch pie crust, baked

Melt butter in top of double boiler. Stir in sugar, cornstarch or flour, and salt. Blend thoroughly. Add lemon juice and rind. Add egg yolks and stir until smooth. Cook over simmering water, stirring constantly, 8-10 minutes or until mixture is thick. Cool. Soften 1 pint ice cream at room temperature and smooth into pie crust. Freeze until firm. Spread half the lemon sauce over frozen layer of ice cream. Return to freezer until firm. Repeat with remaining ice cream and sauce. Freeze until firm.

Meringue
3 egg whites
¼ teaspoon cream of tartar, or
   pinch baking powder

⅓ cup sugar

Beat egg whites and cream of tartar until soft peaks form. Gradually beat in ⅓ cup sugar. Continue beating until sugar is dissolved and meringue is stiff and glossy. Cover top of pie with meringue, being careful to seal edges. Place pie on a board. Bake at 475° F. for 3 minutes or until lightly browned. Return to freezer. Allow to stand 10 minutes at room temperature before serving. Serves 8-10.

Mrs. Gavin M. Gentry (Mary Jane Coleman)

Macaroon Angel Delight

1	package angel food cake mix	12	almond macaroons
½	gallon vanilla ice cream	⅓	cup dry sherry
		1½	cups heavy cream, whipped

The day before assembling cake, bake angel food cake according to package directions. Next day, soften ice cream. In a large bowl, soak macaroons in sherry for 30 minutes; stir in ice cream. Slice off 1-inch of top of cake with serrated knife. Set aside. Make tunnel inside by removing bits of cake, leaving ½ inch of sides and bottom. Pack ice cream mixture into tunnel; replace top. Set in freezer for 1 hour before icing cake with whipped cream. Return to freezer. When cream is hard, wrap in foil and store in freezer until ready to use. A few minutes before serving, remove from freezer and unwrap foil. Serves 12.

Elegant but easy! Can be decorated for any occasion—tint ice cream green and decorate with shamrocks for St. Patrick's Day; or tint pink and set glass in center to be filled with roses for a birthday; or tint yellow and use jonquils for spring!

Mrs. William A. Coolidge, Jr.

Peppermint Brownie Cake

Cake

1 23-ounce package brownie
    mix

2 teaspoons vanilla
½ gallon peppermint ice cream

Prepare brownie mix following directions for cake-like brownies, adding vanilla. Line bottom of greased 13x9x2-inch pan with waxed paper and spread with batter. Bake at 350° F. for 20 minutes. Cool in pan 10 minutes. Invert on rack and peel off paper. Cool. Chill in freezer 1 hour or until hard. Cut cake crosswise in 3 equal pieces. Spread one piece with ½ of ice cream. Top with layer of cake, remainder of ice cream and cake. Wrap airtight and freeze. Serve with Hot Fudge Sauce. Serves 8-10.

Hot Fudge Sauce

5½ tablespoons butter
2 squares unsweetened
    chocolate
2 squares semi-sweet
    chocolate

1 cup sugar
1 cup heavy cream
⅛ teaspoon salt
2 teaspoons vanilla

Melt butter and chocolate in top of double boiler. Blend in sugar, cream and salt. Cook, stirring constantly, for 5 minutes or until sugar is dissolved. Remove from heat and stir in vanilla. Serve warm. Yields 2⅓ cups.

Mrs. Scott May (Linda Morse)

Caramel Cream Supreme

½ cup dark brown sugar
½ cup quick oatmeal
2 cups flour
1 cup chopped pecans
2 sticks butter, melted

½ gallon vanilla ice cream,
    softened
1½ jars caramel or chocolate
    sauce

Mix first 5 ingredients to resemble cookie dough. Spread and pat on cookie sheet. Bake at 400° F. for 15 minutes. Crumble with spoon while hot. Spread ½ crumbs in 9x13-inch pan. Pour ½ jar of sauce over crumbs. Spread this with ice cream. Top with remaining crumbs and sauce. Freeze. Set out 5-10 minutes before serving. Cut into squares. Serves 10-12.

Mrs. Harte J. Thomas (Patty Jenkins)

Evelyn's Angel Food Dessert

3 eggs, separated
1 cup sugar
2 cups milk
1½ envelopes unflavored
   gelatin, softened in ¼ cup
   cold water
1 cup heavy cream, whipped
1 small angel food cake,
   broken in small pieces

1 cup coarsely chopped pecans
1 8-ounce can crushed
   pineapple
1 6-ounce bottle maraschino
   cherries
1 cup heavy cream, whipped,
   for icing

Mix beaten egg yolks with milk and sugar. Bring to boil. Add gelatin. When cool, fold in stiffly beaten egg whites. When cold, fold in 1 cup of whipped cream. Add remaining ingredients. Pour mixture into angel food cake pan. Refrigerate until set. Unmold on platter and ice with another cup of whipped cream, sweetened to taste. Serves 12.

Mrs. Dorsey Mathis, Jr. (Margaret Jones)

Island Angel Dessert

4 eggs, separated
2 cups milk
2 tablespoons flour
⅛ teaspoon salt
1 cup sugar
1 envelope unflavored gelatin

¼ cup cold water
4 cups heavy cream, whipped
1 angel food cake
   Sherry, rum or brandy to
   taste
1 package coconut

Make custard of beaten egg yolks, milk, flour, salt and sugar; mix well. Cook, stirring constantly over low heat until thickened. Soften gelatin in cold water and add to custard, stirring until dissolved. Cool. Beat egg whites until stiff. Fold egg whites and 2 cups of cream, whipped, into custard. Line tube pan with waxed paper. Trim angel food cake by cutting slices around the outside. Use these slices to line bottom and sides of tube pan. Break up remaining cake into pieces. Pour some custard into pan. Add layer of cake pieces. Repeat until pan is full, ending with cake on top. Refrigerate overnight. Ice with remaining 2 cups of cream, whipped and flavored with brandy, rum or sherry. Cover top and sides with coconut. Serves 24.

Decorate with fresh flowers in the center of cake!

Mrs. Harte Thomas, Jr. (Patty Jenkins)

Mrs. John Franklin Holmes (Jeanie Hobby)

Chocolate Marvel

1½ cups chopped pecans
1½ cups graham cracker crumbs
1½ cups packed light brown
   sugar

2 sticks butter, melted
1 package devil's food cake
   mix
2-3 cups heavy cream, whipped

Combine pecans, crumbs, sugar and butter. Into each of four 9-inch round pans, put ¼ of mixture. Pat down evenly. Prepare cake mix as label directs. Divide batter into the 4 pans. Bake 30 minutes at 350°F., staggering pans in oven. Cool for 10 minutes. Loosen edges and invert each layer on wire rack to cool completely. Place one layer on cake plate, crumb side up; top with whipped cream. Repeat layers, ending with whipped cream. Refrigerate. Serves 16.

Very rich!

Mrs. John A. Stemmler (Marsha Miller)

Chocolate Éclair Dessert

16-18 graham crackers
2 3-ounce packages vanilla
   instant pudding
8 ounces Cool Whip
2¼ sticks butter
2 squares semi-sweet
   chocolate

2¼ cups powdered sugar
3 tablespoons white Karo
   syrup
1 teaspoon vanilla
1½ tablespoons cool water

Line 9x13-inch pan with whole graham crackers. Prepare pudding, according to directions, and fold in Cool Whip. Pour over graham crackers. Melt butter and chocolate on low heat in saucepan. Remove from heat and add all other ingredients. When chocolate mixture is smooth and creamy, pour on top of pudding mixture. Refrigerate overnight. Serves 12.

Mrs. Burdette Russ (Scottie McCord)

Patrician Loaf

½ pound semi-sweet chocolate,
   cut in small pieces
¼ cup rum
2 sticks unsalted butter,
   softened
2 tablespoons sugar
2 eggs, separated

1½ cups grated blanched
   almonds
⅛ teaspoon salt
12 ladyfingers, cut into
   1x½-inch pieces
Powdered sugar
½ cup heavy cream, whipped

Lightly grease bottom and sides of 1½-quart loaf pan with vegetable oil; invert pan over paper towels to drain. Melt chocolate over low heat, stirring constantly. When chocolate is dissolved, stir in rum and remove from heat. Cool to room temperature. Cream butter in large mixing bowl until light and fluffy. Beat in sugar and egg yolks, one at a time. Stir in almonds and cooled chocolate. In a separate bowl, beat egg whites and salt until stiff enough to form soft peaks; fold into chocolate mixture. When no streaks of white show, gently fold in ladyfingers. Spoon mixture into loaf pan and smooth top. Cover tightly with plastic wrap and refrigerate for at least 4 hours, or until loaf is very firm. Unmold loaf 1 hour before serving onto chilled serving platter. Smooth top and sides of unmolded loaf and return to refrigerator. Just before serving, sift powdered sugar over top. Cut loaf into thin slices and serve, if desired, with whipped cream. Serves 8.

Mrs. Jim Nichols
Chesterfield, Missouri

Bavarois Aux Amandes
(Almond Bavarian Cream)

2 tablespoons butter
24 ladyfingers
½ cup cold milk
2 envelopes unflavored gelatin
6 egg yolks
¼ cup sugar
2 cups milk, scalded
1 8-ounce can imported almond
paste

½ cup hot milk
1 tablespoon vanilla
6 egg whites
⅛ teaspoon cream of tartar
Dash of salt
¼ cup sugar
1½ cups heavy cream, whipped
Toasted slivered almonds

Using butter, grease two 6-cup molds. Line molds with ladyfingers and place in refrigerator. Soften gelatin in ½ cup cold milk. Combine yolks, sugar and milk in top of double boiler and cook over simmering water until it coats a spoon. Stir constantly but do not boil. Blend almond paste with ½ cup hot milk. With wire whisk, add dissolved almond paste to custard and blend until smooth. Pour hot almond mixture over softened gelatin and stir to blend. Add vanilla and refrigerate. As soon as mixture starts to set, beat whites with cream of tartar and salt until stiff but not dry. When whites are stiff, add other ¼ cup sugar, 1 tablespoon at a time. Have whipped cream ready. Gently fold whipped cream and egg whites alternately into almond custard, which is partly set. Pour mixture into refrigerated molds and chill until firm. Garnish with toasted almonds. Serves 12-14.

Mrs. Frank Jemison (Peggy Boyce)

Charlotte Russe

2 envelopes unflavored gelatin
¾ cup sugar
¼ teaspoon salt
4 eggs, separated
2 cups milk, scalded
⅓ cup brandy

12 ladyfingers, split
2 cups heavy cream, whipped
9 strawberries
Heavy cream, whipped, for garnish

Combine first 3 ingredients in double boiler. Add egg yolks and slowly stir in milk. Cook, stirring constantly, until mixture coats spoon. Cool. Add 3 tablespoons brandy and refrigerate until mixture congeals slightly. Sprinkle remaining brandy over ladyfingers and line mold. Fold gelatin mixture into beaten egg whites. Fold in cream and pour into lined mold. Refrigerate at least 8 hours. Unmold and garnish with strawberries and whipped cream. Serves 10-16.

A light and lovely dessert.

Mrs. Max Ostner, Jr. (Mary Margaret Buffa)

Chocolate-Almond Dessert

1 tablespoon butter
12 ladyfingers, split
3 squares semi-sweet chocolate
1 square unsweetened chocolate
2 tablespoons instant coffee
¼ cup hot water

1 cup sugar
2 cups almonds
¼ cup Cointreau
½ teaspoon vanilla
2 sticks butter, softened
1 cup heavy cream, whipped
Whipped cream for garnish

Lightly butter bottom and sides of 9-inch springform pan and arrange ladyfingers, slightly overlapping, around sides. Melt chocolate. Dissolve instant coffee in ¼ cup hot water. Cool. Add chocolate. In food processor, finely grind almonds and sugar. Add Cointreau and vanilla. Transfer to mixing bowl. With mixer, beat in butter, 2 tablespoons at a time. Continue beating until very fluffy. Mix in chocolate and fold in whipped cream, ½ cup at a time. Fill mold with mixture. If necessary, trim ladyfingers even with top of mold. Cover with foil and heavy plate. Chill overnight. To serve, release from pan and garnish with whipped cream flavored with Cointreau. Serves 12.

Mrs. Max Ostner, Jr. (Mary Margaret Buffa)

Chocolate Richesse

3 sticks butter
2 cups powdered sugar
12 eggs, separated
4 squares unsweetened
   chocolate, melted

1 teaspoon vanilla
1½ cups chopped pecans
18 ladyfingers
48 macaroon cookies, crumbled
1 cup heavy cream, whipped

Cream butter and sugar for 20 minutes. Beat egg yolks well. Add chocolate, vanilla, egg yolks and pecans to butter mixture. Line large springform pan with ladyfingers. Alternate layers of crumbled macaroons and chocolate mixture 3 times, ending with macaroons. Refrigerate overnight. Cover top with whipped cream and decorate with chocolate shavings. Serves 12.

Mrs. Charles E. Frankum (Linda Lacey)

Lemon Mousse

4 eggs
1 cup sugar
½ cup lemon juice
1 envelope unflavored gelatin

½ cup cold water
2 cups heavy cream
24 ladyfingers

Separate eggs. Beat yolks until thick and add sugar gradually. Add lemon juice. Soften gelatin in cold water and dissolve over heat. Add to egg mixture. Beat whites until they peak. Whip cream. Fold in whites and cream with egg mixture. Line bowl with ladyfingers, split side up. Cover with custard and put ladyfingers on top. Let stand 24 hours in refrigerator. Serves 12.

Mrs. Philip H. Strubing (Ginny Muller)

Lemon Celestial

30 lemon wafers, or brown edge
    wafers
4 egg yolks
½ cup lemon juice
¼ cup sugar
1½ tablespoons grated lemon
    peel

4 egg whites
⅛ teaspoon cream of tartar
⅛ teaspoon salt
¾ cup sugar
1½ cups heavy cream

Line bottom and sides of 9-inch springform pan with wafers. Combine next 4 ingredients and blend well. Set aside. Beat egg whites until foamy. Add cream of tartar and salt and beat until soft peaks form. Gradually add remaining sugar, beating constantly until stiff. Whip cream until stiff. Fold whites and cream into yolk mixture and pour into pan. Cover with foil and freeze. Before serving, let soften in refrigerator for 1 hour. Serves 10-12.

Mrs. Charles D. Schaffler (Mickey Pooley)

Rich Chocolate Ice Cream

2 cups milk
1 tablespoon flour
1 cup sugar
¼ teaspoon salt
2 egg yolks, slightly beaten

2 ounces unsweetened
    chocolate
¼ cup hot water
2 cups heavy cream
1 tablespoon vanilla

Scald 1½ cups milk in small saucepan. While milk is scalding, mix flour, sugar and salt in the top of double boiler. Stir remaining ½ cup cold milk into dry ingredients. Add scalded milk and cook in double boiler for 7 minutes, stirring constantly. Stir hot mixture slowly into beaten egg yolks. Melt chocolate and add hot water. Stir into hot custard. Allow to cool and stir in cream and vanilla. Freeze in ice cream freezer.

Mrs. Robert Mednikow

Crème de Menthe Ice Cream

2 eggs, beaten
3 cups heavy cream
1 cup milk
½ cup sugar
¼ cup light corn syrup

1 teaspoon vanilla
¼ teaspoon salt
⅓ cup crème de menthe
2 squares semi-sweet chocolate, shaved

Combine first 7 ingredients and stir until sugar dissolves. Add crème de menthe. Pour into ice cream freezer and freeze according to appliance directions. Stir in chocolate and cover. Pack with 1 part salt to 4 parts ice. Refrigerate for 3 hours. Makes 5 cups.

Mrs. William T. Black (Lida Willey)

Lemon Ice Cream

4 lemons
1 cup sugar

1 cup heavy cream
2 cups milk

Squeeze lemons and dissolve sugar in juice. Slice one lemon very thinly. Beat cream until thick but not stiff. Combine all ingredients and freeze. Serves 8.

Lemon slices may be omitted for smoother ice cream!

Mrs. J. Richard Walker (Margaret Bullington)

Lotus Ice Cream

1 cup fresh lemon juice, or one 8-ounce bottle frozen lemon juice
3¼ cups sugar
5 cups milk
2 cups light cream
1 cup heavy cream

1 teaspoon vanilla
2 teaspoons almond extract
1 lemon, very thinly sliced, then slices quartered
1 cup sliced almonds, toasted and chopped

Mix lemon juice and sugar in metal can of electric ice cream freezer. Add milk, creams, vanilla and almond extract. Add more milk if necessary to fill container ¾ full. Let sit overnight in refrigerator. Freeze in ice cream freezer. When mixture becomes mushy, stop and stir in lemon pieces and almonds. Let sit packed in ice for about 2 hours to firm up. Makes 1 gallon.

Mrs. Otis Warr, III

Food Processor Ice Cream

1 16-ounce bag frozen whole
strawberries

1 cup sugar
1 cup heavy cream

Put all ingredients in food processor. Using steel blade, process until strawberries are completely blended and mixture has consistency of ice cream. Place in freezer. Makes 1 quart.

Mrs. David Alexander
Claremont, California

Homemade Fruit Ice Cream

Juice of 3 oranges and 3
lemons
3 cups sugar
3 cups milk
1½ cups heavy cream

1½ cups light cream
2 10-ounce packages frozen
strawberries, or equal
amount of peaches or
bananas

Mix all ingredients together. Freeze in ice cream freezer using machine instructions.

Mrs. John Lay
Savannah, Tennessee

Mint Sherbet

1½ cups sugar
1½ cups water
2 cups packed fresh mint
leaves, washed and
drained
2 cups milk

2 cups heavy cream
1 cup light Karo syrup
1 tablespoon lemon juice
2 cups pineapple juice
1 cup crushed pineapple
¼ cup crème de menthe

Dissolve sugar and water in saucepan and boil for 5 minutes. Purée mint and small amount of syrup. Return mint-mixture to rest of syrup and cook for 3 more minutes. Cool. Pour milk and cream into ice cream freezer container. Strain mint-syrup into freezer container and mix well. Add next 5 ingredients to freezer container and mix well. Freeze according to freezer directions. Makes 1 gallon.

Mrs. Dayton Smith (Justine Holloway)

Apricot and Lemon Sherbet

2 cups water
1 3-ounce package lemon
   gelatin
1 17-ounce can apricots,
   drained, juice reserved

1 cup sugar
1 cup heavy cream, whipped
   Fresh mint or strips of lemon
   rind for garnish

Bring water to boil. Dissolve gelatin in water. Purée apricots in blender or food processor. Add apricots, 1 cup apricot juice and sugar to gelatin mixture. Cool and add whipped cream. Freeze in electric freezer. Serve topped with mint or lemon rind. Makes about 1½ quarts.

Mrs. John S. Palmer (Nancy Moore)

Italian Ice

2 cups warm water
¾ cup sugar
one of the following:
½ cup lemon juice & 1 teaspoon
   rind
½ cup lime juice & 1 teaspoon
   rind

1 cup puréed strawberries
½ cup grated, semi-sweet
   chocolate, melted
Maraschino cherries with
   stems, whole strawberries,
   or shaved chocolate for
   garnish

In a saucepan, dissolve sugar in water. Add fruit juice, strawberries, or chocolate. If adding fruit juice, let stand 5 minutes, then strain out rind. Pour mixture into freezer tray and freeze, stirring frequently until mixture is thick and mushy. Serve in chilled champagne glasses with appropriate garnish. Serves 4.

Perfect light dessert after a heavy meal.

Mrs. Frank E. Reid (Diana Mann)

Caramel Icing

3½ cups sugar
1 cup water
1½ cups heavy cream

⅛ teaspoon salt
4 tablespoons butter
1 teaspoon vanilla

Caramelize ½ cup sugar with water in heavy skillet. This process will take approximately 10 minutes over high heat. In large saucepan, mix remaining sugar, cream and salt. Pour in caramelized sugar and cook to soft ball stage. Add butter and vanilla. Cool. Beat well and spread on cake.

Mrs. Aimee Gianotti (Aimee Guthrie)

Eloise's Caramel Icing

2½ cups sugar
1 cup heavy cream
1 teaspoon cornstarch

1 teaspoon vanilla
⅛ teaspoon salt

Put 2 cups sugar, heavy cream and cornstarch in a double boiler and bring to a rolling boil. Place ½ cup sugar in heavy skillet and let caramelize. When cream mixture has boiled 2-3 minutes, pour caramelized syrup into it. Let boil until it forms a soft ball in water. Remove from heat and add vanilla and salt. Beat until cool and spread on a yellow cake. Decorate with pecan halves.

Mrs. William A. Watson, III (Pattie Walker)

Creamy Chocolate Frosting

1 egg
5½ tablespoons butter, softened
1½ cups powdered sugar

6 tablespoons cocoa
1 teaspoon vanilla

Whip egg until frothy. Beat in butter and continue beating while adding remaining ingredients.

Excellent, quick frosting for brownies.

Mrs. Joseph W. Teagarden, III (Diana Wilborn)

Cocoa Fudge Frosting

1 stick butter
½ cup cocoa
2 cups powdered sugar

7 tablespoons evaporated milk
1 teaspoon vanilla

Melt butter in saucepan with cocoa. Heat one minute or until smooth, stirring constantly. Pour into small mixing bowl. Alternately add powdered sugar and milk. Beat in vanilla. Enough to fill and frost two 9-inch layers or 1 sheet cake.

Mrs. Alan Carey (Nancy Brunson)

Grandmother's Coconut Icing

½ stick margarine
½ cup milk

1 cup sugar
2 teaspoons coconut flavoring

Mix all ingredients in saucepan and bring to a boil. Boil for 1 minute. Pour hot icing over pound cake. Make holes in top of cake to allow icing to soak through.

Mrs. Harold Webb Jenkins, Jr. (Janice Cochran)

Carol's Glaze

1 cup sugar
1 stick butter

½ cup buttermilk
½ teaspoon soda

Mix all ingredients and bring to rolling boil. Let boil 3 minutes, stirring constantly. Make holes in cake with toothpick and pour on icing while cake is still in pan. Make sure glaze goes down sides and center hole. After turning out cake, top with more glaze.

Carol Brantley Henderson

Grama's Pineapple Glaze

1 egg yolk
  Rind of ½ lemon, grated
2 tablespoons butter, melted
2 tablespoons pineapple juice

3 tablespoons crushed
  pineapple, drained
1¼ cups powdered sugar

Beat egg yolk 1 minute on high speed. Pour in remaining ingredients. Beat 2 minutes until smooth. Serve over cake.

Especially good on angel food cake.

Mrs. Jon K. Thompson (Susan Taylor)

Miss Lacey's Lemon Cake Filling

2 lemons, juice and grated
  rinds
2 egg yolks, beaten
2 cups sugar
5 tablespoons flour

1 cup boiling water
1½ tablespoons butter
2 egg whites, beaten

Combine lemon juice, rind and yolks. Blend in sugar, flour, water and butter and cook until thickened. Cool mixture and fold in egg whites. This will fill a 4-layer cake.

A real lemon treat for plain yellow cake.

Mrs. Lacey Tucker Scott

Rum Fruit Filling

4 egg yolks
½ cup sugar
½ stick butter, melted
¼ cup dark rum
1½ cups chopped pecans

½ cup chopped raisins
¼ cup chopped pitted dates
¼ cup chopped maraschino
  cherries

Beat egg yolks and sugar together and add melted butter. Cook in top of double boiler over low heat for about 10 minutes or until thickened. Add rum. Cool. Stir in pecans and fruits. Serve over French vanilla ice cream or use as a filling for butter cake.

Also wonderful as icing.

Mrs. Frank E. Reid (Diana Mann)

English Custard Sauce

⅓ cup sugar
1 tablespoon cornstarch
2 cups milk
2 tablespoons butter

6 egg yolks
1½ teaspoons vanilla
½ cup heavy cream

Combine sugar and cornstarch in a medium saucepan. Gradually add milk; stir until smooth. Add butter. Cook over medium heat, stirring constantly, until thick and comes to a boil. Boil one minute. Remove from heat. In a medium bowl, slightly beat egg yolks. Gradually add a little of the hot mixture, beating well. Stir yolks into rest of hot mixture. Cook over medium heat, stirring just until it boils. Remove and stir in vanilla. Strain. Cool in refrigerator, covered. When cool, stir in cream. Chill. Makes 2½ cups.

Mrs. Leo J. Fairchild
Monroe, Michigan

Delicious Fudge Sauce

½ cup cocoa
1 cup light Karo syrup
1 cup sugar
½ cup light cream

3 tablespoons butter
¼ teaspoon salt
1 teaspoon vanilla

Combine all ingredients, except vanilla, in a large saucepan and bring to boil. Boil 5 minutes. Remove from heat and add vanilla. Makes 2 cups.

This is good hot or cold. Keeps well in refrigerator.

Mrs. John C. Moss (Ethel Merrin)

Chocolate Fondue Sauce

1 12-ounce package chocolate
    chips

1 cup heavy cream
1-2 tablespoons kirsch

Melt chocolate chips in a small amount of cream. Gradually add remainder of cream, mixing well. Add kirsch and mix well. Serve warm over ice cream or as a dip for fruit or sponge cake.

Mrs. William C. Harris (Ann Clark Quinlen)

One-Two-Three Chocolate Sauce

1 13-ounce can evaporated milk

2 cups sugar

3 squares unsweetened chocolate

Pour a little of the milk and all of the chocolate in a double boiler. When melted, stir in sugar and remaining milk. Mix well. Cook until thick, stirring occasionally. Serve warm over desserts.

Mrs. William L. Quinlen, Jr. (Ann Clark Miller)

Praline Sauce

1½ cups light brown sugar
⅔ cup white Karo syrup
4 tablespoons butter

1 5.33-ounce can evaporated milk
Pecans

Mix first 3 ingredients and heat to boiling. Remove from heat and cool. When lukewarm, add milk and blend well. Store in jar in refrigerator. Serve over ice cream with pecans sprinkled on top. Makes 3½ cups.

Keeps for a long time. Can be reheated over and over again.

Mrs. John Stemmler (Marsha Miller)

Granola

2 cups uncooked oatmeal
1 cup wheat germ
1 cup pecans
½ cup sesame seeds
1 cup shredded unsweetened coconut

½ cup chopped dates or raisins
½ cup honey
2 tablespoons oil
½ cup chopped dried apples

Combine first 6 ingredients in a 9x9-inch shallow pan. Mix honey and oil in a small saucepan and heat, stirring lightly. Pour over oatmeal mixture. Bake at 325° F., turning from bottom with a spatula every 5 minutes. Bake 20 minutes. Cool and add chopped apples. Store in containers in refrigerator or freezer. Serves 6-8.

Good as topping for ice cream!

Mrs. Huey L. Holden (Barbara Hopper)

Illicium anisatum

C. Grivich

Beverages

Beverages

Many of the following recipes came from the collection of Lafayette Draper, Jr., legendary bartender formerly at the Memphis Country Club.

Simple Syrup

Sugar   **Water**

Mix and boil 2 parts sugar to 1 part water until sugar is dissolved. Cool and store in refrigerator. Keeps indefinitely. One spoon of syrup equals 1 spoon of sugar in any recipe.

Lafayette Draper

Hiccup Special

2 ounces lemon juice   **½ ounce simple syrup**

Combine ingredients and serve chilled.

Sure cure for the hiccups!

Lafayette Draper

Banana Cow

1 dash bitters   **⅛ teaspoon vanilla**
1 ripe banana   **3 ounces milk**
½ ounce simple syrup   **1 ounce light rum**

Combine all ingredients and serve over shaved ice.

Great cure for a hangover.

Lafayette Draper

Old Fashioned

1½ ounces bourbon or Scotch   **1 teaspoon simple syrup**

Combine ingredients and serve over crushed ice. Garnish with an orange slice and a cherry.

Lafayette Draper

Bourbon Toddy

1½ ounces bourbon
½ ounce simple syrup
Dash of bitters

Splash of club soda
Lemon twist

Combine all ingredients and serve with a twist of lemon. This may be served hot or cold.

Lafayette Draper

Mint Julep

Fresh mint
1½-2 ounces bourbon

½ ounce simple syrup
Crushed ice

Crush mint sprig in bottom of julep cup. Add bourbon, syrup and fill cup with crushed ice. Garnish with another sprig of mint.

Lafayette Draper

Tom Collins

1½ ounces gin
1 ounce lemon juice

½ ounce simple syrup
Club soda

In an 8-ounce glass, add all ingredients except soda. Add ice and fill glass with soda. For a John Collins, substitute bourbon for gin and garnish with an orange slice and cherry.

Lafayette Draper

Orange Blossom

1½ ounces gin
1½ ounces orange flower water

1½ ounces orange juice
Orange slice

Combine all ingredients, except orange slice, and serve in champagne glass. Float orange slice on top.

Lafayette Draper

Daiquiri

1½ ounces light rum
1 ounce lime juice

½ ounce simple syrup

Blend ingredients with ice, strain and serve in champagne glass. To make this a frozen daiquiri, put all ingredients in a blender, fill with crushed ice and blend. One cup of strawberries, bananas or peaches may be added to the blender.

Lafayette Draper

Hot Buttered Rum

1½ ounces light rum
½ ounce simple syrup

Boiling hot water
Butter

Combine rum and syrup in coffee mug and fill with boiling water. Top with a pat of butter.

Lafayette Draper

Piña Colada

1½ ounces white rum
1 ounce coconut cream

3 ounces pineapple juice,
   chilled

Blend ingredients and serve chilled in a frosted glass.

Lafayette Draper

Planter's Punch

1½ ounces dark rum
½ ounce simple syrup
1 ounce pineapple juice

1 ounce lemon juice
1 ounce orange juice

Combine all ingredients. Add ice and serve in 12-ounce frosted glass.

Lafayette Draper

Country Club Special

1½ ounces light rum   ½ ounce simple syrup
1   ounce gin
1   ounce fruit juice, recipe
      below

Combine ingredients and serve over ice in a 12-ounce frosted glass.
Garnish with a cherry and an orange slice.

Fruit Juice
1   ounce orange juice   1   ounce lemon juice
1   ounce pineapple juice

Combine all juice ingredients.

Lafayette Draper

Zombie

1½ ounces dark rum   1   ounce orange juice
1½ ounces light rum   1   ounce pineapple juice
1   ounce Jamaica rum   ½ ounce simple syrup
1   ounce lemon juice

Combine and chill all ingredients. Serve over crushed ice.

Lafayette Draper

Margarita

Salt   1   ounce lemon juice
1½ ounces tequila   ½ ounce triple sec or Cointreau

Rim chilled champagne glass with salt. Combine rest of ingredients,
chill and pour into glass.

Lafayette Draper

Harvey Wallbanger

1½ ounces Galliano   Orange juice
1½ ounces vodka

Pour Galliano and vodka in an 8-ounce glass. Add ice cubes. Fill glass with orange juice, and goodnight!

Lafayette Draper

Wine Cooler

¾ cup red wine   Lime juice to taste
¼ cup tonic water

Combine all ingredients and serve chilled in a wine glass. May also be served over ice.

Charles D. Schaffler

Wine Spritzer

4 ounces white wine   Lime twist
4 ounces club soda

Combine ingredients and serve with a twist of lime. May also be served over ice.

Mrs. Gwin Scott (Wynn Skipper)

Mitch's Summertime Special

4 ounces Burgundy   2 ounces dark rum
1 ounce grenadine   Squeeze of lemon or lime
1½ ounces simple syrup   Ice cubes
2 ounces orange juice

Combine first 6 ingredients in blender. Add enough ice cubes to reach 4-cup mark. Blend until slushy. Yields two 8-ounce glasses.

Absolutely wonderful! Caution is advised.

Frank Mitchell
University Club of Memphis

Kahlua

2 ounces instant coffee
4 cups sugar
4 cups water

1 vanilla bean
1 fifth vodka

Combine coffee, sugar and water. Boil mixture for 6 minutes. Remove from heat and add vanilla bean. Cool. Add vodka. Cover and let stand for 2 weeks. Yields 2 fifths.

Mrs. Jere Fones (Ellen Kimbrough)

Black Russian

1½ ounces vodka

1 ounce Kahlua

Combine ingredients and serve over ice in an old fashioned glass. For a White Russian, follow the above recipe and add 2 ounces of heavy cream.

Lafayette Draper

Golden Cadillac

1 ounce Galliano
1 ounce white crème de cacao

2 ounces heavy cream

Blend all ingredients, chill and serve in cocktail glass.

Lafayette Draper

Grasshopper

2 ounces heavy cream
1 ounce green crème de menthe

1 ounce white crème de cacao

Blend all ingredients with ice. Strain and pour into champagne glass.

Lafayette Draper

Rusty Nail

1 ounce Drambuie   3 ounces Scotch

Combine Drambuie and Scotch. Serve over ice.

Lafayette Draper

Stinger

1½ ounces brandy   1 ounce white crème de menthe

Chill ingredients with ice and strain into cocktail glass.

Lafayette Draper

Velvet Hammer

1 ounce white crème de cacao   1 ounce vodka
1 ounce triple sec or Cointreau 2 ounces heavy cream

Blend all ingredients with ice. Strain and pour into cocktail or 8-ounce glass.

Lafayette Draper

Brazilian Coffee

Coffee   Grenadine
Brandy   Heavy cream, whipped
Tia Maria

To each cup of coffee add 1 ounce each of brandy and Tia Maria and ¼ ounce of grenadine. Top with whipped cream.

Mrs. Robert M. Williams, Jr. (Julia Gray)

Dorothy Special

1½ ounces brandy
2 teaspoons Kahlua
1 teaspoon Cointreau or
   triple sec

1 cup vanilla ice cream,
   softened

Mix all ingredients in blender. Serves 1.

Wonderful dessert!

Mrs. Jere Fones (Ellen Kimbrough)

Charlie's Wha-Ha Punch

8 6-ounce cans frozen
   Hawaiian Punch, thawed
2 bottles frozen lemon juice, or
   juice of 12 lemons
½ gallon sauterne

1 pint brandy
1 fifth light rum
½ pint sloe gin
6-8 bottles dry champagne

In a very large pot or kitchen wastebasket, mix Hawaiian Punch according to directions. Add lemon juice. Add next four ingredients and mix well. Fill a punch bowl ½ full of ice. Add 6-8 cups of the punch base to bowl. Then add 1 bottle champagne. To refill, just repeat ice, punch base and champagne. Serves approximately 50.

Makes you want to say WHA-HA!

Charles H. House
New York, New York

Scorpion

1½ fifths light rum
2 ounces gin
2 ounces brandy
1 pint lemon juice

½ pint orange juice
½ pint orgeat syrup
1 split dry white wine
2 sprigs mint

Combine all ingredients and pour over ice. Let stand 2 hours, add more ice and serve.

Lafayette Draper

407

Party Bloody Marys

2 46-ounce cans V-8 juice
19 ounces vodka
18 tablespoons Worcestershire
    sauce
9 dashes Tabasco

9 shakes celery salt
½ 5-ounce jar horseradish
3 tablespoons parsley flakes
    Juice of 4 lemons or limes

In a gallon jar mix all ingredients together. Refrigerate. Stir well before serving. Makes twenty-two 6-ounce drinks.

Mrs. Frank E. Reid (Diana Mann)

Whiskey Sour Punch

4 cups bourbon
4 6-ounce cans frozen
    lemonade, thawed
2 quarts apple juice or cider

2 quarts ginger ale
1 10-ounce bottle maraschino
    cherries

Combine all ingredients. Serves 20.

Mrs. Robert M. Williams, Jr. (Julia Gray)

New Orleans Breakfast (Milk Punch)

⅔ cup milk
⅓ cup heavy cream
1 tablespoon sugar, or to taste
1 teaspoon vanilla
1 tablespoon brandy or
    whiskey

1 teaspoon Tia Maria (optional)
    Crushed ice
    Nutmeg

Combine milk and cream and sweeten to taste. Add remaining ingredients. Blend in a blender or shaker jar until frothy. Pour into tall, chilled glass. Sprinkle with nutmeg. Makes 1 large serving.

Mrs. Michael Lynch (Susan Corcoran)

Eggnog

5 eggs, separated
5 tablespoons sugar
½ pint bourbon

2 cups heavy cream, whipped
Nutmeg

Beat egg yolks until foamy. Add sugar, and slowly stir in bourbon. Fold in whipped cream and stiffly beaten egg whites. When serving, sprinkle with nutmeg. Serves 8.

Mrs. Richard Walker (Margaret Bullington)

Hot Spiced Wine

½ gallon red wine
½ cup sugar
½ orange stuck with 3-4 cloves

½ lemon
1 cinnamon stick

Heat all ingredients together until mixture almost boils. Never let it boil. Cook over low heat for 20 minutes or until flavors blend. Serves 8-10.

A German holiday favorite!

Mrs. Lee L. Wardlaw (Mary Linda Lewis)

Refreshing Iced Tea

4 tablespoons tea or 4 small
   tea bags
2 cups sugar
⅓ cup mint sprigs, crushed
   slightly

1 quart boiling water
1 12-ounce can frozen orange
   juice
1 7½-ounce bottle frozen lemon
   juice

Combine tea, sugar and mint. Add boiling water, and let stand for 15 minutes, stirring occasionally. Strain tea into gallon container and add thawed juices and enough water to fill container. Stir and chill. Yields sixteen 8-ounce glasses.

Mrs. John W. Dillard, Jr. (Ann Rogers)

Spiced Tea

2 cups Tang
2 cups sugar
1 0.47-ounce package
   lemonade mix

½ cup unsweetened instant tea
1 teaspoon ground cloves
2 teaspoons cinnamon

Mix ingredients. Store in covered jar. To serve, use 2 tablespoons of spiced tea per cup of boiling water.

Mrs. Tony M. Parker (Judith Greene)

Prohibition Punch

6 cups water
⅞ cup sugar
1 12-ounce can frozen
   lemonade

1 12-ounce can frozen orange
   juice
1 46-ounce can pineapple juice
1 quart ginger ale

Dissolve sugar in 2 cups boiling water. Add remaining water and fruit juices. Freeze. Three hours before serving, put frozen mixture into punch bowl and add ginger ale. Punch will be slushy. Yields 30 cups.

Could be served hot.

Mrs. Thomas Holloman (Jayne Pressgrove)

Patio Cooler

1 cup sugar
2 cups strong tea
1 cup water
2 cups unsweetened pineapple
   juice

4 cups orange juice
1 28-ounce bottle ginger ale

In a large pitcher, dissolve sugar in hot strong tea. Add remaining ingredients except ginger ale, and chill. Add ginger ale just before serving. Serves 10-12.

Garnish with orange slice for pretty summer drink.

Mrs. John Albritton (Patsy Thomas)

410

Sunshine Orange Drink

1 egg
1 cup milk
1 6-ounce can frozen orange
   juice

4 ice cubes
1-2 teaspoons sugar

Place all ingredients in blender and whip until smooth. Serves 2.

Great breakfast treat!

Sarah Pearce Ramey

Herb and Spice Glossary

Allspice
Native to Latin America, the reddish-brown seed of the Allspice fruit tastes like a mixture of nutmeg, cinnamon, cloves and pepper and is used, whole or crushed, in broths, gravies and desserts and in preserving meat and fish.

Anise
The licorice-like seeds and cuttings of this Chinese magnolia are used especially as flavoring in sweets and as breath fresheners.

Basil
This sweet, aromatic, multi-variety member of the mint family is a staple of salads, Italian dishes, sauces and snuff.

Bay
Pungent and spicy, the leaves of this Mediterranean member of the rose family are added to vinegar; meats, fish and poultry; vegetables and stews.

Caraway
The roots of this variety of parsley are eaten as a vegetable; the leaves are used as seasoning. The seeds' oil is used in perfumes, gargles and soaps; the seeds themselves, in cakes, rye breads, cheeses and applesauce.

Cardamom
A sweet, pungent seed of the ginger family, cardamom often flavors pastries, liqueurs, coffee, perfume and curry powder.

Cayenne
The red fruit of this nightshade plant, from the Greek "to bite," is bitingly hot and seasons eggs, beans and many hot dishes.

Celery Seed
Of the parsley family, this slightly bitter herb is an ingredient in mixtures as diverse as bird food and gourmet dishes.

Chives
This diverse, onion-like perennial of the lily family is used both fresh and dried as a complement to meat, egg and vegetable dishes; in broths; and in puddings and pies.

Cinnamon
A bushy evergreen, sweet cinnamon is probably the most important of baking spices, and in stick form is used in hot drinks, pickling, and stewing.

Cloves
An evergreen from the myrtle family, this highly aromatic herb is used in desserts and to flavor meats and fruits.

Coriander
From the parsley family, coriander, mild and sweet, is used in candy, meats and liquors.

Cumin	A strong and hot member of the parsley family, cumin is used to season sauces, soups, breads and cheeses.
Dill	This member of the parsley family, similar to caraway, can be used either whole or ground. Good in seafoods, salads and breads.
Fennel	Also from the parsley family, fennel is excellent with fish. The seeds are used in pickles, breads and soups.
Garlic	Garlic comes from the lily family and is used to season a variety of dishes. The oil is used in making vinegar.
Ginger	Sweet and spicy, ginger is used in cookies, breads, puddings and some oriental dishes.
Horseradish	This member of the mustard family is very hot. The crushed roots are used in many sauces for seafood and beef.
Marjoram	This member of the mint family is used in meat and vegetable dishes.
Mustard Seed	A very hot, hearty spice of the mustard family, the seeds are used as a seasoning.
Nutmeg	Strong and aromatic, this tropical spice is used ground in baked goods and to flavor beverages. The oil is used medicinally.
Onion	Strong and pungent, from the lily family, onion is mainly used in cooking.
Oregano	From the mint family, spicy oregano is used in tomato dishes, salads, vegetables and stews.
Paprika	The cured, dried pods of this nightshade plant are used as a colorful garnish for egg, fish and meat dishes.
Parsley	A very mild spice, parsley garnishes and flavors salads and sauces.
Pepper	A climbing evergreen vine, pepper is a warm, spicy seasoning of limitless uses.
Poppyseed	A delicious topping on breads and pastries, poppy seeds add a nut-like flavor to salads and vegetables.
Rosemary	This fragrant herb from the mint family is used in soups, vegetables, potatoes and lamb dishes.
Saffron	Of the iris family, this cooking spice is used in breads, cakes and rice dishes. Harvested by hand, 600,000 slivers of saffron weigh one pound.
Sage	Sage is a warm and bitter member of the mint family used in stuffing, poultry and cheese dishes.

Tarragon	From the sunflower family, tarragon is used in vinegars, salads, pickles, meats and vegetables.
Thyme	This aromatic and pungent herb from the mint family is used in soups, meats and vegetables.
Turmeric	Of the ginger family, turmeric is used in cheeses, butters, curry powder and fruit drinks.
Vanilla	This member of the orchid family is used as a flavoring in desserts.

Sauce Chart

Sauces	Butter	Flour	Milk	Onion	Eggs	Cheese	Wines	Stock or Sauce	Directions
Cream or White (Basic)	2 T.	2 T.	1 c.						Melt butter. Add flour gradually, stirring constantly over low flame, for 3-5 minutes. Add scalded milk slowly. Cook, stirring constantly until smooth and thick.
Béchamel (Basic)	2 T.	2 T.	1 c.	1 T.					Sauté onion in butter. Add flour and cook slowly. Add milk and stir until smooth. Add ¼ t. salt, 3 peppercorns and a sprig of parsley. Cook over low heat until thick and smooth.
Mornay (Fish, poultry, eggs)	2 T.				3 yolks	2 T. Parmesan or Swiss		2 c. Béchamel	Mix egg yolks with a little cream and combine with Béchamel sauce. Cook, stirring constantly, until boiling. Add butter and cheese.
Velouté (Basic)	2 T.	2 T.						1 c. chicken	Melt butter. Add flour and cook a few minutes. Add chicken stock, ½ t. salt and a little pepper. Cook, stirring constantly, until thick.
Soubise (Fish, lamb, veal, sweetbreads)	1 T.		1 c. cream	1 c.				2 c. Béchamel	Parboil onions 3-4 minutes. Drain, then cook in saucepan with butter until soft but not brown. Add Béchamel and cook for 15 min. Strain. Return to fire and add the cream little by little.
Hollandaise (Fish, vegetables)	8 T.				4 yolks		2 t. lemon juice		Divide butter into 3 parts. Put egg yolks and 1 part of butter in top of double boiler over hot but not boiling water. Stir constantly, and when melted add 2nd piece. When melted add 3rd piece. Add lemon and pinch of white pepper. If mixture curdles add 2 T. boiling water and beat.
Béarnaise (Broiled meats, fish)	16 T.			1 T. shallots	3 yolks		1c. white wine 1 T. tarragon vinegar		Combine wine, vinegar, shallots, parsley sprig, 2 stalks tarragon chopped, sprig chervil chopped & 2 bruised peppercorns. Cook over hot fire until reduced to ⅔ of original volume. Cool slightly before adding egg and beating in butter piece by piece as it melts. When thick & blended, strain. Finish with a dash cayenne & 1 t. each of tarragon and chervil
Supreme (Meats, vegetables, eggs, poultry)			1 c. cream					1 pt. chicken stock 1 c. velouté	Cook chicken stock with 3 sliced mushrooms until reduced to ⅓ originial volume. Combine with velouté. Bring to a boil and reduce to 1 cup. Add cream, stirring constantly. Correct seasoning with salt and cayenne. Strain.

Sauce Chart

Sauces	Butter	Flour	Milk	Onion	Eggs	Cheese	Wines	Stock or Sauce	Directions
White Wine (Poached fish)	1½ T.	1½ T.		1 t.	3 yolks		3 T. tarragon vinegar		Reduce 3 c. strained fish stock made with white court-bouillon to ½ volume. Thicken with butter & flour. Add 2 t. tomato purée. Simmer. Cook 1 t. each finely chopped onion & chervil or parsley, & 3 crushed peppercorns in 3 T. tarragon vinegar until nearly all vinegar is absorbed. Add to sauce—bring to boil. Remove from heat & beat in 3 yolks, 1 at a time, beating well. Return to fire—bring to boil, stirring. Strain. Stir in ½ t. each chopped tarragon & chervil & 1½ T. truffles.
Newburg (Fish, seafood)	2 T.	1 T.	1 c. cream		2 yolks		2 T. sherry		Heat butter in saucepan. Blend with flour & gradually add hot cream, stirring constantly until thick & smooth. Do not boil. Season with salt & cayenne—pour slowly over well-beaten egg yolks, stirring. Place sauce over boiling water and cook, stirring, for 3 minutes. Flavor with 2 T. sherry.
Berry (Fish)	2 T.			1 T. shallots		¼ c. white wine		¼ c. fish stock ½ c. velouté	Melt 2 T. butter in saucepan. Sauté shallots until transparent. Add wine & fish stock and cook until reduced by ½. Stir in fish velouté. Finish with 1 T. each of butter and parsley.
Poulette (Fish, poultry, calf brains)	1 T.		½ c. cream	2 shallots	2 yolks			½ c. Béchamel	Cook 6-8 minced mushrooms in butter until almost brown. Add chopped shallots & cream. Cook until reduced by ½, add Béchamel and bring to boil. Add egg yolks, lightly beaten & mixed with a little cream. Bring to boil stirring constantly. Do not boil. Add juice of ½ lemon & ½ t. chopped parsley.
Brown Espagnole (Basic)	1½ T.	1½ T.						2 c. beef consommé	Melt butter in saucepan. Add flour & cook slowly, stirring occasionally, until blended & brown. Moisten gradually with bouillon or consommé, bring to boil and stirring, cook 3-5 minutes. Lower flame and simmer gently for 30 minutes.
Madeira (Beef, veal, poultry, ham)							⅓ c. Madeira	2 c. Brown	Cook brown sauce until reduced to 1 cup. Add Madeira and bring to boil. Remove immediately.
Diable (Broiled poultry, meat)				3 shallots			⅓ c. white wine	½ c. tomato	Add 3 chopped shallots and 8 crushed peppercorns to dry wine (or vinegar) and cook until reduced to a paste. Add brown sauce, 1 t. Worcestershire sauce and ½ t. chopped parsley.

Sauce Chart

Sauces	Butter	Flour	Milk	Onion	Eggs	Cheese	Wines	Stock or Sauce	Directions
Piquante (Veal, bland meats)				1 t. shallots			1½ T. vinegar 3 T. white wine	1 c. Brown	Reduce over high heat the dry wine & vinegar & minced shallots by ½. Stir in brown sauce, bring to boil and cook 5 minutes. Remove from heat and stir in 1½ T. finely chopped sour pickles, 1 T. chopped chives & parsley and a pinch of tarragon.
Robert (Pork, leftover meat)	1 T.			2 onions			⅓ c. white wine	1 c. Brown	Cook finely chopped onion in butter until golden. Add dry wine & 1 T. vinegar and reduce to ¾ original volume. Add brown sauce & 2 T. tomato sauce & cook slowly 10-15 min. Before serving add 1 T. prepared mustard, 1 T. chopped sour pickle and 1 t. chopped parsley.
Portugaise (Meats, poultry)	2 T.			1 shallot			¼ c. red wine	½ c. Brown ½ c. tomato	Melt butter in saucepan, add finely chopped shallot and wine. Cook until reduced to ⅓ original quantity. Add 2 tomatoes peeled & seeded & chopped and cook until soft. Add ½ c. each of brown sauce & tomato sauce, ½ t. chopped parsley, ½ t. salt and a little pepper. Bring to boil.
Chasseur (Chicken or veal)	4 T.			2 shallots			½ c. white wine	1 c. Brown 2 T. tomato sauce	Add 1 lb. of mushrooms, capped & thinly sliced, to melted butter. Salt and pepper to taste and sauté until golden brown. Add shallots & dry wine and cook until reduced by ½. Add the brown sauce, tomato sauce and ½ t. each of parsley & tarragon, both chopped.
Lyonnaise (Meats, vegetables)	2 T.			2 onions			⅓ c. white wine	1 c. Brown	Put butter in saucepan. Add finely chopped onions and cook until golden. Add wine and reduce to ½; add brown sauce and cook slowly for 15 minutes. Add 1 t. chopped parsley.

Compiled by Dr. Richard J. Reynolds, Jr.

Frequently Used Food Measurements

1 tablespoon	= 3 teaspoons	1 cup	= 16 tablespoons or 8 fluid ounces
1 fluid ounce	= 2 tablespoons		
¼ cup	= 4 tablespoons	1 pint	= 2 cups
⅓ cup	= 5⅓ tablespoons	1 quart	= 2 pints or 4 cups
½ cup	= 8 tablespoons	1 gallon	= 4 quarts or 16 cups or 128 ounces
⅔ cup	= 10⅔ tablespoons		
¾ cup	= 12 tablespoons		

Equivalents, Substitutions and Yields of Common Foods

Bread . . . . 3 to 4 slices bread = 1 cup bread crumbs, dry

Butter or Margarine . . . . . . 1 pound = 2 cups
2 tablespoons = 1 ounce
1 stick = ¼ pound or ½ cup (8 ounces)

Cream, Heavy, Whipping . . . . . . 1 cup = ⅓ cup butter plus about ¾ cup milk
= 2 cups whipped cream

Chocolate . . . . 1 square = 1 ounce
= 3 tablespoons cocoa plus 1 tablespoon butter or margarine

Cheese . . . . ¼ pound = 1 cup shredded
Cottage . . . . 8 ounces = 1 cup or ½ pound
Cream . . . . 6 tablespoons = 3 ounces

Coffee . . . . 1 pound = about 40 servings (2 tablespoons to each ¾ cup water)

Eggs . . . . 1 whole = 3 tablespoons
Whites . . . . 1 = 1½ to 2 tablespoons
4-6 = ½ cup
Yolks . . . . 1 = 1 tablespoon
6-7 = ½ cup

Measurements

Flour

All-purpose .....1 pound = 4 cups sifted

Cake ....1 pound = 4½ cups

1 cup = 1 cup minus 2 tablespoons all purpose flour

Self Rising ......1 cup = 1 cup plain flour plus 1½ teaspoons baking powder and ½ teaspoon salt

Whole-wheat ....1 pound = about 3½ cups unsifted

Graham Crackers .

11 finely crumbled crackers = 1 cup

Gelatin ....1 ounce unflavored = 4 tablespoons (4 envelopes)

Honey ....1 cup = 1 cup sugar—to use in recipe reduce ⅓ cup of liquid

Lemon Juice ......1 medium = 3 tablespoons

Milk ....1 cup whole = ½ cup evaporated milk plus ½ cup water
= 1 cup reconstituted nonfat dry milk plus 2½ teaspoons butter or margarine

1 cup sour or buttermilk = 1 tablespoon lemon juice or vinegar plus sweet milk to make 1 cup (let stand 5 minutes.)

Oats ....1 cup (quick or old-fashioned) = 2 cups oatmeal, cooked

Cornstarch (for thickening) .....1 tablespoon = 2 tablespoons flour, or 4 teaspoons quick cooking tapioca

Baking Powder ...1 teaspoon = ¼ teaspoon baking soda plus ½ cup buttermilk or sour milk (to replace ½ cup of liquid called for in recipe.)
= ⅓ teaspoon baking soda plus ½ teaspoon cream of tartar

Rice (White,
parboiled or
brown) ....1 cup = 3 to 4 cups, cooked

Yeast Compressed

1 cake = 2 teaspoons active dry yeast,
or 1 scant tablespoon

Tomato Juice ......1 cup = ½ cup tomato sauce plus
½ cup water

Salad Oil ....16 ounces = 2 cups

Sugar,
granulated .....1 pound = 2 cups
1 cup = 1 cup molasses plus ¼ to ½
teaspoon soda. Omit baking
powder (for baking only)
= ½ cup maple syrup and ¼
cup corn syrup. Lessen liquid
by 2 tablespoons (baking only)

brown ....1 pound = 2¼ cups
powdered ....1 pound = 3½ cups

Measurements

Liquid Measure

Cups, quarts, ounces, pounds and their metric equivalents (Nearest convenient equivalents)

Cups Spoons	Quarts Ounces	Metric Equivalents
1 teaspoon	1/6 ounce	5 milliliters 5 grams
2 teaspoons	1/3 ounce	10 milliliters 10 grams
1 tablespoon	1/2 ounce	15 milliliters 15 grams
3 1/3 tablespoons	1 3/4 ounces	50 milliliters
1/4 cup (4 tablespoons)	2 ounces	60 milliliters
1/3 cup (5 1/3 tablespoons)	2 2/3 ounces	79 milliliters
1/3 cup plus 1 tablespoon	3 1/2 ounces	100 milliliters
1/2 cup (8 tablespoons)	4 ounces	118 milliliters
1 cup (16 tablespoons)	8 ounces	1/4 liter 236 milliliters
2 cups	1 pint 16 ounces	1/2 liter less 1 1/2 tablespoons 473 milliliters
2 cups plus 2 1/2 tablespoons	17 ounces	1/2 liter
4 cups ..... (1 quart)	32 ounces	946 milliliters
4 1/3 cups	1 quart, 2 ounces	1 liter 1000 milliliters

Dry Measure and the Metric Equivalent

Pounds and Ounces
(Most convenient approximation)

	Metric
⅙ ounce	5 grams
⅓ ounce	10 grams
½ ounce	15 grams
1 ounce	28 grams
1¾ ounces	50 grams
2⅔ ounces	75 grams
3½ ounces	100 grams
¼ pound (4 ounces)	114 grams
4⅛ ounces	125 grams
½ pound (8 ounces)	227 grams
¾ pound (12 ounces)	250 grams
1 pound (16 ounces)	454 grams
1.1 pounds	500 grams
2.2 pounds	1 kilogram
	1000 grams

Metric Conversion Table

To convert teaspoons to milliliters, multiply the teaspoons by 5
To convert tablespoons to milliliters, multiply the tablespoons by 15
To convert fluid ounces to milliliters, multiply the fluid ounces by 30
To convert cups to liters, multiply the cups by .24
To convert pints to liters, multiply pints by .47
To convert quarts to liters, multiply the quarts by .95
To convert ounces to grams, multiply the ounces by 28.3
To convert pounds to kilograms, multiply the pounds by .45
To convert grams to ounces, multilply the grams by 0.352
To convert liters to quarts, multiply the liters by 1.056
To convert milliliters to fluid ounces, multiply the milliliters by 0.033

Home Metric-Aid

Spoonfuls
¼ teaspoon .....1.25 milliliters
½ teaspoon ......2.5 milliliters
¾ teaspoon .....3.75 milliliters
1 teaspoon .... 5 milliliters
¼ tablespoon ...3.75 milliliters
½ tablespoon ....7.5 milliliters
¾ tablespoon ..11.25 milliliters
1 tablespoon ..... 15 milliliters

Cups
¼ cup .... 59 milliliters
⅓ cup .... 78 milliliters
½ cup .... 118 milliliters
⅔ cup .... 157 milliliters
¾ cup .... 177 milliliters
1 cup .... 236 milliliters

Weight in Ounces
¼ ounce .... 7.1 grams
½ ounce .... 14.17 grams
¾ ounce .... 21.27 grams
1 ounce .... 28.35 grams

Fluid Ounces
¼ ounce ....7.5 milliliters
½ ounce .... 15 milliliters
¾ ounce ....22.5 milliliters
1 ounce .... 30 milliliters

Pounds
¼ pound .... 113 kilograms
½ pound .... 227 kilograms
¾ pound .... 340 kilograms
1 pound .... 454 kilograms
2.205 pounds ...... 1 kilogram

Pints-Quarts-Gallons
½ pint .... 236 milliliters
1 pint .... 473 milliliters
1 quart .... 946 milliliters
1 gallon .... 3785 milliliters

Length
1 inch .... 2.54 centimeters
1 foot .... 30.48 centimeters
1 yard .... 91.44 centimeters
100 feet ....30.48 meters
1 mile .... 1.609 kilometers
50 mph .... 80.45 kilometers/hr

Temperature
32°F. ....0° Celsius
68°F. .... 20° Celsius
212°F. .... 100° Celsius

Compliments of The University of Tennessee Agricultural Extension Service.

424

Index

Index

Index

Index

Index

Index

Index

Index

Index

Index

Index

LES PASSEES PUBLICATIONS
40 South Idlewild
Memphis, Tennessee 38104

Please send me _____ copies of *Well Seasoned* at $17.95 per copy, plus $3.00 for postage and handling. (For Tennessee delivery add $1.48 sales tax per book.) ISBN # 0-939114-42-9

Name: _____

Address: _____

City:_____State: _____ Zip: _____

Make checks payable to **Les Passees Publications**.

Proceeds for the sale of books will be used directly for the benefit of the Les Passees Children's Services Center, Memphis, Tennessee.

LES PASSEES PUBLICATIONS
40 South Idlewild
Memphis, Tennessee 38104

Please send me _____ copies of *Well Seasoned* at $17.95 per copy, plus $3.00 for postage and handling. (For Tennessee delivery add $1.48 sales tax per book.) ISBN # 0-939114-42-9

Name: _____

Address: _____

City:_____State: _____ Zip: _____

Make checks payable to **Les Passees Publications**.

Proceeds for the sale of books will be used directly for the benefit of the Les Passees Children's Services Center, Memphis, Tennessee.

LES PASSEES PUBLICATIONS
40 South Idlewild
Memphis, Tennessee 38104

Please send me _____ copies of *Well Seasoned* at $17.95 per copy, plus $3.00 for postage and handling. (For Tennessee delivery add $1.48 sales tax per book.) ISBN # 0-939114-42-9

Name: _____

Address: _____

City:_____State: _____ Zip: _____

Make checks payable to **Les Passees Publications**.

Proceeds for the sale of books will be used directly for the benefit of the Les Passees Children's Services Center, Memphis, Tennessee.